THE POLITICS OF URBAN EDUCATION

The Politics of Urban Education

EDITED BY

MARILYN GITTELL

AND

ALAN G. HEVESI

FREDERICK A. PRAEGER, *Publishers*
New York • Washington • London

FREDERICK A. PRAEGER, PUBLISHERS
111 Fourth Avenue, New York, N.Y. 10003, U.S.A.
5, Cromwell Place, London S.W.7, England

Published in the United States of America in 1969
by Frederick A. Praeger, Inc., Publishers

© 1969 by Frederick A. Praeger, Inc.

Library of Congress Catalog Card Number: 69-15747

Printed in the United States of America

To
Rose and Jules Jacobs
and
To Carol

PREFACE

This collection of readings seeks to examine a major functional area of urban decision-making in the hope of developing an understanding of the political processes that are relevant to American cities. Public education is one of the most controversial issues and, perhaps, one of the most important vehicles for finding solutions to the problems of the urban poor. It is therefore essential for scholars and public officials to comprehend the struggle for power that is occurring daily in our nation's urban school systems.

We are indebted to several persons who have been most helpful in providing us with research assistance and valuable recommendations as to the direction and thrust of this volume. (The opinions offered, however, are the sole responsibility of the authors of the articles in this collection and of the editors in their introductory sections.) We are grateful for the aid of Miss Frances Gottfried and Mr. Maurice Berube, and particularly to Mrs. Marian Wood, who reviewed the entire manuscript and offered invaluable assistance in its preparation. Additionally, Mr. Frederick Zolna and Mrs. Adele Spier gave us important research assistance. We are, of course, also indebted to the authors and publishers, who have given us permission to use their original materials.

Finally, we wish to give special acknowledgement to Carol Hevesi and Irwin Gittell, whose moral support and forbearance exceeded any limits we had a right to expect.

MARILYN GITTELL
ALAN G. HEVESI

CONTENTS

THE POLITICS OF URBAN EDUCATION

EDITORS' INTRODUCTION:
THE POLITICS OF URBAN EDUCATION

The Urban Setting

Over the last two decades, we have witnessed extensive changes in the composition of our urban population—changes that have greatly intensified the problems of our city school systems. The exodus of middle-class whites and the movement of lower-class nonwhites to the cities have effected radical changes in the school population; in many of our large cities, a majority of the lower-school population is now nonwhite.[1] Of the new families, many are first-generation urban dwellers, and a large proportion of these are still rurally oriented; their cultural traditions differ significantly from the standard middle-class values embedded in city school systems and professed by teachers and school administrators.

City institutions have yet to adjust to the changing character of the city population. Pressing needs have been met with limited responses. Over the last three decades, cities have expanded their services and, to cope with this growth, city bureaucracies have doubled in size. Unfortunately, growth and expansion have not been paralleled by any fundamental change in basic structure and environment; urban school systems are but a case in point.[2] Economy and efficiency, civil service reform, professionalism, and centralization have characterized the major movements in urban government. All of these factors contribute to the development of a remote, static bureaucratic structure, ill equipped to handle the demands of a new population. The old mechanism for immigrant entree to the city political structure is gone; the political party no longer serves as the community welfare agency, a channel for achieving status or power.[3] Today, government jobs are restricted by professional standards and examination procedures; the poor nonwhite, newly arrived and badly educated, is shut out of the system.

With the expansion of the nonwhite population in the cities, segregation in housing has intensified. This has meant increased isolation, with the result that communication and meaningful contact between black and white are now less possible than during previous periods.[4]

3

Added to this isolation are the expectations of the deprived, which now far exceed what present programs, set up to correct past inequities, can offer. Consequently, open conflict has become commonplace.

The only source of power for the ghetto community is ethnic solidarity—for which voting provides only a minor outlet. Within the ghetto, there is increasing interest and hope in getting "a piece of the action," and this means a redistribution of power in the city to allow the ghetto community a greater role in the policy process.[5] For cities all over the country, effective action will depend on a breaking down of the structure and a re-evaluation of the ideology that has governed that structure and that denies so large a segment of the population a voice in its own affairs. As constituted, the large, remote city structure cannot be responsive to the needs of local communities; it cannot provide that "piece of the action" the new city population demands.

The survival of America's urban communities will depend upon their ability to respond to these pressures; somehow, they must make the adjustments necessary to accommodate these demands. One of the first areas of attack will be the city school systems because these represent so essential a part of the total structure and so important a link to mobility in American society.

The Urban School System

If the urban poor are to effect a restructuring of the educational system, they must overcome the opposition of those elements with a vested interest in maintaining the status quo. An appreciation of the extent of this problem requires a familiarity with the operational structure of the urban school system.

City school systems are legal entities created to operate independently from the city governments in whose geographic jurisdiction they are located. Education is a state function, controlled by state law. Many school systems are fiscally independent of government and are empowered to raise revenues themselves; others must depend upon general tax revenues granted by city and state governments. The tradition of independence of the school system is historically a strong one; it can be traced to a commitment to keep politics separate from education. Nonetheless, urban school systems are political systems,[6] governed, at least nominally, by local school boards, whose members are usually elected, though sometimes appointed. Board members are unsalaried, and their effectiveness in initiating and implementing policy depends, to a large extent, on the personal skills in negotiating, bargaining, and persuading that they can bring to their positions. Generally, board members have minimal staff assistance and must depend upon professional administrators for information and direction. Joseph Pois's study of the Chicago School Board indicates the mushrooming frustrations of board members pressed to make decisions in an environment that permits them little time and gives them few resources.[7] Under such conditions, the role of the school superintendent becomes pivotal. Concomitantly the reliance of school boards upon their superintendents makes such appointments a vital part of the board's functions.

Generally, a superintendent is recruited from within the school system; he is, traditionally, an educator with some administrative experience. As the system's chief administrator, the superintendent is responsible for a variety of tasks, and, since education decisions are becoming increasingly visible, his powers often relate to decisions of a most sensitive political nature.[8] To a large extent, in attending to these tasks, the superintendent depends on an ever increasing professional bureaucracy at central headquarters and a field staff of school administrators.

The headquarters staff and the bureaucracy probably have more significant resources for affecting the outcome of policy questions than does any other set of actors in the urban educational system. They have permanence and tradition. Moreover, professionalism has developed a strong foothold in the policy process in education, so that the bureaucracy jealously guards the power it has developed over the years.[9]

In the name of professionalism, educational administrators have organized urban school systems in a manner that effectively restricts lay access to the points of decision-making. They have mustered the general support of those nonprofessional actors in the system who are content with the educational outputs of the system. The best example of their ability to control education in most communities is their legal power to dictate standards of professional conduct and the licensing requirements of teachers and administrators. This power permits an almost total restriction of access for those who do not conform to the standards imposed. Such restrictive recruitment, structured and employed by professionals within the system, has sometimes been of questionable merit; often the standards mandated are based on values unrelated to demands or needs in the school environment.

If administrators are now deeply involved in the policy process, so too are teachers. During the past several years, teachers have become considerably more militant and have succeeded in forming themselves into professional organizations and unions of great strength. Where they have developed real cohesion, teachers' unions have become powerful actors in urban educational systems; in such instances, they play an increasingly important role in determining the direction of policies that, officially, emanate from the boards of education and the bureaucracies.[10] In some cities, union contracts contain major statements of educational policy. Teacher organizations that have operated within the framework of the existing systems and that have succeeded in capturing a portion of the power available from those systems are not generally receptive to demands for restructuring educational institutions. In fact, they are often allied with administrators in efforts to maintain the system. They, too, have become defenders of the status quo. Part of the explanation for this state of affairs may be found in the life patterns of the teachers themselves. Most city teachers come from backgrounds that have placed great value on achieving professional status. They are, naturally, reluctant to depreciate the role of the professional, particularly in education. Teachers reared on the concepts of merit examination, competition, discipline, and hierarchical administrative control cannot accept changes that would jeopardize a system built upon these values.

In addition to administrators and teachers, there are a variety of nonprofessional groups involved in education, though these affect educational policy only peripherally. The school parent associations form one such group. These associations are primarily concerned with individual school problems; generally, they are not interested in action based upon an overview of the entire school system. In another category are those civic groups interested in "good education." These are analogous in aim and function to good-government groups; they usually phrase their desires in terms of the value of centralization, specialization, and professionalism. Both parent groups and civic groups generally are supportive of existing systems, representative of middle-class citizenry, and committed to using traditional techniques in order to solve the problems of educating the poor.[11] Finally, in the larger cities, specialized education-oriented interest groups are common; these tend to be staffed by professionals, who generally reinforce their counterparts in the school system.

The newest set of actors in the educational system are the civil rights groups and community organizations. Their involvement has been the stimulant for considerable conflict; their demands have triggered a rethinking of basic educational priorities. The entrance of these groups into the educational arena has overturned the traditional notion of school systems as apolitical and untouchable entities subject only to the sanctity of professional decision-making. Their quest for educational parity has exposed the school systems to public view and, in turn, has created a demand for greater visibility in what had generally been a closed political process. Because of their actions, social scientists have begun to study school systems as political systems, viewing school policy as basic political and social policy.

The Call for Integration

The 1954 U.S. Supreme Court decision ordering integration of public schools was one of the most dramatic and far-reaching events of our generation. It propelled public education into the open political arena; it led to attempts to revise our traditional methods of school administration; and, perhaps more important, it enabled ghetto parents to perceive, for the first time, that the schools were failing ghetto children.

The organization by activists—both black and white, both for and against integration of public schools—led to major political conflict in the 1950's and the early 1960's. This conflict reflected the general racist atmosphere in American cities and the alienation of the black community from the mainstream of society. Reactions of middle-class communities, even to minor plans for integration, were violent. The movement for change stimulated a reaction based upon latent economic and racial bias. Federal and state orders for implementing integration through such programs as open enrollment, school pairing, and the busing of school children were roundly defeated in the localities. Almost every effort was forestalled by bureaucratic inaction or public disapproval.[12]

Integration has failed. In most cities, school segregation has intensified; the political conflict continues. The tremendous resistance of parent groups, as well as many school administrators and teachers, has engulfed those attempting to implement the orders of the courts. State legislatures and city councils have been swamped with bills prohibiting forced busing or redistricting of school boundaries for the purpose of attaining racial balance. Even where minimal pairing has been imposed, the resulting racially balanced schools have, all too often, been segregated within the classrooms. Local school boards have been voted out of office for attempting to put integration programs into effect. Teacher groups and administrators have eschewed meaningful change in the system.

The hostile reaction to integration has, with very few exceptions, been overwhelming. As a result, civil rights groups that once urged integration have virtually tabled their demands. Recognizing the political character of the struggle, these groups are now aware that they lack the power to produce change. They have also come to understand that integration per se cannot solve the problem of reducing inequities that result from cultural and sociological deprivation. A variety of studies have revealed that the attitudes of teachers and administrators affect the learning success of students.[13] The imposition of such programs as "tracking" has further differentiated the advantaged middle-class white student from the slum child by segregating according to performance within the classroom. In addition, compensatory education programs, attempting to add to the deprived child's school experience through summer, after-school, and preschool sessions, have also failed to produce the desired effect of raising pupil performance.[14]

The accumulated evidence indicates a basic sickness in the school structure: The total environment of the system prevents progress and changes that would meet new situations and serve new populations. Studies analyzing all aspects of city school systems have identified as the fundamental malady an insensitive system unwilling to respond to the demands of the community.[15] With this new understanding, the insulated centralized bureaucratic structure has come increasingly under attack, and school-reform movements have replaced the efforts for integration.

Community Control of the Schools

The failure of integration plans and compensatory education programs has led those concerned to look to a reform of urban educational institutions for solutions; such reform would create new structures, thus providing a new and healthier environment. One group of reformers emphasizes administrative change; its proposals are concerned with readjustment of bureaucratic practices, new recruitment policies, and new systems of organization.[16] The proponents of these concepts are generally professionals who recognize the need for some change but cannot radically revise their own values to accept fundamental change. The other, more vocal, group of reformers is predominantly made up of nonprofessionals living in, or identified with, the ghettos. They are, to a large extent, community leaders and ghetto dwellers who reject administrative reform and demand a complete redistribution of power; to effect such a redistribution, they stress the techniques of decentralization of school systems and community control.[17]

The reformers in this latter group no longer accept the values imposed on educational systems by middle-class reformers of past decades, the purpose of which was the separation of education from partisan politics. They reject the traditional middle-class reform ethos that stressed nonpartisan elections, public authorities, and professional control of public policy. They argue that these values, laudable within the context of their original purpose, answer neither the needs of the 1960's nor the interests of a powerless, uninvolved population. Moreover, the ends sought by middle-class reform tradition—standardized procedures, merit promotions, appointment through objective examinations, specialization of function, and centralized leadership[18]—are now considered instruments of maintaining the system; they are the means whereby ghetto residents are excluded from a role in that system and they are contributory factors in the educational failure of ghetto children.

The frustration that has resulted from professionalization and political insulation stems from the way in which these are used to close off access to the centers of decision-making. The poor, increasingly alienated from the institutions of society that are failing them and finding access routes blocked, turn in frustration either to apathy or to militancy. The educational system is not alone in this trend toward overcentralization and overprofessionalization. It is also evident in many noneducational institutions and groups that, although deeply involved in the policy process, have become less and less receptive to public participation in policy-making precisely at a time when an increasing segment of the population is alienated from these institutions and groups. For example, the medical profession has monopolized public policy with respect to the establishment of health standards, the administration of health institutions, the training of professionals, and even the determination of the extent of government participation in insuring the financial liability of citizens burdened with the financial trauma of illness. The logical response to these circumstances is the call for community control—the means for achieving "a piece of the action."

Community Control: The Controversy

Those who support decentralization criticize centralized control of decision-making because they believe it excludes from participation those elements that are essential to a workable system: the parents and the community.[19] They deny the validity of the concept of professionalism as the absolute and exclusive value upon which a power system should be based. To them, professionalism has come to mean bureaucracy in its most rigid form, and this, in turn, has resulted in the alienation of parents and the community. Community control does not mean an abandonment of professional competence in administering schools. Rather, it means that parents will have policy-making power in broad terms and will participate in determining the general direction of educational policy in their communities. Advocates of this position recognize that professionals will always retain a monopoly of the skills and expertise that are of primary importance in policy determination, but they suggest that professionals should not be allowed complete control over the system, nor should the application of co-optive self-serving standards to school conditions be their first priority.[20] Hence, a central goal of the proponents of decentralization is the revision of existing mechanisms of professional dominance—such as the rigid merit system and the civil service examination—that restrict access to positions of responsibility, barring those who, despite their demonstrated ability to contribute much to the education of slum children, are unable to meet the "objective," culture-laden standards.

Supporters of community control also believe that the administration of education on a centralized city-wide basis automatically prevents the adjustment of educational programs to particular local needs. There are, they suggest, compelling problems growing out of the varying cultures, backgrounds, languages, and levels of deprivation that can no longer be ignored; these problems cannot be approached through educational policies emanating from a single source that is geared to the median level of performance of hundreds of thousands of students.

Opposition to community control comes from several areas and is founded on a variety of reasons. Many have concluded that decentralization and community control constitute the radical proposals of a militant minority intent on challenging American traditions. They do not believe that increased public participation in policy-making will aid in finding solutions to school problems and they remain pessimistic about the stimulation of broader involvement under any circumstances. Studies made by social scientists of the distribution of urban power generally rationalize elitist—that is, professional—control in functional areas as satisfying the demands of democratic theory because the elites are multiple and do not overlap.[21] These studies, abandoning the notion of a participatory system, serve as a continuing reinforcement of the existing system. At no point do they explore the possibility that the failure of our cities to make the necessary adjustments for resolving growing racial problems is related to a failure of the multiple-elite structure.

Within the cities, an increasing number of groups oppose community control because they fear it is a euphemism for black racism. Often these fears are aroused by minority-group efforts to secure increased representation for themselves. In some situations, however, extremism does pose a legitimate threat to established concepts of behavior.

There are many who oppose community control because they believe that it tolls the death knell of integration. This is a position that engenders much sympathy; yet, with every study pointing to both the failure of integration and the intensification of segregation in all major cities, the argument is, at best, well intentioned but invalid and, at worst, specious. Interestingly, many of those who bitterly fought attempts at integration in cities throughout the country now invoke integration as an argument against community control.[22] Faced with this argument, advocates of community control claim that integration is much more likely to occur when the poor are better able to compete in society—that is, when they reach a material level of security on a par with the middle class; then, and only then, will the white middle class begin to accept integration with black people. Nonetheless, supporters of community control do not accept the argument that decentralization is incompatible with effective integration. A central school agency must exercise the power to adjust school-district lines in a manner designed to attain a level of racial balance that conforms to a court order. A decentralized school system, legally, has the same sanction to integrate as has a centralized school system. The key issue still is—as it has always been—the desire and the ability, considering urban population shifts, to integrate.

Opponents of community control and decentralization also fear that it will lead to a damaging parochialism. Proponents of decentralization counter with the argument that localizing decision-making will certainly produce *greater* conflict among groups in the local community; because local control can be a technique for developing community identity and encouraging active participation in the institutions of a community, it is likely to foster greater diversity. Such a development, they suggest, is particularly important for disadvantaged groups who share common feelings of alienation, mistrust, frustration, and helplessness. Parents and community representatives in, for example, New York City's three experimental decentralization districts have taken a much greater interest in their schools since the program emphasizing community participation began. In each of the districts—and all are poverty areas—voter turnout in school board elections has been relatively high, attendance at school meetings is surprisingly large, and an identity with the schools is now voiced by parents for the first time.

The greatest benefit to be reaped from community control, according to advocates of the movement, is the willingness of the community's people to experiment and to innovate in the attempt to find solutions to educational problems that are local in nature. Centralized school systems have been notoriously inflexible in dealing with the overwhelming problems confronting them today. Local control is a more visible alternative that offers greater opportunity for change.[23]

Attempts to restructure any system are likely to meet enormous resistance from those with a vested interest in maintaining the status quo. Since the forces calling for change are generally powerless, they must organize for direct action. This may take the form of the direct vote, political pressure, and/or the formation of alliances with other groups. When these approaches fail, direct confrontations against official power groups become the only recourse of the powerless groups. This has been the case with respect to the politics of reform of urban schools. Community groups have met resistance from administrators, teachers, and those parent groups that fear dramatic change. Elected officials favoring change have had to suffer charges that their actions were "political"— that they were really trying to restore a discredited patronage system.

Because education is a state function, and because the pressure on local boards to resist change will be enormous, the issue most probably will be settled through legislative mandate. This requires activity throughout the entire political system by those attempting to initiate a radical restructuring of school systems. So far, such attempts have not succeeded; for example, in New York and Michigan, both far-reaching and compromise legislation failed to be enacted in the 1968 sessions of the state legislatures. Should a restructuring be effected, however, what could one, on the basis of present plans, expect to find?

A restructured school system would mean the end of city-wide control and the establishment of relatively independent local school districts. Each district would have to be granted significant power over such crucial items as budget, personnel, and curriculum—subject, of course, to standards set by the state. This would require allocation of funds directly to the local districts according to an equitable formula. It might also jeopardize such mechanisms of vested power as the city-wide union contract; and, in fact, the loss of city-wide bargaining power by a teachers' union is one fundamental reason union leaders oppose decentralization. Under any meaningful decentralization plan, local school boards would have to be given some power to negotiate directly with the union, particularly in regard to hiring and firing rules, tenure rights of teachers, supplemental salary arrangements, and so forth. Such a situation would mean a preponderance of power in the hands of local shop chairmen, operating within their own districts; undoubtedly, the union would eventually become a confederation of autonomous local shops and the influence of the city-wide union leadership would be shattered. It is unlikely that unions will ever compromise on this question. In fact, it is probable that otherwise neutral unions representing public employees would totally support the teachers in this case.

An immediate shift in the balance of power through state legislation to restructure city school systems is unlikely. What is more probable is the passage of compromise plans that, while vesting certain powers in the local boards, would retain a central education agency with control over standards, district lines, special schools, coordination of programs at the request of local boards, or some combination thereof. No plan for decentralization and community control, however, can have meaning if the local boards do not have substantial control over budget, personnel, and programs.[24]

A Case in Point

Activity in New York City for a change in school policy-making seems traditionally to precede activity in other urban areas. Such was the case with most of the plans for integration and with the programs for compensatory education; such also is the case with respect to decentralization and community control. The movement for community control in New York City has intensified in the last two years and a battle is being waged on several fronts.

Part of the struggle over decentralization occurred as a result of the 1967 decision of the New York Board of Education to create "experimental" decentralized school districts in Harlem, Ocean Hill–Brownsville, and lower Manhattan. These districts became the focal point of conflict over the powers to be granted to the elected governing boards and the administrators of the districts.[25] The community groups felt that they had been given the structure of change but not the reality of power. The board claimed that it could not, under the education law of the state, delegate power to the districts. There were several headline-making incidents as the experimental districts attempted to assert power.*

Most significantly, the mayor of New York, the governor, and the New York State Board of Regents have joined in sponsoring legislation to decentralize the New York City school system. The proposal—called the Regents Plan—incorporates the basic ideas of a scheme proposed by the Advisory Panel on Decentralization of the New York City Schools, which had been appointed by the mayor prior to the 1968 legislative session. The panel, chaired by McGeorge Bundy, President of the Ford Foundation, recommended dividing the New York system into from thirty to sixty school districts, with the election of local boards empowered to regulate budget, personnel, and curriculum. The plan proposed retention of a central education agency whose functions would have included the creation of basic standards, control over capital expenditures, and the provision of certain control services. The Regents Plan had the support of ghetto groups, several good-government organizations, The New York Times, and a prestigious group of citizens who formed a committee for the purpose of supporting the plan. Opposition

---

* At the same time, Harlem CORE introduced legislation into the New York State Legislature that would have created an independent school district for the Harlem community. Failing to gain passage in 1967, CORE reintroduced the bill in the 1968 session, with the same result. Nonetheless, CORE continues to identify the creation of the independent district as a major program.

was led by the United Federation of Teachers (UFT), the Council of Supervisory Associations, and some middle-class parent and civic groups.[26] The legislature, sitting in a crucial election year, refused to pass the Regents Plan; instead, it put through a bill that, in effect, postponed action until the following year (1969). The bill that was enacted empowered the mayor to appoint four additional members to the New York City Board of Education, thus expanding its membership to thirteen; it also ordered the board to recommend a decentralization plan to the legislature the following year. In December, 1968, the board submitted the required plan. It provided for some community control but, because of the conflict over the Ocean Hill–Brownsville experimental district, the plan proposed retaining existing personnel procedures so as to avoid antagonizing the UFT.

The political struggle for school reform in New York City very likely reflects the character of the struggle as it will emerge throughout America's urban centers. Legislation for independent districts and for community control has been introduced during the last two years in California, Massachusetts, Michigan, and Kentucky. In addition, interest in similar plans has developed in such cities as Boston, Detroit, Chicago, Los Angeles, Minneapolis, Philadelphia, and Washington, D.C.

The Study of Educational Decision-Making

There is, as yet, little empirical evidence to prove systematically that maximum public participation will automatically lead to maximum educational quality. The central reason for this deficiency is obvious: we still lack truly decentralized urban school districts that would permit significant parent and community involvement and control. Nonetheless, several recent studies indicate that increased participation has been a factor in the introduction of innovative programs and techniques into relatively stagnant educational systems; this seems to be the case, for example, in both Detroit and Philadelphia.[27] In part, however, our lack of information results from a general satisfaction with our system of nonparticipatory control of policy-making.

City school systems are political subsystems that provide a substantial laboratory for analyzing the political forces that have shaped policy and, as such, they offer the social scientist an opportunity to test the validity of some of our current social and political theories. Political scientists are now debating whether multiple-elite structures provide a sound foundation for democratic processes.[28] The final evaluation, however, depends on the output of the system—its ability to meet demands and resolve conflicts. Whether broader participation in the political process is necessary, or even possible, can be determined only by an in-depth analysis of the major areas of public policy. Specialization of function is so integral a part of our system that it would seem natural for social scientists to test their hypotheses by more comprehensive studies of political subsystems in areas of broad policy.

Social scientists have only recently begun the systematic study of educational decision-making and the power relationships of actors in the urban school system. Prior to 1954, research in education stressed teaching techniques, psychological motivation of students, educational programs, and the like. Since 1954, however, researchers have slowly but increasingly begun to ignore the taboos that surrounded educational policy-making and that protected it from critical scrutiny. Although a great deal needs to be done in the area of scholarship, the signs of change are encouraging.

The political movement in education may very well foreshadow a total movement for reform of city government. The ghetto communities throughout the country may provide the impetus for restructuring remote and obsolete city governments that have lost sight of the fundamental needs of their clienteles. It is also possible that this movement toward revitalizing the role of the citizenry will suggest the failure of elitist structures—be they multiple or professional. The test of any political system must come in its ability to meet demands and adapt to change; the ability to change and the process of change itself are vital to a viable political system. The viability of city school systems is currently being challenged. To an extent, the failure of public education in American cities is the result of the failure of educational techniques and practices, but, fundamentally, this failure reflects the deeper conflicts in American society, especially in American cities. Hence, the response that these school systems offer to the challenges they are now faced with will have relevance for the survival of all our American cities.

This compilation of readings on the politics of urban school systems intends to review major developments in a critical area of public policy: education. Chapter I, which deals with recent studies of urban power structures, provides the theoretical framework for many of the materials that follow. The selections in this chapter illustrate divergent schools of democratic theory. On the one side are those who claim that multiple-elite structures satisfy the basic tenets of democratic theory. In practical terms, they support increased bureaucratic and political specialization and reliance on professional expertise in each area of government policy. On the other side are those who are critical of limited participation in the shaping of important public policy; they consider broader public participation integral to the democratic process and see the narrowing of the public role as a violation of democratic theory.

The politics of education, particularly in relation to power structures and the development of public policy, is the subject of the remaining chapters. Chapter II is concerned with integration, the most significant political issue in public education in the last decade. The selections in this chapter describe the character of the political controversy over integration and offer some insights into the resultant political processes. Chapter III employs the case-study method to analyze the political processes inherent in educational decision-making. The variety of experiences found in these studies is significant.

The evaluation of school systems as political systems—after a half century of insulation from critical scrutiny—is the focus of the selections in Chapter IV. These selections review school structure: Some are more obviously political, while others retain a deeper concern for the educational process. Chapter IV offers some immediate structural proposals for change, with the Bundy Report providing the first indication of a need for broadening the base for political participation.

Chapter V describes the more recent movements toward greater community control and the call for a breakup of existing systems. The selections in this final chapter generally describe programs that reject present-day systems and attempt to revitalize participatory democracy. Community control is offered as an alternative to elite professionalism.

The course of the politics of education charted by the selections in this volume is important to an understanding of urban politics in general. The political structure of our cities, and of our society as a whole, is now being brought to task for its failures. Much that has happened in the politics of public education already challenges traditional assumptions, and the continuing failure to resolve basic educational conflicts is leading to a further rejection of many heretofore readily accepted concepts in American political theory. It is certain that future political theorists will have to face the evidence of such studies as these in making judgments on the effectiveness of political systems.

Notes

1. The Research Council of the Great Cities Program for School Improvement, *Status Report 1967* (Chicago, 1967), p. 7.

2. Marilyn Gittell and T. Edward Hollander, *Six Urban School Districts: A Comparative Study of Institutional Response* (New York: Frederick A. Praeger, 1968), p. 53.

3. Robert Merton, *Social Theory and Social Structure* (rev. ed.; Glencoe, Ill.: The Free Press, 1957), pp. 72–82.

4. Roger Kahn, "White Man, Walk Easy," in *Politics in the Metropolis: A Reader in Conflict and Cooperation*, ed. Thomas R. Dye and Brett W. Hawkins (Columbus, Ohio: Charles E. Merrill, 1967), pp. 78–91; and Robert S. Browne, "The Case for Two Americas—One Black, One White," *The New York Times Magazine*, August 11, 1968, p. 12.

5. Robert A. Dahl, *Who Governs? Democracy and Power in an American City* (New Haven: Yale University Press, 1961), pp. 11–62.

6. Thomas H. Eliot, "Towards an Understanding of Public School Politics," *The American Political Science Review*, LIII (December, 1959), 1032–51.

7. Joseph Pois, *The School Board Crisis: A Chicago Case Study* (Chicago: Aldine Press, 1964).

8. Allan R. Talbot, "Needed: A New Breed of School Superintendent," *Harper's Magazine*, February, 1966, pp. 81–87.

9. Marilyn Gittell, *Participants and Participation: A Study of School Policy in New York City* (New York: Frederick A. Praeger, 1967), pp. 23–41.

10. Marilyn Gittell, "Teacher Power and Its Implications for Urban Education," *Theory Into Practice*, VII (April, 1968), 80–82; and Richard Karp, "School Decentralization in New York: A Case Study," *Interplay* (August–September, 1968), pp. 9–14.

11. Wallace S. Sayre and Herbert Kaufman, *Governing New York City: Politics in the Metropolis* (New York: Russell Sage Foundation, 1960), p. 258; Dahl, *op. cit.*, pp. 155–159; and Gittell, *Participants and Participation*, pp. 15–16.

12. New York City Public Schools, *Blueprint for Further Action Toward Quality Integrated Education*, Recommendations of the Superintendent of Schools to the Board of Education, 1965; Robert L. Crain, *The Politics of School Desegregation* (Chicago: Aldine Publishing Co., 1968), pp. 106 and 111; and the article by Peter Schrag on Boston, in Chapter III, below.

13. Robert Rosenthal and Lenore F. Jacobson, "Teacher Expectations for the Disadvantaged," *Scientific American*, April, 1968, pp. 19–24; Kenneth B. Clark, *Dark Ghetto* (New York: Harper & Row, Publishers, 1965), p. 128; Jonathan Kozol, *Death at an Early Age: The Destruction of the Hearts and Minds of Negro Children in the Boston Public Schools* (Boston: Houghton Mifflin Co., 1967); and Herbert Kohl, *36 Children* (New York: New American Library, 1967).

14. James S. Coleman *et al.*, *Equality of Educational Opportunity* (Washington, D.C.: U.S. Department of Health, Education, and Welfare, Office of Education, 1966), p. 12; and a passage by Mario Fantini, in "Discussion: Implementing Equal Educational Opportunity," *Harvard Educational Review*, XXXVIII (Winter, 1968), 163–64.

15. Sloan R. Wayland, "Old Problems, New Faces, New Standards," in *Education in Depressed Areas*, ed. A. Harry Passow (New York: Teachers College, Columbia University, 1963), pp. 46–47; and Schrag, *op. cit.*

16. See, for example, the Odell Report, in Chapter IV, below; and Robert J. Havighurst, *The Public Schools of Chicago* (Chicago: The Board of Education of the City of Chicago, 1964).

17. Five State Organizing Committee for Community Control to the Office of Metropolitan Educational Sub-Systems, *Position Statement* (January 25, 1968), p. 3.

18. Sol Cohen, *Progressives and Urban School Reform* (New York: Teachers College, Columbia University, 1964).

19. See Marilyn Gittell, "Community Control of Education," in Chapter V, below; and the Passow Report, in Chapter IV, below.

20. Marilyn Gittell, "The Balance of Power and the Community School" (Paper presented at the Conference on the Community School, The Brookings Institution, Washington, D.C., December 12–13, 1968).

21. Dahl, *op. cit.*, p. 305; and Nelson W. Polsby, *Community Power and Political Theory* (New Haven: Yale University Press, 1963).

22. See Gittell, "Community Control of Education."

23. Mayor's Advisory Panel on Decentralization of the New York City Schools [Bundy Report], *Reconnection for Learning: A Community School System for New York City* (November, 1967), pp. 16–17.

24. Gittell, *Participants and Participation*, pp. 24–31.

25. Martin Buskin, "Local Control of Schools Gets Test in City Slums," *Newsday*, April 8, 1968; and Karp, *op. cit.*, pp. 9–14.

26. Sydney H. Schanberg, "Teachers' Union Reportedly Blocking Mild Decentralization Plan in Albany," *The New York Times*, May 24, 1968, p. 35.

27. See the relevant chapters in Gittell and Hollander, *op. cit.*

28. Peter Bachrach, *The Theory of Democratic Elitism* (Boston: Little, Brown & Co., 1967).

I

Community Power Structure

It has become increasingly important for students of politics to analyze functional areas of policy in order to come to an understanding of political processes and the nature of the distribution of power in society. The focus of this volume is an analysis of one such functional area: public education. It is nonetheless important to place such an analysis within the framework of the general approaches to the study of community power that have concerned social scientists in recent years. Accordingly, this chapter offers selections that investigate and comment upon both the various schools of thought regarding the manifestation of community power and the differing methodological approaches that social scientists have employed in the study of power. The debate among social scientists as to the validity of the various methodological approaches has contributed to an expanding concern with the reality of the power structures of American localities.

Stephen Hencley's article defines the basic difference in approach between those who support the use of reputational methods that prove the existence of single-elite power structures and those who, attacking the theories of the single elitists, support techniques that perceive the existence of multiple elites in community life. Hencley begins with a discussion of the motivation, theoretical assumptions, and methodology of Floyd Hunter, whose study of Regional City is a landmark of the elite school. Analyzing the reactions of the pluralist school to Hunter—and, in particular, emphasizing such works as Robert Dahl's study of New Haven—Hencley goes on to contrast the two positions, to review the strengths and weaknesses of the pluralist school, and to suggest avenues for future study of community power.

Nelson Polsby's article is a defense of the pluralist position and in it he sharply defines pluralist criticisms of the single elitists. Although written in 1960, the article is still relevant to the issues and provides a clear challenge to both the basic assumptions of the reputationalists and the methods that they employ.

In the article that follows, Richard Merelman discusses what he calls the third phase of the dispute: the renewal of the debate by the "neo-elitists," who attack pluralist analysis for ignoring the broad areas of non-decision-making in which the role of single elites becomes dominant. Merelman investigates the neo-elite argument both in terms of its logic and in terms of the American political experience.

Jack Walker adds a new dimension to the dispute by criticizing those who defend elites—whether single or multiple—out of a belief that elites satisfy democratic assumptions by providing the kind of stability that permits peaceful and orderly change. Underlying elitist thinking, Walker argues, is the assumption that democratic systems must be based on a generally apathetic citizenry that accepts control by elites possessing wealth, organizational power, expertise, traditional status, or other special attributes. This is a highly conservative approach to democratic theory and, for Walker, it is a distortion of the original norms and values of democracy.

The dispute charted in this chapter is exceptionally relevant to the study of the politics of urban school systems. The assumptions that form the bases both for the various elitist schools of thought and for those who support a more radical conception of democracy constitute the theoretical underpinnings for much of what is occurring in our city education systems. Questions of who should control the schools of America and of what purposes the schools should serve are very much tied to these significant philosophical problems.

1. THE STUDY OF COMMUNITY POLITICS AND POWER

STEPHEN P. HENCLEY

For more than a decade, spirited controversy has characterized the work of researchers engaged in the analysis of political and power systems operating in American communities. Two major schools of thought have emerged during this time: (1) the reputational school, based primarily on sociology, and (2) the pluralist school, structured largely upon political science. Studies of community power based on these schools have revealed marked differences, not only in terms of conceptual and theoretical underpinnings, but also in terms of favored research strategies and methodologies.

Characteristically, such differences have been welcomed in academic circles. Divergences in thought and theory have often launched new scholarly movements that have culminated in fertile additions to, or refinements of, accepted bodies of knowledge. Seldom, however, have differences of this kind been elevated to the point (1) where they have become ideological in nature (as in the case of recent attacks and counterattacks among proponents of the aforementioned schools) or (2) where the defense of a particular point of view appeared fully as important as scholarship and the pursuit of new knowledge. Yet, in the eyes of some observers, this is precisely what has happened during the continuing debates between adherents of the reputational and pluralist schools. Anton has observed that "the point has now been reached where studies are no longer undertaken to 'discover' and 'understand' the nature of political systems; they are undertaken to 'disprove' another man's theories, not in a scientific sense, but in an ideological and political sense."[1]

Whether a *rapprochement* between the two schools is possible at this point must necessarily be considered in light of the major disagreements that have precipitated controversy. The central concern of both schools

Reprinted from *The Politics of Education*, edited by Robert Cahill and Stephen Hencley (Danville, Ill.: Interstate Printers, 1964). Reprinted with the permission of the author and the publisher.

—to gain increased understanding of processes and patterns of political decision-making—is, however, of primary concern to every person interested in civic development who has felt a sense of impotence in dealing with formally organized systems of government. As the frustration of an increasingly complex society leads more citizens to express hostilities and aggressions toward many important community functions, the need to understand more about the political systems of local communities assumes vital importance.

The Reputational School

Floyd Hunter's study of community power structure, using reputational techniques,[2] serves as the landmark for the study of community political decision-making. He was not the first to probe beyond the formal organization of a community's governmental structure. However, this work serves as the best dividing line between two types of studies: (1) contemporary investigations based on a concern for power systems which are invisible to those who focus their attention only on formal institutions and agencies of local government and (2) the traditional investigation of the type which Plato and Aristotle initiated in their examination of the public rules and behavior of the ancient Greek city-state. It is not accidental that Hunter's work was initiated shortly after the close of World War II. . . . The 1930's and the early 1940's had seen the development of cooperative and collaborative federal-state programs of development in such areas as highways and hospitals and housing, but by the end of World War II it had become evident to many that the local community need was greater than the earlier expansion in the scope of national government would allow.

As "big government" continued its development in the 1930's and the 1940's, the role of administrators and experts continued to assume increasing importance, not only in administrative decision-making, but in political decision-making as well. The good community was being increasingly envisaged as one wherein experts in various aspects of public health, welfare, and education would have a larger domain in which to pursue the best "principles" of public administration at all levels of the community—federal, state, and local. Moreover, professionalization was proceeding with leaps and bounds so that relatively new professional groups were assuming positions of importance in community life (e.g., city managers and city planners). Traditional groups (e.g., schoolteachers and administrators) were also self-consciously developing a professional perspective and organization. The so-called administrative state was seen by a number of observers as having arrived and by others as rapidly arriving.[3]

It was in this context that in the late 1940's and the early 1950's professionals and political analysts began to be disturbed by the discrepancies between what they were observing in the development of programs (or in attempts to develop programs) of civic improvement and what they conceived as the new political influence of experts in civic improvement. Hunter himself was originally a social worker. Later, as a sociologist, he began to analyze and interpret what he had observed in his former role. He found major discrepancies between the model of a productive community political decision-making system, responsive to, and leading the community to, a better life, and the sometimes frustrated set of professionals in the ongoing life of a large city in the Southeast. As a result, he joined other analysts of community life and practitioners in asking who really runs our cities. This question apparently was not motivated (as in the case of Lincoln Steffens and the muckrakers of the first decade of this century) by a middle-class feeling of guilt over civic corruption and lower-class oppression but by a very insistently felt need to provide necessary public services at a level consistent with the private benefits supplied by an affluent society.

Hunter merely put into print the question that disturbed many community professionals in all fields of service. If they were to be effective representatives of the needs of the community in their areas of specialization, could they confine their activities exclusively to government employees on the one hand and the voters on the other? Years of experience as a social worker, capped by rigorous studies as a social scientist, left no doubt in Hunter's mind. If a community were to move forward, it could do so only if progress had on its side the men who controlled the means—the goods and services—by which progress could be implemented into concrete programs. Other social scientists who followed Hunter's lead called these crucial individuals the "economic dominants" and, like Hunter, stressed that the role of economic dominants in community decision-making depended upon the type of issue at stake. When it came to the big issues of urban development, level of taxation, public housing, major innovations in education, or any other such policy area which would affect the significant life chances of great numbers of a community's population, little could be initiated, let alone completed, without the approval and guidance of these economic dominants, whose influence was felt in every area of civic life. Lesser issues, such as the specific location of a hospital, were sometimes left to the professionals and the experts. If these lesser issues infringed upon larger problems, such as race relations, the civic professionals were again limited in their freedom of decision-making action.

The bases for Hunter's findings (i.e., that Regional City was controlled by a monolithic power structure and that community power was centralized in, and exercised by, a small and atypical proportion of the citizenry) appear to be grounded in a number of theoretical propositions and hypotheses enunciated in the introduction to *Community Power Structure*. The influence of sociological theories of stratification and of the concept of the community as a social system is evident throughout the propositions and hypotheses advanced.

To Hunter, *power* was "an abstract term denoting a structural description of social processes,"[4] in relation to "the ability of men to command the services of other men."[5] Power, moreover, was definable structurally because individual power "must be structured into associational, clique, or institutional patterns to be effective,"[6] and "power involves relationships between individuals and groups, both controlled and controlling."[7] Additional propositions and corollaries advanced by Hunter held (1) that power is a relatively "constant factor in social relationships with policies as variables," (2) that "wealth, social status, and prestige are factors in the 'power constant,'" and (3) that "variation in the strength between power units, or a shift in policy within one of these units, affects the whole power structure."[8] To these propositions and corollaries, Hunter added three hypotheses. The exercise of power, he stated, was not only (1) "a necessary function in social relationships" but was (2) "limited and directed by the formulation and extension of social policy within a framework of socially sanctioned authority." Finally, Hunter hypothesized that (3) "a smaller number of individuals will be found formulating and extending policy than those exercising power."[9]

With these propositions and hypotheses serving as a "mental backdrop," it is clear that Hunter viewed the community as a system of action (i.e., a social system) in which the roles were *structured, interdependent, and unequal in power*. To get at the question of who exercised community power, it became necessary to identify those roles that were both salient and centrally involved in determining community policies. Hunter's methodology for identifying the salient roles—the so-called reputational technique—made extensive use of panel techniques: nominations of reputedly powerful community figures were obtained from individuals who were at the centers of communications and organizational life in Regional City.[10]

Hunter's findings on the basis of his study of Regional City indicated that a relatively few people made all of the crucial decisions in this city, i.e., that a monolithic power structure was in control of political decision-making processes. "It became evident," Hunter stated, "that certain men, even within the relatively narrow range of decision leaders with whom I was dealing, represented a top layer of personnel,"[11] and "the 'little fellows' are continually moved to perform their proper tasks by those above them."[12] Moreover, Hunter observed a close working relationship between politics and business:

"In the normal course of events the actions of the private citizen, at least on a policy-making level of power, are almost indistinguishable from those of formally designated officials. The dual relationship between government and economic operations tends to blur into one process."[13]

Other studies have tended to buttress Hunter's findings. Schulze and Blumberg,[14] for example, found that in one small city the reputational technique for identifying the powerful decision-makers produced substantially the same list of nominees regardless of who did the nominating. D'Antonio, Form, Miller, and others[15] have also used reputational measures of power (which deviate little from Hunter's original techniques) for comparative studies of several communities. Moreover, the proposition advanced by Mills, that a powerful ruling elite exercises substantial control of the political system at the national level,[16] appears to parallel Hunter's description of controlled political processes at the community level in Regional City.

Some Salient Issues

Hunter's handbook for progressive-minded civic professionals has been questioned by other social scientists on several accounts. Such political scientists as Kaufman and Jones[17] believed that the role of government officials had been seriously underestimated in such analyses as Hunter's in Regional City. Professional students of public administration sought to point out that the innovating ideas must come from imaginative experts and not from power-oriented economic dominants who are dependent upon the professional substructure to suggest alternatives for action. The man of power could still pick and choose, but the range of alternatives from which he could select was profoundly shaped by the ideas proposed by the professionals. Shaping the developing debate over the character of community political systems was the fact that some of those whose commitment to the democratic ideal had been enhanced by the cold war found it difficult to believe that any one group, economic dominants or whoever, could hold sway over so wide a range of human activity within democratic community politics. Others were disturbed by the pessimistic implications about democracy which a reading of Hunter presented.

Criticism of Hunter's work proceeded on several fronts. Social scientists of the pluralist school questioned (1) whether monolithic power structures could be defended as accurate representations of community political systems in American cities, (2) whether reputational techniques resulted in accurate assessments of power distributions in communities, and (3) whether unity in both the values and the economic and social backgrounds of top leaders really existed.

MONOLITHISM VERSUS PLURALISM

Rossi[18] questioned Hunter's assumption that American communities have monolithic political systems, i.e., that power is centralized in the hands of a relatively small and atypical proportion of the citizenry. Granted the top leaders may come from similar social and economic backgrounds in society, it remains possible that they represent divergent ideologies and that "it is precisely to these deviants on the upper occupational levels that the popular support of the lower strata of the community may be attracted." In other words, a group that may seem to have an identity of interest opposed to other group interests may in reality be divided enough in values, although from a similar class background, for some of their members to represent interests of groups or classes other than their own. Thus the picture of a monolithic power structure might be misleading.

Similarly, Sayre and Kaufman,[19] in their study of New York City, saw not only a pluralistic society but a polity wherein elected government officials and appointed administrators were a relatively independent, autonomous group in political decision-making in the city. Their conclusion, that "no single ruling elite dominates the political and governmental system of New York City," would appear to be diametrically opposed to the hierarchical, political elite systems described by Hunter and others.

Other community analysts have also voiced objections in relation to Hunter's position. In criticizing the work of the reputational school, Dahl[20] appeared convinced that what Hunter had identified in Regional City was not a ruling-elite system but rather a group that possessed *high potential* for control. His own study of New Haven had indicated to Dahl "that the small group that runs urban redevelopment is not the same as the small group that runs public education, and neither is quite the same as the two small groups that run the two parties."[21] How anyone could have signified the dominance of a power elite in a community "without basing his analysis on the careful examination of a series of concrete decisions"[22] was, to Dahl, a mystery. Moreover, as Polsby pointed out in a later article, "most of the reputational researchers, by their failure to specify scopes in soliciting reputations for influence, assume that the power of their leader-nominees is equal for all issues."[23] To pluralists, this assumption is of dubious validity, for "it is improbable . . . that the same people who decide which houses of prostitution are to be protected . . . also plan the public school curriculum."[24]

In summary, pluralists questioned Hunter's picture of monolithic control in Regional City because (1) he had confused potential power with actual power, (2) he had failed to examine the role of economic dominants in the actual resolution of community issues, and (3) he had assumed that the crucial decision-makers remained the same from issue area to issue area.

THE REPUTATIONAL TECHNIQUE

How is it possible to explain findings by political analysts which show American community politics as monolithic and run by economically dominant elites and, at the same time, as pluralistic and run by several political groups with governmental officials being at least one of the important sectors of the governing leadership? One valid explanation may be that investigators have chosen to study different communities: their descriptions of the functioning of community politics in different situations may, in fact, be accurate. Until comparative studies are the rule (rather than the exception), it would appear unwise to discount this possibility.

A second common explanation, however, attributes the discrepancy to a bias of Hunter's methodology, particularly the so-called reputational technique. Hunter assumed that a relatively few people made all of the crucial decisions; then he set out to identify the responsible individuals by asking for a limited number of nominations from people at the centers of communications and organizational life in the community. Although Schulze and Blumberg found that this technique produced substantially the same list of nominees regardless of who did the nominating, pluralists have pointed out that the reputational method had some elements of a self-confirming prophecy. The validity of the method, i.e., the extent to which the reputedly powerful (however consensual the judgments of nominators) were actually powerful, was in doubt.

Validity of the reputational method has been questioned by community analysts on various grounds. First, pluralists have argued that the use of citizen panels for verification of power figures may result in the identification of the *reputed*, rather than *actual*, power wielders. Secondly, since ordinary citizens usually possess inadequate knowledge about actual power systems in communities, their responses have doubtful validity and may not represent "anything more than a report of public opinion on politics."[25] Third, the reputational method leads to the identification of both *status* figures and *power* figures and offers no means for distinguishing between these types. Pluralists have argued that there is no reason to suppose that status and power are synonymous.[26] Finally, the reputational method fails to make required distinctions among friends and foes in the elite system; there is a presumption of unity among members of the power structure.

Some of the research subsequent to the Regional City study has attempted to clarify certain deficiencies seen in Hunter's approach. The researchers argued that it was necessary to examine a number of issues independently to ascertain the extent to which the same individuals had control over policy rather than assume that they had the same degree of control in a wide range of areas. They supplemented nominations of the reputedly influential people by asking the nominees whether in fact they had been active in a selected set of political issues. In a recent restudy of Regional City, Cleveland and Jennings[27] have concluded that Hunter's portrait of this city needs some amendment. The political leadership, apart from its unity or diversity in preferences about the scope of government, is more specialized in decision-making activity than might have been thought.

.   .   .   .

The Pluralist School

Although pluralists would agree that power and influence are always relationships among people, they have questioned a priori assumptions about the invariable correlation between power and social structure variables, such as wealth, status, and position. Polsby has pointed out that the pluralist position holds "that nothing categorical can be assumed about power in any community. [The pluralist position] rejects the stratification thesis that *some* group necessarily dominates a community."[28] Moreover, Polsby has indicated that findings concerning the existence of a community power structure are untenable unless "there exist high degrees of overlap among issue areas in decision-making personnel, or of institutionalization in the bases of power in specified issue areas, or of regularity in the procedures of decision-making . . ."[29]

The essence of the pluralist position might be summarized as follows:

(1) sociological assumptions about the invariable correlation between *power* and variables such as position, wealth, and prestige are open to question; (2) correlations between power and the variables associated with status can be established only through empirical test; (3) the assessment of community power requires intensive study of the actions of participants in processes of community decision-making and issue resolution; (4) the determination of overlap among decision-making personnel is possible only if several issue areas are selected for study in a community; and (5) community power is accorded to individuals and groups, *not* on the basis of their perceived status or reputation, but rather on the basis of their participation in decision-making processes and their actual impact in affecting decisional outcomes.

Conceiving of political leadership in terms of participation and impact in processes of decision-making has several important consequences. The selection of decision-making processes for study shapes the character of the power structure observed. If processes are selected that involve mass sharing in decision-making or political power, the analyst's picture of the community polity will tend to be that of a broadly based power structure. If processes are selected that involve only a few decision-makers, the analyst's picture will show a narrow, restricted distribution of political power.

This means that some of the controversy over the scope of power structures in American communities has been due to the fact that analysts have selected different types of processes in different communities. It also means that the role of government officials, administrators, and experts in community power structures will vary as different sets of decisional processes are at the focus of attention of the analyst.

STRENGTHS OF PLURALIST POSITION

Although pluralist theory and methodology have not escaped criticism,[30] the work of this school has tended to strengthen the study of community decision-making in a number of ways.

1. *Pluralists have made available evidence about community political systems in process.* Studies by pluralists exhibit strength in their concern for (a) systematic observation of political processes, (b) precision in data collection and data analysis, and (c) strict attention to significant problems of evidence. The pluralist methodology offers an alternate means for identifying community rulers which is dependent neither upon analyses of reputations nor upon data extrapolations derived from analyses of formal structures.

2. *Pluralists offer a methodology for the development of a range of propositions in relation to community political systems.* The pluralist

position appears not to rule out the possibility that some American communities are ruled by a monolithic power elite. Empirical tests using the pluralist methodology may, in fact, signify that such a conclusion is justifiable. On the other hand, neither does the method rule out the possibility that in other communities power is more widely dispersed. The important point here is that the pluralist methodology offers an avenue for mapping the total domain of community power *types*, i.e., for developing typologies of power that can be subjected to test and verification in a wide range and number of communities.

SHORTCOMINGS OF PLURALIST POSITION

A number of shortcomings of the pluralist position should also be cited.

1. *Although pluralist studies have presented excellent pictures of community political systems in process, few hypotheses have been generated about interrelationships between the political behavior and the social-structure characteristics of communities.* Intensification of efforts toward relating diverse structural characteristics of communities[31] to various resource bases that determine community power distributions appears to be in order.

2. *The use of isolated case studies, together with a concentration on small numbers of issues, has limited the productivity of a heuristic methodology.* Comparative community studies would do much to increase the generalizability of findings about community political systems. Moreover, studies based on greater numbers of significant issues would tend to increase confidence in findings about power structures in different types of communities.

3. *There is a need to identify both structural and institutional contexts which have tended to generate either identical or divergent systems of political participation and power.* An acute need at this time is to develop typologies of community power systems which can be related to similarities or differences in (a) community social structures and (b) existing political systems. Whether pluralist theory and methodology are adequate to meet these challenges is a moot question which will undoubtedly engage the attention of both analysts and researchers for some time to come.

.   .   .   .

Students of community decision-making have spent much time questioning one another's methods, perhaps in the realization that their conclusions, which seem to differ so much, might be artifacts of the assumptions and techniques of different investigators. The field seems not only ready for, but very much in need of, the adoption of a set of methods based on a few explicitly stated assumptions which will allow investigators to study many different communities—not only simultaneously, but also over time—in order to assess the extent to which decisions do vary from city to city and issue to issue, and to determine whether there are any common patterns of community life within particular communities and among categories of communities which are linked to one or another type of decision-making process.

To make studies of community decision-making even more productive than they have been in the past will require movement in several directions. The following appear to be among the most salient avenues for forward movement:

1. *Realization that the controversy between pluralists and members of the reputational school has been both unproductive and beside the point.* Other than on an individual basis, the question of whether American communities have monolithic or pluralistic power structures is unresolvable. Given the current state of knowledge about community political systems—as derived from a handful of studies based on *different* communities and *differing* methodologies—the answers to significant questions concerning the prevalence of various types of political systems among American communities are moot. Hunter's comment on Dahl's findings in New Haven appears apropos on this point. Said Hunter, "O.K. Who knows New Haven better at this time than Dahl? He has just finished a study there which must stand until the next investigator takes a look."[32] The important point is this: It is premature (and unscientific) to seek closure on the questions that have precipitated debate. A great deal more research (using both reputational and pluralist techniques) appears necessary before questions of this kind can be confronted in intelligent fashion.

2. *Sustained effort to generate more viable approaches to the study of community politics and power.* Random effort in research has long been detrimental to the continuity, generalizability, and cumulative impact of knowledge generated through disciplined inquiry. The field of community studies appears to have suffered from the shortcomings of random research efforts. The need for research patterns that circumvent inadequacies and discontinuities appears clear and compelling.

Extended use of comparative and/or cooperative experiments would appear to offer at least one pattern that would help to alleviate the shortcomings of random approaches. Sustained attention should be directed toward (a) developing new approaches to large-scale experimentation in the field of community studies, (b) focusing conscious interdisciplinary attention upon important and significant problems and variables requiring research attention, and (c) developing conceptual frameworks and theoretical models to guide disciplined inquiry in large-scale experimentation.[33]

Large-scale comparative and cooperative approaches to the study of community political systems appear to be needed for several reasons: (a) to ensure the continuity that is lacking in random approaches, (b) to secure not only the contribution of each individual but also the additional information that can be generated through combining the results of many studies, (c) to open the possibility for pursuing a multiplicity of objectives and aims in research designs, (d) to make possible more efficient utilization of experimental resources, (e) to ensure that knowledge generated through disciplined inquiry will be more cumulative in nature, and (f) to lay a research base to produce results that will have much wider generality.

As noted earlier, large-scale experimentation should be structured on common theory with explicitly stated assumptions and should make provisions for analysts to study communities both simultaneously and over time. Moreover, attention should be given both to a careful delineation of the dimensions of the political system to be encompassed (economic, social, political) and to the development of common methodologies.

3. *Deliberate attempts to come to grips with the concept of "community."* Although both sociologists and political scientists have, for some time, been engaged in community studies, neither discipline has attempted a serious delineation of the various foci for community identification. The lack of explicit conceptions and definitions has led, as Anton has observed, to a state of affairs where "pluralists talk about issues which may or may not be community issues, while the followers of Hunter talk about power, which may or may not be community power."[34]

4. *Continuous effort to ascertain the relationship between differing political systems and the structural and institutional contexts in which they become manifest.* Rogers[35] has suggested that one starting point for beginning this work is to "construct 'ideal-type' models of community power structures, from the most monolithic to the most pluralistic, and attempt to ascertain the structural conditions that correspond with and perhaps give rise to these various types."[36] Important goals in this work would be (a) movement toward more specific mapping of the total universe of community power types, (b) the identification of critical variables that are strongly associated with either monolithic or pluralistic power structure, and (c) the formulation of typologies of community power that can be tested and verified in communities of various kinds.

Notes

1. Thomas J. Anton, "Rejoinder," *Administrative Science Quarterly*, VIII (September, 1963), 268. See also Thomas J. Anton, "Power, Pluralism, and Local Politics," *Administrative Science Quarterly*, VII (March, 1963), 425–57; and Robert A. Dahl, "Letter to the Editor," *Administrative Science Quarterly*, VIII (September, 1963), 250–56.

2. Floyd Hunter, *Community Power Structure* (Chapel Hill, N.C.: University of North Carolina Press, 1953).

3. The writer does not wish to imply that the development of principles of public administration and theories of the administrative state was occasioned by the development of big government in the 1930's and the 1940's. Many public administration doctrines go back further in time to the so-called reform movement that swept the country roughly between 1890 and 1920.

4. Hunter, *op. cit.*, p. 2.

5. *Ibid.*, p. 4.

6. *Ibid.*, p. 6.

7. *Ibid.*

8. *Ibid.*

9. *Ibid.*, p. 8.

10. *Ibid.*, pp. 262–71.

11. *Ibid.*, p. 66.

12. *Ibid.*, p. 110.

13. *Ibid.*, p. 171.

14. Robert O. Schulze and Leonard U. Blumberg, "The Determination of Local Power Elites," *American Journal of Sociology*, LXIII (November, 1957), 290–96; Robert O. Schulze and Leonard U. Blumberg, "Economic Dominants in Community Power Structure," *American Sociological Review*, XXIII (February, 1958), 3–9; and Leonard U. Blumberg, "Community Leaders: The Social Bases and Social-Psychological Concomitants of Community Power" (Microfilmed Ph.D. dissertation, University of Michigan, 1955).

15. William H. Form and William V. D'Antonio, "Integration and Cleavage Among Community Influentials in Two Border Cities," *American Sociological Review*, XXIV (December, 1959), 804–14; Delbert C. Miller, "Industry and Community Power Structures: A Comparative Study of an American and an English City," *American Sociological Review*, XXIII (February, 1958), 9–15; William V. D'Antonio, *et al.*, "Institutional and Occupational Representations in Eleven Community Influence Systems," *American Sociological Review*, XXVI (June, 1961), 440–46; and Orrin E. Klapp and Vincent L. Padgett, "Power Structure and Decision-Making in a Mexican Border City," *American Journal of Sociology*, LXV (January, 1960), 400–406.

16. C. Wright Mills, *The Power Elite* (New York: Oxford University Press, 1956).

17. Herbert Kaufman and Victor Jones, "The Mystery of Power," *Public Administration Review*, XIV (Summer, 1954), 205–12.

18. Peter H. Rossi, "Community Decision-Making," in Roland Young (ed.), *Approaches to the Study of Politics* (Evanston, Ill.: Northwestern University Press, 1958), pp. 363–82.

19. Wallace S. Sayre and Herbert Kaufman, *Governing New York City* (New York: Russell Sage Foundation, 1960).

20. Robert A. Dahl, "A Critique of the Ruling Elite Model," *American Political Science Review*, LII (June, 1958), 463–69.

21. *Ibid.*, p. 466.

22. *Ibid.*

23. Nelson W. Polsby, "Three Problems in the Analysis of Community Power," *American Sociological Review*, XXIV (December, 1959), 797.

24. *Ibid.*

25. Raymond E. Wolfinger, "Reputation and Reality in the Study of Community Power," *American Sociological Review*, XXV (December, 1960), 642.

26. *Ibid.*, p. 640.

27. Frederic Cleveland and Kent Jennings (MS, University of North Carolina).

28. Nelson W. Polsby, "How To Study Community Power: The Pluralist Alternative," below, pp. 35–36.

29. *Ibid.*, p. 40.

30. See, for example, Anton, "Power, Pluralism, and Local Politics," pp. 448–56.

31. Such as population size, industrial development, scope of local government, salience of local party organizations, homogeneity or heterogeneity of community inhabitants in terms of ethnic origin, religious preferences, and occupations, etc.

32. Floyd Hunter, "Book Review," *Administrative Science Quarterly*, VI (March, 1962), 517–19.

33. Examples of efforts to come to grips with these problems would be the research seminar on "Processes of Community Decision-Making and Change and Their Influence on Education," held at the University of Oregon, August 5–24, 1963; and the Kansas City Comparative Community Study Conference, sponsored by Community Studies, Inc., June 14–17, 1961.

34. Anton, "Power, Pluralism, and Local Politics," p. 456. For an extended discussion of the problems involved in defining "community," see Luvern L. Cunningham, "Community Power: Implications for Education," in Robert S. Cahill and Stephen P. Hencley (eds.), *The Politics of Education in the Local Community* (Danville, Ill.: The Interstate Printers & Publishers, 1964), chap. ii.

35. David Rogers, "Community Political Systems," in Bert E. Swanson (ed.), *Current Trends in Comparative Community Studies* (Kansas City, Mo.: Community Studies, Inc., 1962), pp. 31–48.

36. *Ibid.*, p. 37.

2. HOW TO STUDY COMMUNITY POWER: THE PLURALIST ALTERNATIVE

NELSON W. POLSBY[1]

Political scientists are beginning to view certain major contributions to the study of community politics less favorably than one would have expected after hearing the fanfare surrounding the original acceptance of these works.[2] Often billed as studies of "community power structure," these works have been produced mostly by sociologists, whose orientation has been to study the politics of American communities as a subsidiary aspect of social structure.[3] "The political organization of Jonesville," writes one such scholar, "fits the rest of the social structure . . . curving or bulging with the class outlines of the body politic."[4]

The faults which critics have found with studies following this general conception of politics as an epiphenomenon of social stratification are many, varied, and serious. They include the charges that this conception encourages research designs which generate self-fulfilling prophecies[5] and that it leads to the systematic misreporting of facts[6] and to the formulation of ambiguous and unprovable assertions about community power.[7] It would be gratuitous for me to re-explore these criticisms here. It would be more profitable, instead, to describe some of the ways in which students have evaded—apparently with success—the various disabilities of the stratification approach to the study of community power. With judicious unoriginality, I shall call the alternative research strategy to be outlined here the "pluralist" approach. Old, familiar pluralistic presumptions[8] about the nature of American politics seem to have given researchers strategies for the study of community power which are both feasible to execute and comparatively faithful to conditions in the real world.[9] What follows is an attempt to explain why this seems to be the case for pluralist studies, but not for stratification studies.

The first, and perhaps most basic, presupposition of the pluralist approach is that nothing categorical can be assumed about power in any

Reprinted from the *Journal of Politics*, XXII (August, 1960), 474–84, by permission of the author and the *Journal of Politics*.

35

community. It rejects the stratification thesis that *some* group necessarily dominates a community.[10] If anything, there seems to be an unspoken notion among pluralist researchers that at bottom *nobody* dominates in a town, so that their first question to a local informant is not likely to be "Who runs this community?," but rather "Does anyone at all run this community?" It is instructive to examine the range of possible answers to each of these questions. The first query is somewhat like "Have you stopped beating your wife?," in that virtually any response short of total unwillingness to answer will supply the researchers with a "power elite" along the lines presupposed by the stratification theory.[11] On the other hand, the second question is capable of eliciting a response which *could* lead to the discovery of a power elite (i.e., "Yes"), or any of an infinite number of stable, but nonelitist, patterns of decision-making (i.e., "No, but . . ."; "Yes, but . . ."), or total fragmentation, or disorganization (i.e., "No").

What sort of question is likely to follow "Who runs the community?" in a questionnaire? Obviously, something like "How do the people named in the above response run the community?" This entirely probable pattern of investigation begs the question of whether or not those said to rule actually do rule. In the pluralist approach, on the other hand, an attempt is made to study specific outcomes, in order to determine who actually prevails in community decision-making. Consonant with the desire to study actual outcomes, which requires arduous and expensive field work, outcomes in a few (but, for reasons of expense, usually only a few) issue areas are studied closely. More than a single issue area is always chosen, however, because of the presumption among pluralist researchers that the same pattern of decision-making is highly unlikely to reproduce itself in more than one issue area. In this expectation, pluralist researchers have seldom been disappointed.[12] They recognize, however, the possibility that the same pattern *could* reproduce itself in more than one issue area. Since actual behavior is observed, or reconstructed from documents, witnesses, and so on, it is possible to determine empirically whether or not the same group rules two or more issue areas. The presumption that the existence of a power elite is unlikely does not, in other words, prevent the finding of such an elite if the data so indicate.

A superficially persuasive objection to this approach might be phrased as follows: "Suppose research in a community discloses different patterns of decision-making in each of three issue areas. This does not rule out the possibility that all other issue areas in the community are dominated by a single power elite." How can pluralists meet this objection? First, it is necessary to acknowledge the *possibility* that this is the case. However, pluralists can (and do) protect themselves in part by studying significant issues. In the New Haven study, for example, of which this paper is an outgrowth, we studied (1) nominations by the two political parties, which determine which persons hold public offices; (2) the New Haven Redevelopment program, which is the largest in the country (measured by past and present outlay per capita); (3) public education, which is the most costly item in the city's budget; and (4) a campaign to revise the city charter.[13] In Bennington, Scoble studied political nominations and elections, the issue of consolidation of various municipal governments, the formation of a union high school district, and the construction of a new high school building.[14] A pilot study, by Long and Belknap, of a large eastern city embraced the problems of transportation, race relations, traffic, urban redevelopment, and recreation,[15] while, in the San Francisco Bay area, Belknap studied the issues of urban redevelopment, transportation, and race relations.[16] None of these issues was trivial; they probably were, in fact, the most important issues before these communities during the time these studies were being carried out. What sort of a power elite is it—it may appropriately be asked—which asserts itself in relatively trivial matters, but is inactive or ineffective in the most significant areas of community policy-making?

Stratification theory holds that power elites fail to prevail only on trivial issues.[17] By preselecting as issues for study those which are generally agreed to be significant, pluralist researchers can test stratification theory without searching endlessly in one issue area after another, in order to discover some semblance of a power elite. After all, it cannot be reasonably required of researchers that they validate someone else's preconceived notions of community power distributions. If the researcher's design is such that any power distribution has an equal chance of appearing in his result, his result may not properly be criticized on the grounds that it did not conform to expectations. The burden of proof is clearly on the challenger in such a case to make good his assertion that power is actually distributed otherwise.[18]

Another presumption of the pluralist approach runs directly counter to stratification theory's presumption that power distributions are a more or less permanent aspect of social structure. Pluralists hold that power may be tied to issues, and issues can be fleeting or persistent, provoking coalitions among interested groups and citizens ranging in their duration from momentary to semipermanent. There is a clear gain in descriptive accuracy involved in formulating power distributions so as to take account of the dimension of time, as pluralists do,[19] since it is easily demonstrated that coalitions *do* vary in their permanency. To presume that the set of coalitions which exists in the community at any given time is a timelessly stable aspect of social structure is to introduce systematic inaccuracies into one's description of social reality.

Why do pluralists reject the idea that *some* group necessarily dominates every community? The presumption that communities are likely to be less, rather than more, permanent in their patterns of decision-making is no doubt part of the answer, but another part is an even more fundamental conception of human behavior as governed in large part by inertia. This view leads pluralists to put a high value on overt activity as indicative of involvement in issues and to look upon the collection of "reputations" for leadership as a much less desirable research procedure.[20]

Pluralists consider as arbitrary the inclusion of certain groups as being "implicated" in decisions when these groups themselves reject such involvement.[21] For pluralists, "false class consciousness" does not exist, because it implies that the values of analysts are imposed on groups in the community. They reject the idea that there is any particular issue or any particular point in the determination of an issue where a group must assert itself in order to follow its expressed values. Rather, the pluralist assumes that there are many issues and many points at which group values can be realized. Further, pluralists presume that there are certain costs in taking any action at all. This refers not simply to the possibility of losing, of making political enemies, and so on, but also to the costs in personal time and effort involved in political mobilization, in becoming informed, in lobbying or campaigning, and in taking the trouble to vote.[22]

It is a demonstrated fact that public activity of all sorts is a habit more characteristic of the middle and upper classes than of the lower classes.[23] Vidich and Bensman, for the first time in a community study, depicted the life of the lowest-class groups in the community sufficiently well so that the personally functional aspects of withdrawal from the community were revealed.[24] The presumption of inertia permits the researcher to regard the public sector of activity as but one facet of behavior capable of giving people satisfaction and discourages the inappropriate and arbitrary assignment of upper- and middle-class values to all actors in the community.

The presumption of inertia also helps put economic and social notables into perspective. If a man's major lifework is banking, the pluralist presumes he will spend his time at the bank, and not in manipulating community decisions. The presumption holds until the banker's activities and participations indicate otherwise. Once again, it is very important to make the point that this assumption is not scientifically equivalent to its opposite. If we presume that the banker is "really" engaged in running the community, there is practically no way of disconfirming this notion, even if it is totally erroneous. On the other hand, it is easy to spot the banker who really *does* run community affairs when we presume he does not, because his activities will make this fact apparent. In the absence of the requisite activities, we have no grounds for asserting that the banker, in fact, does run the community.[25]

The pluralist emphasis on the time-bounded nature of coalitions and on the voluntary aspect of political participation leads to a further contrast with stratification theory, since pluralists hold that the "interest group" and the "public" are the social collectives most relevant to the analysis of political processes. In the sociologist's patois, politically important groups would be called phenomena of "collective behavior" rather than of "social structure."[26] Social classes in stratification theory are populations differentially ranked according to economic or status criteria, which embrace the entire community. Everyone in a community is a member of at least one, but no more than one, class at any given moment, and no one in the community falls outside the system. This is a legitimate heuristic construction; however, it is a mistake to impute to the apparently inescapable fact of class membership any sort of class consciousness. This sociologists have long recognized.[27] But they seem less willing to grant that it is equally incorrect to presume that those sharing similar market or status positions are also equidistant to all the bases of political power or, in fact, share class interests. American society has never been noted for its interclass warfare, a fact often reported with a great show of surprise in stratification studies of American communities.[28]

Pluralists, who see American society as fractured into a congeries of hundreds of small "special interest" groups, with incompletely overlapping memberships, widely differing power bases, and a multitude of techniques for exercising influence on decisions salient to them,[29] are not surprised at the low priority which Americans give to their class membership as bases of social action. In the decision-making of fragmented government—and American national, state, and local governments are nothing if not fragmented—the claims of small, intense minorities are usually attended to.[30] Hence it is not only inefficient but usually unnecessary for entire classes to mobilize when the preferences of class members are pressed and often satisfied in a piecemeal fashion. The empirical evidence supporting this pluralist doctrine is overwhelming,[31] however much stratification theorists may have missed its significance for them; namely, that the fragmentation of American governmental decision-making and of American society makes class consciousness inefficient and, in most cases, makes the political interests of members of the same class different.

Pluralist research is not interested in ascertaining an actor's ranking in a system presumed to operate hierarchically. Rather, pluralists want to find out about leadership *roles*, which are presumed to be diverse and fluid, both within a single issue area over time, and as between issue areas. Long and Belknap, for example, identify the following leadership roles in community decision-making: initiation, staffing and planning, communication and publicity, intra-elite organizing, financing, and public sanctioning.[32]

By describing and specifying leadership roles in concrete situations, pluralists are in a position to determine the extent to which power structure exists. If there exist high degrees of overlap among issue areas in decision-making personnel, or of institutionalization in the bases of power in specified issue areas, or of regularity in the procedures of decision-making, then the empirical conclusion is justified that some sort of a "power structure" exists. By specifying leadership roles and activities, the pluralist research strategy makes it possible for an empirical determination of the bounds and durability of a community power structure—if one exists—to be described, and the stratification theory presumption that community power is necessarily general and relatively immutable can be discarded as arbitrary.

The final contrast I want to make between the pluralist and stratification methods has to do with their differing conceptions of what is meant by "power." I have already noted that stratification theorists emphasize the cataloguing of power bases, meaning the resources available to actors for the exercise of power.[33] Pluralists, on the other hand, concentrate on power exercise itself. This leads to two subsidiary discoveries. First, there are a great many different kinds of resources which can be turned to use in the process of community decision-making—many more resources, in fact, than stratification theorists customarily take account of. One list, for example, includes money and credit; control over jobs; control over the information of others; social standing; knowledge and expertness; popularity, esteem, and charisma; legality, constitutionality, and officiality; ethnic solidarity; and the right to vote.[34]

The second product of the pluralist emphasis on power exercise is the discovery that resources are employed only with variations in degree of skill. The elaboration of the ways in which resources are employed enables the pluralist researcher to pay attention to what practical politicians customarily see as the heart of their own craft: the processes of bargaining, negotiation, salesmanship, brokerage, and leadership in mobilizing resources of all kinds. This approach also makes possible a more realistic evaluation of the actual disposable resources of actors. A corporation may be worth millions of dollars, but its policies and liquidity position may be such that it cannot possibly bring those monetary resources into play in order to influence the outcome of a community decision—even one in which the corporation is vitally interested. And interest itself, as noted above, is differentially distributed in a pattern which pluralists assume is rational for most actors, most of the time. For example, Long and Belknap observe:

> Just as business organizations may be disinterested in community affairs because of the national scope of its [sic] operations, individual businessmen who move or are shifted from city to city may have little opportunity or incentive to participate in community affairs. Some businesses have strong pressures on them to give attention to community and metropolitan problems. Large department stores are particularly tied up with the destiny of the city and must decide whether to keep to the central city or decentralize in suburban shopping centers. Businessmen with a "metropolitan view" would thus be expected to be found here rather than in the branch office of a national corporation.[35]

What practical recommendations emerge from this comparison of stratification and pluralist approaches to the study of community power?[36] First, the researcher should pick issue areas as the focus of his study of community power. Second, he should be able to defend these issue areas as being very important in the life of the community. Third, he should study actual behavior, either at firsthand or by reconstructing behavior from documents, informants, newspapers, and other appropriate sources. There is no harm in starting with a list of people whose behavior the researcher wishes to study vis-à-vis any issue area. The harm comes, rather, in attributing some mystical significance to such a list, so that the examination of activity and of actual participation in decision-making becomes superfluous. This recommendation is not meant to discourage the researcher from collecting information about the reputation of actors, or their intentions with respect to community issues, or their evaluations about the "meanings" of community incidents. All of these kinds of data are of immeasurable value in tracing patterns of decision-making. However, these cultural data must be accompanied by information about behavior so that the researcher has some way of distinguishing between myths and facts.

The final recommendation is of the same order; researchers should study the outcomes of actual decisions within the community. It is important, but insufficient, to know what leaders want to do, what they intend to do, and what they think they can do. The researcher still has to decide on the basis of his own examination of the facts what actually emerges from these various intentions, and not conclude prematurely that the combination of intentions and resources inflexibly predetermines outcomes.

Notes

1. This article is a paper of the New Haven Community Leadership Study and owes a great deal to Robert A. Dahl and Raymond E. Wolfinger. I am also grateful to George M. Belknap, Norton E. Long, and Robert O. Schulze, but none of these gentlemen should be held responsible for the notions presented here.

2. For indications that disenchantment is setting in among political scientists, see the following: Robert A. Dahl, "A Critique of the Ruling Elite Model," *American Political Science Review*, LII (June, 1958), 463–69; Herbert Kaufman and Victor Jones, "The Mystery of Power," *Public Administration Review*, XIV (Summer, 1954), 205–12; Norton E. Long, "The Local Community as an Ecology of Games," *American Journal of Sociology*, LXIV (November, 1958), 251–61; Nelson W. Polsby, "The Sociology of Community Power: A Reassessment," *Social Forces*, XXXVII (March, 1959), 232–36, and "Three Problems in the Analysis of Community Power," *American Sociological Review*, XXIV (December, 1959), 796–803; and Raymond E. Wolfinger, "Reputation and Reality in the Study of Community Power," *American Sociological Review*, XXV (December, 1960), 636–44. Sociologists also seem to be re-examining studies of community power. See, for example, Reinhard Bendix and Seymour M. Lipset, "Political Sociology," *Current Sociology*, VI (1957), 79–99; and Peter H. Rossi, "Community Decision-Making," *Administrative Science Quarterly*, I (March, 1957), 415–43. Writings praising community power studies are quite extensive, and include the following: Gordon Blackwell, "Community Analysis," in Roland Young (ed.), *Approaches to the Study of Politics* (Evanston, Ill.: Northwestern University Press, 1958), pp. 305–17; William J. Gore and Fred S. Silander, "A Bibliographical Essay on Decision-Making," *Administrative Science Quarterly*, IV (June, 1959), 106–21; and Lawrence J. R. Herson, "The Lost World of Municipal Government," *American Political Science Review*, LI (June, 1957), 330–45.

3. For example, Robert S. Lynd and Helen M. Lynd, *Middletown* (New York: Harcourt, Brace and Co., 1929), and *Middletown in Transition* (New York: Harcourt Brace and Co., 1937); Floyd Hunter, *Community Power Structure* (Chapel Hill, N.C.: University of North Carolina Press, 1953); August B. Hollingshead, *Elmtown's Youth* (New York: John Wiley & Sons, 1949); W. Lloyd Warner *et al.*, *Democracy in Jonesville* (New York: Harper & Bros., 1949); C. Wright Mills, "The Middle Classes in the Middle-Sized Cities," *American Sociological Review*, XI (October, 1946), 520–29; Robert O. Schulze, "Economic Dominants and Community Power Structure," *American Sociological Review*, XXIII (February, 1958), 3–9; Roland Pellegrin and Charles H. Coates, "Absentee-Owned Corporations and Community Power Structure," *American Journal of Sociology*, LXI (March, 1956), 413–19; and Delbert C. Miller, "Industry and Community Power Structure," *American Sociological Review*, XXIII (February, 1958), 9–15, and "Decision-Making Cliques in Community Power Structure," *American Journal of Sociology*, LXIV (November, 1958), 299–310.

4. Warner *et al.*, *op. cit.*, p. xviii.

5. See, e.g., Kaufman and Jones, *op. cit.*

6. See Polsby, *op. cit.*

7. See *ibid.*; Dahl, *op. cit.*; and Kaufman and Jones, *op. cit.*

8. I am well aware that for other purposes the "pluralist" approach can be divided into several schools of thought. However, all variations of pluralist theory contrast effectively with stratification theory. Pluralist presumptions can be found, for example, in the writings of de Tocqueville and Madison, and in Arthur Bentley, *The Process of Government* (Chicago: University of Chicago Press, 1908); E. Pendleton Herring, *The Politics of Democracy* (New York: W. W. Norton & Co., 1940); David B. Truman, *The Governmental Process* (New York: Alfred A. Knopf, 1953); and V. O.

Key, Jr., *Politics, Parties and Pressure Groups* (4th ed.; New York: Thomas Y. Crowell Co., 1959).

9. Among the researchers who have found pluralist presumptions about the nature of the political system useful are Robert A. Dahl, "The New Haven Community Leadership Study," ("Working Paper No. 1," mimeo., December, 1957), Harry Scoble, "Yankeetown: Leadership in Three Decision-Making Processes," paper presented at the meeting of the American Political Science Association, 1956; George M. Belknap; and Norton E. Long. See Long, *op. cit.*; Norton E. Long and George M. Belknap, "A Research Program on Leadership and Decision-Making in Metropolitan Areas" (New York: Governmental Affairs Institute, mimeo., 1956); George M. Belknap and John H. Bunzel, "The Trade Union in the Political Community," *PROD*, II (September, 1958), 3–6; and George M. Belknap, "A Plan for Research on the Socio-Political Dynamics of Metropolitan Areas," paper presented before a seminar on urban leadership of the Social Science Research Council, New York, August, 1957. See also a paper presented to this same seminar by Peter H. Rossi, "The Study of Decision-Making in the Local Community."

10. I present some of the characteristics of a stratification theory of community power in other papers, e.g., "Power in Middletown: Fact and Value in Community Research" (March, 1960); and "Power as a Variable of Social Stratification" (November, 1959).

11. See Kaufman and Jones, *op. cit.*

12. Wolfinger, *op. cit.*, pp. 7 ff, has summarized findings on this point.

13. See Dahl, "The New Haven Community Leadership Study"; Polsby, *op. cit.*; Wolfinger, *op. cit.*; and forthcoming publications of the New Haven Community Leadership Study.

14. Scoble, *op. cit.*

15. Long and Belknap, *op. cit.*

16. Belknap, *op. cit.*

17. See, for example, Pellegrin and Coates, *op. cit.*; and Lynd and Lynd, *Middletown in Transition*, p. 89.

18. See Dahl, "A Critique of the Ruling Elite Model."

19. See, for example, Belknap, *op. cit.*, for an explicit discussion of this point. One stratification writer who has attempted to take account of the time factor is Jerome K. Myers, "Assimilation in the Political Community," *Sociology and Social Research*, XXXV (January–February, 1951), 175–82. Myers plots a secular trend which indicates slow increases in the number of Italians and Italian-descended persons employed by New Haven municipal government over a fifty-year period ending in 1940. Myers claims to have discovered "discrimination" against Italians, because they did not participate in city-government jobs to an extent proportional with their representation in the total population of the city. His conclusion was that "the early or quick assimilation of New Haven Italians in the political system does not seem very probable. . . . All indications are that political assimilation is inevitable, although it is at least several generations away."

By taking account of shorter-term cyclical movements within the allegedly "basic" structure, we may be able to explain the delay in the political assimilation of Italians.

First, New Haven Italian-Americans were and are predominantly Republican in local politics, because in New Haven the Republican organization early and energetically courted the Italian-American vote. From 1920 to 1940, years in which that ethnic group would "normally" have been expected to come into their own as a politically significant minority group, the city government was in Democratic hands two-thirds of the time. It might be expected, therefore, that Italian-Americans would be less well represented among officeholders than if these circumstances were reversed. Second, in 1945, a Republican of Italian descent was elected mayor, whereupon Italian-Americans invaded the top echelons of city government to such an extent that the mayor pleaded in vain with one who was a candidate for president of the city council to withdraw in favor of a Yankee Republican, on the grounds that there were "too many Italians" in City Hall and that the Yankee members of the Republican coalition should have some recognition.

20. See, especially, Wolfinger, op. cit.

21. See C. Wright Mills, op. cit.; and Polsby, "The Sociology of Community Power: A Reassessment," on this point.

22. See Anthony Downs, An Economic Theory of Democracy (New York: Harper & Bros., 1957); Robert E. Lane, Political Life: How People Get Involved in Politics (Glencoe, Ill.: The Free Press, 1959); and Samuel Stouffer, Communism, Conformity, and Civil Liberties (New York: Doubleday & Co., 1955), pp. 58 ff.

23. Lane, op. cit., pp. 220–34.

24. Arthur J. Vidich and Joseph Bensman, Small Town in Mass Society (Princeton: Princeton University Press, 1958), pp. 69–70 and 290–91. Studies of social status have been hampered by a similar problem of upper-class centeredness. See the criticism of Warner on this point by Seymour M. Lipset and Reinhard Bendix, "Social Status and Social Structure," British Journal of Sociology, II (June, 1951), especially 163 ff.

25. See Bentley, op. cit., pp. 175–222. Note, on p. 202: "If we can get our social life stated in terms of activity, and of nothing else, we have not indeed succeeded in measuring it, but we have at least reached a foundation upon which a coherent system of measurements can be built up. . . . We shall cease to be blocked by the intervention of unmeasurable elements, which claim to be themselves the real causes of all that is happening, and which by their spook-like arbitrariness make impossible any progress toward dependable knowledge."

26. Only one sociologist seems to have realized what this implies for the methods and conclusions of political analysis. See Rudolf Heberle, Social Movements: An Introduction to Political Sociology (New York: Appleton-Century-Crofts, 1951). The relevant theory is compactly expounded by Herbert Blumer, "Collective Behavior," in Alfred McClung Lee (ed.), Principles of Sociology, (New York: Barnes & Noble, 1953), pp. 167–220.

27. Indeed, Max Weber, the most important "founding father" of modern stratification analysis, makes just this point. See Weber's "Class, Status, Party, in Hans Gerth and C. Wright Mills (eds.), From Max Weber: Essays in Sociology (New York: Oxford University Press, 1946), pp. 180–195, especially p. 184.

28. See, for example, Lynd and Lynd, Middletown in Transition, pp. 454–55 and 509; Alfred W. Jones, Life, Liberty and Property (Philadelphia: J. B. Lippincott Co., 1941), pp. 336–54; Warner et al., op. cit., p. 27; and C. Wright Mills, op. cit. Compare also Richard H. Centers, The Psychology of Social Classes (Princeton: Princeton University Press, 1949), and note the extent to which his conclusions outrun his data.

29. See, for example, Truman, op. cit., passim; and Alexis de Tocqueville, Democracy in America (New York: Alfred A. Knopf, 1944), especially Vol. I, pp. 181–205 and 281–342, and Vol. II, pp. 114–35.

30. See Robert A. Dahl, A Preface to Democratic Theory (Chicago: University of Chicago Press, 1956).

31. Truman, op. cit., summarizes a tremendous amount of this material.

32. Long and Belknap, op. cit., pp. 9–11. See Polsby, "The Sociology of Community Power: A Reassessment"; and Edward C. Banfield, "The Concept 'Leadership' in Community Research," paper delivered at the meeting of the American Political Science Association, 1958, for similar lists.

33. In papers cited in note 10, above.

34. Robert A. Dahl, "The Analysis of Influence in Local Communities" (May, 1959), p. 10.

35. Long and Belknap, op. cit., pp. 13–14. This corresponds to the findings—but not the interpretations—of Schulze, op. cit.; and of Pellegrin and Coates, op. cit.

36. This presumes that the researcher wants to make some generalizations about the "normal" distributions of power in community decision-making.

3. ON THE NEO-ELITIST CRITIQUE
OF COMMUNITY POWER

RICHARD M. MERELMAN[1]

Introduction

The process of inquiry occasionally exhibits a dialectical pattern in which a series of assertions is advanced and then attacked. A third phase, which consists of an attempt to salvage the first set of assertions, often ensues. The study of American community power has followed this sequence almost classically, and today we find ourselves in the third phase of the dialectic. The first period marked the contemporary emergence of community power as a distinct field of study, mainly through the investigations of Hunter, Mills, and their followers. These observers contended that communities were controlled by "elites," usually economic, who imposed their will, often covertly, on nonelites. The second phase was marked by the challenge of another group of observers, the "pluralists." Pluralists contended that the methods and premises of the "elitists" predisposed them to conclusions about community power which were unjustified. Elitists commonly reached their conclusions either by investigating the reputations for power of various members of the community or merely by assuming that all who possessed certain presumed sources of power were in fact powerful. The pluralists claimed that reputations did not guarantee control and demanded evidence that community *decisions* on political issues, major and minor, were controlled by a reputed elite. The pluralists, after studying community decisions on a variety of subjects, concluded that shifting coalitions of participants drawn from all areas of community life actually controlled local politics. Rarely could a single elite be discovered imposing itself in each area of decision, policy, and conflict.[2]

Many observers felt that the pluralists had won the day. Their methodology studied actual behavior, stressed operational definitions, and turned up evidence. Most important, it seemed to produce reliable con-

Reprinted from the *American Political Science Review*, LXII (June, 1968), 451–60, by permission of the author and the American Political Science Association.

clusions which met the canons of science. Recently, however, new considerations have been introduced which intend to prop up the elitist Humpty Dumpty on a more substantial wall of theory than the one from which it had previously tumbled. The beginnings of a new position on community power appear in the work of those responsible for the third phase, the "neo-elitists," as I shall call them.[3] That position forms the subject of this analysis.

Generally speaking, neo-elitists differ with pluralists over the conclusions which can legitimately be drawn from the study of community decisions in issue areas. Such decisions, say the neo-elitists, actually represent much less than the pluralists suspect. Decisional methodology and pluralist premises are alleged to be deficient in the three following major respects:

1. *Pluralists misunderstand the way influence expresses itself in the community.* According to the neo-elitists, nonelites are encased in values foisted on them by the elite. Elites transmit these values to nonelites by a conscious and unconscious "mobilization of bias."[4] Therefore, nonelites are not even conscious of having major differences with the elite. A "false consensus,"[5] created by the elite, limits conflicts and decisions in the community to unimportant matters which do not threaten the elite.

2. *Pluralists are most successful in assessing power when conflict is occurring.* However, there are many situations in which individuals, despite their disagreements with the powerful, anticipate that they have no chance to profit by raising an issue. They realize that their powerful opponents would crush them. In this case, the power of the opponents expresses itself through the phenomenon of anticipated reactions.[6] Under these conditions, there is no conflict, no visible issue, and no decision and the decisional methodology is useless. According to Bachrach and Baratz, the major figures among the neo-elitists, "To measure relative influence solely in terms of the ability to initiate and veto proposals is to ignore the possible exercise of influence or power in limiting the scope of initiation."[7] In another context, Bachrach and Baratz define power solely to cover situations in which individuals act or do not act in anticipation of the sanctions others may exert upon them.[8] We shall accept the definition to facilitate discussion.

3. *Pluralists unduly stress decisions made in the governmental realm.* However, such emphasis is unwarranted. Even if the anticipation situation breaks down and issues are initiated, they may never reach the stage of governmental decision-making. A variety of coercive devices and sanctions—organizational, ideological, and procedural—may be used to prevent such concerns from being acted on by government. Threats by, and anticipation of, the powerful give way to the application of sanc-

tions which obliterate alternatives to desisting. Bachrach and Baratz define this situation as one involving the actual application of force.[9] Again, we will accept this definition for discussion.

In summation, nonelites are not even conscious of important differences with the elites. Even if they are, they anticipate that they could only lose by making trouble, and so they bow to the power of the elite. Or the application of force prevents them from having their concerns acted on by government. Each of the situations occupies a position on a "nondecision-making" continuum. "When the dominant values, the accepted rules of the game, the existing power relations among groups, and the instruments of force . . . effectively present certain grievances from developing into full-fledged issues which call for decisions, it can be said that a nondecision-making situation exists."[10]

The "False Consensus" Argument

The argument on the problem of false consensus, as it is presently stated, is not an empirical argument, though it makes certain dubious empirical assumptions. Rather, it is a purely deductive, tautological theory which, if one accepts its empirical assumptions, does not admit of empirical proof or disproof. Therefore, it is of limited utility in the actual exploration of community power structure. Furthermore, the peculiar structure of the argument incorporates a logical fallacy which is inadmissible. Finally, any conditions which can be introduced to make the argument subject to empirical validation indicate its lack of utility. These are serious charges; let us see if they hold.

The argument claims that the conflicts studied by the pluralists are unimportant. Why are they unimportant? Because they do not threaten an elite. We need not consider the conflicts studied by the pluralists unimportant if we don't presume the existence of an elite. But the presumption itself is not justified unless the theory specifies some independent reasons for us to believe an elite exists. The argument specifies no such independent reasons. Therefore, we need not believe an elite exists and, without an elite, we cannot have a false consensus.[11]

More generally, the terms of the argument make it impossible to disprove the existence of an elite under conditions of conflict and, as we shall see, under any conditions. If a conflict is unimportant (i.e., "does not threaten an elite"), an elite exists. If a conflict *does* threaten an elite (impossible under the terms of the theory), then an elite also exists, but in this case it will probably be observable since it will be threatened into action. In all cases of conflict an elite exists. Therefore, *only by definition*, the existence of an elite in cases of conflict is "proved."

The set of problems outlined stems directly from the general nature of the argument. The *absence* of an event, conflict which threatens an elite, is taken as the evidence for the existence of an elite. However, we have no reason for accepting the absence of an event as evidence for any particular cause, unless it can be demonstrated that the cause (in this case, an elite) produced the absence of the event (threatening conflict). To do so, some threatening conflict must precede the coming of false consensus. But such threatening conflict is incompatible with false consensus as defined. Therefore, false consensus does not admit the evidence to support itself. To put the point differently, no conflict existing under conditions of false consensus threatens an elite; therefore, no such conflict will cause an elite to show itself. We can never get empirical evidence that an elite exists. The argument reduces itself to a statement of faith.

Furthermore, the argument does not allow us to distinguish between "real" and "false" consensuses. Presumably, a "real" consensus would be defined as a nonelite-controlled consensus. However, since nonelites, under the terms of the theory, are controlled by the mobilization of bias from an elite to them, a real consensus is impossible unless an elite does not exist. But the theory presumes the existence of an elite. Therefore, there can be no real consensus. Finally, joining the two sides of our argument, elites exist in all cases of consensus and in all cases of conflict. The argument cannot be falsified.[12]

The theory also suffers in its chief empirical assumption. It contends that nonelites are encased in a series of values which they assimilate from the elite. No evidence for this assertion is proffered. We now have, instead, good reason to doubt the presence of consensus on many fundamental rules and values of the democratic system.[13] Whatever consensus on fundamental values exists, therefore, seems to pertain to values so far not studied. Is it possible that political scientists could have ignored completely those values which *are* shared and which produce false consensus? Possible, certainly, but unlikely.

Finally, another premise of the argument needs to be explored. The argument assumes that the mobilization of bias operates only downward, from elite to mass. Since little actual *behavior* of the elite is considered in the theory, it is understandable that no specification of mechanisms whereby the elite transmits its values is forthcoming. Therefore, within the bounds of the argument, no evidence to support the downward mobilization of bias is adduced. But a more fundamental problem exists. In the absence of evidence to the contrary, it is just as plausible that any consensus we *do* find is not controlled by an elite. One can argue that nonelites do not differ with elites precisely because the former's values are so well embodied by the latter.[14] The neo-elitist critique provides no reason to reject this assertion. Indeed, as Vidich and Bensman admit in their study of nondecision-making, when elite members do not reflect and conform to widely held values of nonelites, significant conflicts may erupt, in which case power and force come to control.[15]

Because the false consensus argument is deductive, nonfalsifiable, and ridden with undemonstrated assumptions, it is necessary to imagine empirical conditions which might produce an elite-controlled false consensus. In the real world, what conditions are necessary for an elite to erect a successful false consensus? The logic of the argument suggests that the following conditions must hold: (1) the elite must succeed in producing consensus on values within the community as a whole and (2) such values must control policy choice.

What factors affect the attainment of these conditions? First, there must be consensus on a wide variety of points within the elite. Value cleavage within the elite may encourage elite factions to look for support outside. If such conflict extends itself, consensus on community values will disintegrate rapidly. Also, value consensus within the elite must control policy choice. If a particular set of approved values does not dictate policy choice, conflicts can again be extended beyond the elite to the community. Should values continue to permit policy conflict, the way lies clear for the introduction of competing values to justify and express policy conflicts. In order to attain value and policy consensus, the elite must adhere to some procedure designed to obtain agreement on values and priorities, thereby preventing differences from affecting the community. The substantive and procedural elite consensus required here defies complete and continuous attainment. Conflict within the elite is likely.[16]

Elite consensus is itself partially dependent upon a second factor, system autonomy. Individuals in the system, either elite or nonelite, who have some of their needs provided outside the system, may develop competing allegiances and alternative values. Outside contacts offer new means for obtaining goals, new goals, and new models of behavior. External contacts thereby loosen elite controls wherever they exist.[17] And conflict will probably erupt, shattering whatever false consensus exists.

The legal relationships between local, state, and federal governments in the United States, as well as the informal political connections emanating from these arrangements, break down the system autonomy necessary for attainment of false consensus. These arrangements not only provide a forum for the airing and institutionalization of value differences in a community, but also *introduce* competing value sets, priorities, and procedures into communities. Lack of political autonomy for communities lessens the opportunity for local elites to construct a false consensus. Lack of community economic autonomy, increasingly characteristic of American towns and cities, produces a similar effect.[18] In short, neither economic nor political self-sufficiency exists in most localities; therefore, this determinant of false consensus is absent also.

Of course, lack of autonomy is intimately related to community stability at its most fundamental levels. The preservation of elite consensus and local autonomy depends partially upon the extent to which demographic, ecological, and sociological characteristics of the community can be controlled. Changes in birth and death rates, economic patterns, and life expectancies are in varying degrees uncontrollable by political leadership in the United States. Such social changes make demands upon local political systems and leaders as constantly and significantly as, in their turn, local political leaders structure community needs. Often, they require dependence of local organs of government upon national levels.[19] I do not assert, however, that temporary consensuses on policy are impossible or even improbable; I merely suggest the likelihood that any consensus we do find is not "false."

The Power Argument

The conditions for the creation of a successful false consensus seem unattainable, and the logic and assumptions of the false consensus argument are faulty. Therefore, we may conclude that power and force control most community decision-making. Let us look at the next alternative, that of the application of power to prevent community issues from being initiated. This argument, like that of false consensus, suffers both in its statement and in its application to the real world.

The neo-elitist critique suggests that power cases of nondecision are most characteristic of situations in which those with little—anticipating reactions from, and responding to, threats from those with much—do not act. In fact, however, the application of power to forestall action involves all sorts of groups. Therefore, we can conclude little from the mere existence of nondecisions arising from the application of power. For example, the logic of the deterrence formula in American military policy, as Snyder demonstrates,[20] is based on a virtually infinite regress of anticipated reactions. Why are so many anticipated reactions, and the inaction based on such anticipation, necessary? Precisely because the parties to the deterrence situation view themselves as equally able to decimate each other. Nor may those with much ignore the possible reactions of those with little. Under most conditions, as Blau shows,[21] those with much buy legitimacy by anticipating possible unfavorable reactions to their behavior. When such reactions seem imminent, those with much may well not act. Therefore, power cases of nondecisions provide no criteria *by themselves* for saying anything meaningful about community political patterns.

On the other hand, even if those planning to initiate policies hostile to an "elite" become subject to its power and are constrained to desist, they have still exerted power of their own. The elite has been forced to anticipate *them* and exert power in return. The power to get others to veto behavior has policy consequences for the others, a fact which neo-elitists often ignore. For all these reasons, the existence of power cases of nondecisions tells us less about community power than the neo-elitist suspects.

Granting the ubiquity and inconclusiveness of power cases of nondecision-making, the neo-elitist may shift the grounds of his argument. He may contend that those with much need desist only on issues in which they have relatively little at stake. On the other hand, he might say, those with little must desist when they have relatively much at stake. If we accept this contention, we now have a way of measuring power by examining what was at stake for each group controlled by the anticipated sanctions of others. But this argument leads us in an unfortunate direction. Must we conclude that a group's power varies whenever it is involved in decisions or nondecisions of varying import? Surely not. Rather, we are concerned with the ability of a group to get what it wants no matter what the character of the encounter in which it finds itself.

Furthermore, we may argue that power cases of nondecision-making for *all* are equally likely to occur when only marginal gains and losses are at stake. Power cases of nondecisions require that there be sufficient precedents to guide all participants, so that they can assess meaningfully whatever threats are made. In cases where there are such precedents, more often than not established programs already exist, thereby restricting current actions to marginal gains and losses. Wildavsky's discussion of the budgetary process provides many examples of the importance of anticipated reactions in governing marginal allocations for well-established programs.[22] Normally, few ordinary citizens or creative leaders are interested in such areas. Therefore, we need not conclude a priori that groups subject to power cases of nondecisions are losing much.

We might also argue that when there are new programs at stake designed to meet pressing problems which yield few guidelines for policy-makers, control by anticipated reactions often gives way to applications of force. Not only are these issues crucial to group survival, thereby necessitating vigorous action, but they are also lacking in those precedents which might provide meaningful assessments of threats. To sum up, those with much anticipate those with little; those with little, those with much; and they relatively equal each other when both important and unimportant matters are at stake. The power argument cannot be reformulated to tell us anything a priori about community power.

The logic of the power case has two further weaknesses that require exploration. Elites, we are told, are able, through the application of power, to prevent issues which threaten them from being initiated. But one might argue the exact contrary of this position, using the logic of the argument itself. If the major concern of the elite is to keep threatening issues from being initiated and reaching government, then only the most conflictful, the most intense, the most pressing will be able to mobilize enough support to pass the barriers of power and force erected by the elite. In this case, one could perfectly well argue that the neo-elitist critique strengthens rather than detracts from the pluralist emphasis on governmental decision-making. As presently stated, the power argument leads as plausibly to this conclusion as to the conclusion adopted by the neo-elitists. The point is, of course, that the neo-elitist interpretation of the power case takes only that side of the phenomenon which supports its conclusions.

But suppose we assure ourselves that the issues which are decided through one governmental agency are relatively harmless to an elite and of little interest to the nonelite. Suppose, further, that the elite has threatened the nonelite with sanctions if it pursues issues which might change the status quo. May this set of facts be taken as validation of the neo-elitists' power argument? No. After all, the initiators may anticipate not only that they will not get a hearing from an agency, but also that the agency is too weak to help them. For example, in some large cities the great number of decision-making organs produces as much inaction and nondecision-making as does the application of power aimed at preventing initiation.[23] In addition, one could only affirm the importance of the nondecision-making process in this case if the nonelite were unable to find a hearing in other governmental agencies which could aid it. In Springdale, for example, the unwillingness of the village board to handle potentially threatening issues ultimately was [balanced] by the availability of competent state, local, and national agencies to which recourse was had successfully.[24]

More generally, even though a group attempts to prevent an issue from reaching a governmental agency, and the issue does not, we need not assume that the group has succeeded. The availability of other outlets limits the extent to which we can say that an elite has succeeded in applying power to prevent decision. The American political system maximizes outlets for decisions, thereby lessening the ability of an elite to produce nondecision-making through the application of power.

So much for ambiguities, unjustified assumptions, and problems of interpretation in the power argument; equally as serious are the difficulties that remain when we attempt to apply the argument to the conduct of research. Ironically enough, both the study and the logic of anticipated reactions as a phenomenon drive us back to research premises virtually identical to those already employed by the pluralists.

In order to meet the problem of anticipated reactions, the pluralist focus on decisions must be expanded to cover patterns of *communication* within policy areas. If power, defined by Bachrach and Baratz as being based on anticipation, is exercised to "limit the scope of initiation," the powerful must communicate policy preferences and threatened sanctions to the less powerful. Bachrach and Baratz themselves specify that power exercise requires communication.[25] A few nondecisions might be based on inferences about elite preferences in the absence of contemporaneous communication, but such situations seem unlikely. If preferences are initially strong enough, potential initiators will make certain that the current desires of those who count are ascertained through some sort of overt communication. Communication is an empirically investigable phenomenon and can be studied through an expansion of the pluralist framework.

But by expanding the scope of inquiry from decisions to communications, we do not skirt all our problems. Having discovered the pattern of communication, we still must infer the controlling pattern of anticipated reactions. Merely knowing who communicated with whom in an issue area over a period of time and who threatened sanctions or promised rewards does not reveal whose anticipated reactions actually carried weight. How can we solve this problem?

We could, of course, simply ask those involved in an issue area what their actual anticipation of reactions is or, in cases of retrospective research, was. But this procedure is both incomplete and unreliable. We know that many people are often unclear about the influences to which they respond. Many simply forget; others have good reason to lie. Still others rationalize in such a way as to convince themselves that decisions thrust on them from external sources were really their own. For example, Bachrach and Baratz have no difficulty believing that economic dominants who take no role in a decision do so from their own disinterest in the issues at stake.[26] However, it may instead be true that, anticipating a defeat, they downgrade the importance of the issues. Rationalization is a ubiquitous and powerful defense mechanism.

We are unable to draw the sorts of conclusions about community power from an investigation of communication that would satisfy either the neo-elitists or others. Is there no way of supplementing the study of communication with an additional factor which will allow us to identify, at least fairly well, the determining pattern of anticipated reactions? I submit that we can use the pattern of actual, observable, past and present force applications as a guide to the present pattern of anticipated reactions. These applications of force will occur most often in community conflicts. Such conflicts, of course, are those most likely to be uncovered by a traditional pluralist methodology.

Why should force situations provide our springboard? The answer is that the reactions of a group are anticipated mainly when current or past experience with the group demonstrates that its reactions must be reckoned with. Such experience comes only from the actual application, rather than simply the threat, of sanctions. As Dorwin Cartwright laconically observes, "It appears . . . that if a person possesses power he will be inclined to use it."[27] Nor was Machiavelli insensitive to the importance of demonstrations of power through sanction application.[28] Even Bachrach and Baratz concede that "the *use* of force in one situation increases the credibility of *threats* to use it in others."[29] However, as we have seen, the major thrust of the Bachrach and Baratz argument runs counter to these notions. To repeat, *we have little reason to expect that any group will be listened to unless it has been tested and been forced to apply some of the sanctions it threatens.* We must conclude that the only answer to the problem of anticipated reactions in nondecisions is to rely, in practice, on the pluralist investigation of forceful conflict. The power argument in the neo-elitist critique does not suggest a viable alternative.

But, it may be argued, even if we find, either in the community's political history or present political life, a rough index of the operative pattern of anticipated reactions, our problem is not solved. The essence of the anticipated reactions problem, the argument goes, is that no two situations are alike. For example, labor leaders may demand publicly that politicians press legislation governing working conditions. Politicians remember that in the past business leaders, though threatening sanctions, actually did little to impede similar labor legislation governing wages and hours. Nor have they done more than threaten in the current case. But the past and present are unreliable guides to the future. Perhaps business leaders feel more strongly about working conditions. Therefore, we cannot use either past or current experience as an infallible index to present, controlling patterns of anticipated reactions or to subsequent behavior.[30] This argument is true as far as it goes; strictly speaking, of course, we cannot.

But let us look at the matter from the perspective of the politicians caught in the middle. They are faced with public pressures from labor leaders who have made commitments to their followers. Against this present pressure the neo-elitist critique assumes that politicians will weigh more heavily the private threats of other groups in the community who have a history of failing to carry out their threats. We may grant that politicians will consider such threats, but we may wonder how seriously they will view them. One may argue more plausibly that they will heavily discount these threats because they doubt that they are meaningful. Lacking demonstrations of seriousness by those business leaders with whose motives and intentions they are concerned, politicians would rationally support labor. When the businessmen commit themselves and actually apply pressures and sanctions, they make their threats credible. By so doing, of course, they also bring the conflict into view of pluralist methodology. In politics, as in poker, "put up or shut up" expresses a major formula for decision-makers. Also, in politics as in poker, bluffs work consistently only with novices and for short periods. The actions of politicians tend to redeem the utility of pluralist methodology.[31]

The Force Argument

It would appear, from the analysis of the power argument, that force holds the major empirical relevance in the area of nondecisions. As a matter of research strategy, it appears clear that applications of force are both easier to study than any behavior falling under the power case and also more likely to structure the pattern of anticipated reactions. A traditional pluralist approach uncovers applications of force which produce nondecision-making; therefore, we need be concerned only with the implications and interpretations of the force argument. The neo-elitist interpretation of the force argument is, I feel, neither entirely justified nor complete.

Suppose we discover that the application of elite force prevented some of a certain group's major concerns from reaching the stage of governmental policy-making. Few would deny that this process occurs. Indeed, a variety of techniques can be used to assure this outcome. Procedural tactics can be employed to sidetrack issues. Talk about whether to put a matter on the agenda can go on endlessly. Resort to precedent can be used to deny the legitimacy of an issue for governmental decision. Access to precedents, records, and other useful material can be denied the initiators. In extreme cases, intimidation of the initiators may be undertaken. Channels of communication can be closed.[32] All these applications of force coerce the initiators into acceptance of the status quo. However, inferences about these tactics are not as straightforward as the neo-elitists suggest.

We may, of course, infer that the neo-elitist critique has been confirmed. However, we may also infer something else; namely, that the elite has been coerced into exerting sanctions. Initiators have severely restricted the elite's alternatives. Should we not consider this situation evidence of the strength of the initiators as well as of the elite? The neo-elitists may dismiss this interpretation by suggesting that, regardless, the governmental process continues to favor the elite. But the process rewards the elite, as far as one can tell, only when the elite asks nothing from it but protection from outside interference. Whether, in fact, the governmental process would favor the elite, should it want *positive* concessions from government, remains a moot point.

Of course, the neo-elitist might reply, "So what? Those who get the most of what there is to get won't need government to aid them, but only to prevent others from hurting them. Only losers go to government actually to get something positive."[33] This reply, it should be immediately apparent, is an assertion, not a demonstration. Indeed, we have good reason to suspect that government is an aid in getting things for both winners and losers. If so, we may wonder why the elite itself chooses not to use government for something positive. There are two possible answers to this question. First, we may argue that elites, because of their favored positions, have fewer needs than those who wish to use government. But, on the other hand, their great power should make it easier for them to work through government to get what little they still want. Second, we may argue that the elite members do not feel they could win in attempts to use government. If, in fact, elites can only prevent others from using government, but feel themselves similarly unable to use it, few of us would wish to label the situation truly "elitist."[34] Therefore, we can conclude little from the force argument, unless and until the "elite" itself succeeds in gaining something positive from government.

Neo-elitists ignore the fact that nonelites can often enhance their power by forcing their opponents to use force against them. Nonelites may try to force elites to deny them access to government, hoping that they will gain public sympathy, publicity, and, ultimately, political support. What may at first appear to be simply an instance of an elite forcing nonelites into acquiescence may, on deeper examination, turn out to be the opening wedge in a campaign to unseat the elite. No responsible analyst should ignore all the possible interpretations and aspects of force application.

The neo-elitist may wonder if the situation just described bears any relation to the real world. Why, he may say, should individuals be attracted to a cause which has just been forcibly denied even a governmental hearing? The neo-elitist formulation of nondecision-making conceals the answer to this question, because it emphasizes only those values which contribute to elite control and support the status quo. But are there no "dominant values," no "accepted rules of the game," which favor the initiators of issues? Are there no Americans who feel that the role of government is to handle grievances put to it? Is not one "rule of the game" that government officials should handle legitimate protests which arise within society, and not conspire to force initiators of such protests to desist? Though we do not have conclusive evidence, there is reason to believe that values and beliefs favoring initiators do exist.[35] They constitute both a check on the nondecision-making process and a lever by which those groups discriminated against by nondecision-making acquire supporters and resources. Such groups can occasionally activate these values by forcing elites to deny them the use of government. We need not assume that all the "values," all the "rules of the game," favor the status quo.

What has so far been said leads to another deficiency in the force argument. The argument ignores the political costs of nondecision-making, especially by force, but also by power. Such costs affect governmental agencies, public officials, and members of the elite itself. Ultimately, they undercut rule by forceful nondecision-making.

Perhaps the major cost of continued forceful nondecision-making is the lessened possibility of *any* sort of positive decision-making by the governmental agency in question. Taking an extreme example, Vidich and Bensman note that, as a consequence of its continued unwillingness to hear grievances, "the [Springdale] village board is not usually in a position to act when pressing action is required."[36] There are two reasons why continued nondecision-making, whether by force or power, decreases the possibility of positive decision-making.

First, the refusal of one agency to exercise its legal jurisdiction means that other governmental agencies supplant it and, despite legalities, expand their own operative spans of control. Vidich and Bensman indicate that this reorientation of power occurred even in insular Springdale.[37] As organizational and bureaucratic theory would suggest, competing centers of power tend to expand their jurisdictions as much as possible.[38] Second, and equally costly to agencies engaged in nondecision-making, the effect of an agency's inaction tarnishes its image. Officials of the agency, as well as the general public, lose faith in the decision-making process. Vidich and Bensman report of the members of the Springdale village board:

> They are not . . . able to assess their relationship to a constituency, and this lack of skill leads to the indecision which results in incompetence. What is more, the picture of their performance which emerges to the public level is generally regarded as reflecting a do-nothing, incompetent

government agency. The incompetence of the board members is an open and widespread subject of public discussion among all groups in the community, and elected board members are themselves quick to admit to the outside observer that they "don't know much" about village government.[39]

The good burghers of Springdale seemed not at all unhappy to preside over the dissolution of village-board authority and power in the town. At the behest of economic notables they aided in destroying the power and prestige of village government. Most politicians, however, will not contemplate so passively and sanguinely either their own stained images or the decayed prestige of their organization. They, perhaps even more than the general public, share those values which suggest that the role of a political body is to decide, pro or con.[40] These values provide an important check on their propensity to practice nondecision-making. It is at least possible that, at some point, public officials will act to protect their dying prestige. One of the ways they can do so is by assuring groups with grievances that they will at least receive an official decision, should they reactivate their demands. In so doing, whatever nondecision-making process formerly existed would be destroyed.

Nor do the costs of forceful nondecision-making fall easily on the elite. Unanimity within the elite is relatively easy to maintain when only threats are involved. But actual application of sanctions, with all the unforeseen consequences of such application, will not elicit so unanimous a response. Indeed, once force is necessary to prevent issues from reaching government, it is quite possible that the elite will be on its way to dissolution. It is not as easy to conceal actual sanction application as it is threats. Nor is it easy to ward off reactions to overt, forceful nondecision-making. We can therefore conclude that the costs of nondecision-making to governmental agencies, public officials, and local elites assure that control by forceful nondecision-making will be inherently unstable and, probably, of short duration.

The neo-elitist critique of community power focuses on the problem of nondecision-making. Nondecision-making may proceed through the application of power, force, or the construction of a "false consensus." However, the neo-elitist statement of nondecision-making has logical and empirical problems as formulated. The false consensus argument is nonfalsifiable and, therefore, not amenable to scientific investigation. The power and force cases are construed in ways which lead to unwarranted conclusions. A pluralist methodology must be adopted to meet the major contentions raised by the power case, because anticipated reactions will be based upon observable instances of force application. However, applications of force are not always understandable in the terms posited by the neo-elitist critique, nor can we expect that forceful nondecision-making will provide conclusions that support the critique. For these reasons, we have reason to believe that research based on pluralist premises leads to a reasonably accurate picture of community power. We also have reason to believe that no "elite" can operate for long solely on the basis of nondecision-making.

Notes

1. I am indebted to Stephen Stephens, Fred Greenstein, and James Eisenstein for cogent comments on earlier drafts of this paper.

2. For good statements of positions, see Nelson W. Polsby, *Community Power and Political Theory* (New Haven: Yale University Press, 1963); Delbert C. Miller, "Democracy and Decision-making in the Community Power Structure," in William D'Antonio and Howard J. Ehrlich (eds.), *Power and Democracy in America* (Notre Dame, Ind.: University of Notre Dame Press, 1961), pp. 25–73; Robert A. Dahl, "Equality and Power in American Society," in *ibid.*, pp. 73–91; and Raymond Wolfinger, "Reputation and Reality in the Study of Community Power," in Nelson W. Polsby, Robert A. Dentler, and Paul A. Smith (eds.), *Politics and Social Life* (Boston: Houghton Mifflin Co., 1963), pp. 703–12. The literature in this area is voluminous. Obviously, not all those who use the reputational method come to elitist conclusions, nor do all those who use the decisional approach come to pluralist conclusions. For example, see Robert E. Agger, Daniel Goldrich, and Bert E. Swanson, *The Rulers and the Ruled* (New York: John Wiley & Sons, 1964). However, it is fair to say that most investigators using the reputationalist approach start off with elitist premises and most investigators using the decisional approach begin with pluralist assumptions. Hence, I will oversimplify a bit and consider approach and premises as coextensive. Indeed, as John Walton shows, decisional theorists do tend to find pluralist power situations and reputationalists, elite situations. This is only partially due to the different arenas they have examined. See John Walton, "Substance and Artifact: The Current Status of Research on Community Power Structure," *American Journal of Sociology*, LXXI (January, 1966), 430–39. It is important to note that, for the most part, in the discussion to follow I take the notion of "elite" as given and meaningful. The substance of my argument does not turn in any crucial way on the obvious difficulties, which have been explicated elsewhere, with definitions of community power elites.

3. The neo-elitist critique relies primarily on the notion of nondecision-making. In particular, I will be treating the writings of Peter Bachrach and Morton S. Baratz, "Two Faces of Power," *American Political Science Review*, LVI (December, 1962), 947–52, and "Decisions and Non-decisions: An Analytical Framework," *American Political Science Review*, LVII (September, 1963), 632–42; E. E. Schattschneider, *The Semisovereign People* (New York: Holt, Rinehart & Winston, 1960); and Arthur J. Vidich and Joseph Bensman, *Small Town in Mass Society* (Garden City, N.Y.: Doubleday & Co., 1960). These writings relate closely to theory exemplified in Felix Oppenheim, *Dimensions of Freedom* (New York: St. Martin's Press, 1961), chap. iii; and Carl J. Friedrich, *Man and His Government* (New York: McGraw-Hill Book Co., 1963), chap. iii. Recent influential writings which embody traces of "nondecision" theory include Richard E. Neustadt, *Presidential Power* (New York: John Wiley & Sons, 1962), *passim*; and Karl W. Deutsch, *The Nerves of Government* (New York: The Free Press of Glencoe, 1963), pp. 110–11, *et passim*.

4. Schattschneider, *op. cit.*, chaps. i–iii, *et passim.*

5. "False consensus" is a term borrowed from Robert A. Dahl, "A Critique of the Power Elite Model," *American Political Science Review*, LII (June, 1958), 463–69, especially 468.

6. For complex examples of the phenomenon of anticipated reactions, see an unpublished paper by Robert A. Dahl, "The Power Analysis Approach to the Study of Politics," (April, 1965), 27–28; and James G. March, "An Introduction to the Theory of Measurement of Influence," *American Political Science Review*, XLIX (June, 1955), 431–51, especially 443–44.

7. Bachrach and Baratz, "Two Faces of Power," p. 952.

8. Bachrach and Baratz, "Decisions and Non-decisions: An Analytical Framework," p. 637.

9. *Ibid.*, p. 636.

10. *Ibid.*, p. 641.

11. For a similar criticism of the elitists, see Polsby, *op. cit.*, p. 24.

12. On the criterion of falsifiability in theory construction, see Karl R. Popper, *The Logic of Scientific Discovery* (London: Hutchinson, 1959), chap. iv.

13. See, especially, Herbert McClosky, "Consensus and Ideology in American Politics," in Edward C. Dreyer and Walter Rosenbaum (eds.), *Political Opinion and Electoral Behavior* (Belmont, Calif.: Wadsworth Publishing Co., 1966), pp. 37–64; and Robert A. Dahl, *Who Governs? Democracy and Power in an American City* (New Haven: Yale University Press, 1961), chap. xxviii.

14. For a discussion of a variety of constraints on elites, see Polsby, *op. cit.*, pp. 128 ff. Put in a rather simplified form, the neo-elitist critique accepts a "Great Man" theory of leadership much at variance with current studies of leadership which indicate the extent to which leaders are constrained to conform to group values. See, for example, the theory of E. P. Hollander, "Emergent Leadership and Social Influence," in Luigi Petrillo and Bernard Bass (eds.), *Leadership and Interpersonal Behavior* (New York: Holt, Rinehart & Winston, 1961), pp. 30–48.

15. See the discussion of the challenge to the village elite launched by James West, in Vidich and Bensman, *op. cit.*, 162–71. I will rely heavily on the Vidich and Bensman study, not through a paucity of other useful material, but rather because it is interpreted primarily as support of the nondecision argument.

16. The major difficulty stems from specialization of leadership roles, which leads to conflict. The most obvious example is the conflict inherent between staff and line in a bureaucracy. Even the insular, homogeneous elite in Springdale could not continually maintain consensus (see *ibid.*, pp. 46–53).

17. For a theoretical statement of the same proposition, see Richard Emerson, "Power-Dependence Relations," *American Sociological Review*, XXVII (1962), 31–41, especially 32.

18. For a case study, see Robert O. Schulze, "The Bifurcation of Power in a Satellite City," in Morris Janowitz (ed.), *Community Political Systems* (Glencoe, Ill.: The Free Press, 1961), pp. 19–81.

19. This has become especially true of American cities and metropolitan areas, but it is also becoming true for smaller towns wishing to make use of urban renewal funds available from the federal government. On this point see the figures of Martin Anderson, *The Federal Bulldozer* (Cambridge, Mass.: The MIT Press, 1962), p. 44.

20. Glenn Snyder, *Deterrence and Defense* (Princeton: Princeton University Press, 1961), pp. 9–53.

21. Peter Blau, *Exchange and Power in Social Life* (New York: John Wiley & Sons, 1964), chap. viii.

22. Aaron Wildavsky, *The Politics of the Budgetary Process* (Boston: Little, Brown & Co., 1964), chaps. ii and iii.

23. See, especially, the case of New York, in Wallace S. Sayre and Herbert Kaufman, *Governing New York City* (New York: W. W. Norton & Co., 1965), chap. xix.

24. I speak here not only of governmental agencies, to which reference will be

made later, but to the role of the Community Club at the local level (see Vidich and Bensman, *op. cit.*, pp. 133–35).

25. Bachrach and Baratz, "Decisions and Non-decisions: An Analytical Framework," p. 634.

26. Bachrach and Baratz, "Two Faces of Power," p. 950.

27. Dorwin Cartwright, "A Field Theoretical Conception of Power," in Dorwin Cartwright (ed.), *Studies in Social Power* (Ann Arbor, Mich.: University of Michigan Press, 1959), p. 202. Here it seems clear that Cartwright is thinking about the disposition to demonstrate power forcefully and visibly when such demonstration is feasible and inviting.

28. "And men have less scruple in offending one who makes himself loved than one who makes himself feared; for love is held by a chain of obligation which, men being selfish, is broken whenever it serves their purpose; but fear is maintained by a dread of punishment which never fails" (Machiavelli, *The Prince and the Discourses* [New York: The Modern Library, 1940], p. 61).

29. Bachrach and Baratz, "Decisions and Non-decisions: An Analytical Framework," p. 636.

30. Of course, no index is "infallible." What we look for is an index which will be reliable under most circumstances. To put it another way, past and present demonstrations of power are a less fallible index of present anticipations on policy matters than any other index we could use.

31. Theory underlying these formulations is drawn primarily from David Braybrooke and Charles E. Lindblom, *A Strategy of Decision* (New York: The Free Press of Glencoe, 1963), chaps. iv–vi; and Thomas Schelling, *The Strategy of Conflict* (Cambridge, Mass.: Harvard University Press, 1960), chap. ii.

32. For examples of many of these and other techniques, see Vidich and Bensman, *op. cit.*, *passim*. For an examination of the ways in which rules governing decisional priorities are generated and operate in a decision-making body, see James David Barber, *Power In Committees* (Chicago: Rand McNally & Co., 1966), chaps. ii and iii.

33. Schattschneider makes this argument about intrabusiness conflict: "It is the *losers in intrabusiness conflict who seek redress from public authority. The dominant business interests resist appeals to the government*" (Schattschneider, *op. cit.*, p. 40 [italics his]).

34. This formulation is reminiscent of Riesman's "veto groups" concept. See David Riesman *et al.*, *The Lonely Crowd* (Garden City, N.Y.: Anchor Books, 1953), pp. 246–51.

35. Evidence is only suggestive and scattered. However, we can note that more Americans (22 per cent) preferred firm and aggressive leadership, honesty and sincerity, to other leadership qualities in a 1960 Roper poll (see Roper Commercial Poll, No. 101, question 21). Similarly, we may note the familiar upsurge of support for a President after his forceful intervention in foreign affairs. This response was most recently exploited by President Johnson in the Tonkin affair. Nor is it any accident that most of those who write on "great" Presidents ordinarily talk about activists such as Lincoln, Roosevelt, etc. The evaluation of greatness arrived at by scholars is reflected in the opinions of most Americans. Support for governmental initiators may well reflect a deeper support for initiators throughout the system.

36. Vidich and Bensman, *op. cit.*, p. 131.

37. *Ibid.*, p. 136.

38. For a sophisticated treatment of conflict strategies and expansionist tendencies in governmental bureaucracies, see Matthew Holden, Jr., " 'Imperialism' in Bureaucracy," *American Political Science Review*, LX (December, 1966), 943–52.

39. Vidich and Bensman, *op. cit.*, p. 118.

40. Indications are that political activists are much more likely to be strongly ideological than their followers. Therefore, they will be even more likely than their followers to use the political process actively as a vehicle for obtaining their values. See Herbert McClosky, *et al.*, "Issue Conflict and Consensus Among Party Leaders

and Followers," *American Political Science Review*, LIV (June, 1960), 406–27. Also, see Lester Milbrath, *Political Participation* (Chicago: Rand McNally & Co., 1965), chap. iii, for a review of the literature relating political participation to the development of ideological thinking. Finally, the idealistic, activist self-conceptions of federal bureaucrats are noted in W. Lloyd Warner *et al.*, *The American Federal Executive* (New Haven: Yale University Press, 1963), chap. xiii. Such role identities seem entirely incompatible with perpetual nondecision-making.

4. A CRITIQUE OF THE ELITIST THEORY OF DEMOCRACY

JACK L. WALKER

During the last thirty years, there have been numerous attempts to revise or reconstitute the "classical" theory of democracy: the familiar doctrine of popular rule, patterned after the New England town meeting, which asserts that public policy should result from extensive, informed discussion and debate.[1] By extending general participation in decision-making the classical theorists hoped to increase the citizen's awareness of his moral and social responsibilities, reduce the danger of tyranny, and improve the quality of government. Public officials, acting as agents of the public at large, would then carry out the broad policies decided upon by majority vote in popular assemblies.

Although it is seldom made clear just which of the classical democratic theorists is being referred to, contemporary criticism has focused primarily on the descriptive elements of the theory, on its basic conceptions of citizenship, representation, and decision-making.[2] The concept of an active, informed, democratic citizenry, the most distinctive feature of the traditional theory, is the principal object of attack. On empirical grounds it is argued that very few such people can be found in Western societies. Public policy is not the expression of the common good as conceived of by the citizenry after widespread discussion and compromise. This description of policy-making is held to be dangerously naive because it overlooks the role of demagogic leadership, mass psychology, group coercion, and the influence of those who control concentrated economic power. In short, classical democratic theory is held to be unrealistic; first, because it employs conceptions of the nature of man and the operation of society, which are utopian and, second, because it does not provide adequate, operational definitions of its key concepts.

Since contemporary scholars have found the classical theory of democracy inadequate, a "revisionist" movement has developed, much as it has among contemporary Marxists, seeking to reconstitute the the-

Reprinted from the *American Political Science Review*, LX (June, 1966), 286–95, by permission of the author and the American Political Science Association.

ory and bring it into closer correspondence with the latest findings of empirical research. One major restatement, called the "elitist theory of democracy" by Seymour Martin Lipset,[3] is now employed in many contemporary books and articles on American politics and political behavior and is fast becoming part of the conventional wisdom of political science.

The adequacy of the elitist theory of democracy, both as a set of political norms and as a guide to empirical research, is open to serious question. It has two major shortcomings: first, in their quest for realism, the revisionists have fundamentally changed the normative significance of democracy, rendering it a more conservative doctrine in the process; second, the general acceptance of the elitist theory by contemporary political scientists has led them to neglect almost completely some profoundly important developments in American society.

Normative Implications of the Elitist Theory

At the heart of the elitist theory is a clear presumption of the average citizen's inadequacies. As a consequence, democratic systems must rely on the wisdom, loyalty, and skill of their political leaders, not on the population at large. The political system is divided into two groups: the elite, or the "political entrepreneurs,"[4] who possess ideological commitments and manipulative skills; and the *citizens at large*, the masses, or the "apolitical clay"[5] of the system, a much larger class of passive, inert followers who have little knowledge of public affairs and even less interest. The factor that distinguishes democratic and authoritarian systems, according to this view, is the provision for limited, peaceful competition among members of the elite for the formal positions of leadership within the system. As Joseph Schumpeter summarized the theory, "the democratic method is that institutional arrangement for arriving at political decisions in which individuals acquire the power to decide by means of a competitive struggle for the people's vote."[6]

Democracy is thus conceived primarily in procedural terms; it is seen as a method of making decisions which insures efficiency in administration and policy-making and yet requires some measure of responsiveness to popular opinion on the part of the ruling elites. The average citizen still has some measure of effective political power under this system, even though he does not initiate policy, because of his right to vote (if he chooses) in regularly scheduled elections. The political leaders, in an effort to gain support at the polls, will shape public policy to fit the citizens' desires. By anticipating public reaction the elite grants the citizenry a form of indirect access to public policy-making, without the creation of any kind of formal institutions and even in the absence of any direct communication. "A few citizens who are non-voters, and who for some reason have no influential contact with voters, have no indirect influence. Most citizens, however, possess a moderate degree of indirect influence, for elected officials keep the real or imagined preferences of constituents constantly in mind in deciding what policies to adopt or reject."[7] An ambiguity is created here because obviously leaders sometimes create opinions as well as respond to them, but since the leaders are constantly being challenged by rivals seeking to gain the allegiance of the masses it is assumed that the individual citizen will receive information from several conflicting sources, making it extremely difficult for any one group to "engineer consent" by manipulating public opinion. As Lipset puts it, "Representation is neither simply a means of political adjustment to social pressures nor an instrument of manipulation. It involves both functions, since the purpose of representation is to locate the combinations of relationships between parties and social bases which make possible the operation of efficient government."[8]

There has been extensive research and speculation about the prerequisites for a democratic system of this kind. There is general agreement that a well-developed social pluralism and an extensive system of voluntary groups or associations is needed, along with a prevailing sense of psychological security, widespread education, and limited disparities of wealth. There must be no arbitrary barriers to political participation, and "enough people must participate in the governmental process so that political leaders compete for the support of a large and more or less representative cross section of the population."[9]

Elitist theory departs markedly from the classical tradition at this point. Traditionally it was assumed that the most important prerequisite for a stable democracy was general agreement among the politically active (those who vote) on certain fundamental policies and basic values, and widespread acceptance of democratic procedures and restraints on political activity. Political leaders would not violate the basic consensus, or "democratic mold," if they wished to be successful in gaining their objectives, because once these fundamental restraints were broken the otherwise passive public would become aroused and would organize against the offending leaders. Elitist theorists argue instead that agreement on democratic values among the "intervening structure of elites," the very elements which had been seen earlier as potential threats to democracy, is the main bulwark against a breakdown in constitutionalism. Writing in 1959, David Truman discards his notion of "potential groups," a variation of the traditional doctrine of consensus, and calls instead for a "consensus of elites," a determination on the part of the leaders of political parties, labor unions, trade associations, and other voluntary associations to defend the fundamental procedures of democracy in order to protect their own positions and the basic structure of society itself from the threat of an irresponsible demagogue.[10] V. O. Key, Jr., in his *Public Opinion and American Democracy*, concludes that "the critical element for the health of a democratic order consists in the beliefs, standards, and competence of those who constitute the influentials, the opinion-leaders, the political activists in the order."[11] Similarly, Robert Dahl concludes in his study of New Haven that the skillful, active political leaders in the system are the true democratic "legitimists."[12] Since democratic procedures regulate their conflicts and protect their privileged positions in the system the leaders can be counted on to defend the democratic creed even if a majority of the voters might prefer some other set of procedures.[13]

It has also been suggested by several elitist theorists that democracies have good reason to fear increased political participation. They argue that a successful (that is, stable) democratic system depends on widespread apathy and general political incompetence.[14] The ideal of democratic participation is thus transformed into a "noble lie" designed chiefly to ensure a sense of responsibility among political leaders. As Lester Milbrath puts it: "it is important to continue moral admonishment for citizens to become active in politics, not because we want or expect great masses of them to become active, but rather because the admonishment helps keep the system open and sustains a belief in the right of all to participate, which is an important norm governing the behavior of political elites."[15]

If the uninformed masses participate in large numbers, democratic self-restraint will break down and peaceful competition among the elites, the central element in the elitist theory, will become impossible. The principal aim of the critics whose views we are examining has been to make the theory of democracy more realistic, to bring it into closer correspondence with empirical reality. They are convinced that the classical theory does not account for "much of the real machinery"[16] by which the system operates, and they have expressed concern about the possible spread among Americans of either unwarranted anxiety or cynical disillusionment over the condition of democracy. But it is difficult to transform a utopian theory into a realistic account of political behavior without changing the theory's normative foundations. By revising the theory to bring it into closer correspondence with reality, the elitist theorists have transformed democracy from a radical into a conservative political doctrine, stripping away its distinctive emphasis on popular political activity so that it no longer serves as a set of ideals toward which society ought to be striving.[17]

The most distinctive feature, and the principal orienting value, of classical democratic theory was its emphasis on individual participation in the development of public policy. By taking part in the affairs of his society the citizen would gain in knowledge and understanding, develop a deeper sense of social responsibility, and broaden his perspective beyond the narrow confines of his private life. Although the classical theorists accepted the basic framework of Lockean democracy, with its emphasis on limited government, they were *not* primarily concerned with the *policies* which might be produced in a democracy; above all else they were concerned with *human development*, the opportunities which existed in political activity to realize the untapped potentials of men and to create the foundations of a genuine human community. In the words of John Stuart Mill: "the most important point of excellence which any form of government can possess is to promote the virtue and intelligence of the people themselves. The first question in respect to any political institutions is how far they tend to foster in the members of the community the various desirable qualities, . . . moral, intellectual, and active."[18]

In the elitist version of the theory, however, emphasis has shifted to the needs and functions of the system as a whole; there is no longer a direct concern with human development. The central question is not how to design a political system which stimulates greater individual participation and enhances the moral development of its citizens, but how "to combine a substantial degree of popular participation with a system of power capable of governing *effectively* and *coherently*."[19]

The elitist theory allows the citizen only a passive role as an object of political activity; he exerts influence on policy-making only by rendering judgments after the fact in national elections. The safety of contemporary democracy lies in the high-minded sense of responsibility of its leaders, the only elements of society that are actively striving to discover and implement the common good. The citizens are left to "judge a world they never made, and thus to become a genteel counter-part of the mobs which sporadically unseated aristocratic governments in eighteenth- and nineteenth-century Europe."[20]

The contemporary version of democratic theory has, it seems, lost much of the vital force, the radical thrust, of the classical theory. The elitist theorists, in trying to develop a theory which takes account of the way the political system actually operates, have changed the principal orienting values of democracy. The heart of the classical theory was its justification of broad participation in the public affairs of the community; the aim was the production of citizens who were capable enough and responsible enough to play this role. The classical theory was not meant to describe any existing system of government; it was an outline, a set of prescriptions for the ideal policy which men should strive to create. The elitist theorists, in their quest for realism, have changed this distinctive prescriptive element in democratic theory; they have substituted stability and efficiency as the prime goals of democracy. If these revisions are accepted, the danger arises that in striving to develop more reliable explanations of political behavior, political scientists will also become sophisticated apologists for the existing political order. Robert Lane, in concluding his study of the political ideologies of fifteen "common men" in an Eastern city, observes that they lack a utopian vision, a well-defined sense of social justice that would allow them to stand in judgment on their society and its institutions.[21] To some degree, the "men of Eastport" share this disability with much of the American academic elite.

The Elitist Theory as a Guide for Research

The shortcomings of the elitist theory are not confined to its normative implications. Serious questions also arise concerning its descriptive accuracy and its utility as a guide to empirical research. The most unsatisfactory element in the theory is its concept of the passive, apolitical common man who pays allegiance to his governors and to the sideshow of politics while remaining primarily concerned with his private life, evenings of television with his family, or the demands of his job. Occasionally, when the average citizen finds his primary goals threatened by the actions or inactions of government, he may strive vigorously to influence the course of public policy, but *homo civicus*, as Dahl calls him, "is not, by nature, a political animal."[22]

It was the acceptance of this concept that led the elitist theorists to reject the traditional notion of consensus. It became implausible to argue that the citizenry is watchful and jealous of the great democratic values while at the same time suggesting that they are uninvolved, uninformed, and apathetic. Widespread apathy also is said to contribute to democratic stability by insuring that the disagreements that arise during campaigns and elections will not involve large numbers of people or plunge the society into violent disorders or civil war.

No one can deny that there is widespread political apathy among many sectors of the American public. But it is important to ask why this is so and not simply to explain how this phenomenon contributes to the smooth functioning of the system. Of course, the citizens' passivity might stem from their satisfaction with the operation of the political system, and thus they would naturally become aroused only if they perceived a threat to the system. Dahl, for one, argues that the political system operates largely through inertia, tradition, or habitual responses. It remains stable because only a few "key" issues are the objects of controversy at any one time, the rest of public policy having been settled and established in past controversies which are now all but forgotten. Similarly, Nelson Polsby argues that it is fallacious to assume that the quiescent citizens in a community, especially those in the lower-income groups, have grievances unless they actually express them. To do so is to arbitrarily assign "upper- and middle-class values to all actors in the community."[23]

But it is hard to believe, in these days of protest demonstrations, Black Muslims, and the Deacons of Defense and Justice, that the mood of cynical apathy toward politics which affects so many American Negroes is an indication of their satisfaction with the political system, and with the weak, essentially meaningless alternatives it usually presents to them. To assume that apathy is a sign of satisfaction in this case is to overlook the tragic history of the Negroes in America and the system of violent repression long used to deny them any entrance into the regular channels of democratic decision-making.

Students of race relations have concluded that hostile attitudes toward a racial group do not necessarily lead to hostile actions, and amicable feelings do not ensure amicable actions. Instead, "it is the social demands of the situation, particularly when supported by accepted authority figures, which are the effective determinants of individual action."[24] This insight might apply to other areas beside race relations. It suggests that a society's political culture, the general perceptions about the nature of authority and the prevailing expectations of significant reference groups, might be a major influence on the political behavior of the average citizen regardless of his own feelings of satisfaction or hostility. There have been sizable shifts in rates of political participation throughout American history which suggests that these rates are not rigidly determined. A recent analysis indicates that rates of voter participation are now *lower* than they were in the nineteenth century, even though the population is now much better educated and the facilities for communication are now much better developed.[25] Other studies indicate that there are marked differences in the political milieu of towns and cities which lead citizens of one area to exhibit much more cynicism and distrust of the political system than others.[26] Although the studies showed no corresponding changes in feelings of political competence, cynical attitudes might inhibit many forms of participation and thus induce apathy.

Political apathy obviously has many sources. It may stem from feelings of personal inadequacy, from a fear of endangering important personal relationships, or from a lack of interest in the issues; but it may also have its roots in the society's institutional structure, in the weakness or absence of group stimulation or support, in the positive opposition of elements within the political system to wider participation—in the absence, in other words, of appropriate spurs to action or in the presence of tangible deterrents.[27] Before the causes of apathy can be established with confidence much more attention must be directed to the role of the mass media. How are the perceptions of individual citizens affected by the version of reality they receive, either directly or indirectly, from television, the national wire services, and the public schools,[28] and how do these perceptions affect their motivations? Political scientists have also largely neglected to study the use of both legitimate and illegitimate sanctions and private intimidation to gain political ends. How do the activities of the police,[29] social workers, or elements of organized crime affect the desires and the opportunities available for individual political participation?

Certainly the apparent calm of American politics is not matched by our general social life, which is marked by high crime rates, numerous fads and crazes, and much intergroup tension.[30] One recent study showed that during the civil rights protests in Atlanta, Georgia, and Cambridge, Maryland, crime rates in the Negro communities dropped substantially.[31] A finding of this kind suggests that there is some connection between these two realms of social conflict and that both may serve as outlets for individual distress and frustration. High crime (or suicide) rates and low rates of voting may very well be related; the former may represent "leakage" from the political system.[32]

Once we admit that the society is not based on a widespread consensus, we must look at our loosely organized, decentralized political parties in a different light. It may be that the parties have developed in this way precisely because no broad consensus exists. In a fragmented society which contains numerous geographic, religious, and racial conflicts, the successful politician has been the man adept at negotiation and bargaining, the man best able to play these numerous animosities off against each other and, thereby, to build *ad hoc* coalitions of support for specific programs. Success at this delicate business of coalition-building depends on achieving some basis for communication among the leaders of otherwise antagonistic groups and finding a formula for compromise. To create these circumstances sharp conflicts must be avoided; highly controversial, potentially explosive issues must be shunned. Controversy is shifted to other issues or the public authorities simply refuse to deal with the question, claiming that they have no legitimate jurisdiction in the case or burying it quietly in some committee room or bureaucratic pigeonhole.[33]

In other words, one of the chief characteristics of our political system has been its success in suppressing and controlling internal conflict. But the avoidance of conflict, the suppression of strife, is *not* necessarily the creation of satisfaction or consensus. The citizens may remain quiescent, the political system might retain its stability, but significant differences of opinion remain, numerous conflicts are unresolved, and many desires go unfulfilled. The frustrations resulting from such deprivations can create conflict in other, nonpolitical realms. Fads, religious revivals, or wild, anomic riots such as those which occurred in the Negro ghettos of several large American cities during the summers of 1964 and 1965—phenomena not directly related to the achievement of any clearly conceived political goals—may be touched off by unresolved tensions left untended by the society's political leaders.

The American political system is highly complex, with conflicting jurisdictions and numerous checks and balances. A large commitment in time and energy must be made, even by a well-educated citizen, to keep informed of the issues and personalities in all levels of government. Most citizens are not able or willing to pay this kind of cost to gain the information necessary for effective political participation. This may be especially true in a political system in which weak or unclear alternatives are usually presented to the electorate. For most citizens the world of politics is remote, bewildering, and meaningless, having no direct relation to daily concerns about jobs or family life. Many citizens have desires or frustrations with which public agencies might be expected to deal, but they usually remain unaware of possible solutions to their problems in the public sphere. This group within our political system are citizens only from the legal point of view. If a high degree of social solidarity and sense of community are necessary for true democratic participation, then these marginal men are not really citizens of the state. The polity has not been extended to include them.[34]

For the elitist theorist widespread apathy is merely a fact of political life, something to be anticipated, a prerequisite for democratic stability. But for the classical democrat political apathy is an object of intense concern because the overriding moral purpose of the classical theory is to expand the boundaries of the political community and build the foundations for human understanding through participation by the citizens in the affairs of their government.

Leaders and Followers

While most elitist theorists are agreed in conceiving of the average citizen as politically passive and uncreative, there seems to be a difference of opinion (or at least of emphasis) over the likelihood of some irrational, antidemocratic outburst from the society's common men.

Dahl does not dwell on this possibility. He seemingly conceives of *homo civicus*, the average citizen, as a man who consciously chooses to avoid politics and to devote himself to the pleasures and problems of his job and family. "Typically, as a source of direct gratifications political activity will appear to *homo civicus* as less attractive than a host of other activities; and, as a strategy to achieve his gratifications indirectly political action will seem considerably less efficient than working at his job, earning more money, taking out insurance, joining a club, planning a vacation, moving to another neighborhood or city, or coping with an uncertain future in manifold other ways."[35]

Lipset, on the other hand, seems much more concerned with the danger that the common man might suddenly enter the political system, smashing democratic institutions in the process, as part of an irrational, authoritarian political force. He sees "profoundly antidemocratic tendencies in lower-class groups,"[36] and he has been frequently concerned in his work with Hitler, McCarthy, and other demagogic leaders who have led antidemocratic mass movements.

Although there are obviously some important differences of opinion and emphasis concerning the political capacities of average citizens and the relative security of democratic institutions, the elitist theorists agree on the crucial importance of leadership in ensuring both the safety and viability of representative government. This set of basic assumptions serves as a foundation for their explanation of change and innovation in American politics, a process in which they feel creative leadership plays the central role.

Running throughout the work of these writers is a vision of the "professional" politician as hero, much as he is pictured in Max Weber's essay "Politics as a Vocation." Dahl's Mayor Lee, Edward Banfield's Mayor Daley, Richard Neustadt's ideal occupant of the White House, all possess great skill and drive, and are engaged in the delicate art of persuasion and coalition-building. They are actively moving the society forward toward their own goals, according to their own special vision. All of them possess the pre-eminent qualities of Weber's ideal-type politician: "passion, a feeling of responsibility, and a sense of proportion."[37] As in Schumpeter's analysis of capitalism, the primary source of change and innovation in the political system is the "political entrepreneur"; only such a leader can break through the inherent conservatism of organizations and shake the masses from their habitual passivity.

It is obvious that political leaders (especially chief executives) have played a very important role in American politics, but it is also clear that the American system's large degree of internal bargaining, the lack of many strong hierarchical controls, and its numerous checks and balances, both constitutional and political, place powerful constraints on the behavior of political executives. American Presidents, governors, and mayors usually find themselves caught in a web of cross pressures which prevent them from making bold departures in policy or firmly attaching themselves to either side of a controversy. The agenda of controversy, the list of questions which are recognized by the active participants in politics as legitimate subjects of attention and concern, is very hard to change.

Just as it can be argued that the common citizens have a form of indirect influence, so it can also be argued that the top leaders of other institutions in the society, such as the business community, possess indirect influence as well. As Banfield suggests in his study of Chicago, the top business leaders have great potential power: "if the twenty or thirty wealthiest men in Chicago acted as one and put all their wealth into the fight, they could easily destroy or capture the machine."[38] The skillful politician, following Carl Friedrich's "rule of anticipated reactions,"[39] is unlikely to make proposals which would unite the business community against him. The aspiring politician learns early in his career, by absorbing the folklore which circulates among the politically active, which issues can and cannot be exploited successfully. It is this constellation of influences and anticipated reactions, "the peculiar mobilization of bias" in the community, fortified by a general consensus of elites, that determines the agenda of controversy.[40] The American political system, above all others, seems to be especially designed to frustrate the creative leader.

But as rigid and inflexible as it is, the political system does produce new policies; new programs and schemes are approved; even basic procedural changes are made from time to time. Of course, each major shift in public policy has a great many causes. The elitist theory of democracy looks for the principal source of innovation in the competition among rival leaders and the clever maneuvering of political entrepreneurs, which is, in its view, the most distinctive aspect of a democratic system. Because so many political scientists have worn the theoretical blinders of the elitist theory, however, we have overlooked the importance of broadly based social movements, arising from the public at large, as powerful agents of innovation and change.

The primary concerns of the elitist theorists have been the maintenance of democratic stability, the preservation of democratic procedures, and the creation of machinery which would produce efficient administration and coherent public policies. With these goals in mind, social movements (if they have been studied at all) have usually been pictured as threats to democracy, as manifestations of "political extremism." Lipset asserts that such movements typically appeal to the "disgruntled and the psychologically homeless, to the personal failures, the socially isolated, the economically insecure, the uneducated, un-sophisticated, and authoritarian persons at every level of society."[41] Movements of this kind throw the political system out of gear and disrupt the mechanisms designed to maintain due process; if the elites were overwhelmed by such forces, democracy would be destroyed. This narrow, antagonistic view of social movements stems from the elitist theorists' suspicion of the political capacities of the common citizens,[42] their fear of instability, and their failure to recognize the elements of rigidity and constraint existing in the political system. But if one holds that view and at the same time recognizes the tendency of the prevail-ing political system to frustrate strong leaders, it becomes difficult to explain how significant innovations in public policy, such as the social security system, the Wagner Act, the Subversive Activities Control Act of 1950, or the Civil Rights Bill of 1964, ever came about.

During the last century American society has spawned numerous social movements, some of which have made extensive demands on the political system, while others have been highly esoteric, mystical, and apolitical. These movements arise because some form of social disloca-tion or widespread sense of frustration exists within the society. But dissatisfaction alone is not a sufficient cause; it must be coupled with the necessary resources and the existence of potential leadership which can motivate a group to take action designed to change the offending circumstances.[43] Often such movements erupt along the margins of the political system, and they sometimes serve the purpose of encouraging political and social mobilization, of widening the boundaries of the polity.[44] Through movements such as the Negroes' drive for civil rights, the Midwestern farmers' crusade for fair prices in the 1890's, the Ku Klux Klan, or the "radical right" movements of the 1960's, "pre-political people who have not yet found, or [have] only begun to find, a specific language in which to express their aspirations about the world"[45] are given new orientation, confidence, knowledge, sources of informa-tion, and leadership.

Social movements also serve, in Rudolf Heberle's words, as the "cre-ators and carriers of public opinion."[46] By confronting the political au-thorities, or by locking themselves in peaceful—or violent[47]—conflict with some other element of the society, social movements provoke trials of strength between contending forces or ideas. Those trials of eco-nomic, political, or moral strength take place in the court of public opinion and sometimes place enormous strain on democratic institu-tions and even the social fabric itself. But through such trials, as tumul-tuous as they may sometimes be, the agenda of controversy, the list of acceptable, "key" issues may be changed. In an effort to conciliate and mediate, the political leaders fashion new legislation, create unique regulatory bodies, and strive to establish channels of communication and accommodation among the combatants.

Of course, members of the political elite may respond to the movement by resisting it, driving it underground, or destroying it; they may try to co-opt the movement's leaders by granting them privileges or by accepting parts of its program, or even by making the leaders part of the established elite; they may surrender to the movement, losing control of their offices in the political system in the process. The nature of the political leader's response is probably a prime determinant of the tactics the movement will adopt, the kind of leadership that arises within it, and the ideological appeals it develops. Other factors might determine the response of the leadership, such as the existence of competing social movements with conflicting demands, the resources available to the political leaders to satisfy the demands of the movement, the social status of the participants in the movement, the presence of competing sets of leaders claiming to represent the same movement, and many other elements peculiar to each particular situation. In this process social movements may be highly disruptive and some institutions may be completely destroyed; the story does not always have a happy ending. But one major consequence (function, if you will) of social movements is to break society's log jams, to prevent ossification in the political system, to prompt and justify major innovations in social policy and economic organization.[48]

This relationship of challenge and response between the established political system and social movements had gone without much systematic study by political scientists. Sociologists have been concerned with social movements, but they have directed most of their attention to the causes of the movements, their "natural history," and the relationship between leaders and followers within them.[49] Historians have produced many case studies of social movements but little in the way of systematic explanation.[50] This would seem to be a fruitful area for investigation by political scientists. But this research is not likely to appear unless we revise our concept of the masses as politically inert, apathetic, and bound by habitual responses. We must also shift our emphasis from theories which conceive of the "social structure in terms of a functionally integrated system held in equilibrium by certain patterned and recurrent processes" to theories which place greater emphasis on the role of coercion and constraint in the political system and which concentrate on the influences within society which produce "the forces that maintain it in an unending process of change."[51] The greatest contribution of Marx to the understanding of society was his realization that internal conflict is a major source of change and innovation. One need not accept his metaphysical assumptions to appreciate this important insight.

In a society undergoing massive social change, fresh theoretical perspectives are essential. Political theorists are charged with the responsibility of constantly reformulating the dogmas of the past so that democratic theory remains relevant to the stormy realities of twentieth-century American society, with its sprawling urban centers, its innumerable social conflicts, and its enormous bureaucratic hierarchies.

In restating the classical theory, however, contemporary political scientists have stripped democracy of much of its radical *élan* and have diluted its utopian vision, thus rendering it inadequate as a guide to the future. The elitist theorists generally accept the prevailing distribution of status in the society (with exceptions usually made for the American Negro) and find it "not only compatible with political freedom but even . . . a condition of it."[52] They place great emphasis on the limitations of the average citizen and are suspicious of schemes which might encourage greater participation in public affairs. Accordingly, they put their trust in the wisdom and energy of an active, responsible elite.

Beside these normative shortcomings the elitist theory has served as an inadequate guide to empirical research, providing an unconvincing explanation of widespread political apathy in American society and leading political scientists to ignore manifestations of discontent not directly related to the political system. Few studies have been conducted of the use of force or informal, illegitimate coercion in the American political system, and little attention has been directed to the great social movements which have marked American society in the last 100 years.

If political science is to be relevant to society's pressing needs and urgent problems, professional students of politics must broaden their perspectives and become aware of new problems which are in need of scientific investigation. They must examine the norms that guide their efforts and guard against the danger of uncritically accepting the values of the going system in the name of scientific objectivity. Political scientists must strive for heightened awareness and self-knowledge; they must avoid rigid presumptions which diminish their vision, destroy their capacities for criticism, and blind them to some of the most significant social and political developments of our time.

Notes

1. For discussions of the meaning of the classical theory of democracy, see George Sabine, "The Two Democratic Traditions," *The Philosophical Review*, LXI (1952), 451–74, and *A History of Political Theory* (New York: Holt, Rinehart & Winston, 1958), especially chaps. xxxi and xxxii. See also J. Roland Pennock, *Liberal Democracy: Its Merits and Prospects* (New York: Holt, Rinehart & Winston, 1950); and

Sheldon Wolin, *Politics and Vision* (Boston: Little, Brown & Co., 1960), especially chaps. ix and x.

2. Criticism of the descriptive accuracy of the classical theory has been widespread in recent years. The best statement of the basic objections usually made is Joseph Schumpeter, *Capitalism, Socialism and Democracy* (New York: Harper & Bros., 1942), Part IV. See also Bernard Berelson *et al.*, *Voting* (Chicago: University of Chicago Press, 1954), chap. xiv; articles by Louis Hartz and Samuel Beer, in W. N. Chambers and R. H. Salisbury (eds.), *Democracy in the Mid-Twentieth Century* (New York: The Macmillan Co., 1960); Seymour Martin Lipset, *Political Man: The Social Bases of Politics* (New York: Doubleday & Co., 1960); Robert A. Dahl, A *Preface to Democratic Theory* (Chicago: University of Chicago Press, 1956), and *Who Governs? Democracy and Power in an American City* (New Haven: Yale University Press, 1961), especially pp. 223–325; V. O. Key, Jr., *Public Opinion and American Democracy* (New York: Alfred A. Knopf, 1961), especially Part VI; Lester W. Milbrath, *Political Participation: How and Why Do People Get Involved in Politics?* (Chicago: Rand McNally & Co., 1965), especially chap. vi; and, for a general summary of the position, Henry Mayo, *An Introduction to Democratic Theory* (New York: Oxford University Press, 1960).

3. See the Introduction by Lipset to the Collier Books paperback edition of Robert Michels, *Political Parties* (New York: Collier Books, 1962), p. 33.

4. The phrase is Dahl's, in *Who Governs?*, p. 227.

5. *Ibid.*, p. 225.

6. Schumpeter, *op. cit.*, p. 269.

7. Dahl, *Who Governs?*, p. 164.

8. Lipset, Introduction to Michels, *op. cit.*, p. 34.

9. Robert A. Dahl and Charles E. Lindblom, *Politics, Economics, and Welfare: Planning and Politico-Economic Systems Resolved into Basic Social Processes* (New York: Harper & Bros., 1953), p. 309.

10. David Truman, "The American System in Crisis," *Political Science Quarterly* (December, 1959), pp. 481–97. See also a perceptive critique of Truman's change of attitude in Peter Bachrach, "Elite Consensus and Democracy," *The Journal of Politics,* XXIV (1962), 439–52.

11. Key, *op. cit.*, p. 558. See also Key's "Public Opinion and the Decay of Democracy," *The Virginia Quarterly Review,* XXXVII (1961), 481–94.

12. Dahl's position on this issue seems to have undergone a transformation somewhat similar to Truman's. Compare Dahl and Lindblom, *op. cit.*, chap. xi, with Dahl, *Who Governs?*, Books IV, V, and VI.

13. Dahl, *Who Governs?*, pp. 311–25. It is important to note that these conclusions about the crucial function of an elite consensus in democracy were based on little empirical evidence. Truman, Key, and Dahl seem to rely most heavily on Samuel Stouffer, *Communism, Conformity, and Civil Liberties* (New York: Doubleday & Co., 1955), a study based on national opinion surveys which was concerned with only one issue (McCarthyism) and did not investigate the relationship between the expressed opinions of its subjects and their behavior under stress; and James Prothro and Charles Grigg, "Fundamental Principles of Democracy: Bases of Agreement and Disagreement," *Journal of Politics,* XXII (1960), 276–94, a study of attitudes in two small cities. More recently, however, Herbert McClosky has produced more convincing data in his "Consensus and Ideology in American Politics," *American Political Science Review,* LVIII (1964), 361–82. McClosky concludes that widespread agreement on procedural norms is not a prerequisite to the success of a democratic system: "Consensus may strengthen democratic viability, but its absence in an otherwise stable society need not be fatal, or even particularly damaging" (p. 377). McClosky's conclusions are called into question by data presented by Samuel Eldersveld, *Political Parties: A Behavioral Analysis* (Chicago: Rand McNally & Co., 1964), pp. 183–219; and Edmond Constantini, "Intra-party Attitude Conflict: Democratic Party Leadership in California," *Western Political Quarterly,* XVI (1963), 956–72.

14. See Bernard Berelson, *et al.*, *op. cit.*, chap. XIV; Lipset, *op. cit.*, pp. 14–16; and W. H. Morris-Jones, "In Defense of Apathy," *Political Studies*, II (1954), 25–37.

15. Milbrath, *op. cit.*, p. 152.

16. Louis Hartz, "Democracy: Image and Reality," in Chambers and Salisbury (eds.), *op. cit.*, p. 26.

17. Several articles have recently appeared which attack the elitist theory on normative grounds. The best and most insightful is Lane Davis, "The Cost of Realism: Contemporary Restatements of Democracy," *Western Political Quarterly*, XVII (1964), 37–46. See also Graeme Duncan and Steven Lukes, "The New Democracy," *Political Studies*, XI (1963), 156-77; Steven W. Rousseas and James Farganis, "American Politics and the End of Ideology," *British Journal of Sociology*, XIV (1963) 347–60; and Christian Bay, "Politics and Pseudopolitics," *American Political Science Review*, LIX (1965), 39–51. The subject is also treated in Henry Kariel, *The Decline of American Pluralism* (Stanford, Calif.: Stanford University Press, 1961), chaps. ix and xi; T. B. Bottomore, *Elites and Society* (London: Watts & Co., 1964), pp. 108–10; Robert Presthus, *Men at the Top: A Study of Community Power* (New York: Oxford University Press, 1964), pp. 3–47; and Robert Agger, Daniel Goldrich, and Bert Swanson, *The Rulers and the Ruled: Political Power and Impotence in American Communities* (New York: John Wiley & Sons, 1964), pp. 93–99 and 524–32. For an insightful critique of the work of Dahl and Mills, conceived of as opposing ideological positions, see William E. Connolly, "Responsible Political Ideology: Implications of the Sociology of Knowledge for Political Inquiry" (Ph.D. dissertation, University of Michigan, 1965), pp. 18–39. This section of this article depends heavily on Lane Davis' analysis.

18. John Stuart Mill, *Considerations on Representative Government* (New York: Oxford University Press, 1947), pp. 39–40.

19. Samuel Beer, "New Structures of Democracy: Britain and America," in Chambers and Salisbury (eds.), *op. cit.*, p. 46.

20. Davis, *op. cit.*, p. 45.

21. Robert Lane, *Political Ideology* (New York: The Free Press of Glencoe, 1962), p. 475. See also the comments on the same topic in Donald Stokes, "Popular Evaluations of Government: An Empirical Assessment," in Harlem Cleveland and Harold D. Lasswell (eds.), *Ethics and Bigness*, published for the Conference on Science, Philosophy, and Religion (New York: Harper & Row, 1962), p. 72.

22. Dahl, *Who Governs?*, pp. 225.

23. Nelson W. Polsby, *Community Power and Political Theory* (New Haven: Yale University Press, 1963), p. 117.

24. Herbert Blumer, "Recent Research [on Race Relations in the] United States of America," *International Social Science Bulletin*, X (1958), 432.   Similar arguments concerning the relationship of beliefs and action can be found in J. D. Lohman and D. C. Reitzes, "Deliberately Organized Groups and Racial Behavior," *American Sociological Review*, XIX (1954), 342–44; and Earl Raab (ed.), *American Race Relations Today* (Garden City, N.Y.: Doubleday & Co., 1962).

25. Walter Dean Burnham, "The Changing Shape of the American Political Universe," *American Political Science Review*, LIX (1965), 7–28.

26. Robert Agger, Marshall Goldstein, and Stanley Pearl, "Political Cynicism: Measurement and Meaning," *The Journal of Politics*, XXIII (1961), 477–506; and Edgar Litt, "Political Cynicism and Political Futility," *The Journal of Politics*, XXV (1963), 312–23.

27. For a brief survey of findings on this subject, see Milbrath, *op. cit.*; and for a clear, brief summary, see Morris Rosenburg, "Some Determinants of Political Apathy," *Public Opinion Quarterly*, XVIII (1954–55), 349–66. See also David Apter (ed.), *Ideology and Discontent* (New York: The Free Press of Glencoe, 1964), especially chapters by Converse and Wolfinger, *et al.*

28. A major study of the influence of secondary schools on political attitudes is underway at the University of Michigan under the direction of M. Kent Jennings

29. An extensive investigation of the role of the police and the courts in city politics is being conducted at Harvard University by James Q. Wilson.

30. It is very difficult to compare crime rates or other indications of social disorganization in the United States with those in other countries. For a discussion of some of the difficulties, see *Report on the World Social Situation* (New York: UNESCO, 1963).

31. Frederic Solomon, Walter L. Walker, Garrett O'Connor, and Jacob Fishman, "Civil Rights Activity and Reduction of Crime Among Negroes," *Archives of General Psychiatry*, XII (March, 1965), 227–36.

32. For an excellent study of the Black Muslims which portrays the movement as a nonpolitical outlet for the frustration and bitterness felt by many American Negroes, see the study by an African scholar, E. V. Essien-Udom, *Black Nationalism: A Search for an Identity in America* (Chicago: University of Chicago Press, 1962).

33. Herbert Agar makes a similar analysis and argues for the retention of the system in *The Price of Union* (Boston: Houghton Mifflin Co., 1950). He states: "The lesson which Americans learned [from the Civil War] was useful: in a large federal nation, when a problem is passionately felt, and is discussed in terms of morals, each party may divide within itself, against itself. And if the parties divide, the nation may divide; for the parties, with their enjoyable pursuit of power, are a unifying influence. Wise men, therefore, may seek to dodge such problems as long as possible. And the easiest way to dodge them is for both parties to take both sides" (p. 689).

34. For a study of several important factors affecting the degree of participation in American politics, see E. E. Schattschneider, *The Semisovereign People* (New York: Holt, Rinehart & Winston, 1960), especially chaps. v and vi.

35. Dahl, *Who Governs?*, p. 224.

36. Lipset, *op. cit.*, p. 121.

37. Hans Gerth and C. Wright Mills (eds.), *From Max Weber: Essays in Sociology* (New York: Oxford University Press, 1946), p. 115.

38. Edward C. Banfield, *Political Influence* (New York: The Free Press of Glencoe, 1961), p. 290.

39. Carl Friedrich, *Constitutional Government and Democracy* (Boston: Little, Brown & Co., 1939), pp. 17–18.

40. This point is made persuasively by Peter Bachrach and Morton S. Baratz, "Two Faces of Power," *American Political Science Review*, LVI (1962), 947–52. See also their "Decisions and Non-decisions: An Analytical Framework," *American Political Science Review*, LVII (1963), 632–42; and Thomas J. Anton, "Power, Pluralism, and Local Politics," *Administrative Science Quarterly*, VII (1963), 425-57.

41. Lipset, *op. cit.*, p. 178.

42. Ruth Searles and J. Allen Williams, in a study of Negro students who took part in the sit-in demonstrations, found no evidence that they were authoritarian or posed threats to democracy: "Far from being alienated, the students appear to be committed to the society and its middle class leaders" ("Negro College Students' Participation in Sit-ins," *Social Forces*, XL [1962], 219). For other studies of this particular social movement, see Robert Coles, "Social Struggle and Weariness," *Psychiatry*, XXVII (1964), 305–15; and three articles by Frederic Solomon and Jacob Fishman, "Perspectives on Student Sit-in Movement," *American Journal of Ortho-psychiatry*, XXXIII (1963), 872–82, "Action and Identity Formation in First Student Sit-in Demonstration," *Journal of Social Issues*, XX (1964), 36–45, and "Psycho-social Meaning of Nonviolence in Student Civil Rights Activities," *Psychiatry*, XXVII (1964) 91–99. See also the October, 1964, issue of *The Journal of Social Issues*, entitled "Youth and Social Action," edited by Frederic Solomon and Jacob Fishman; and Jack L. Walker, "Protest and Negotiation: A Case Study of Negro Leaders in Atlanta, Georgia," *Midwest Journal of Political Science*, VII (1963), 99–124.

43. Sociologists usually study social movements under the rubric of collective behavior. For general treatment, see Herbert Blumer, "Collective Behavior," in Joseph

B. Gittler (ed.), *Review of Sociology* (New York: John Wiley & Sons, 1957); Rudolph Heberle, *Social Movements: An Introduction to Political Sociology* (New York: Appleton-Century-Crofts, 1951); Lewis Killian, "Social Movements," in Robert Faris (ed.), *Handbook of Modern Sociology* (Chicago: Rand McNally & Co., 1964); Charles King, *Social Movements in the United States* (New York: Random House, 1956); Kurt Lang and Gladys E. Lang, *Collective Dynamics* (New York: Thomas Y. Crowell Co., 1961); Neil Smelser, *Theory of Collective Behavior* (New York: The Free Press of Glencoe, 1963); and Ralph Turner and Lewis Killian, *Collective Behavior* (Englewood Cliffs, N.J.: Prentice-Hall, 1957). For a brief historical sketch of some American social movements, see Thomas Greer, *American Social Reform Movements: Their Pattern Since 1865* (Englewood Cliffs, N.J.: Prentice-Hall, 1946).

44. For a book which investigates social movements which have served this function among Italian peasants, see Eric J. Hobsbawm, *Primitive Rebels* (Manchester, Eng.: Manchester University Press, 1959). See also Vittorio Lanternari, *The Religions of the Oppressed: A Study of Modern Messianic Cults* (New York: Alfred A. Knopf, 1963), for a study of the relationship of messianic cults and revolutionary movements on five continents; and George Rude, *The Crowd in History, Seventeen Thirty to Eighteen Forty-Eight* (New York: John Wiley & Sons, 1964), for a study of popular uprisings in England and France from 1730–1848.

45. Hobsbawm, *op. cit.*, p. 2.

46. Heberle, *op. cit.*, pp. 417–18.

47. American political scientists have not been sufficiently concerned with the role of violence in the governmental process. Among all the articles published in the *American Political Science Review* between 1906 and 1963, there was only one whose title contained the word "violence," only one with the word "coercive" (it concerned India), and none with the word "force." During the same period there were forty-nine articles on governmental reorganization and twenty-four on civil service reform. See Kenneth Janda (ed.), *Cumulative Index to the American Political Science Review* (Evanston, Ill.: Northwestern University Press, 1964). Efforts to retrieve this situation have begun in Harry Eckstein (ed.), *Internal War* (New York: The Free Press of Glencoe, 1964).

48. Lewis Coser has discussed the role of conflict in provoking social change in his *The Functions of Social Conflict* (Glencoe, Ill.: The Free Press, 1956), and in his "Social Conflict and the Theory of Social Change," *British Journal of Sociology*, IX (1957) 197–207. See also Irving Louis Horowitz, "Consensus, Conflict and Cooperation: A Sociological Inventory," *Social Forces*, XLI (1962), 177–88.

49. For an insightful and stimulating example, see Joseph Gusfield, *Symbolic Crusade: Status Politics and the American Temperance Movement* (Urbana, Ill.: University of Illinois Press, 1963), which makes an excellent analysis of the causes of the temperance movement and changes in its leadership, but makes only brief mention of the movement's impact on the government and the responses of political leaders to its efforts.

50. John Higham is somewhat of an exception to this generalization. See his *Strangers in the Land: Patterns of American Nativism 1860–1925* (New York: Atheneum Publishers, 1963). See also his "Another Look at Nativism," *Catholic Historical Review*, XLIV (1958), 147–58, and his "The Cult of the 'American Consensus'; Homogenizing Our History," *Commentary* (February, 1959), p. 159.

51. Ralf Dahrendorf, *Class and Class Conflict in Industrial Society* (Stanford, Calif.: Stanford University Press, 1959), p. 159.

52. Sabine, "The Two Democratic Traditions," p. 459.

II

Education and Race

The decision of the Supreme Court, in 1954, to order integration of the public schools of America triggered political demands for changes in existing school systems that ranged far beyond the original integration issue. Integration became the call for those interested in improving educational quality as well as for those concerned with racial balance. The subsequent moves to implement school integration policy became primary elements in the politics of educational decision-making in the 1950's and the 1960's. Concern with educational change roused a general interest in questions such as who was running the schools, how were they being run, were they performing their functions adequately, who was advantaged and who disadvantaged by existing systems, and so forth. When civil rights organizations entered the arena, the answers to such questions often became rallying cries for more radical change. Civil rights activity stimulated political controversy over school decision-making and made scholarly analysis of the politics of educational policy-making more acceptable and legitimate.

The selections in this chapter relate to the extent of segregation in our urban schools, the values inherent in racially segregated and racially integrated systems, the ramifications of integration, and the political context in which specific questions of integration have been and are being decided. The emphasis is on integration as a political as well as a sociological and educational question.

James Kent reviews the landmark study *Equality of Educational Opportunity*, which was directed by James Coleman. Known as the Coleman Report, the study is one of the most significant and controversial analyses of public education to be made in generations. Kent describes the general thrust of the Coleman Report's conclusions and discusses some of the major commentaries made by critics of the study.

Thomas Dye's comparative study of desegregation in urban schools notes the variety of patterns of desegregation and analyzes some of the major variables leading to such differences. He compares the impact of the southern tradition of legal segregation with that of *de facto* segregation in northern cities and analyzes government's role in attempting to influence these conditions.

Robert Crain and David Street view desegregation as the result of political decisions. Their comparative study of eight large northern school systems traces the general pattern of conflict resulting from attempts to implement integration proposals.

David Rogers' article is a case study of the unsuccessful attempts to integrate New York City's schools over the past decade. He examines the motivation of the various actors in the political system and the reaction of core decision-makers, such as the board of education, to the resultant pressures. His analysis of the role of the various participants in the integration struggle can be compared with experiences in other large cities, some of which are treated in the next chapter.

5. THE COLEMAN REPORT:
OPENING PANDORA'S BOX

JAMES K. KENT

Recently created to foster interdepartmental conversations among graduate students, the doctoral Colloquium Board of the Harvard Graduate School of Education focused its fall conference on James S. Coleman's devastating report, *Equality of Educational Opportunity*. The topic chosen was eminently appropriate, for the Coleman Report stands majestically as a seminal document in the history of American education. Increasingly, educational research, discussions, decisions, and even time are measured as pre–Coleman Report or post–Coleman Report.[1]

Heretofore, the traditional notion of what constituted equality of educational opportunity was placidly assumed to be such school factors as the teacher-pupil ratio, per pupil expenditure, laboratory facilities, number of volumes per student in the library, and several measures of quality of curriculum. The report's findings exploded many sacrosanct myths. These physical and economic school factors appear to have a uniform effect on student achievement and are relatively unimportant insofar as their effects on student learning are concerned: "Differences in school facilities and curriculum . . . are so little related to differences in achievement levels of students, that, with few exceptions, their effects fail to appear even in a survey of this magnitude" (p. 316).

While controversy surrounds the report, a totally different definition of equality of educational opportunity has been forged. This new concept embraces the effects or results of school learning rather than spurious measures of resource inputs. As Coleman told the Harvard audience: "The crucial point is that effects of inputs have come to constitute the basis for assessment of school quality (and thus equality of opportunity), rather than the mere *definition* of particular inputs as being measures of quality (e.g., small classes are better than large, higher-paid teachers are better than lower-paid ones, by definition)."[2] To be blunt, the conventional wisdom of administrators, teachers, school

Reprinted from the *Phi Delta Kappan* (January, 1968), pp. 242–45. Reprinted by permission of Phi Delta Kappa.

boards, professional organizations, and legislators has been undermined, and henceforth those who are asked to finance public education must increasingly evaluate school quality and equality of educational opportunity by the results of schooling instead of by arbitrary input measures.

The Coleman speech at Harvard was an elaboration upon this new concept of equality of educational opportunity. Coleman sees that the burden and function of the public school have dramatically shifted in the past ten years. Formerly, the schools merely played a passive role by providing free public resources. It was the responsibility of the child and his family to take advantage of these free resources. This responsibility has been completely reversed. Now,

> the responsibility to create achievement lies with the educational institution, not the child. The difference in achievement at grade 12 between the average Negro and the average white is, in effect, the degree of inequality of opportunity, and the reduction of that inequality is a responsibility of the school. This shift in responsibility follows logically from the shift of the concept of equality of educational opportunity from school resource inputs to effects on schools.[3]

Coleman seeks to clarify his new definition by noting that

> this does *not* imply that all students' achievement comes to be identical, but only that the *averages* for two population groups that begin at different levels come to be identical. . . . These questions concern the *relative intensity* of two sets of influences; those which are alike for the two groups, principally the school, and those which are different, such as those in the home or neighborhood. . . . The concept becomes one of degree of proximity to equality of opportunity. This proximity is determined, then, not merely by the *equality* of educational inputs, but by the *intensity* of the schools' influences. That is, equality of opportunity is not so much determined by equality of the resource inputs, but by the power of these resources in bringing about achievement.[4]

Given this new definition of equality of educational opportunity, schools will be expected to achieve the desired academic results and schoolmen will be held accountable by concerned parents and community groups.

While the Colloquium Board Conference participants concurred with Coleman's opinion that a new definition of equality of educational opportunity has emerged and that it is directly related to the results of school learning, there were numerous divergent views as to how society could best achieve this equalitarian ideal. The report stressed that the factors most highly correlated with student achievement were the student's home environment, the social composition of the student body, and the quality of teachers. Some conference speakers argued along the line advanced by the U.S. Commission on Civil Rights in its publication *Racial Isolation in the Public Schools*. Proponents of school integration asserted that since schools do not have strong effects on achievement that are independent of the student's home, neighborhood, and peer environment, the pervasive influences of social class and race cannot be avoided or explained away; just the opposite. Almost a year ago Daniel P. Moynihan declared:

> Because race is the single most inclusive (although not, of course, complete) determinant of class . . . I will argue that Coleman's data represent the most important demonstration of the absolute necessity of racial integration in education that has ever been assembled. He has shown that the achievement of lower-class students is raised when they are included in a predominantly middle-class school, and that the corresponding achievement of the middle-class students is not thereby lowered. . . . The evidence is that if we are going to produce equality of educational opportunity in the United States in this generation, we must do so by sending Negro students, and other minority students as well, to majority white schools.[5]

While in sympathy with Moynihan's argument for integration, Coleman sees the problem in slightly different perspective, as his most recent article in *The Public Interest* indicates. He rejects the view that *only* through racial integration will Negroes' achievement compare favorably with [that of] whites. The goal of racial integration

> does not conflict with, and to some degree aids, the goal of increasing the educational achievement of lower-class children. But these two goals are not identical. The task of increasing achievement of lower-class children cannot be fully implemented by school integration, even if integration were wholly achieved—and the magnitude of racial and class concentration in large cities indicates that it is not likely to be achieved soon.[6]

Yet another line of argument was taken at the conference by Harvard economist Samuel Bowles. Coleman to the contrary, Bowles supports the position that the quality of school resources does have a "statistically significant effect" on student achievement. In his reanalysis of the Coleman data Bowles concluded that "the achievement levels of Negro students are particularly sensitive to the quality of the teaching staffs assigned to them." But, he emphasized, the upgrading of teachers of minority-group children is not enough; a massive societal attack on racism, unemployment, job discrimination, and poverty must be devised and vigorously implemented. The educational system alone cannot achieve equality of educational opportunity, and therefore Bowles calls for a radical redistribution of political power to include the poor of this nation and especially the members of the Negro community.

Whatever divergent views men like Coleman, Moynihan, and Bowles may have relative to the means by which equality of educational opportunity is to be achieved, they would all stress the unique importance of people—students, teachers, parents, community. While differing on which remedial alternative should receive what priority, there was general agreement expressed at the conference that the Coleman Report has lasting significance for American intergroup relations and that educators who continue to think of equality in terms of "things" such as buildings, books, and curriculum do so at their peril.

There are many Americans, however, who maintain that the Coleman Report has no relevance whatsoever to them. John Alexander, president of the Orange, New Jersey, Board of Education and a Negro, condemned the report as dealing a "death blow to all black children. If this report [were] accepted as fact, all black children would never have a chance to be educated." Integrated education is a physical impossibility in large urban areas and it is impossible due to pronounced antiblack feelings among whites. Alexander believes, in short, that the report is merely another piece of paper designed to show black inferiority, and charged that the "whiteness-is-rightness" bias reflected in Coleman's study is anathema to the black community in 1967 America.

Preston Wilcox carried Alexander's line of argument even further with his own version of "functional anger." Wilcox, a professor of social work who was identified with the Harlem parents' movement at I.S. 201, stated that the real issue was not integration or segregation but community control of schools. "I don't subscribe to the view that a black kid must sit next to a white kid to learn. The report is based on the myth of white supremacy. Schools improve only when educators become advocates of their students and not the system." He blamed low Negro achievement on "WASP Nationalism," which has made "WASPism" and "Americanism" the same thing to blacks. This has historically undermined black self-confidence and sense of identity, and Wilcox proclaims that black control of schools will resolve the blacks' problem of low achievement.

Indeed, there is Coleman data that at least partially supports this essentially Black Power argument: "Of all the variables measured in the survey, the attitudes of student interest in school, self-concept, and sense of environmental control show the strongest relation to achievement" (p. 319). And, "a pupil attitude factor which appears to have a stronger relationship to achievement than do all the 'school' factors together is the extent to which an individual feels that he has some control over his destiny" (p. 23). Time will tell whether this Black Power claim and demand for community control of schools will in fact raise achievement scores and whether minority-group children will gain a feeling of control over their environment and destiny. In this light New York City's proposed decentralization plan will be closely watched by black and white Americans alike.

The Alexander-Wilcox position of total rejection of the Coleman Report, while not unexpected given the present mood of black militancy, nonetheless raises another issue that should be touched upon in passing. Simply put, in recent years minority groups have assumed that social science research findings would automatically support claims for action which minority groups believed in. When the published data is at odds, however, with the prevailing mood of the minority group under study, the "facts" are summarily rejected as "false" and the social scientists who conducted the research are likewise held up to ridicule and scorn. The parallel between the controversy that enveloped the 1965 Moynihan Report is strikingly similar to that which now surrounds the Coleman findings; yet are there any men in academic life more devoted to scholarly knowledge and to the cause of social justice? Louis Wirth once tried to explain this phenomenon:

> The distinctive character of social science discourse is to be sought in the fact that every assertion, no matter how objective it may be, has ramifications extending beyond the limits of science itself. Since every assertion of a "fact" about the social world touches the interests of some individual or group, one cannot even call attention to the existence of certain "facts" without courting the objections of those whose very *raison d'être* in society rests upon a divergent interpretation of the "factual" situation.[7]

The Coleman Report does not lend itself to easy solutions, as these observations of the Harvard Conference attest, but the report's findings, albeit controversial, directly challenge the very structure and moral fabric underpinning public education. Future policy decisions cannot lightly dismiss the Coleman data. No responsible person can now deny that our public schools are becoming increasingly segregated by race and social class and that children who survive this "education" are largely unable to cope in our technology-oriented, multiracial world. Simply pouring more money down the present educational drainspouts is an answer doomed to failure. As Senator Ribicoff declared over a year ago: "The Coleman Report is pregnant with implications that are the deepest that this nation has ever faced in its educational system; we as a people would neglect this at the peril of the future of our country."[8] The questions raised about the Coleman Report at the Harvard Conference ultimately come down to whether Americans are willing to move our society toward the goal of effective equality of educational opportunity. To date, the answer from the white community that verbally espouses the rhetoric of the Great Society is clear. Just look around.

Notes

1. Some of the recent reviews of the Coleman Report include James S. Coleman, "Educational Dilemmas: Equal Schools or Equal Students?," *The Public Interest* (Summer, 1966); Robert A. Dentler, "Equality of Educational Opportunity: A Special Review," *The Urban Review* (December, 1966); Christopher Jencks, "Education: The Racial Gap," *The New Republic*, October 1, 1966; and Robert C. Nichols, "Schools and the Disadvantaged," *Science*, December 9, 1966 (reprinted in the June, 1967, *Phi Delta Kappan*). Page numbers in the text refer to the Coleman Report.

2. Speech delivered to the Harvard Colloquium Board Conference by James S. Coleman, *Harvard Educational Review*, XXXVIII (Winter, 1968), 7–22. This special issue is devoted to the concept of equality of educational opportunity.

3. *Ibid.*, p. 22.

4. *Ibid.*, p. 21.

5. Daniel P. Moynihan, "Education and the Urban Poor," lecture delivered to the Harvard Club of New York City, February, 1967.

6. James S. Coleman, "Toward Open Schools," *The Public Interest* (Fall, 1967).

7. Louis Wirth, Preface to Karl Mannheim, *Ideology and Utopia: An Introduction to the Sociology of Knowledge* (New York: Harcourt, Brace and Co., 1936).

8. Senator Abraham Ribicoff, testimony concerning the Coleman Report, held before the Subcommittee on Executive Reorganization of the Committee on Government Operations, *U.S. Senate Proceedings*, August, 1966.

6. URBAN SCHOOL SEGREGATION: A COMPARATIVE ANALYSIS

THOMAS R. DYE

By means of comparative analysis, this article attempts to provide a systematic explanation of public school segregation in large cities. Such an approach entails the comparison of school segregation patterns in a number of cities for the purpose of discovering the social, economic, and political conditions associated with variations in the extent of segregation.

Although racial segregation of public school pupils is widespread throughout the nation, there are marked differences among states and cities in the degree of school segregation. The U.S. Civil Rights Commission reports that 75 per cent of the Negro elementary pupils in seventy-five large cities attended nearly all-Negro schools (at least 90 per cent of enrolled students were Negro) in the 1965–66 school year.[1] However, the range of variation in this measure of segregation ran from New York City, with only 21 per cent of its Negro pupils attending predominantly Negro schools, to Buffalo, with 77 per cent of its Negro students attending such schools; of the Negro students of Tuscaloosa, Alabama, 99 per cent attended predominantly Negro schools, while, in Corpus Christi, Texas, this was true for only 31 per cent of the Negro students. In short, there are significant differences in school segregation patterns; this presents both an opportunity and a challenge for comparative policy research.

What accounts for these differences in the degree of racial segregation in public schools? Are segregation patterns exclusively a product of Negro population percentages? What role do the education, occupation, and income levels of a city's white and Negro populations play in determining the degree of school segregation? How sharply do northern and southern cities differ in the actual extent of school segregation? Do cities with large ethnic populations have more or less Negro segregation? How do political variables affect school segregation? Does an increase

Reprinted from *Urban Affairs Quarterly*, IV (December, 1968), 141–65. Reprinted by permission of Sage Publications, Inc. and the author.

in voter participation reduce the extent of racial segregation? Are cities that vote Democratic more, or less, segregated than those that vote Republican? Does it make any difference in segregation patterns whether a city has partisan or nonpartisan elections? Does it make any difference whether the school board is elected or appointed, or whether it is selected at large or by wards? Do the same social, economic, or political factors that affect school segregation in northern cities also affect school segregation in southern cities? These are some of the questions that will be dealt with through comparative analysis.

School Segregation as Public Policy

Our conceptualization of public school segregation as a policy output of political systems assumes that racial segregation in both northern and southern cities is not the result of fortuitous circumstances unrelated to the activities of political systems. (Following the practice of the U.S. Civil Rights Commission, this paper operationally defines public school segregation on a basis of the per cent of total Negro elementary pupils in schools that are 90–100 per cent Negro and the per cent of total Negro elementary teachers assigned to schools that are 90–100 per cent Negro.) While the segregation of Negro pupils and teachers in southern communities is generally recognized as a product of the past or present actions of political systems, it is often contended that "racial isolation" in northern communities is unrelated to public policy; hence, the phrase *"de facto* segregation." This contention has some support in law. Several U.S. circuit courts have held that the equal protection clause of the Fourteenth Amendment does not create an affirmative duty for school districts to correct racial imbalance resulting from a neighborhood school plan that was not conscientiously constructed to segregate the races. Since the Fourteenth Amendment has been held to prevent state action specifically designed to segregate the races, the implication of these holdings is that *de facto* segregation is not really public policy—that is, it is not really a product of the actions of states or school districts. In the leading case of *Bell v. School City of Gary*, the U.S. Supreme Court refused certiorari in a lower federal court decision that had upheld the Gary, Indiana, neighborhood school plan.[2] That plan, drawn to accord with a racially segregated housing pattern, had resulted in racial imbalance in the public schools.

Yet, the existence of racial imbalance in public schools testifies to the absence of any effective policy to eliminate segregation. Our measures of segregation reflect "nondecisions," and public policy can reasonably be defined to include nondecisions as well as decisions. The maintenance of neighborhood schools in a city with a segregated housing pattern is a public policy, inasmuch as there is no physical or technological reason why children need to be assigned to neighborhood schools. The U.S. Civil Rights Commission[3] points out several policy options for school districts wishing to desegregate: the "pairing" or merging of attendance areas of two or more schools; the establishment of central "educational parks" integrating students from throughout the school district; and the closing of predominantly Negro schools and the dispersal of their students among other schools in the community. The only technological innovation these policies call for is the school bus and, since 75 per cent of all public school children in the nation already ride buses, the feasibility of the bus seems beyond question.

There is, moreover, no constitutional bar to racial classification schemes designed to overcome school desegregation. In *Fuller v. Volk*, a federal district court rejected the arguments of white parents that the decision of the Englewood, New Jersey, School Board consciously to assign children to schools and classes on the basis of race in order to eliminate *de facto* segregation violated the equal protection clause.[4] The court held that "a local board of education is not constitutionally prohibited from taking race into account in drawing or redrawing school attendance lines for the purpose of reducing or eliminating *de facto* segregation in its public schools." While this district court decision is hardly a strong precedent, it is unlikely that the Supreme Court would overturn a racial classification scheme designed to overcome *de facto* segregation. Although the Supreme Court has taken the position that racial classification schemes are "inherently suspect," all of the racial classification practices it has overturned as a violation of the equal protection clause have operated to the detriment of the minority race; there have been no Supreme Court holdings that racial classification designed to improve the conditions of a minority are unconstitutional.

Several states have made more or less official policy pronouncements against *de facto* segregation. Massachusetts has taken the strongest policy stand of any state. Its Racial Imbalance Act of 1965 provides that a school district, upon notification by the state board that one of its schools is racially imbalanced (in this case, 50 per cent or more Negro pupils), must prepare and file with the board a plan to eliminate the imbalance.[5] If the school district fails, within a reasonable time, to show progress in eliminating racial imbalance, the commissioner of education must refuse to certify state school aid for that school district. New York, New Jersey, and Illinois have general laws guaranteeing equal educational opportunity and these have been construed by state boards and commissioners of education as mandating the elimination of racial imbalance in the selection of school sites and the drawing of attendance lines. However, the sanctions available to enforce these policies are vague and ill-defined. In California, the state Board of Education has issued regulations to school boards to avoid racial imbalance, but it is not clear whether the board has any sanctions it may impose in the event of a failure to comply. At the very least, these state actions suggest that alternative policies to school segregation do exist.

It is sometimes argued that central cities of large metropolitan areas that have a very large proportion of Negro pupils cannot be desegregated because of the physical absence of white students; hence, segregation in these cities is said to be a physical necessity rather than a public policy. Actually, however, with the exception of Washington, D.C., no city as yet has so few white pupils that it is physically unable to bring an end to segregation as we have defined it. In 1965–66, more than 90 per cent of the public elementary school pupils in Richmond, Baltimore, and St. Louis were Negro; these are the highest Negro enrollments in large-city school systems in the nation and there are still enough white pupils in these cities to abolish the predominantly Negro schools if the white pupils are spread around. Of course, it is true that the greater the Negro proportion of the school population, the more extensive the policy changes required to accomplish desegregation. But it is not impossible.

Federal policy neither encourages nor discourages school segregation outside of the southern and border states. In other words, federal policy to date constitutes a nondecision in support of *de facto* segregation in northern cities. Title VI of the Civil Rights Act of 1964, which authorizes the withholding of federal funds from programs that are operated in a racially discriminatory manner and which has been the most effective instrument of desegregation in the South, specifically excludes *de facto* segregation from its purview. It defines the word "desegregation" as "the assignment of students to public schools and within such schools without regard to their race, color, religion or national origin, but . . . not . . . the assignment of students to public schools in order to overcome racial imbalance."[6] It also provides that nothing "shall empower any official or court of the United States to issue any order seeking to achieve a racial balance in any school by requiring the transportation of pupils or students from one school to another or one school district to another in order to achieve such racial balance."[7] That Congress felt the need to state what was not its policy is further evidence that nonpolicy is policy.

In short, superimposing a policy of geographical attendance zoning on a pattern of residential segregation insures public school segregation. It is plainly the agents of the state and its political subdivisions who select school sites, define attendance areas, and assign Negro pupils and teachers to schools that are racially isolated. The maintenance of segregated schools by states and school districts is certainly a nondecision and is, equally, public policy.

Related Research

The U.S. Civil Rights Commission examined the consequences of racial segregation in a 1967 report entitled *Racial Isolation in the Public Schools.*[8] The commission relied heavily on a study that James Coleman had done for the U.S. Office of Education.[9] Coleman's study suggested that even when segregation is *de facto*, the adverse effects on Negro students are still significant. In northern urban school districts, the commission reported that predominantly Negro schools were less likely to have good libraries or advanced classes in the sciences and mathematics, and more likely to have overcrowded classrooms, poorly trained teachers, and teachers who were dissatisfied with their schools. Negro students attending predominantly Negro schools had lower achievement scores and lower aspiration levels than Negroes from similar economic backgrounds who attended predominantly white schools. In fact, Negroes in segregated schools were more than two years behind the students from the same kinds of families who attended white schools. On the other hand, the achievement level of white students in classes that were half Negro was no different than that of a control group of students in all-white schools. The commission rejected compensatory education programs in segregated schools as a solution to Negro educational problems, citing research that indicated such programs were less effective in raising achievement and aspiration levels of Negro students than were integrated classrooms. The report, primarily an argumentative and prescriptive document, dealt with the causes of racial isolation in a general rather than a systematic fashion. It concluded with a call for affirmative steps by school districts, states, and the national government to end racial isolation in the schools.

A systematic study of this subject has been done by Donald Matthews and James Prothro, who examined the environmental and political factors associated with desegregation policy in 997 southern counties.[10] Of the environmental variables, Matthews and Prothro concluded that desegregation is most likely in an urban setting in which Negroes and whites receive relatively high incomes and Negroes are relatively well educated. In addition, a large Negro population was a distinct barrier to desegregation. Apparently, the presence of large numbers of Negroes in an area stimulates white resistance to desegregation.

Matthews and Prothro also found that political variables were much less influential in accounting for school desegregation policy than were environmental variables. Moreover, their data indicated that most of the correlation between political variables and school desegregation policy was really a product of the relationship between political variables and environmental variables.

A study of school desegregation in eleven southern states made by the author corroborates the findings of Matthews and Prothro. The study concluded that a large Negro population strengthened the position of the segregationists; whereas large Negro populations appeared to stimulate resistance to desegregation, wealth and urbanism appeared to have the opposite effect.

Urban Environmental Variables and School Segregation

SECTIONALISM

The single most influential variable affecting school segregation is still sectionalism. The roots of racial attitudes in the South are too deep to examine here, but the impact of past legal segregation and the lingering traditions of the "southern way of life" are clearly visible more than a decade after *Brown v. Board of Education*. After years of Negro migration from the South to the North, the Negro proportion of public school students in northern cities is not much different from that in southern cities. The average proportion of Negro public elementary school pupils in the northern cities that this study sampled[11] was 32.5; in southern cities it was 31.5. This means that differences existing in the degree of school segregation between northern and southern cities cannot be attributed to differences in Negro school population percentages.

Northern and southern cities differed markedly in the extent of pupil and teacher segregation in public schools. Southern cities in the sample had an average of over 85 per cent of their Negro pupils in schools that were 90–100 per cent Negro, while northern cities had an average of only about 46 per cent of their Negro pupils in these predominantly Negro schools. The Civil Rights Commission reported: "The extent of racial isolation in northern school systems does not differ markedly from that in the South."[12] This statement is, at best, very misleading and is at variance with the figures supplied by the commission itself.

One of the interesting consequences of legal segregation was that it provided employment for Negro teachers in southern states. Southern cities actually employ more Negro teachers than do northern cities; southern cities employ roughly the same proportion of Negro teachers as there are Negro pupils, while northern cities employ a much smaller proportion of Negro teachers than there are Negro pupils. Of course, the vast majority of Negro teachers in southern cities (almost 95 per cent) teach in predominantly Negro schools, whereas only 45 per cent of Negro teachers in northern cities are assigned to such schools.

TABLE 6-1

AVERAGES FOR NORTHERN AND SOUTHERN CITIES ON PUPIL AND
TEACHER SEGREGATION MEASURES[a]

	Southern Cities	Northern Cities
Negro pupils (as per cent of total)	31.5	32.5
Negro teachers (as per cent of total)	27.3	19.8
Negro pupil segregation	86.7	45.5
Negro teacher segregation	94.5	45.0

[a] In public elementary schools that are 90–100 per cent Negro.

Segregation in southern cities is decreasing with time, however slight the decreases. Even though pupil and teacher segregation measures for southern cities run much higher than those for northern cities, they represent a decrease from the nearly 100 per cent segregation in existence in 1954. In contrast, available evidence indicates that school segregation in northern cities is increasing over time. While data that go back over time are not complete for many cities, available data compiled by the Civil Rights Commission suggest that not only are larger numbers of Negro pupils now attending segregated schools, but also larger percentages of Negro pupils are now attending such schools. Table 6-2 shows the growth of Negro pupil segregation in selected cities over time.

TABLE 6-2

CHANGES IN PUPIL SEGREGATION IN SELECTED CITIES[a]

City	Year	Number of Negro Students	Percentage of Total Negro Students	Year	Number of Negro Students	Percentage of Total Negro Students
Cincinnati	1950	3,981	43.7	1965	11,155	49.4
Milwaukee	1950	1,316	51.2	1965	14,344	72.4
Philadelphia	1950	29,555	63.2	1965	66,052	72.0
Pittsburgh	1950	3,226	30.4	1965	9,226	49.5
Indianapolis	1951	7,837	83.2	1965	15,426	70.5
Cleveland	1952	12,369	57.4	1965	41,034	82.3
Oakland	1959	1,110	7.7	1965	9,043	48.7
Detroit	1960	62,391	66.9	1965	77,654	72.3
Buffalo	1961	9,199	80.5	1965	13,106	77.0
San Francisco	1962	1,579	11.6	1965	3,031	21.1
Harrisburg	1963	2,103	58.1	1965	2,075	54.0
Springfield	1963	0	0.0	1965	567	15.4
New Haven	1963	1,196	22.5	1965	2,171	36.8

[a] In 90–100 per cent Negro schools.

Not only does the extent of school segregation differ markedly between northern and southern cities, but the determinants of segregation patterns also differ as between North and South. Political and environmental variables that may be influential in determining the extent of segregation in northern cities are not necessarily influential in shaping segregation in southern cities. For this reason, northern and southern cities are examined separately in the analysis that follows.

NEGRO ENROLLMENT

The most commonly accepted hypothesis about school segregation is that it varies inversely with the proportion of Negroes enrolled in the public schools. Comparative analysis reveals that, indeed, Negro pupil percentages are the single most important determinant of pupil and teacher segregation in both northern and southern cities. Table 6-3 pre-

TABLE 6-3

ENVIRONMENTAL VARIABLES AND PUBLIC SCHOOL SEGREGATION IN NORTHERN AND SOUTHERN CITIES[a]

	SEGREGATION MEASURES							
	Northern Cities				Southern Cities			
	NEGRO PUPILS		NEGRO TEACHERS		NEGRO PUPILS		NEGRO TEACHERS	
	Simple	Partial	Simple	Partial	Simple	Partial	Simple	Partial
Negro pupils (*as per cent of total*)	.76*	.60*	.79	.67	.46	.66	.35	.36
Status characteristic of city populations								
Adult education	−.46*	−.34*	−.51	−.42	.20	.52*	−.03	.63*
White-collar employment	−.56*	−.44*	−.57	−.51	.12	.32*	−.08	.58
Family income	−.04	−.25	−.15	−.25	.06	.05	−.10	.29
Status characteristics of Negro populations								
Adult education	−.42*	−.20	−.46*	−.12	.05	.11	−.07	.20
White-collar employment	−.14	.19	−.13	.27	.33*	.46*	.16	.27
Family income	−.05	.13	−.19	.05	.02	.10	.19	.05
Ethnicity	−.31*	−.21	−.39*	−.39*	−.24	−.40*	−.43*	−.62*
Size of city	.49*	.37*	.43*	.38*	.16	.21	.06	.24
Age of city	.54*	.32*	.53*	.38*	.12	−.11	−.10	−.44*
Private school enrollment	.25	.17	.22	.02	.35		.17	.59

[a] Figures are simple and partial correlation coefficients for the relationships between pupil and teacher segregation measures and environmental variables for northern and southern cities respectively. Partial coefficients show the influence of each environmental variable while controlling for *all* other environmental variables, including Negro pupil percentages. An asterisk indicates a significant relationship.

sents simple and partial correlation coefficients for a series of urban environmental variables and Negro pupil and teacher segregation measures for both northern and southern cities. Simple coefficients indicate that Negro pupil and teacher segregation is more closely associated with Negro pupil percentages than with any other environmental variable. The strong partial coefficients indicate that this relationship is an independent one—that is, it does not depend upon the intervening effect of some other environmental variable. Our findings contradict the Civil Rights Commission assertion that the pattern of school segregation does not vary according to the proportion of Negroes enrolled in the school system. School segregation does vary according to the proportion of Negroes in the school system, and this is particularly true in northern cities. The commission, however, accurately observed that Negroes constitute 26 per cent of the elementary school enrollment in Milwaukee and almost 60 per cent of the enrollment in Philadelphia: yet, in both cities, almost three out of every four Negro children attend nearly all-Negro schools. Hartford has a Negro enrollment of 43 per cent, whereas Buffalo has only 37 per cent; yet in Hartford, only 9 per cent of the Negro students attended predominantly Negro schools, while 77 per cent of the Negro students in Buffalo did so.

These examples are evidence that segregation is not a *necessary* result of large Negro enrollments; yet large Negro enrollments certainly generate strong demands and place important constraints on school systems in racial matters. Apparently, it is far more difficult to adopt an effective policy of desegregation in cities with large Negro enrollments. This suggests that an interesting measure of public policy toward school segregation would be the degree to which cities *deviate* from the general proposition that school segregation is a function of Negro enrollment percentages. What accounts for variations in the degree of segregation among cities with the same proportions of Negro enrollment? In other words, controlling for the effect of Negro enrollment, what accounts for differences among cities in school desegregation?

Figure 6-1 permits us to observe which cities segregate more or less of their Negro pupils than predicted from their Negro enrollment. Figure 6-1 is a scatter diagram of the relationship between the proportion of Negro pupils enrolled and the per cent of Negro students assigned to predominantly Negro schools. Among northern cities, Milwaukee and Buffalo are much more segregated than one would expect on the basis of their Negro enrollment. They segregate a larger percentage of their Negro pupils than cities such as Pittsburgh, Cincinnati, Rochester, and Akron, which have roughly the same proportion of Negro students. In contrast, New York City, Wilmington, and especially Hartford, are

Figure 6-1
DISTRIBUTION OF NORTHERN AND SOUTHERN CITIES
BY NEGRO ENROLLMENT AND
PUPIL SEGREGATION PERCENTAGES[a]

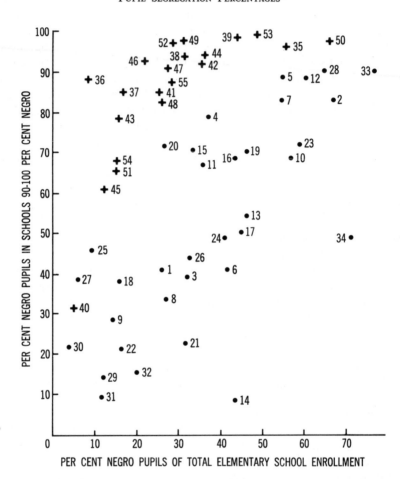

[a] Northern cities are identified by a dot; southern cities, by a cross. The cities and their corresponding numbers in the figure are as follows: *Northern Cities:* 1. Akron, 2. Baltimore, 3. Boston, 4. Buffalo, 5. Chicago, 6. Cincinnati, 7. Cleveland, 8. Columbus, Ohio, 9. Denver, 10. Detroit, 11. Flint, 12. Gary, 13. Harrisburg, 14. Hartford, 15. Indianapolis, 16. Kansas City, 17. Lexington, 18. Los Angeles, 19. Louisville, 20. Milwaukee, 21. New York, 22. Peoria, 23. Philadelphia, 24. Pittsburgh, 25. Portland, 26. Rochester, 27. St. Joseph, Mo., 28. St. Louis, 29. San Diego, 30. San Francisco, 31. Seattle, 32. Springfield, Mass., 33. Washington, D.C., 34. Wilmington; *Southern Cities:* 35. Atlanta, 36. Amarillo, 37. Austin, 38. Charleston, 39. Columbia, 40. Corpus Christi, 41. Dallas, 42. Houston, 43. Knoxville, 44. Little Rock, 45. Lubbock, 46. Oklahoma City, 47. Miami, 48. Nashville, 49. Raleigh, 50. Richmond, 51. San Antonio, 52. Texarkana, 53. Tuscaloosa, 54. Wichita Falls, 55. Winston-Salem.

more integrated than one would predict on the basis of their Negro enrollment.[13]

Cities with generally higher-status populations might be expected to experience more public school desegregation, not only because these cities have fewer Negroes, but also because higher-status populations may be more willing to accept integration than may lower-status populations. Whites with higher education, income, and occupational characteristics are said to be more "public-regarding" than those of the lower middle class and working class. "Public-regardingness" is said to involve both concern for "the public interest" and for the "welfare of the community."[14] This suggests that desegregation might be associated with higher educational, income, and occupational levels among urban populations.

In northern cities, the extent of racial segregation in public schools is significantly correlated with the educational and occupational levels of the urban population, but not with income levels. Increases in adult education and white-collar employment are associated with decreases in Negro pupil and teacher segregation. These relationships appear in both simple and partial coefficients, suggesting that these environmental variables independently affect school segregation.

There are, however, no systematic differences in the extent of desegregation in southern cities that can be attributed to variations in over-all status characteristics of urban populations. In short, status characteristics of urban populations affect segregation patterns in northern cities but not in southern cities.

STATUS CHARACTERISTICS OF URBAN POPULATIONS

What other variables, aside from Negro pupil percentages, might be expected to affect school desegregation? In examining the influence of other environmental and political variables on school desegregation, it is particularly important to observe partial coefficients that control for the effect of Negro pupil percentages. While Figure 6-1 identifies cities having more or less desegregation than expected on the basis of their Negro enrollment, only partial coefficients can systematically assess the impact of other environmental and political variables while controlling for Negro pupil percentages.

STATUS CHARACTERISTICS OF NEGRO SUBPOPULATIONS

The educational, occupational, and income levels of the Negro populations within large cities might also be expected to affect segregation patterns. The well-educated, middle-class Negro populations should be in a better position economically and politically to reduce segregation. They should know how to make their demands felt in the political system. Moreover, we might expect Negro children from families with higher education, occupation, and income levels to be more "acceptable" to whites and, therefore, less likely to inspire white resistance to desegregation.

On the whole, however, comparative analysis fails to reveal any strong independent relationships between status levels of Negro subpopulations in cities and the extent of segregation. While the simple coefficients in Table 6-3 show a significant relationship between adult education levels of Negro subpopulations in northern cities and pupil segregation, this relationship tends to "wash out" when other variables are controlled. In other words, it is difficult to show that Negro educational levels *independently* assist in desegregation, although northern cities with well-educated adult Negro populations are somewhat less segregated than northern cities with less-educated Negro populations. In southern cities, there are no significant relationships between the characteristics of Negro subpopulations and the extent of school desegregation.

ETHNICITY

It was originally hypothesized that the existence of large white ethnic subpopulations, particularly in northern cities, might constitute an obstacle to desegregation. Private-regardingness, as opposed to public-regardingness, is said to be a characteristic of white working-class ethnic subpopulations.[15] These private-regarding subpopulations are felt to be less concerned with the plight of the Negro. They are often in competition with Negroes for housing and jobs. Therefore, it could be expected that "ethnic" cities—cities with large proportions of persons who are foreign-born or whose parents are foreign-born—would be more segregated than cities without large ethnic subpopulations.

In terms of aggregate comparisons among cities, however, large ethnic subpopulations are associated with *decreases* in school segregation, rather than with increases in it. Ethnicity appears to have some independent relationship with desegregation, even when other variables are controlled; cities with larger ethnic populations tend to be less segregated. This is true in both northern and southern cities, but the relationship is noticeably stronger in southern cities. Southern cities that have experienced some dilution of local white Anglo-Saxon Protestant stock are slightly less segregated than those that have not.

SIZE AND AGE OF CITY

Larger and older cities may be less amenable to policy change than may smaller and younger cities. There is as yet little systematic research regarding this proposition, but there are good a priori reasons for believing that this is true. Increase in size involves expansion in bureaucracy, and large bureaucracies have many built-in mechanisms to resist policy innovations. Increase in size also multiplies the number of interest groups that may exercise veto powers. Age may also tend to immobilize policy. Over time, persons and organizations adjust themselves to circumstances as they find them. The longer these adjustments have been in existence, the greater the discomfort, expense, and fear of unanticipated consequences associated with policy change. Finally, the housing in the core areas of older cities is obsolescent. These visibly deteriorating areas of older cities are likely to constitute well-defined segregated neighborhoods. Housing segregation in newer and younger cities may be less well-defined. All of this suggests that larger and older cities may find it more difficult to desegregate than may smaller and younger cities.

Comparative analysis reveals that among northern cities both size and age are independently associated with segregation policy. Larger and older cities tend to have more pupil and teacher segregation than smaller and newer cities. The partial coefficients in Table 6-3 indicate that these associations exist separately from the influence of Negro enrollment percentages (which are, of course, greater in larger and older cities). In contrast to northern cities, size and age are not associated with segregation in southern cities. Apparently, smaller and newer southern cities are just as segregated as larger and older southern cities.

PRIVATE SCHOOL ENROLLMENT

Private and parochial school enrollments made up only about one-sixth of the total school enrollment in the United States in 1960, but private school enrollment ranges up to 33 per cent of the total school population in Boston, 40 per cent in Philadelphia, and 46 per cent in Pittsburgh. Almost all private school enrollment is white.

The removal of white children from public schools, of course, makes it more difficult for school systems to reduce segregation if they choose to do so. One would expect private school enrollment percentages to be associated with school segregation; yet, this does not turn out to be a very influential determinant of variations in school segregation among cities. There is only a slight relationship between private school enrollment and Negro pupil segregation. Some school systems, like that in

Pittsburgh, with relatively large private school enrollment have less pupil segregation than that in Buffalo, Indianapolis, or Milwaukee, with small private school enrollment; this is true even after controlling for the effects of Negro percentages in public schools. We have sufficient evidence that large private school enrollment does not "cause" *de facto* segregation. Cities with the largest private school enrollment are not the most segregated. The segregation of public school children is not a product of the existence of private schools.

Political Variables and School Segregation

Thus far, attention has been focused on the relationships between environmental variables and school segregation. The effect of the characteristics of the political system on segregation policy remains to be assessed. Of course, in assessing the effect of system characteristics, it is necessary to control for the effect of environmental inputs, since we know that environmental variables shape political systems as well as influence segregation policy.

Matthews and Prothro[16] found that political system variables were less influential than environmental variables in the decisions of southern school districts to desegregate. In general, the results of this study support that finding; political system variables are not as important as environmental variables in shaping school segregation patterns among northern cities; few of the political system characteristics measured correlated significantly with Negro pupil or teacher segregation in northern cities. Those relationships between political system variables and school segregation that do occur in northern cities are either very weak or "wash out" when the effects of environmental variables are controlled.

Surprisingly, however, political system variables are much more closely related to segregation patterns in southern cities. Environmental variables are *less* influential in school segregation in southern cities than in northern cities, but political variables are *more* influential. Most of the political system variables turn out to be significantly related to the extent of Negro pupil and teacher segregation in southern cities. And these relationships do not "wash out" when environmental variables are controlled, which suggests that they do not occur as a result of some intervening environmental conditions.

FORM OF CITY GOVERNMENT AND TYPE OF ELECTION

The mayoral form of city government is said to be more "political" than the commission and manager forms.[17] Manager government—predicated on the belief that cities can and should be governed scientifically, efficiently, and nonpolitically—was designed to remove day-to-day decisions from political pressure. It seems reasonable to hypothesize that insulating government from "politics" might reduce Negro influence since Negroes might feel themselves to be in a less effective bargaining position when dealing with a "nonpolitical," efficiency-minded, middle-class administrator as opposed to dealing with a politically sensitive mayor interested in accommodating minorities. Of course, if white "backlash" were evident in a city, a mayoral government might be *less* interested in accommodating Negro demands than might a manager.

It turns out that there is a slight tendency for cities with mayoral governments to be less segregated than cities with manager governments. This relationship is barely significant among southern cities and just below our level of significance among northern cities. Hence, it is possible that the political environment associated with mayoral government is more conducive to encouraging desegregation than is the nonpolitical environment associated with manager government. This interpretation is reinforced by the relationship between partisan elections and desegregation in southern cities. Southern cities with partisan elections are less segregated than southern cities with nonpartisan elections.

These findings suggest that, in southern cities at least, the more political forms of government—mayoral governments and partisan elections—may result in increased Negro political power and more progress in school desegregation. Nonpolitical forms of government—managers and nonpartisan elections—may suppress effective political action on behalf of desegregation.

SCHOOL BOARD SELECTION

School decisions affecting segregation, including pupil assignments, building locations, busing, teacher assignments, and so on, are usually made by school boards or school administrators who report to these boards. It is not unreasonable to inquire whether segregation is related to the method of selecting these boards.

Most city school boards in the United States are elected rather than appointed. Only about one-quarter of the nation's school boards are appointed. However, appointed school boards are often found in larger cities with larger populations in the lower socio-economic level and with large Negro populations. More importantly, the data suggest that appointed boards are associated with greater pupil and teacher segregation. This association is barely discernible in northern cities, but it is quite marked in southern cities.

This finding lends additional support to our notion that the more political the environment of southern cities, the more progress toward desegregation. On the whole, school systems with elected boards are less segregated than school systems with appointed boards. Moreover, school districts that select their school board members at-large rather than by ward tend to have greater pupil and teacher segregation. Ward elections are generally considered more political than at-large elections, since ward representatives are more directly responsible to a specific electorate than are representatives elected at-large. Cumulatively, these findings increase our suspicion that "nonpolitical" structures of government are associated with nondecisions, which, in turn, support existing patterns of school segregation.

VOTER PARTICIPATION

If the theory that increased political activity leads to desegregation is true, then we should expect segregation to decrease with increased voter participation. Indeed, this is the case: Increases in voter participation are associated with decreases in pupil and teacher segregation. But the relationships are very weak in northern cities and tend to "wash out" when other environmental variables are controlled. These relationships are only slightly stronger in southern cities. Unfortunately, it cannot be said with any confidence that increased voter participation leads to desegregation.

DEMOCRATIC PARTY VOTING

In northern cities, an increase in Democratic Party voting is closely associated with increased segregation of pupils and teachers. This association, however, is clearly a product of intervening environmental variables for it "washes out" when these environmental variables are controlled. Democratic Party voting is strongest in larger cities with larger populations on lower socio-economic levels and with larger concentrations of Negroes. Since these environmental variables are associated with segregation, Democratic Party voting is also associated with segregation. When these environmental variables are controlled, however, there is no relationship between Democratic Party voting and school segregation in northern cities.

However, in southern cities, Democratic party voting is independently related to increases in pupil and teacher segregation. Even when environmental variables are controlled, larger Democratic vote totals mean greater percentages of Negro pupils and teachers assigned to nearly all-Negro schools. Republican Party voting in southern cities is indicative of party competition and, apparently, party competition is independently related to progress in school desegregation. Cities such as Dallas, Nashville, Knoxville, Miami, and San Antonio are more party competitive than cities such as Richmond, Tuscaloosa, and Atlanta. These competitive cities are also less segregated. Hence, V. O. Key's proposition that one-partyism was a bulwark of segregation appears to have some empirical support in correlation analysis.[18] However, the very recent growth of a segregationist Republican element in the South since 1964 is not fully reflected in these figures, and it may be that the relationship between Democratic voting and school segregation will gradually disappear as segregationist strongholds go Republican.

In summary, comparative analysis of aggregate figures on school segregation in large cities reveals a number of interesting correlates of *de facto* public school segregation in both northern and southern cities. Of course, these correlations do not tell us exactly how demands regarding school policy develop out of environmental conditions, how these demands are communicated, how school systems adopt themselves to these demands, or exactly how governmental structures and political variables modify these demands. Nor are these correlations necessarily evidence of cause-and-effect relationships. But they do direct our attention to underlying environmental conditions and political variables that are linked to urban school segregation.

Notes

1. U.S., Commission on Civil Rights, *Racial Isolation in the Public Schools* (2 vols.; Washington, D.C.: Government Printing Office, 1967); hereafter cited as Commission Report.
2. *Bell v. School City of Gary*, 213 F. Supp. 819, aff'd, 324 F. 2d 209 (1963), cert. denied, 377 U.S. 924 (1964). See also "Legal Appendix," in Commission Report, I, 219–36.
3. Commission Report, I, 140–83.
4. *Fuller v. Volk*, 230 F. Supp. 25 (1964); see also *Offerman v. Nitkowski*, 248 F. Supp. 129 (1965).
5. Mass. Gen. Laws, Ch. 71, sec. 37 D (1965).
6. Civil Rights Act of 1964, Title IV, sec. 401; 78 Stat. 346 (1964).
7. *Ibid.*, sec. 407.
8. See note 1, above.
9. James S. Coleman, *et al.*, *Equality of Educational Opportunity* (Washington, D.C.: U.S. Department of Health, Education, and Welfare, Office of Education, 1966).
10. Donald R. Matthews and James W. Prothro, "Stateways versus Folkways: Critical Factors in Southern Reactions to Brown v. Board of Education," in Gott-

fried Dietze (ed.), *Essays on the American Constitution* (Englewood Cliffs, N.J.: Prentice-Hall, 1964), pp. 139–58.

11. The following data is based on a sampling of fifty-five cities. The selection of fifty-five cities was accomplished by what might be euphemistically called nonprobability sampling. The fifty-five cities were selected solely on the basis of availability of data on all of the environmental and political variables and information on pupil and teacher segregation. The U.S. Commission on Civil Rights collected *complete* information on both pupil and teacher segregation in only sixty-seven cities; this sample of cities with complete data was reduced to fifty-five when matched with sources of information on environmental and, particularly, political conditions—elected versus appointed school boards, private school enrollment, etc.

Difficulties arose because the principle sources of data—reports of the U.S. Commission on Civil Rights, the National Education Association, and the U.S. Office of Education—were available only for "selected" cities and school districts. Often the cities and school districts "selected" by one agency were not the same as those "selected by another, thus reducing the number of cities for which complete data was available.

The principle sources of data were the U.S. Commission on Civil Rights Report, cited in note 1, above; Research Division, National Education Association, *Selected Statistics on Local School Systems* (Washington, D.C.: NEA, 1966); H. Thomas James, *Determinants of Educational Expenditures in Large Cities of the United States* (Stanford, Calif.: School of Education, Stanford University, 1966); and U.S., Bureau of the Census, *County and City Data Book 1962* (Washington, D.C.: Government Printing Office, 1962).

12. Commission Report, I, 6.

13. Hartford's "Project Concern" has received national attention as a metropolitan-wide desegregation program. Negro elementary pupils are bused from predominantly Negro schools in Hartford to schools in five surrounding suburban communities. Children from Hartford are placed in the grade that they would have attended in the city without regard to their achievement level, but with a limit of three Hartford students to a class. Special federal and state funds provide professional staff for participating suburban schools in remedial educational activities. This program does not affect large numbers of children and does not itself account for Hartford's position on our segregation measure. But it is indicative of the policy stand of the Hartford community toward segregation. The New York City Board of Education has long been acutely aware of the problems of racial imbalance. Beginning in 1959, New York City consciously undertook to reduce racial imbalance through school attendance boundary changes, busing, and the establishment of educational complexes and educational parks. Whatever else one may say about New York City schools, they have achieved a remarkable degree of desegregation in comparison with other cities. See Connecticut State Department of Education, *Project Concern*, September 20, 1966; and Commission Report, I, 153. See also State Education Commissioner's Advisory Committee on Human Relations and Community Tensions, "Desegregating the Public Schools of New York City," May 12, 1964.

14. James Q. Wilson and Edward C. Banfield, "Public-Regardingness as a Value Premise in Voting Behavior," *American Political Science Review*, LVIII (December, 1964), 876–87.

15. *Ibid.*

16. Matthews and Prothro, *op. cit.*

17. See Edward C. Banfield and James Q. Wilson, *City Politics* (Cambridge, Mass.: Harvard Univesrity Press, 1963), pp. 138–50.

18. V. O. Key, Jr., *Southern Politics* (New York: Alfred A. Knopf, 1949).

7. SCHOOL DESEGREGATION AND SCHOOL DECISION-MAKING

ROBERT L. CRAIN and DAVID STREET

In many ways the school desegregation issue is an ideal context in which to examine the general question of how school systems make policy decisions. First, it is an issue of some importance, so that the decision-making process uncovered can be assumed to be a nontrivial one. Second, it is a relatively new issue, so that the system can make decisions without much reference to traditional decision-making rules; this means that the social scientist need not be greatly concerned with the impact of prior historical accidents. Finally, the issue has arisen in nearly every large city with only minor differences among cities in the way in which it has been raised and with such idiosyncratic factors as the taxing power of the system being of minor importance. This means that the setting is almost ideal for comparative analysis.

This article principally discusses some of the conclusions of a comparative study of integration in eight northern large-city school systems carried out by the National Opinion Research Center (NORC) in 1965.[1] Data were gathered by teams of graduate students who spent ten man-days in each city interviewing school administrators, school board members, civil rights leaders, political leaders, members of the civic elite, and other informants. The cities were selected by a modified random sampling design from cities having a population between 250,000 and 1,000,000 of which at least 10 per cent were Negro. The findings are supplemented by observations made in the course of research on the social organization of the large-city school system carried out principally in the Chicago schools.[2]

Very little research has been devoted to the school desegregation issue as a problem in policy-making. Consequently, almost everyone, including most social scientists, have been dependent upon the popular media

"School Desegregation and School Decision-Making" by Robert L. Crain and David Street is reprinted from *Educating an Urban Population* (Beverly Hills, Calif.: Sage Publications, 1967), pp. 136–54, by permission of the Publisher, Sage Publications, Inc.

for information about the issue. This has produced a widespread acceptance of some important misconceptions. Perhaps the most common is the view that intense conflict over school desegregation is unavoidable because civil rights leaders want major concessions which the white voters are too prejudiced to give. This statement contains, we believe, three errors. First, our findings indicate that in some circumstances intense conflict is avoidable. In the eight cities studied, three (Newark, Baltimore, and St. Louis) have at least temporarily resolved their conflict with the civil rights movement. In three other cities (Pittsburgh, San Francisco, and Buffalo), the controversy has cooled down and shows promise of being resolved. In the two remaining cities, the controversy is still raging. Second, our data indicate that most civil rights leaders will be satisfied (or at least call off their attacks) if they receive even minimal concessions. Third, survey data have indicated relatively little opposition to school desegregation in national samples of white voters.[3]

In short, the school system has some freedom to establish a policy which will prevent conflict. This is not the same as saying that the school system has the power to develop a policy which will actually alter the basic nature of the schools' treatment of Negro students; indeed, we doubt that any big-city school system can do this. Thus, it will be necessary to divide our discussion into two sections: first, viewing school desegregation as an issue of symbolic politics, and then looking at the actual outputs of the school system—the extent of school integration and the extent to which educational opportunities can in fact be equalized.

Symbolic Politics: The Demands of the Civil Rights Movement

Traditional civil rights groups have pressed for school integration in all eight cities studied in the NORC research. To these groups the integration issue means two things: (1) the prevention of discrimination in allocating students to schools and (2) the acceptance on the part of the school system of the principle that integration is desirable. Beyond these rather minimal goals, the civil rights leaders would prefer, of course, a maximum amount of actual integration, but most of them view true integration as a nearly unattainable goal.[4] If the school system can be persuaded to make racial integration one of its major goals, the civil rights groups will have achieved an important victory, for this commitment exerts normative pressure on the total community to accept the principle of racial equality and to define the efforts to segregate Negroes as illegitimate. Thus, for the traditional civil rights movements, the written policies and pronouncements of the school system are important regardless of their impact. (Of course, if the system took no efforts to implement the policy, the civil rights leaders would raise the cry of hypocrisy.) The civil rights groups would probably endorse the definition of integration given by the Pittsburgh Urban League: "We regard a community as integrated when opportunities for the achievement of respect and the distribution of material welfare are not limited by race."

One is tempted to draw parallels between the school desegregation issue and labor-management negotiations. The major difference is that the corporation is required by law to negotiate with a labor union, while the school board is not. The school board is in the position of the corporation of four decades ago, when management had to decide whether it was wise or morally proper to negotiate with labor unions. The northern school board is not required to recognize the civil rights movement as legitimate and, indeed, many whites who appear otherwise unprejudiced do not consider it so. But another problem is that even when the school system decides that negotiation is proper, the question remains of whom to recognize as the true spokesmen for the civil rights movement. For these two reasons, actual back-room negotiations with the civil rights movement are not common. In our eight cities, only two school systems have been able to maintain this sort of communication with the civil rights groups. This means that we will have to analyze the school systems' policy-making as taking place with only limited private, face-to-face communications between the "negotiators."

THE FIRST STAGE OF THE DESEGREGATION DECISION:
THE SCHOOL SUPERINTENDENT AS DECISION-MAKER

We shall see that the policy decision on desegregation is made by the school board, not the superintendent. However, in each case the board attempted to avoid making a decision for as long as possible. The typical school board seems to operate in a highly pragmatic, fire-fighting fashion. It has limited time, resources, and information with which to make policies, and the result is that it seems not to have a clear policy perspective, but primarily makes *ad hoc* decisions as issues become "hot."[5] In the case of desegregation, none of the eight school boards took action when the issue was first raised, and this placed the burden of decision-making on the superintendent. Of ten superintendents who served in the eight cities during the racial controversy, seven can be said to have acted autonomously without board direction to reject demands made by the civil rights movement, while three urged the board to take a liberal position. This comes as no surprise. It is now fashionable to accuse superintendents as a group of being narrow-minded and arrogant in their dealings with civil rights leaders. As our data indicate, superintendents do not uniformly reject civil rights demands, but enough do to require us to discuss this point.

The statements of school superintendents frequently stress three themes. The first is that the appropriate stance should be "color blindness"—the refusal to pay any attention to race. This sometimes leads to statements that racial census of school children is illegal or at least immoral. Coupled with this concern with color blindness is the stress placed on a narrow definition of the function of the school as "educational" rather than "social." The third theme which recurs (although with somewhat less frequency) is an extreme defensiveness and an intolerance for "lay" criticism. Lay persons are dismissed as unqualified to make recommendations, and their criticisms are frequently answered with flat disagreement or with vague, overly detailed, and off-the-point replies.

Of course, these reactions are common to all organizations which must meet criticism, but the educators go further than most public officials in reacting defensively to political demands. Educational administrators are insistent on defining themselves as professionals and have an entrenched ideology that grants lay control but stresses the importance of the teaching certificate and "educational experience" as the boundary between the expert and the layman. In part, the response to the demands for integration is only another instance of the professionals' tendency—developed through generations of conflict over political interference, progressive education, charges of Communism in the schools, and other issues—to perceive any criticism as an "attack upon education."

Further, civil rights demands also strike deeply at one of the most firmly held tenets of the ideology of the large-city superintendent: universalism. In the development of the large-city schools, insistence on equality of programs for all populations in the city marked a dramatic accomplishment, as it gave the schools protection from the pleas for special treatment from various political and ethnic groups. Without this universalism, northern schools would be more segregated than they are; even after World War I, biracial high schools still discriminated against their Negro students in extracurricular activity participation.[6] Yet, demands by the civil rights movement give the lie to the assumption of universalism, thereby provoking a defensiveness around a highly salient theme and, often, the administrators' counterattack that civil rights demands are themselves a case of special pleading. The defensive response may also be increased by the superintendent's knowledge that, even if he were wholly committed to making integration a prime value of the schools, many of his personnel are too traditionalistic, too prejudiced, or too recalcitrant to make the needed adjustments without great resistance.

Thus, we can understand the superintendents' initial defensive response. But, in most cases, the school board has little difficulty taking control of the decision from the superintendent. Why is this? The answer seems to lie in what areas the superintendents can make believable claims to expertise. On many issues—for example, curriculum construction, textbook selection, or design of facilities—the superintendents' judgments generally go unchallenged, not only because they usually fall into areas of indifference but also because the superintendents' accumulation of detailed information, his technical background, and his appeals to standard or good practice argue well for honoring his professional claims. On such issues, the superintendent in effect runs the schools. Any criticism in these areas may cause the superintendent to accuse the board of interference with his administrative role.

But it is only in the extreme case of Benjamin C. Willis in Chicago that a superintendent has been willing to take the stand that he must have autonomy or he will resign over a racial issue.[7] This is understandable, for there is not truly marketable expertise on racial integration anywhere, and there is certainly little claim possible in this area from within the education profession. Therefore, the superintendent, after his initial negative response, often finds his upstaging by the board to be the least awkward exit.

In addition, the origins and backgrounds of the large-city superintendents generally do not provide them with a sensitivity to urban social change and problems and to the current revolution of rising racial expectations in the large cities which would lead these men to play a leadership role in the absence of professional claims. Evidence bearing on this point comes from the biographies of the eleven big-city superintendents contained in *Who's Who*. Of the ten whose birth dates were given, the mean age was fifty-seven. Nine of the eleven began as teachers, and only one finished graduate school before beginning his career. Six of the ten American-born superintendents were from very small cities or farms, and none of the eleven attended a first-rank undergraduate college. Seven of the eleven began their teaching in small towns, and much of the administrative experience of all but four had been outside the large cities.

While many of these men had been administrators in smaller, suburban, and often vanguard or experimental school systems, their experiences in the large cities have not stimulated their desire to be experimental. The financial problems of the large-city systems, the sheer administrative problems of size, scale, and change, and the often inert middle-level personnel and principals (who frequently are political appointees left over from an earlier era) tend to move these superintendents toward an emphasis upon a traditionalistic philosophy of education that stresses the three R's, the standard neighborhood school, and "sound programs." When racial and other social changes place new demands on the schools, these superintendents generally are unable to articulate a leadership ideology dealing with integration and broadened welfare goals.

THE SECOND STAGE OF THE CONTROVERSY: THE SCHOOL BOARD TAKES OVER

In the typical city studied, the civil rights movement first approaches the board cautiously over a period of a year or two, making statements and testifying at hearings. In general, the school system does not respond to this; the issue is still below the level of saliency. The integrationists then step up their campaign, and their demands are rejected by the school superintendent at this point. When the movement replies to this with demonstrations or threats of demonstrations, the school board begins to take the issue seriously and responds in a variety of ways. At this point, the second stage of the controversy has begun. The board has taken over racial policy-making. In six of the eight cities, it is possible to find a point at which the superintendent's recommendations were ignored or a point when he was instructed to alter his policy. In the other two cases, the system changed superintendents without changing its policy, so that we must assume that the board supplied policy continuity to the system.

The first response made by the school system during this second phase we call the "key response," because it sets the tone for the remainder of the conflict. This key response by the board seems to be made with almost complete autonomy. One might expect the community political and civic elites to exert great influence, but we have only one clear case where this was done successfully. In two cases, the school board seemed to ignore the recommendations of the mayor; in another case, the community's most prominent industrialist was flatly rebuffed. It is not possible to describe all the actions taken by various actors in this short article, but in general it seems clear that there is less direct influence exerted on the board than one would expect and that attempts to influence the board usually are not very successful.

The most complex question is: To what extent can the civil rights movement control the outcomes of the school desegregation decision by their use of power? The evidence seems to indicate that they have surprisingly little influence. The civil rights movement can force the school system to deal with the issue, of course; few if any of these systems would have done anything about civil rights if they had not been pressured by the movement. Generally, the movement is successful in part—that is, the system will usually desegregate schools to some limited extent, and all of the eight cities have adopted a policy statement advocating integration. But concessions may be minimal and may come so late and be given so grudgingly as to be nearly meaningless.

Apparently, there is little that the civil rights leadership in a typical city can do to prevent this. Once the key response of the board is taken, the process is "locked in." If the key response is conciliatory, continued low-keyed civil rights activity will extract additional concessions; if the key response is negative, the civil rights movement will retaliate with demonstrations, but this usually leads to an escalation of the conflict and the school board's subsequently becoming more reluctant to negotiate or make additional concessions. The only way in which the movement can control the outcome is by introducing a new authority—for example, the state government may step in to order desegregation—and this is sometimes very effective.

Altogether, the findings mean that the school board usually is nearly autonomous in its policy-making on racial issues. It generally is not effectively influenced by political or civic leadership, by its superintendent, or even by the behavior of the civil rights movement, despite the fact that the decision on race is probably the issue of greatest immediate importance to the largest number of actors.

In order to demonstrate this conclusion, the research staff of the eight-city study ranked the cities on four variables: the level of civil rights activity prior to the key response, the level of civil rights activity after the key response, the degree to which the key response indicated a willingness to acquiesce to the civil rights demands, and the final level of acquiescence of the board to the demands made. Acquiescence is based on the number of demands met and the general public tone taken by the schools with respect to the civil rights movement. Put another way, the research staff attempted to rank the cities according to the degree to which a typical civil rights leader would feel satisfied with the response of the school system. The eight cities varied greatly in their acquiescence. In Pittsburgh, for example, the school board reacted very early to civil rights demands with a transfer plan which integrated two previously all-white schools. When demands for integration reappeared later, the school board committed itself, in a long and candid statement, to integration; adopted some short-range integration programs; and began planning for large-scale educational parks as the long-run answer to the integration question. In Baltimore, a demand for the elimination of overcrowding in Negro schools led to a summer of negotiation between the civil rights leaders and the school board, resulting in a decision to transport 4,000 Negro students and eliminate all double-shift schooling in the system, effective only six months after the issue was first raised. These two school systems are scored at the top of the acquiescence scale. At the opposite extreme, two school boards have refused to meet any of the demands for integration made, despite repeated demonstrations and pressure from other governmental officials. These two systems are located at the bottom of the scale.

Figure 7-1 diagrams the rank-order correlations between the initial level of civil rights activity, the acquiescence of the key response, the level of civil rights activity following the key response, and the total level of acquiescence of the school system. The correlations indicate that the key response is not dependent upon the level of civil rights activity directed at the board and also that the key response predicts quite accurately the final amount of acquiescence of the school system. If the rank correlations are accurate, they indicate that the civil rights movement principally responds to the behavior of the school system rather than being a cause of the character of the school system's behavior.

Figure 7-1
RANK-ORDER CORRELATIONS BETWEEN CIVIL RIGHTS ACTIVITY AND ACQUIESCENCE OF SCHOOL BOARDS TO CIVIL RIGHTS DEMANDS

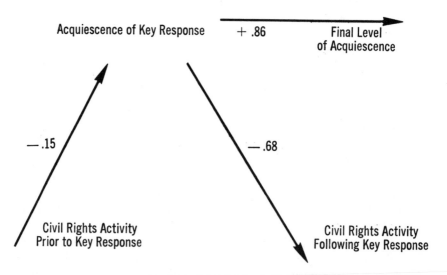

This is only indirect evidence that the boards can be quite autonomous in their decision. We also have some direct evidence of this. In Figure 7-2, the eight boards have been ranked by a combination of two closely correlated variables: the percentage of the board members having high socio-economic status (men from large businesses, corporation lawyers, or professionals) as against the percentage who are professional politicians or related in other ways to the political parties in their city. (High-status men are, of course, generally independent of the parties.) This single variable predicts quite well the final level of acquiescence of the school system. Since the variable is clearly independent of the actual decision situation, this seems to be strong evidence.

The autonomy of the nonpolitical board is not so surprising. However, the five boards which are partly or wholly made up of political appointments are also largely autonomous. Two of these boards are elected boards in cities where political power is quite decentralized. In a third city, the mayor's recommendations seem to have been largely ignored. In

Figure 7-2
STATUS AND POLITICAL ACTIVITY OF SCHOOL BOARD MEMBERS AND ACQUIESCENCE TO CIVIL RIGHTS DEMANDS

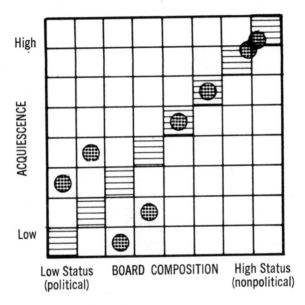

Note: The two boards in the upper right are tied on both rankings.

another, the mayor's appointments have disagreed strongly with each other and have involved the city in a lengthy controversy. In the fifth city, the mayor seems to have maintained control over the school system, and here the board has been persuaded twice to change its position on a racial issue.

It is usually assumed that political leaders wish to maximize their power and, therefore, detachment from school politics may seem surprising; but the mayor who tries to run the schools would be taking a great risk for a very small reward.

Before considering the implications of these findings, we also should consider why it is that the civic board is more acquiescent than the political board. The answer is a simple but empirical one: On our measures, the civic board members are more liberal on racial issues and the political board members are more conservative. This is not a trivial statement, because it is certainly not necessary that there be a high correlation between the personal attitude of government officials and their public actions. In fact, a similar study of southern school boards indicates that there is at best a weak correlation between racial attitudes and behavior regarding school desegregation.[8] The presence of this high correlation in the North indicates the extent to which the school desegregation issue is unstructured. In the absence of clear legal guidelines for action, of efficient communication between the contesting parties, and of a coherent educational ideology to draw upon, the school board members are "on their own" in deciding what to do. Board members are very conscious of this; more than one has publicly appealed for a decision by a local or federal court to clarify the situation. Buffalo, New York, furnishes a striking example of what this kind of clarification by an authority can do. The state Commissioner of Education, James E. Allen, demanded that the board desegregate the schools, and immediately the board became a cohesive decision-making body, even though it had been torn by internal conflict for well over a year prior to his intervention.

The lack of structure and clarity in the civil rights arena is, we think, also reflected in the fact that heterogeneous school boards and boards with a history of internal conflict have the greatest difficulty in meeting civil rights demands. Only two of the eight boards have contested elections for membership (five are appointed, while another is de facto appointed by a slating committee); these two boards were the least acquiescent, probably because of their heterogeneity and the pressures on the boards to make their disagreements public. The board with internal conflict cannot acquiesce to the demands made on it for two reasons. First, it cannot agree on what is being asked of it and what strategies are available to it; second, it cannot prevent public controversy which polarizes the community and further limits the alternatives available to it.

The great debate over community power structure hinges about the amount of autonomy which governmental officials have and the extent to which the civic elite are able to influence policy. The findings of this research suggest that it is possible for government officials to have great autonomy and at the same time for the civic elite to have great influence. In the case of the schools, the nature of the local civic elite is a principal factor in determining the composition of the school board, and thus the elite indirectly controls policy, even though it makes little or no effort to influence any single decision (and probably could not do so if it tried).

The three most acquiescent cities all have high-status school boards, and the civic elite in all three cases plays an important role in locating school board members. These three cities have elites which are highly active across a wide range of local policy issues. In the other five cities, the elites are weaker, and the result is that school board members are selected either from the ranks of the political parties, from the leadership of voluntary organizations, or in order to represent various ethnic groups.

Even the degree of heterogeneity and internal conflict in the school board has its roots in the structure of the political parties and the nature of the elite. The conflict-ridden boards which resist desegregation appear in cities with weak political parties, for example. Thus, the school board is autonomous in its decision-making procedure, yet the degree of acquiescence of the school system is determined by the over-all political structure of the city.

Symbolic Politics and Real Outputs

To this point, we have not discussed the real outputs of the school system's racial policy—the actual changes in quality of education or the actual increase in the number of students in integrated schools. It is not difficult for a school system to adopt a racial policy which will partially satisfy civil rights leaders without actually making a large impact on the operation of the schools. (These symbolic victories may have a considerable impact on the attitudes and behavior of individual Negro students, but this is outside the range of the two studies.) Conversely, it is also possible for the school system to have in operation policies which increase school integration without satisfying the civil rights groups. In two cities, Negro students were routinely bused into white schools, but the school adamantly refused to state that such integration was desirable, and the board in each case was subject to a great deal of attack.

The actual amount of integration is, of course, small. Among the eight cities, the greatest acquiescence, as judged by the research staff, was in Pittsburgh, Baltimore, and St. Louis. In Pitsburgh, the school system has succeeded in remaining on cordial terms with the civil rights leaders and has committed itself wholeheartedly to integration; but, to date, Pittsburgh has done little to increase integration. St. Louis and Baltimore have adopted busing programs which have successfully relieved overcrowded Negro schools, but less than 5 per cent of the Negro students are directly involved. In the eight cities, the proportion of Negro elementary school children attending schools which are at least 90 per cent Negro varies from a low of 30 per cent in San Francisco to a high of 86 per cent in St. Louis; the median for the eight cities is 68 per cent. If the largest cities—Chicago, Detroit, Cleveland, Philadelphia, Washington, and New York City—had been included in the study, the picture would look even bleaker.

The school board may commit itself to a policy of integration but find its efforts to implement this policy restricted by a number of factors outside of its control. The superintendent may undermine the design and implementation of the policy through his role in developing technical details of the plan. Voluntary plans for pupil transfer may have a minimal effect because of a lack of interest among Negro parents, or may even further segregation by allowing whites to transfer out of integrated schools. (This is another example of universalism; transfer plans explicitly based on the race of the pupils involved are quite avant-garde.) Track systems or practices of homogeneous grouping, discriminatory or not, may segregate pupils rigidly within the "integrated" school. And in cities where racial tensions are especially high, such as in Chicago and Cleveland, Negro students attending white schools have been assaulted, and it is often a community prophecy (and in a part a self-fulfilling one) that integrated schools will become all Negro.[9]

More important, the school system cannot control its own personnel. The heart of successful integration is the classroom teacher, and many big-city teachers do not feel comfortable teaching Negro students or handling an integrated class. Further, it is a big-city tradition that the integrated school is a "changing" school, where teachers transfer out, morale drops, and high-level programs are phased out as no longer appropriate to the clientele.

The difficulties encountered by the school systems in implementing effective integration go beyond the particular personality problems of the individual actors. They are tied to basic inadequacies in the organizational capacities of the large-city school systems for adapting to social change. Briefly, these inadequacies include the following:

1. A *bureaucratic rigidity flowing from the statutory and quasi-legal restrictions placed on the school systems by states and accrediting associations*. These restrictions limit the scheduling of the school year, prescribe certain courses and curricula, bureaucratize teacher recruitment, etc. This rigidity is related to the great emphasis upon universalism, a stress which in large part is a heritage of many cycles of reform. The result is administration by numbers: an attempt at innovation becomes merely an elaborate formula for assigning X numbers of specialists to Y numbers of schools. Another example is the procedure of allowing teachers to pick whatever schools they want on the basis of seniority, a practice which usually undermines the "difficult" school. And a crucial result is the highly standardized curriculum, which exists despite obvious differences in the needs of different schools.

2. *The fact that teachers are basically solo practitioners*. Unlike most

professions, teaching offers relatively little opportunity for collegial contact which could provide the opportunity not only for respite but for communication of new practices and the development of new attitudes. In-service training tends to be restricted to short-term workshops which are likely to have a minimal impact on teacher attitudes relevant to racial change. Yet, intensive resocialization procedures are apparently essential because of the conventional perspectives with which persons enter teaching.[10] Further, rewards for the teachers are largely ascriptive, based on seniority and on graduate work which in most schools of education is not oriented to the problems of urban education. As solo practitioners, the teachers frequently are reluctant to have anyone enter their classrooms, including subprofessionals or volunteers who could play a significant role. Principals and middle-level administrators face similar problems of poor lateral and vertical communication, except on purely administrative matters.

3. *Given these patterns, the large-city school systems have very primitive mechanisms of control, which limit them severely in producing change.* These systems are overcentralized in the sense that standardized curricula and administration by formula do not provide enough fiscal and administrative autonomy to permit "decentralized" administrators to vary their programs to local needs with any real facility. Yet they are undercentralized in the sense that it is very difficult for decisions made at the top of the organization to alter the traditional operating procedures. This is particularly the case in cities where principals or other personnel have become highly entrenched in their positions; the man who has been principal of the same school for twenty years is not responsive to supervision. Commitment to the status quo is often heightened by inbreeding and by the associations of principals and other personnel which act as mutual protective associations.[11]

4. *Also limiting the school system in producing innovations in racial practices and programs for the deprived is their general weakness in research and development.* The large systems have numerous special projects for dealing with Negro pupils, and many have generated a sense of success and excitement. But evaluation research is usually poor and attempts to expand the program to other schools are so haphazardly administered that few survive to become incorporated into standard operating procedure.

Cumulatively, these characteristics of the large-city school system imply that more adequate integration of the large-city schools will require not only higher levels of leadership in broadening and pursuing educational goals, but also substantial transformations in the organizational format.

It has often been said that in a large and complex organization the leadership does not have control over the operation of the system. These data indicate that there is considerable truth in this. Control over the classroom teacher is limited by the fact that she cannot be supervised directly and by the nature of her contract and the character of her professional organization. Control over individual principals is limited because supervision must be from a distance and by a strict universalism in administration. The board cannot supervise a school superintendent unless he supplies information to them, presents the full range of policy alternatives, and permits the board to believe that it knows something about how to run a school system. Similarly, the men who select the school board members must defer to them as "experts" once the selection has been made.

On the other hand, we do see a clear line of influence which runs from the top of the system to the bottom. When members of the mayor's staff or members of the civil elite choose school board members (and in most cities they do choose them), they have in mind an operational image when they say they want a "good man" for the job. It is hardly a surprise that they get the kind of man they want most of the time. These men then control the schools' "image" on racial matters and to a limited extent this style can filter down to the classroom. The board selects the superintendent, and some boards have definite criteria in mind; if he does not meet them, he may then be subject to what one board member called a "learning experience." And the superintendent, through his choice of subordinate administrators and his use of policy directives and public relations, can project a "style" into the school system. Granted there is no close isomorphism between this "style" and the actual day-to-day operations of the schools, but at least there is some order in the system.

Notes

1. This research is reported in Robert L. Crain, Morton Inger, Gerald A. McWorter, and James J. Vanecko, *School Desegregation in the North: Eight Comparative Case Studies of Community Structure and Policy Making* (Chicago: National Opinion Research Center, 1965), Report #110A. The research was sponsored by the U.S. Office of Education. Of the eight cities in the study, six are mentioned in the text: Pittsburgh, San Francisco, Baltimore, Buffalo, Newark, and St. Louis. The remaining two cities requested that their identities not be revealed. For purposes of discussion, they have been given fictitious names: Lawndale and Bay City.

2. This research was supported by the Russell Sage Foundation. Major findings will be reported in David Street, *The Public Schools and Metropolitan Change*, forthcoming publication.

3. For a general review of these and other survey data, see Paul B. Sheatsley, "White Attitudes Toward the Negro," *Daedalus*, XCV (Winter, 1966), 217–38;

and Harriet B. Erskine, "The Polls: Race Relations," *Public Opinion Quarterly,* XXVI (1962), 137–48.

4. It is for this reason that we have chosen to use "desegregation," rather than "integration," in the title of this paper.

5. Support for this hypothesis is provided by L. L. Cunningham, "Decision-making Behavior of School Boards," *American School Board Journal* (February, 1962).

6. J. H. Tipton points out that in the late 1940's Negro students were not allowed to use the swimming pool in one high school in Gary, Indiana. See his *Community in Crisis* (New York: Teachers College, Columbia University, 1953).

7. Willis's temporary resignation was apparently triggered by a taxpayer's suit charging that he had arbitrarily changed a voluntary transfer plan designed by the board to further integration. The incident is described in Joseph Pois, *The School Board Crisis* (Chicago: Aldine Press, 1964), pp. 109–14.

8. See Robert L. Crain, Morton Inger, and Gerald A. McWorter, *School Desegregation in New Orleans: A Comparative Study in the Failure of Social Control* (Chicago: National Opinion Research Center, 1965), Report #110B.

9. Each of these problems is potentially subject to remediation, as shown, for example, in St. Louis's ability to bus approximately 2,600 Negro students into white schools in 1965–66. The busing program seems to have an informal "quota"; none of the integrated schools is over 40 per cent Negro. After the initial shock, there has been virtually no opposition in this border city, and busing of Negro students is now taken for granted.

10. The tendency for even city-bred teacher trainees to have quite negative orientations toward the challenges of "problem schools" in the inner city is described in Bryan Roberts, "The Effects of College Experience and Social Background on Professional Orientations of Prospective Teachers" (Ph.D. dissertation, University of Chicago, 1964). Findings of an experiment conducted by Bruno Bettelheim in cooperation with the Russell Sage project indicate that teachers' difficulties in dealing with Negro children who present behavior problems flow not principally from racial prejudice but from social-class views in which the teacher assumes that the children are unlikely to learn. The Bettelheim work also seems to demonstrate that really intensive in-service training can produce a reduction in these stereotypic views.

11. For a discussion of the power of this sort of clique, see Wallace S. Sayre and Herbert Kaufman, *Governing New York City* (New York: W. W. Norton & Co., 1965), pp. 279–80.

8. OBSTACLES TO SCHOOL DESEGREGATION IN NEW YORK CITY: A BENCHMARK CASE

DAVID ROGERS

Though more than a decade has passed since the historic Supreme Court decision supposedly outlawing school segregation, the extent of segregation has remained almost the same as it was in 1954, in the North as well as in the South. In fact, it has increased markedly in many northern cities, partly as a result of the demographic and residential changes they have experienced. Yet there have been variations, both in extent of segregation and of receptivity to desegregation plans in large northern cities.

Little is known, however, about the "mix" of conditions associated with such differences.[1] One way to find out is through comparative study. Another important way, the one I have followed, is to generate hypotheses about conditions related to action or inaction by school officials from an intensive study of a single case. My case is New York City.

A case-study strategy is perhaps especially appropriate at this time, since there haven't been enough studies or codifications of evidence to even suggest what all the relevant variables may be. My purpose is to develop hypotheses to explain New York City's experience, calling attention to the range of variables that should be taken into account in any study of school desegregation.[2]

The Relevance of New York City

Some students of comparative politics see New York City's problems as idiosyncratic. Nonetheless, it is a very strategic case for several reasons. First, its school system has often been a model for those in other cities.

"Obstacles to School Desegregation in New York City" by David Rogers is reprinted from *Educating an Urban Population* (Beverly Hills, Calif.: Sage Publications, 1967), pp. 155–84, by permission of the Publisher, Sage Publications, Inc.

It is generally further along in the formulation of desegregation plans and their implementation on a selective, local basis than any other large northern city. The successes and failures of strategy of its school and political officials and of various civic groups involved in desegregation controversies are taken into account by their colleagues elsewhere and become guidelines for their actions.

Second, regardless of some impediments to change inherent in its fragmented and highly bureaucratized governmental institutions, New York City has long been a center of cosmopolitan values, of progressive politics, and of innovation in many fields.[3] Its present lay board reflects this, dominated as it is by people with a long record of support for progressive labor and civil rights causes. They share an egalitarian, social reformist outlook that has been a hallmark of the city's political life. If school desegregation is not taking place in New York City, then it would be important to know why, since conditions are more favorable there than in many other cities. Yet the fact is that even in New York City not much desegregation has taken place.

Indeed, despite many plans and programs (e.g., rezonings, open enrollments, Princeton Plan pairings, feeder pattern changes), formulated long before most other northern school officials were ready to move, and despite the liberal traditions of the city and the school board, there was minimal implementation. In fact, the New York City Board of Education has not arrested the trend toward segregation. It may even be moving the other way.

.   .   .   .

A "Political" Interpretation of Increasing School Segregation

The most compelling evidence for the assertion that political forces have served to prevent board action is the wide and growing gap between the board's many policy statements and their implementation. Some of the most "advanced" policy statements ever written on school desegregation (going back as far as 1954, when it was not yet "fashionable," at least in the North) were advanced by the New York City Board of Education. And they recommended basic, not diversionary, strategies, e.g., site selection, changes in feeder patterns, rezoning, and establishing educational complexes and parks. Yet, after more than a decade of such policy statements, there has been little implementation.

A few examples may suffice to make the point. The first major desegregation plan, Open Enrollment, resulted in only the most limited numbers of pupil transfers. Fewer than 10 per cent of those pupils to whom the plan was applicable actually transferred. As the authors of the Allen

Report on the city's desegregation prospects stated: "The [Board of Education's own] Commission on Integration recommendations on the redistribution of pupils through 'permissive zoning' and busing were not implemented."[4]

The board's interpretation for the limited success of open enrollment is that Negro parents did not want to have their children transferred out of their local schools. Undoubtedly, this was the sentiment of some and it will always be true of some. On reviewing the history of how open enrollment was introduced, however, it is unfair and inaccurate to place the responsibility on Negro parents for the small numbers who took advantage of the program.

This is how it generally went: The board did not take initiative in informing the public. It did little to prepare parents, students, staff, and communities participating in the program. And when people were informed, it turned out that local school officials and many headquarters personnel were by and large opposed to the plan. There is no available evidence to suggest, for example, that the board and school officials had pointed out with much conviction the possible advantages of participating in open enrollment. And there is evidence to suggest otherwise.

The first pamphlets encouraging parents to take advantage of the plan were prepared by officials of the Urban League, with the help of the American Jewish Committee and other civic organizations. The board refused to help distribute them. Later, when other city agencies did cooperate and much publicity was given this fact, the Board of Education joined in. In effect, the board followed rather than led public opinion on the issue.

Extensive records and files furnished me by some civic leaders and school officials suggest a widespread pattern of sabotage by principals, teachers, and field superintendents and a very limited publicity campaign from headquarters. The practice of not informing Negro parents in ghetto schools of the new opportunities open to them to send their children to underutilized white schools was so widespread, in fact, that headquarters took over more and more of this function. The further practice of lecturing to Negro parents on the many "costs" of transferring their children out, engaged in by many principals and teachers, and the rather strong urging that parents keep their children in their local schools undoubtedly contributed to the low percentage who participated in open enrollment.[5]

Field sabotage took place in "receiving" as well as in "sending" schools. More often than not, principals in receiving schools, anxious to preserve homogeneous classes, would end up placing incoming Negro pupils in segregated situations. Likewise, the limited preparation of students, parents, school officials, and communities (in receiving schools) for incoming students also served to discourage Negro parents. The limited resources headquarters allocated for such preparation and the failure to sanction principals and teachers who scuttled the plan further contributed to its minimal implementation. To top it all off, sabotage at one end could build on sabotage at the other. Principals in sending schools referred to segregated conditions in receiving schools in urging parents not to transfer their children.

The board's policy statements, however, went well beyond such voluntary plans. They included, as I mentioned, rezoning, changes in feeder patterns, and fundamental changes in the construction program, with schools to be built in "fringe" areas wherever possible. On balance, they simply were never implemented. For example, 39 of the 106 projects in the board's 1964–65 building program were for local school areas where the estimated ethnic composition of the school was 90 per cent or more Negro and Puerto Rican pupils. In short, over one-third of the schools planned were guaranteed to be segregated, though many might have been located in fringe areas to prevent that. The board's most recent construction budget calls for over 55 per cent of its funds for segregated schools.[6] To quote the Allen Report once again: "The school building program as presently set forth reinforces substantially the historic pattern of building on sites within the most segregated areas. This is the case chiefly in Negro residential areas, but it is also true in some mainly White neighborhoods, and thus helps to intensify both forms of segregation."[7]

The consistent board practice has been to "build the schools where the children are," despite continued pressure from civil rights groups and continued encouragement from the state Commission of Education to do otherwise. Indeed, the construction program is a key to the whole segregation problem. Civil rights pressures have continued unabated in this field, but to no avail. In sum, the board's actual school construction and site selection decisions are at wide variance with its stated desegregation policies.

Why is it, then, that even in New York City, though they, at least, get to the policy-making stage, there is so little implementation? Why has the board tended to zone and build schools in a way that followed, rather than ran counter to, the segregated housing pattern? And why have they even zoned in some areas to counteract an integrated housing pattern? To answer these questions is to suggest some of the political forces that have contributed, and I think substantially, to the increased segregation of New York City's schools.

My research suggests the following political forces in New York City preventing much implementation of school desegregation plans: the development of a strong opposition—the result of an unplanned alliance of some school officials, white parents, and real estate interests (supported by key politicians) around the "neighborhood school" slogan; a strategy of caution, vacillation, and ineffective planning by the Board of Education; a politically ineffective integrationist coalition—due in large part to lack of unity among integrationist groups, their inability to mobilize much grass roots support, their limited resources, and their particular political strategies; an unwillingness of powerful "moderate" groups to support many desegregation plans and their successes at scuttling them; the structure and operating codes of the school system itself—leading to poor communications, schisms, and an inability to coordinate their actions, let alone innovate, at key points in the system (e.g., conflicts between the lay board and superintendent, between the board and professional staff, between field and headquarters, across divisions, bureaus, and other functional units as to respective spheres of influence and responsibility); and the fragmented structure of New York City government, preventing any meaningful city-wide educational planning through a coordination of housing, urban renewal, transit, industrial development, and poverty projects with the board's desegregation program. I will discuss briefly the role of each factor, pointing up how they relate to one another. It is obviously difficult in a case study of this nature to assess which of these factors was most significant. At the same time, it is possible to suggest how the degree of leadership and initiative exercised by the board and city officials (e.g., the degree to which they passively reflected or tried to shape public opinion) affected the course of school desegregation controversies in recent years.

The "Neighborhood School" Coalition

One of the biggest obstacles to school desegregation, in New York City as elsewhere, has come from within the education profession itself. The "neighborhood school" tradition, propounded almost three generations ago by the profession to suggest organizational forms especially appropriate for urban school systems, has become the clarion call around which a variety of status quo–oriented interests have united. The concept was originally developed to counter the impersonality, decline of primary group ties, and anomie of urban life. It resulted in a number of policies: building schools very close to home, zoning in a way to minimize travel time, gerrymandering to preserve ethnic and class homogeneity, and constructing smaller schools. All these policies were assumed to have innumerable benefits: quality, economies, security and safety for children, and close school-community relations.[8]

Regardless of how one evaluates such benefits by today's conditions, it seems abundantly clear that powerful professional interests inside the school system (teachers, principals, field superintendents, divisonal heads, key headquarters personnel), local parent associations, homeowners, civic groups, and many public and private real estate interests have supported the concept. And although the doctrine is increasingly viewed as an essentially "fundamentalist" one, given the recognized need for consolidation in fragmented, big-city school systems, it has rallied a large number of followers, even in as cosmopolitan a city as New York.

Thus, a loosely joined coalition in defense of the status quo and having tremendous political resources and influence developed in New York City as school desegregation became more of an issue. It frequently mobilized strong white parent support by raising the spectre of "mandatory, long-distance busing," something that the board never intended. The coalition thus formed was not that motivated and planned. Rather, it was an unintended consequence of the pursuit by each of a number of interests of its own inner agendas. What are they?

White parents in New York City most affected by school desegregation plans tended to feel increasingly crowded by expanding Negro populations and embraced the neighborhood school symbol as a socially acceptable expression of a need to preserve the essentially white, middle-class, and "private" character of their schools. Recent studies in New York City suggest the following profile of interests of white parents supporting the neighborhood schools.[9] They represent lower- and lower–middle-class populations recently migrated from central-city slums and decaying areas. They want to keep their new neighborhood "respectable" by preserving uncrowded, "good" schools and safe living conditions. They are an ethnocentric and highly status-conscious second generation, proud of the way they rose from a proletarian existence through their own efforts. They say that if the Negro had any ambition, he could do the same. Many of these whites are homeowners anxious about declining property values if Negroes move into their area. As parents, they are concerned about the upward mobility and occupational achievement of their children which they see as threatened by forced desegregation and, they reason, a decline in quality of education.

All of these interests predispose them to embrace the neighborhood school concept. They constitute a large, mass base for resistance to desegregation and have been especially susceptible to demagogic appeals in Queens (Parents and Taxpayers), Brooklyn (Joint Council for Better Education), and the Bronx, areas of expanding Negro and Puerto Rican populations. They are especially resentful of the fact that upper-middle-class "white liberals" and civil rights leaders have placed them on the firing line while sending their own children, in many cases, to private schools.

There was a rather striking similarity in social outlook between these white parent populations and many school officials, both at headquarters and in the field, who resisted any implementation of the board's desegregation plans with every conceivable strategy they could muster—both private and public. Many of the same arguments against "forced" integration plans were used by teachers, principals, field superintendents, and some headquarters officials, who came from the same kinds of ethnic origins (Irish, Jewish, Italian) and had the same kinds of latent and not so latent prejudice against lower-class minority-group children.[10] Their resistance illustrates how insulated public school educators have become in recent years, especially in metropolitan centers experiencing such rapid demographic and social changes. They have acted as though they were still dealing with a predominantly white, middle-class clientele, and still training low-income populations for jobs that are disappearing in an automating economy.

Thus, the personal and career interests of many public school officials in New York City converged with the interests of the white parent opposition. Principals' associations, district superintendents, and some headquarters personnel staged heated campaigns, in the press and in private, to forestall nonvoluntary desegregation programs. Desegregation meant a number of changes in their working conditions—in curriculum, in staffing and training requirements, in ethnic composition of schools and classrooms, and even in grade and divisional organization. Many understandably felt much more secure and comfortable following older traditions, even if they were dated. And they were especially enraged with civil rights demands for nonvoluntary desgregation plans, since such plans violated the most "sacred" tradition of all, that of the neighborhood school. It was the tradition that many school officials, especially an older generation, had been taught had so many benefits and virtues.[11]

Finally, a variety of public and private real estate groups, perhaps in a number of unplanned ways, reinforced and gave structural support to the twin goals of maintaining segregated residential areas and neighborhood schools. Though not oriented directly toward educational matters, private developers, local homeowner groups, slum landlords, and even city housing agencies, acting in their perceived economic interests or in accordance with housing codes, tended to perpetuate and expand a segregated housing pattern. The housing politics of Queens, Brooklyn, and the Bronx, for example, are replete with examples of the successes of local homeowner groups in white, middle-class areas in keeping low-income housing projects out of their neighborhoods. Slum landlords have successfully resisted some efforts to renovate or demolish tenements in ghetto areas. Private developers have frequently been insensitive to the pleas of the Board of Education to take into account the school and housing integration implications of their decisions. Finally, federal moneys for low-income housing projects have only been rendered if the projects were located in decaying slum areas. This has served to perpetuate and expand segregated housing patterns.

All these real estate and housing pressures need not necessarily be viewed as some form of "conspiracy." Rather, they may mainly have been a consequence of the pursuit by a number of public agencies and private homeowner and business groups of their economic or political self-interest, divorced from any self-conscious considerations of school segregation. The result, however, has been very clear; namely, the growth and proliferation of ghetto neighborhoods.

The Board's Strategy

A second factor serving as an obstacle has been the Board of Education's strategy for dealing with the desegregation issue and with civil rights demands. This can only be understood within the political context just discussed. Their strategy has been one of caution, in the hope of not alienating the large block of white parents and school officials fearful of compulsory segregation plans; of vacillation (as a reflection of cross-pressures from civil rights and opposition groups); and of ineffective planning and preparation for the policies it finally implemented. Faced with demands from conflicting publics, each asking for services in a situation of perceived scarcity and limited supply, the board's response is understandable. This is not to say that it could not have been quite different. And it certainly contributed to polarizing civil rights groups and the opposition, as well as to the long stalemate on the issue.

A key indicator of the board's caution was their posture of insulation from protest groups, as evidenced by periods of virtually no communication with local civil rights leaders and officials and their refusal to allow for any "outside" mediation in the period just preceding the civil rights–sponsored boycotts of February, 1964.[12] Board President James Donovan dismissed the boycott in a public statement as "Fizzle #1," rather than coming to terms with the fact that all civil rights groups had united to support it and that 445,000 pupils had stayed out of school. Indeed, it was only after some outside parties did intervene and force the board to resume meetings with civil rights groups that they did resume communications.[13]

Another indicator was the manner in which the board handled the controversy over Princeton Plan pairing. Board members and headquarters officials developed a plan for as many as twenty pairings for implementation in September, 1964. They did not decide which of the twenty pairings to implement. Instead, they invited selected parent groups along with district superintendents, principals, and local school boards to private meetings to help the board decide not how, but whether, pairings would be implemented in their local areas. Civil rights groups were not invited nor was the opposition. The case made by local parent associations, with the help of the research staff of their parent organization, United Parents Association (UPA), helped defeat sixteen of the twenty.

The tone of the private meetings was significant. Civil rights groups were denounced for their demands, and, in the course of a few months of such meetings, Princeton Plan pairings were effectively scuttled in New York City. Since civil rights leaders, as well, gave up the pairing idea by the time the board finally came out with its plan for four pairings, it seems unlikely that they will ever be tried on any scale, large or small. Civil rights groups came to an agreement that it was more important to restructure the school system along the lines of the Allen Report recommendations than to continue with pairings. The board's own evaluation of the four pairings, completed over a year ago, has still not been published.*

It is important to note, in passing, that the board did not maintain a posture of insulation from all civic groups. The UPA and local parent associations had obviously been given access before major decisions were made. So too had other moderate organizations and even, in a few isolated cases, the oppositionist Parents and Taxpayers. The general pattern was that the more moderate the organization, the more access it had.

A final example of the board's caution was its response to the Allen Report, which contained recommendations for a number of fairly sweeping structural changes to effect more desegregation (e.g., a 4–4–4 grade organization, educational complexes and, eventually, parks, and changes in the building program).[14] Although the board issued a statement as early as June, 1964, seemingly accepting the Allen Report recommendations, it was then silent on the issue until the following March. Even its present grade reorganization and building plans constitute a fragmentary first step. For example, most of the middle schools it plans to build in the next few years have been sited in the segregated areas. There are, of course, many political pressures to make sure that this segregated building pattern will continue.

On hindsight, it is possible to trace the effects of the board's caution and limited leadership and initiative on the course of the controversy. As the board refused to keep open communications with civil rights groups and refused to move ahead on pairings, it strengthened support for the most militant civil rights leadership, and it thus helped contribute to the first boycott. At the same time, the board dealt equally cautiously with

* A corresponding study is, however, available. See James F. Redmond, *Plans to Reorganize the Chicago Public Schools into Three Administrative Areas* (Chicago, August 21, 1967).—Ed. note.

many white groups as well. In the early months of 1964, for example, before the board had finalized its pairing decisions, rumors, feelers, and leaks through the press were quite common, stirring the already heightened anxieties of white parents in local areas assumed to be possible sites for desegregation plans. Yet, these groups could not get any official word on the state of the board's deliberations. A leadership and information vacuum thus existed, contributing in some degree to the increased organizational strength and militancy of the opposition. As anxious white parents could get little information from school officials on actual plans, opposition leaders were able to exploit the situation and feed on parent concerns in typical demagogic fashion, thus spawning a powerful opposition movement.

As the opposition engaged in demonstrations, protests, and boycotts, this further activated already existent tendencies toward similar public protests and direct-action tactics by militant civil rights groups. The two sides soon became polarized. The holding of numerous public hearings further fanned the conflict and polarized the sides, as each had more publicly sanctioned opportunities to square off against the other, even as neither was quite sure what the board was going to do.

The process did not stop there, however. As the board's intentions and plans were still not clear, groups within the integrationist "camp" became divided and fragmented. Latent divisions among civil rights groups and between them and "white liberal" groups became magnified. With so little to respond to from the board itself, they filled the vacuum and conducted heated discussions within their own ranks, eventually magnifying their own minor strategy differences. An inevitable stalemate followed.

It would seem reasonable to conclude, then, that the board's style of relating to the community did a lot to exaggerate a conflict and some internal divisions that would have occurred anyway but to nowhere near the degree that they did. This became a classic illustration of a generalization suggested by Williams in his codification of studies and community experiences with school desegregation. As Williams noted: "An impression of vacillation and indecision on the part of boards of education or of educational administrators, no matter how it may be communicated to the public at large, tends to increase the likelihood of resistance to desegregation (and thereby, the likelihood of conflict)."[15]

Integrationist Divisions

As insulated as the board tried to be, its strategies and actions were not formulated in a vacuum. They were conditioned themselves by political forces within the city. One such force, and a third factor, was the weakness of the integrationist coalition. The main groups within this camp—civil rights organizations, both national and local (NAACP, Urban League, CORE, City-Wide Committee for Integrated Schools, Parents' Workshop for Equality, Harlem Parents, EQUAL, Conference for Quality Integrated Education, and various *ad hoc* groups); Puerto Rican organizations (Commonwealth of Puerto Rico, Puerto Rican Forum, Puerto Rican Committee on Civil Rights); "white liberal" groups (American Jewish Congress, American Jewish Committee, ADL, Protestant Council, ADA, Catholic Inter-Racial Council, Reform Democrat groups, ACLU, Liberal Party, a few unions); a scattering of city and school officials; some activist academicians; and some militant local parent associations in ghetto areas, other than those above. These groups have rarely been solidly united on any school desegregation issue for any extended time in New York City. Divergent loyalties, status affiliations, leadership clashes, organizational imperatives, and constituent pressures have quite consistently prevented much united action except in periods of extreme crisis or extreme clarity as to the board's intentions and actions.[16] Though not necessarily planned that way, it was to the board's advantage to maintain a degree of uncertainty and confusion as to its intentions and policies.

The civil rights movement has been split between militant, locally based groups (Reverend Galamison's Parents' Workshop, Harlem Parents, EQUAL, local CORE and NAACP chapters) and established national organizations (especially NAACP and Urban League). The divisions have been not so much over goals or even, in many instances, over appropriate strategy, but have been, rather, reflections of leadership struggles, organizational priorities, and limited funds. One important structural condition that helped contribute to the split, for example, was the fact that New York is the headquarters city for all national civil rights organizations. Their boards and large donors are frequently from the "white liberal" New York City community. They stress the need for legal and negotiating strategies and for emphasizing other goals (e.g., attacking discrimination in housing and employment and voter registration drives). This has resulted in national civil rights organizations' taking a more moderate stand on school desegregation in New York City than have many local groups.

Civil rights groups, in turn, have been divided time and again from "white liberal" organizations that have participated only in the most limited way in protest actions and have had considerable difficulty mobilizing much support from their ranks for nonvoluntary desegregation plans. The best examples of this were the decline of two coalitions of Negro and white organizations that attempted to bridge the differences. One such coalition, the Inter-Group Committee, was formed in the early

1950's and was composed of over forty city-wide and local organizations. It dissolved in 1959, partly as a result of many leadership struggles. The other was the Conference for Quality Integrated Education, formed in March, 1964, for the purpose of maintaining unity between Negro and white organizations and of giving support to the civil rights movement from the white community. It too dissolved after little more than a year of operation.

The board capitalized on, and attempted to exploit, such differences. Overtures were made to national civil rights leaders in the hopes of getting them to go along with a board plan, so that they could be (and were) quoted to militant local leaders. The same kinds of overtures were made to leaders in white organizations. They were generally, though not always, rebuffed. Though not necessarily done for conventional "conspiratorial" reasons, they sometimes had the same effect, namely, dividing the coalition. The board understandably felt it had to use some "strategies of defense" during the period of most intense civil rights pressure, and this was one of them.[17]

Another source of political ineffectiveness for civil rights and white integrationist groups was that they, unlike the opposition, had the most limited mass base. For example, Parents and Taxpayers was able to build a grass roots support on already existing homeowners, taxpayers, and neighborhood improvement groups, but civil rights organizations had to deal with a more atomized local population. And they did not have the resources and perhaps the foresight to build grass roots support for their point of view. National civil rights organizations, which have had most of the money, have been quite limited in their funds, relative to the national problems they address themselves to. And as I mentioned above, pressures from within prevented them from committing more of their scarce resources to this problem.

One of the results of limited grass roots mobilization was that Negro parents from ghetto areas expressed themselves at times in public hearings as favoring an upgrading of schools and replacements in their local areas, rather than having their children transferred out. A tightly knit family structure within the Puerto Rican population, accompanied by a similar failure of grass roots mobilization, led to an unwillingness to have their children travel. White parents, even those of a more liberal cast, had grave apprehensions about the effects of desegregation on quality. White liberal organizations had great difficulties in gaining acceptance for desegregation plans from their local chapters and constituents.

Integrationist leaders and activists were in actuality just a handful of people conducting a "liberal monologue" with one another. They were truly "leaders without followers." The board began to sense this and guided its actions accordingly. It should also be said that the board ex-

ercised little effort to educate and persuade the community on the benefits of desegregation. Its public relations and its community relations
programs were quite limited, despite the recommendations of many
commissions and civic groups that it do more in this field.[18]

The Moderates

Even though the opposition was well mobilized and integrationist
groups only partially and sporadically so, there might well have been
more movement, given New York City's progressive traditions, had the
city's powerful "moderate" organizations provided some pressure and
support for the board's desegregation efforts. But moderate organizations,
holding the balance of power on the issue, did little to forward the school
desegregation cause. The most important of these organizations were:
(1) the United Parents Association (UPA), representing as many as 430
local parent and parent-teacher associations and 440,000 mothers and
fathers throughout the city; (2) the Public Education Association
(PEA), representing through its board and coordinating committee some
of the most influential professional and civic groups in the city (Citizens
Budget Commission, Men's and Women's City Clubs, New York City
Bar Association, Citizens Union, League for Industrial Democracy, New
York State Congress of Parents and Teachers); and (3) the Citizens
Committee for Children (CCC), an organization of professional and
lay experts in various fields of child care and development with close ties
both to Mayor Wagner and his administration and to civil rights and
"liberal" organizations (among them, Reform Democrats, the labor
movement, and the New York Post).

Such professional and civic organizations with a social reformist,
"good-government" outlook have gradually come to the position that,
while desegregation may be important, it entails more costs than benefits
if pursued on any scale or too rapidly. They see a decline in quality and
a further intensification of white parent opposition and withdrawal from
the school system as inevitable results of rapid, city-wide desegregation.
Their position is that other goals (quality, increased funds, teacher training, neighborhood school centers, administrative reorganization) should
have priority. They favor compensatory programs for ghetto schools
(Operation Head Start, More Effective Schools, Special Service Schools,
All-Day Neighborhood Schools) as the strategy to follow. And they represent some of the same real estate, education, and local parent interests
as does the opposition, though they express their views in a more rea-
soned and respectable way. Perhaps more to the point, they have the
"ear" of city officials.

All moderate organizations, but especially UPA and PEA, reflect a pattern of middle-class control of the New York City school system. They have privileged access to the board and high-level city officials of a kind that has generally been denied to civil rights and integrationist organizations.[19] Both PEA and UPA have become highly politicized organizations and have built up their private access to top board officials through years of experience. Both were called on in a "consultative" capacity before public hearings and before the board decided on its final desegregation plans. Through informal relations with key board officials they shared in such decision-making. And their views on desegregation were, of course, part of the public record.

They essentially "straddled" and related obliquely to the issue by emphasizing diversionary matters. They would never discuss the merits of the board's particular plans, e.g., pairings or educational parks, as desegregation techniques for New York City. Instead, UPA issued a statement that it was against "mandatory, long-distance busing," and PEA officials would debate with civil rights leaders on the same issue. Long-distance busing was not the issue, however, either in the board's actual or projected plans. UPA's general response was to emphasize an orderly implementation of the board's desegregation plans and to maintain quality in desegregating schools. They never came out as organizations for or against any particular plans. Privately, however, they functioned effectively to water down and curtail any grandiose plans the board might have had in mind.[20]

It was easy for PEA and UPA to denounce public protests by civil rights or opposition groups since they had informal access on a daily basis to key headquarters decisions. While it all sounds much like a "conspiracy" interpretation of New York City public education, this was the way it worked out. To speak of a pattern of middle-class control of the New York City school system, as up to 50 per cent of its pupils are from low-income Negro and Puerto Rican families, is quite accurate. The reasons for such control relate to the tremendous inequalities in political resources of moderate groups as compared with civil rights organizations. Most integrationist organizations, including civil rights groups, are multipurpose organizations, with many commitments and priorities other than school desegregation. Their education staff covering New York City are either volunteers or working on the problem in New York City on a part-time basis.

In sharp contrast to that pattern, UPA and PEA are primarily concerned with public education in New York City. Both are affluent enough to have full-time staff professionals who spend their entire working time on these issues. And both have been involved in "watch dog" activities in the public education field since the turn of the century.

Their professional staffs are experienced in dealing with the board; they know much about the system's operation and are especially cognizant of the many strategies that board officials use when confronted with citizen groups like themselves, making demands on the system for more services. In sum, they have money, personnel, experience, grass roots support, powerful city organizations' support, and many informal relationships with board and city officials. It is no wonder, then, that they are much more powerful than civil rights organizations.

But why have they been so opposed to much desegregation? Part of the explanation lies in their ties to local parent groups and "establishment" organizations that exert pressures for moderate or status quo positions. And much of it lies in the fact that they have as organizations become a part of the decision-making and policy-making apparatus of the Board of Education and have a vested interest in its preservation. The changes the Allen Report recommends threaten that interest.

The Structure and Operating Codes of the Board

If these forces alone did not serve to stack the cards against change, there were two others that just about closed out any prospects. One pertained to organizational characteristics and codes within the school system over and above commitments to the neighborhood school doctrine. The other related to the articulation and dovetailing of decisions and projects of other city agencies with those of the board.

The most relevant characteristics and codes of the Board of Education that prevented much implementation of desegregation plans were the following: an overcentralized, authoritarian structure, accompanied by many levels in its administrative hierarchy, and a principle of "bureaucratic" rather than "collegial" (professional) authority; consequent feelings of distrust and alienation of field personnel toward headquarters and traditions of noncompliance with headquarters directives, leading, in turn, to a wide and continuing gap between "advanced" policy statements and their implementation; much specialization on multiple and sometimes contradictory bases, accompanied by a fragmentation of units and informal "power blocs" at headquarters, seriously limiting prospects for developing a strong enough coalition for innovation (as groups could veto one another's ideas); poor communications between headquarters and the field and across divisions and other units, leading to a minimum of dovetailing and coordination of functions and inefficient implementation of new ideas; an examination system that has led to an inordinate amount of "inbreeding" and to the promotion to high headquarters posts of some people with a minimum of daring and innovativeness; insulation of professional (headquarters and field) staff from lay

review and controls, reflected and rationalized by a "technocratic" my-
thology that education should be kept separate from "politics," and
reflected further in continuing conflicts between the board and superintendent about appropriate spheres of authority; and an almost complete
absence of long-range planning.[21]

In sum, the combination of an unwieldy bureaucracy and particular
personalities and personality clashes (e.g., Superintendent Gross and
Board of Education President Donovan) was another important factor
preventing much desegregation. It is important to note, however, that
this was a bureaucracy that had long resisted innovation. Powerful, "inbred" professional groups (principals' associations, district superintendents, divisional heads) had delayed, watered down, or sabotaged innovation for decades. School desegregation was just the latest of a long series
of changes they had resisted.

New York City Government

If power and resources for change could not be mobilized from the
populace or from within the school system, one of the only other sources
was the mayor and city government. But the fragmentation and pluralism of interest groups in the community and at the board were paralleled
by similar patterns in the political structure of the city. The proliferation
in numbers and expansion in size of city agencies with few mechanisms
for interagency coordination have resulted in drift, a web of bureaucratic
entanglements, and a stifling of city-wide educational planning and innovation. On the school desegregation issue, the Board of Education's options were seriously limited by urban renewal programs, the spread of
low-income housing projects, and the use of desirable sites for industrial
rather than educational parks.

The board and numerous citizen groups have recommended many
times over the creation of a superordinate body to coordinate school,
housing, urban renewal, poverty, and mass transit projects to create a
more integrated, open city. This has never come about. Traditions of
agency autonomy, a preference of city officials for a perpetuation of the
informal bargaining that characterizes interagency transactions, and especially the refusal of the mayor to promote it led to inaction. His role
in school desegregation controversies, in turn, was very consistently one
of withdrawing as much as possible from any direct or indirect participation.

.   .   .   .

But what implications does the New York City experience have for
interpreting that of other cities? Much of the New York City experience

has a familiar ring. A "mix" of conditions, some demographic, some structural, and some behavioral (strategies followed by various key parties) are related to the limited desegregation of schools there. One proposition indicated by my study is that the more the pluralism and fragmentation of interest groups and governmental agencies in a city, the more likely it is to become polarized and then stalemated on such a highly contested issue. One reason is that fragmentation and pluralism frequently result in caution and at times vacillation (weak leadership) from school and city officials, caught as they are in a cross-pressure situation.

Actually, the relation between fragmentation and weak leadership is a reciprocal one. Each reinforces the other. As city officials fail to put forth clear and unambiguous plans for change and press firmly for their implementation, the opposition becomes more mobilized, change-oriented groups become more polarized from them, they become divided from within between "moderates" and "revolutionaries," confusion mounts, and a divided community becomes even more so. This process contributed directly to New York City's stalemate on school desegregation.

Other propositions relating characteristics of the school system, city government, the civil rights movement, and the moderates to the extent of innovation in this field are also suggested from my study. On the Board of Education, for example, its high degree of bureaucratization, especially its militaristic structure, had militated against all kinds of innovations (decentralization, elimination of many headquarters units and of layers in the administrative hierarchy) before desegregation became such a contested issue. Its insulation from lay review and controls, as indicated by the continued weakness and lack of influence of the city board and local boards and by a perpetuation of the power of entrenched, "inbred" interests within the system, worked in the same direction.

The board's relations with the mayor and various city agencies also prevented any implementation of innovations to upgrade quality and foster desegregation. The diffusion of authority and responsibility for major board decisions across so many city agencies (e.g., on school construction and its capital budget) had led to interminable delays and an exercise of so many particularistic, local pressures that there was little opportunity for meaningful planning on a city-wide or at least borough-wide basis. In addition, the unwillingness of the board and other city agencies to join together to coordinate their projects, even as education, housing, poverty, transit, industrial development, and urban renewal decisions were all so interrelated, had also contributed to an absence of meaningful innovation.

The mayor obviously has a key role to play in all these matters—in encouraging and mandating administrative reorganization and planning, both within the Board of Education and in city government. Though there are many political "costs" in his becoming involved in such activities, perhaps the alternative "hands off" policy that New York City mayors have followed in the past is no longer in order, given the increased citizen demands for an expansion and more equitable distribution of vital city services. An infusion of more state and federal funds without major efforts at consolidation and planning may only solidify traditional (fragmented and pluralistic) structures and magnify the city's many problems.

A change in strategy, alliances, and outlook among civil rights and moderate groups would further contribute to some needed innovations. The civil rights movement has allowed its internal divisions to be exploited by the board and other high-level city officials. It has also followed a kind of "conflict strategy" in pressing for racial balance in the city's public schools without pointing up how desegregation could and did relate to other goals (quality, economies) that potential opposition groups thought were closer to their interests. Through pressure for school desegregation through some form of "consensus politics"—and that does not dilute in any way the goals of the civil rights movement—civil rights groups may not activate to the same degree the anxieties and opposition of many white populations. In other words, civil rights groups could be much more effective agents of change than they have been.

Finally, the most powerful civic groups of all, various moderate organizations, may hold the key to any prospects for desegregation. Given their present outlook and commitments to maintain the status quo, in which they have such a vital interest, any increase in support from them for desegregation on a much broader scale seems unlikely.

Perhaps the most significant levers to social change, though, lie in the intervention of outside parties who have not played as big a role as they might. There are three such parties—the mayor, the state education department, and the federal government. It seems quite clear from the history of the school desegregation struggle in New York City that there will not be too much movement on the issue without the strong and direct intervention of these parties. All have been subject in the past to political and economic constraints that have limited their participation. The mayor faced a highly organized voting bloc of irate white populations. The state education commissioner faced pressures from a coalition of upstate legislators and big-city "neighborhood school" advocates, as well as from other agencies of state government. And the federal government has not had the legal powers or the fiscal role (federal funds had only constituted a small part of the Board of Education's moneys) to exert much pressure. Unless these parties are able to shake loose from such traditional constraints and intervene more directly in this controversy, there may be no desegregation.

Perhaps *the* key theme running through my discussion of social forces that have prevented desegregation in New York City is that of pluralism and fragmentation. This relates directly to the role that outside parties can play in fostering change. The mayor can press for consolidation of city government, to effect more city-wide educational planning. The state education commissioner can press for similar changes within the Board of Education. And the federal government can give or withhold funds, depending on how much coordination and planning actually takes place. Such structural changes within the board and in city government can help to eliminate the chaos that so frequently accompanies the implementation of even the most limited desegregation plans. They can also help create some unity in a change-oriented coalition of city and board officials and integrationist groups, thereby diluting the power and effectiveness of the moderates and opposition.[22]

The argument will be made, of course, that the demographic changes of New York City, like those of most other large northern cities, are so inexorable that no such intervention will help effect more desegregation. And some will argue that it may even hasten the withdrawal of whites from the city and the school system. Perhaps it has to be tried and fairly soon, however, to test the validity of these assertions. The continued deterioration in quality and hardening of lines of segregation in New York and all other large northern cities indicate that the long-term benefits of such intervention will probably far outweigh any temporary, short-run costs.

Notes

1. See an unpublished paper by Robin Williams, "Factors Affecting Reactions to Public School Desegregation in American Communities" (April, 1964), for the most comprehensive codification to date of studies in this field. Unfortunately, there were no published studies on the school desegregation experience of very large northern cities for Williams to include in his codification.

2. This study was begun under Grant No. 2857 from the U.S. Office of Education. It was completed with the support of the Center for Urban Education. I am especially grateful to Robert A. Dentler, Deputy Director of the Center, for making it possible for me to complete this study. I am also grateful for the help provided by Rosalyn Menzel and Faith Kortheuer, my research assistants. Ronald Milavsky, Kenneth Lenihan, Ivar Berg, and Theresa Rogers provided helpful criticisms of earlier drafts. The views expressed in this paper are those of the author and do not necessarily reflect those of the Center for Urban Education. My data include informant interviews with school and city officials, leaders and activists deemed most influential on the issue; observation at meetings and public hearings; and a content analysis of press clippings, studies, and public statements of the board and involved civic groups.

My purpose was to trace through the positions taken by every influential party to school desegregation controversies since 1957, when the issue first was contested publicly in New York City; delineate the many coalitions and factions; ascertain the extent of access of various interest groups (school staff as well as civic groups) to decision centers on the issue; and suggest the effects of such patterns of influence on the speed and scope of the board's desegregation efforts.

3. See Wallace S. Sayre and Herbert Kaufman, *Governing New York City* (New York: Russell Sage Foundation, 1960), especially chap. xix.

4. State Education Commissioner's Advisory Committee on Human Relations and Community Tensions, "Desegregating the Public Schools of New York City," May 12, 1964 (reprinted in full in *Integrated Education* [August–September, 1964]), p. 16.

5. One reason so many principals from "sending" schools objected to open enroll-ment was that it might seem to reflect adversely on the quality of their program. If too many Negro parents transferred their children out, some principals feared it might suggest to the board that there was much parent dissatisfaction. Others were against it because they wanted to keep at least a few potentially "high achievers."

6. See an unpublished paper by the City Commission on Human Rights of New York City, "Study of the Effect of the 1964–1970 School Building Program on Segre-gation in New York City's Public Schools" (1964). The main findings and conclu-sions of the study were released to the press and never publicly refuted by the board.

7. "Desegregating the Public Schools of New York City," p. 17.

8. See Allan Blackman's excellent summary of the neighborhood school doctrine, "Planning and the Neighborhood School," *Integrated Education* (August–September, 1964), pp. 49–56.

9. Kurt Lang and Gladys Lang, "Resistance to School Desegregation among Jews," *Sociological Inquiry* (Winter, 1965), pp. 94–123; an unpublished study by David Caplovitz and Candace Rogers, Bureau of Applied Social Research, Columbia Univer-sity, 1965; and David Rogers and Bert Swanson, "White Citizen Response to the Same Integration Plan: Comparisons of Local School Districts in a Northern City."

10. For a sample of the sentiments of some of the supervisory staff within the New York City school system, see "The Integration Crisis," reprinted in *Integrated Educa-tion* (June–July, 1964), pp. 30–35. This was a statement issued by the Council of Supervisory Associations, a group representing 3,000 high school, junior high school, and elementary school principals, department chairmen, administrative assistants in high schools, assistant principals, board examiners, assistant superintendents, and other supervisors. They opposed pairings, feeder pattern changes, and the abolishing of group IQ tests. Their stand even appalled one of the city's most powerful "moder-ate" organizations which hadn't given much support to the integration forces. See the United Parents Association press release, April 20, 1964, in which it referred to the "negative attitude recently advanced in the statement of the Council of Supervisory Associations." My data on staff prejudice come from interviews and observations. See also Kenneth B. Clark, *Dark Ghetto* (New York: Harper & Row, 1965), chap. vi.

11. Junior high school principals were especially opposed to the board's desegrega-tion plans because they included a grade reorganization that would abolish the junior high school division.

12. The Commission on Human Rights had played an important mediating role in August and September of 1963, forestalling a boycott for the opening of school. Through the fall, however, the board refused to meet with Commission officials, ac-cusing them of acting merely as another civil rights group and not as a "sister agency." The board turned down suggestions for other mediators.

13. There were, however, some private meetings between Board President James Donovan and the militant opposition. It should be noted, in passing, that the Board President had considerable power and exercised it constantly throughout the period of greatest controversy (fall, 1963, through June, 1965).

14. "Desegregating the Public Schools of New York City," pp. 14–34.

15. Williams, *op. cit.*, p. 51.

16. Some cases in point for this generalization are the following. Integrationist

groups became much more united in the summer and fall of 1963, after Commissioner Allen made a request that all local school boards throughout the state report to him on the extent of "racial balance" in their districts and what they planned to do to increase it. They reunited again in May, 1964, after the Allen Report was issued. They divided when the board hesitated and delayed in implementing open enrollment, pairings, and the Allen Report.

17. Interviews with several civil rights leaders confirmed this. There are some parallels between the board's strategies of relating to civil rights groups and those of many businessmen to rival labor organizations in the early organizing stages of the labor movement. The strategy of quoting and playing off key leaders against one another was similar to the "whipsawing" tactics of business in labor-management controversies.

18. A few illustrations are the sabotage of open enrollment by principals, the limited publicity it received, and the board's handling of school officials and parents in areas to be paired. On the last, it was the consensus of virtually all the teachers, principals, and district superintendents interviewed in the board's evaluation study that their schools and communities had not been adequately prepared. The board only came out with its decision on pairings in May, 1964. There was little time for staff preparation. A "critical incident" illustrating the board's limited community relations efforts took place a week before the opening of school. One civil rights leader suggested that the board hold some intervisitations of parents and pupils in schools to be paired and have an open-school week. The board responded favorably. One cannot help but wonder why they didn't have the idea themselves.

19. Corroborated in interviews with many school officials and civic leaders and from observation. For a detailed study of PEA, documenting some of these points, see Sol Cohen, *Progressives and Urban Social Reform* (New York: Teachers College, Columbia University, 1964). As Cohen notes: "The PEA enjoyed privileged access to school officials. And as Truman observes, once a political interest group has established access, it will exert tremendous efforts to retain the structural arrangements that have given it advantage."

20. The moderates were an important source of citizen support and money-raising activities for the board. Board officials needed the moderates' support to maintain some stability, and both sides knew it. Had the board moved further to the left, supporting civil rights demands more than it did, it feared a withdrawal of the moderates' support.

21. Space does not permit elaboration of these many points. Many were documented as long ago as 1951 in a study directed by George D. Strayer and Louis E. Yavner, *Administrative Management of the School System of New York City* (2 vols.; New York: Mayor's Committee on Management Survey, 1951). There have been many similar reports since then. All these points are elaborated upon with many "critical incidents" in my book *110 Livingston Street* (New York: Random House, 1968). See also the article by Marilyn Gittell, in Gittell (ed.), *Educating an Urban Population* (Beverley Hills, Calif.: Sage Publications, 1967).

22. These propositions parallel those of Amos Hawley in his studies of community power structures and urban renewal success. Hawley found a direct correlation between the extent of concentration of power in cities and the extent of innovation in urban renewal. See Amos Hawley, "Community Power and Urban Renewal Success," *American Journal of Sociology* (January, 1963), pp. 422–33. On the unwillingness of big-city mayors caught in cross-pressure situations to take risks in supporting controversial proposals for change, see Edward C. Banfield and James Q. Wilson, *City Politics* (Cambridge, Mass.: Harvard University Press, 1963), pp. 121–25.

III

Education and Politics: Case Studies

In the late 1950's and the early 1960's, the integration conflicts in public school systems propelled education into the limelight and generated widespread general concern. The impetus for school reform came from the blossoming interest of academicians not only with the output of school systems but also with the mechanisms for attaining policy decisions. Attention focused on the nearly nationwide insulation of educational decision-making from the normal political processes, and judgments began to be offered concerning the value of such insulation and its impact upon the ability of educational systems to perform their functions adequately.

Thus, the 1960's saw the beginning of analyses based on political assumptions relating both to the problems of the various urban school systems and to the structure of power within those systems. Most of these studies concluded that the schools were failing the new urban minorities —the ghetto dwellers—who were comprising increasingly greater percentages of school populations.

Some of the studies dealing with the general failures of the systems continued to analyze them in terms of technical procedures such as organizational structure, teaching techniques, administrative policy, and so forth. Others, however, focused on the political environment, emphasizing the vested interest of, and the conflict between, various groups in the community. The selections that follow fall into this latter category; they are oriented toward analyses of the policy processes and are inherently political in character.

Robert Dahl's study of the New Haven school system is one of the earlier analyses of urban school politics. Dahl studies the relative influence of such elements in the system as the mayor, the superintendent of schools, the bureaucrats, the teachers, and the parents. His conclusions for New Haven at times differ from those of the other studies offered here; the significant variable might be the time gap between Dahl's work and those that follow. Whether this is the case will have to be determined by subsequent study.

Marilyn Gittell's study is directed at the New York City school system. Examining five sets of decisions and the role of the various actors operating to establish influence in the system in regard to these decisions, Gittell concludes that the system's failures are directly related to the closed nature of the educational decision-making process.

Peter Schrag analyzes the effect of ethnic ties on the style and character of Boston's schools. Describing a basically conservative and inflexible system very resistant to change, his study places much of the blame on the parochialism that results from almost total control of the schools by one ethnic group.

Robert Havighurst investigates the broad social conditions of Chicago and explores the trends of that city in terms of population changes, social mobility, and governmental programs and their relationship to the schools. Discussing the conflict between those who call for the "four-wall school" run by professionals free of the political decision-making processes and those who support the "urban community school" that would effectively break the monopoly of professional control over school policy, Havighurst concludes by offering a set of guidelines for improving Chicago's school system.

The method by which Pittsburgh is attempting to resolve its educational problems—problems that generally resemble those of most urban centers—is discussed by Peter Schrag. He attempts to find out why Pittsburgh has not encountered the violent conflict over schools that other cities have, and he goes on to analyze the prospects for change in the city.

In the last selection in this chapter, Marilyn Gittell and T. Edward Hollander analyze Philadelphia's successful efforts to restructure and reform its school system despite opposition from the existing education officials. They examine the impact of the city's civil rights groups, political reform movement, and state government, as well as the controversy within the educational bureaucracy, the fiscal relations of the school system, and the political process as it interacts with the school system.

9. LEADERS IN PUBLIC EDUCATION

ROBERT A. DAHL

Though leadership in the public school system has many of the characteristics of leadership in the political parties and in urban redevelopment, there are also significant differences. Like the parties, but unlike urban redevelopment, the school system has existed for a long time. Policy-making in the schools is far more routinized than in redevelopment; it is far more professionalized—one might say bureaucratized—than in the parties, in the sense that almost all of the people who make day-to-day decisions about the schools meet certain professional standards and have a strong sense of their own professionalism. The schools are more insulated from electoral politics than are the parties, of course; as with redevelopment, leaders in the schools maintain an aura of nonpartisanship.

As in urban redevelopment and party nominations, there are a number of diverse elements in the political stratum whose educational wants and concerns the leaders attempt to conciliate, anticipate, and satisfy. Insofar as they are organized into self-conscious associations, these elements, the public school interests, are somewhat like the subleaders in the political parties. As in redevelopment, the public school interests possess a strong concentration of purpose. Moreover, most of the associations active in school affairs are specialized around the politics of the public schools and play a minor part in the political parties and in urban redevelopment.

. . . .

The public schools are a large operation. Annual outlays for the public school system run from one-quarter to one-third of all city expenditures and constitute far and away the biggest item in the budget. (By comparison the police and fire departments together amount to only one-

Reprinted from Robert A. Dahl, *Who Governs? Democracy and Power in an American City* (New Haven: Yale University Press, 1961), pp. 141–59. Copyright © 1961 by Yale University. Reprinted by permission of Yale University Press.

fifth of total city expenditures; health and welfare are between one-twentieth and one-tenth.) In 1959 the regular school system employed about 1,250 people, including 924 teachers, 98 administrators, 43 clerks, and 184 janitors, repairmen, etc. In addition, programs in adult education and summer recreation employed over 200 persons. Altogether, one out of every two persons employed by the city government worked in the school system.

The responsibilities placed on the public schools by law, custom, and popular expectations are heavy. The schools are, of course, expected to provide a minimum level of knowledge for all except the mentally retarded and a much higher level for the increasing proportion of students who aspire to higher education. The schools are, and from the time of their establishment have been, expected to prepare the student for a useful calling. In addition, the schools have always been assigned a heavy responsibility for helping to form the character, moral sensibilities, and civic attitudes of the student. In a city of immigrants like New Haven, the last task has necessarily assumed a position of key importance.

Considering the nature of the tasks assigned to the public schools, it is hardly surprising that control over the schools is seen as worth fighting for by leaders of many different groups.

.   .   .   .

An examination of eight different sets of decisions taken between 1953 and 1959 indicates that there are three main centers for initiating or vetoing policies involving the public schools. These are the mayor, the Board of Education, and the superintendent of schools.

In New Haven, the seven members of the Board of Education are appointed for four-year terms by the mayor, who is ex officio an eighth member. Appointments are staggered; hence by the end of his first term in office a mayor will usually have had the opportunity to appoint a majority of the members to the board.

Because the local norms prescribe that the schools should be insulated from politics, a mayor who attempted to press his own policies directly on the school system through the board or the superintendent would antagonize the segments of the political stratum most keenly interested in the schools. Consequently, the mayor ordinarily influences school policy only indirectly through his appointments to the board. Even then, the mayor does not have a free hand. By tradition, members are reappointed as long as they are willing to serve; because of this tradition, it is not always simple to ease out a board member whom the mayor would prefer not to reappoint. Moreover, some ethnic, religious, and professional distribution is assumed to be necessary. In recent years, the board's appointive members have included three Catholic, two Protestants, and two Jews. Among the Catholics were one man of Irish stock and another of Italian stock. Mayor Lee appointed the state head of the AFL–CIO to the board; fear of trade union resentment may henceforth require a trade union man on the board. In response to rising demands from Negroes, Lee also appointed a Negro; probably no future mayor will fail to follow his lead.

Once the mayor has appointed his members, his direct influence is limited. The board members are unpaid. They have careers, goals, and standards of their own. Membership on the board is time-consuming and even onerous. Board members do not feel particularly beholden to the mayor. Hence, the most a mayor can do is to choose people in whom he has confidence and then give them his strong backing when they call for help.

The superintendent of schools is a major official. In 1960 his annual salary of $16,300 was the highest of any official in the city except for the mayor himself. Once appointed, a superintendent is difficult to remove, not only because he builds up his own following among the public school interests, but because he can invoke the support of national professional groups if his removal does not seem to be based on considerations of professional adequacy.

Because of all the constraints on the mayor and the Board of Education, a superintendent in whom they have confidence can be expected to acquire a major, perhaps even decisive, influence on policies relating to essentially internal school matters—that is, policies that do not require extensive negotiations with elements in the political stratum not primarily concerned with the public schools. If the mayor and the board lack confidence in the superintendent, then the direct influence of board members on decisions is likely to increase, as board members substitute their own judgment for his. Finally, if the situation of the schools generates a series of proposals and decisions that require extensive negotiations outside the public school system, then the direct influence of the mayor is likely to increase. Consequently, the relative influence of the mayor, the board, and the superintendent tends to be different at different times and with different kinds of decisions.

Consider now the following scoreboard. In eight different sets of decisions between 1953 and 1959, there were twenty-seven instances in which the initiation or veto of a policy alternative could be attributed to a particular individual, group, or agency. The successful actors included eight individuals, a group of three members of the Board of Education, three official agencies (in cases where the action could not be attributed to any particular individual), and the Teachers' League. Of the twenty-seven instances of successful action on policy, all except three were traceable to participants officially and publicly involved in the school system.

Fifteen, or more than half, were traceable to the mayor or officials who were members of his educational coalition. All the rest were scattered among a variety of individuals and agencies, from the Board of Finance and the Board of Park Commissioners to the superintendent of schools and the president of Yale.

One might suspect the validity of crude measures of this sort, but the conclusions they suggest fit with the qualitative evidence. Taken together, the qualitative and quantitative evidence seems to support three propositions. First, the number of citizens who participate directly in important decisions bearing on the public schools is small—just as it is in the other areas of public life we have examined. Second, direct influence over decisions in public education seems to be exerted almost entirely by public officials. Third, in recent years the chief center of direct influence has been the mayor and his appointees on the Board of Education, rather than the superintendent.

As with urban redevelopment and political nominations, however, it would be a serious error to assume that the individuals and groups with the greatest *direct* influence on decisions are autonomous. On the contrary, they consider the reactions of a number of different public school interests who can, if aroused, make themselves felt in various ways—not least through elections.

The most important of these public school interests are the administrators, the teachers, and the parents of the children in the public schools.

School Administrators

In New Haven, for every nine teachers there is an administrator of some sort—a superintendent, assistant superintendent, supervisor, assistant supervisor, or principal. The school administrators, rather than the teachers, are the elite of the American public school system.

The ambitious teacher, particularly if he is a man, soon learns that greater income and power are to be found in an administrative career; if he remains in teaching, the terminus is plainly visible and not overly attractive. In New Haven, in 1959, the official upper salary limit for a public school teacher was $7,000 (a decade earlier it had been $3,600). The average teacher's salary was about $5,450. By comparison, principals were, on the average, paid half again as much; the highest salary a teacher could receive was over $1,000 less than the average salary paid to a school principal. Three of the four assistant superintendents were paid twice as much as the average teacher. The superintendent was paid three times as much.

Once a teacher obtains a "school of his own" as a principal or moves into the administrative hierarchy as a supervisor, he belongs to an elite group within the school system. In New Haven this is symbolized by the right to belong to a separate association, the Principals' Club.

But to succeed in his new career, the school administrator must obey the First Commandment of the public school administrator: "Thou shalt not alienate teachers, parents, superiors, or professional colleagues." In making his way according to this rule, he brings with him doctrines about education, teaching, and administration that he has learned at his teachers' college, doctrines that he may continue to acquire in annual installments at summer school until he has earned his Ph.D. in education. He also brings his own temperament, experiences, idiosyncrasies, and even neuroses.

The school administrator is faced with two great problems. On the one hand, he depends heavily on the cooperation of others to get the resources he needs to run the schools in a fashion that will insure his professional recognition and advancement. On the other hand, to maintain his professional standards and reputation he must oppose outside interference in the school system, particularly by politicians. Sometimes it is impossible to reconcile these two needs.

The school system gives away education to its pupils (and their parents) and pays for it out of public funds. In New Haven, unlike many other places in the United States, funds for the public schools are appropriated by the city government out of general revenues obtained from taxes, state grants, and loans. Because the city government is subject to a great variety of demands, the views, aims, and strategies of political leaders usually do not coincide entirely with those of citizens and administrators concerned with the schools. The adequacy of school appropriations, therefore, depends in part on the effectiveness of various leaders, including school administrators, in mobilizing the support of the other public school interests and in part on how important the views and actions of these interests are in the calculations of the men who make the decisions on city revenues and expenditures. The teachers, of course, are one key group who can sometimes be mobilized.

Teachers

If the public school system is an important instrument in the Americanization of the immigrant, and if the education provided by the public schools is the first step in a social ladder leading to a social respect and self-respect according to American standards, to become a *teacher* is to take a still higher step. Jobs in the school system have been one of the main avenues to assimilation. When an ethnic group is in its first stage, some of its members become janitors in the schools. Later, as the ethnic group moves into its second stage, schoolteaching is a wedge that permits the group to expand its white-collar segment. Then, in the third stage, members of the ethnic group begin to receive appointments as school administrators.

For this process of assimilation to function effectively, two prerequisites are necessary. First, the training required for teaching must be inexpensive and easily available. Second, teachers from immigrant backgrounds must be free to enter into teaching without discrimination. Normal schools satisfy the first requirement; city elections eventually guarantee the second. Under the prodding of leaders in the public school movement like Henry Barnard, free teachers' institutes were created in Connecticut in 1848. The State Normal School was established the next year.[1] From that time forward a boy or girl with limited means and a high school diploma could become a public school teacher. When city elections began to be won by ethnic candidates, the likelihood of discrimination declined.

Thus, the rate at which an ethnic group is being assimilated can almost be determined from the proportion of its members who are public school teachers. Judging from their names, about two out of three teachers were of Yankee or English stock in 1900; about one-quarter were Irish; there were no Italians. Over the next two decades the proportion of Irish teachers rose as the proportion of Yankee teachers fell. But the time of the Italians had not yet arrived either in politics or in schoolteaching. Even in 1930, the Russians—mainly Russian Jews—outnumbered the Italians. In 1939, however, William Celentano was nominated for mayor; within one generation, 20 per cent of the teachers bore Italian names.

.   .   .   .

In 1947, a report on the New Haven school system described "the median, or typical teacher, [as] about 45 years of age. She was born in New Haven and attended local schools. After graduation from high school, she took her professional training at New Haven State Teachers College graduating . . . from the two-year course. Immediately upon graduation she entered the local system without teaching experience elsewhere and has been teaching here ever since."[2]

Altogether, teachers make up the largest group of municipal employees —nearly one-third of the total. They are organized in two professional associations, the New Haven Teachers' League and the American Federation of Teachers. The Teachers' League is older and larger, claiming two-thirds of the teachers as members; principals are also eligible for membership and are often chosen as presidents. In orientation, the League is a professional association rather than a trade union and is affiliated with the Connecticut Education Association; because it has worked closely with the last two superintendents, it has been called a "company union" by its critics. The smaller, more union-oriented Teachers' Federation is affiliated with the AFL–CIO, accepts only teachers as members, and is less warmly received by the school administration. As a result of an ill-conceived set of recommendations on discipline submitted a few years ago by the Federation, critics have sometimes called it "irreresponsible" and "crackpot." The close ties with the school administration enjoyed by the leaders of the Teachers' League have permitted it to perform functions denied to the Federation, and in general the League has played a more prominent role in important decisions.

The most influential leaders on questions involving public education— the mayor, members of the Board of Education, the superintendent—are constrained in their choices by what they think will be acceptable to the teachers. In 1955, the opposition of the Teachers' League was . . . a major factor in the unexpected defeat of a proposed reform of procedures on appointments and promotions.

Democratic Ritual: The Followings

The greatest ambiguity in the relations of leaders and constituents stems from the fact that individuals who seem to have the greatest direct influence on decisions are themselves influenced in their choices by the need to gain and retain popular support. This ambiguity is further compounded by the fact that leaders do not merely respond to demands; they also help to generate them. In public education, as we have noted, differences in the objectives of leaders and parents induce leaders to develop methods of generating new demands among parents and other citizens. One of these methods is the creation of special associations. Just as the numerous action committees provide a democratic façade and a body of subleaders and followings for leaders in redevelopment and renewal, and the party functionaries and convention delegates furnish auxiliaries for party leaders, so certain citizen organizations provide subleaders and followings for leaders in public education. The Parent-Teachers' Associations fit most obviously into this role.

Ostensibly, of course, a Parent-Teachers' Association (PTA) is a democratic organization of parents and teachers associated with a particular school, brought into being and sustained by their joint interests. In practice, a PTA is usually an instrument of the school administrator. Indeed, an ambitious principal will ordinarily regard an active PTA as an indispensable means to his success. If no PTA exists, he will create one; if one exists, he will try to maintain it at a high level of activity.

The functions of the PTA are rather like those of party subleaders. The PTA supplies a group of people whose loyalty and enthusiasm can occasionally be mobilized for educational purposes important to the leaders. Thus, an energetic principal of a New Haven school in a low-income neighborhood described how he had organized a PTA in order to improve the facilities of the school. He went to an important neighborhood leader, he said, and persuaded her that "the kids in the neighborhood needed help." Together they started a PTA. In order to involve the parents even more heavily, they then induced the PTA to endorse a hot-lunch program; this required PTA members to raise funds and even to hire kitchen help. As participation in the PTA increased, the principal began to work for a new school to replace the old one. When obstacles were raised by the city administration, the principal called a meeting of PTA members and other neighborhood leaders and "gave them a rousing speech asking for their help. Within twenty-four hours they were on the phone and in other ways bringing pressure on the administration. The problem was solved."

It is a rare PTA that ever opposes the wishes of a principal, and its mere existence helps to give a certain legitimacy to the otherwise hierarchical structure of the school system. As long as the principal keeps the active PTA members moderately satisfied, he will appear to have the "backing of the parents" for his programs and policies.

But a PTA is also useful to head off or settle conflicts between parents and the school system. A shrewd principal often uses the PTA to find out what problems are in the parents' minds; he then brings about some adustments in the school's program or perhaps allays the concern of parents simply by discussing the problem with them. PTA meetings also create an atmosphere of friendliness and conviviality that blunts criticism. For many women, in fact, the PTA is obviously an outlet for social needs; PTA meetings furnish opportunities to escape from the home for a few hours, meet neighbors, make new friends, gossip, talk about children, partake of coffee and pastry, and achieve a fugitive sense of social purpose. Some female Machiavellians even look upon PTA activity as a way of assuring favorable treatment for their own children. And they may be right, for the experienced principal or teacher learns from PTA meetings who the most interested parents are, who the "troublemakers" might be, who makes demands on the school system, and who does not. If he is politically sensitive, the principal is likely to conclude that it is safer to ignore the difficulties of a child whose parents are not interested enough to participate in the PTA than the problems of a child whose mother is a PTA activist.

The PTA is also a legitimate channel through which potential leaders may enter into the school system, test themselves, gain experience, and pass into the ranks of the leaders. It is a remarkable fact that three recent appointees to the New Haven Board of Education all became involved in the politics of the public schools via the PTA. To be sure, each of these men had already possessed a strong prior interest in education. But it was when the education of their own children was at stake that they became active in their PTA.

.   .   .   .

Ordinarily a PTA president is a housewife who lacks the time, experience, interest, and drive to move into the real centers of educational influence. Moreover, the focus of the individual PTA is narrow, since parents are more interested in the current education of their own children than in enduring problems of the educational system as a whole. It is probably for these reasons that the individual PTA's and the New Haven Council of Parent-Teachers' Associations have not played a prominent role in important decisions.

It was because of the limitations of the PTA's that Mayor Lee created the Citizens Advisory Committee on Education (CACE) in 1954. . . .

The CACE illustrates nicely the way many citizen committees fit the needs of leaders. The first chairman, John Braslin, was an educator who worked in New York and lived in New Haven; he had been chairman of the PTA at a school located in one of the best residential areas of New Haven. Before World War II, he had taught French at Hillhouse High; he was an old friend of the Mayor—they had even been in the same platoon in basic training during the Mayor's brief stint in the army—and the Mayor turned the task of organizing the committee over to him. Braslin said later,

> What I did was to make a list of about 150 names of people . . . many of whom I knew through Junior Chamber work, through work prior to the war . . . air raid wardens, and activities of that sort. And then I asked representatives of various organizations like the labor unions and the merchants downtown, the League of Women Voters, the PTA council, to recommend names to me who would be members of the CACE and act as liaison with these various civic, social, and service groups in the city. . . . I whittled the list down to 100 names . . . I wanted a large representative group that would really cover a broad section of the city.

The first task of the CACE and probably its most important one was to help arouse support for new public high schools. But it had other jobs to do, too. Braslin said,

> In order to keep this large committee as a functioning group, what I did was to break it down into seven subcommittees and I first appointed a govern-

ing board as an executive board composed of fifteen members. . . . I figured . . . I'll pick these people because these are the ones that I will have to work with, that I will be openly responsible for, and on whom I will depend to lead and encourage and arouse the other members of the over-all committee. So from among these fifteen I was able to draw a chairmanship for each of the seven subcommittees. Then, the executive board first decided on and we picked seven areas of study: personnel, finance, building, school population, and publicity, public relations and the like.

The leaders then sent out a note to the members asking them to indicate the area each was most interested in; they placed the members on subcommittees according to their interests.

From its inception, then, the CACE was an instrument of its leaders for generating support for schools. How effective it was it is difficult to say. There is little doubt that it helped to generate support for new high schools at a time when the mayor badly needed support. It pressed for higher teachers' salaries. It sponsored an improved program for testing the vision of school children that was finally adopted by the Board of Education.

Notes

1. A. R. Mead, *The Development of Free Schools in the United States, as Illustrated by Connecticut and Michigan* (New York: Teachers College, Columbia University, 1918), p. 48.

2. *New Haven's Schools: An Investment in Your City's Future, Report of a Survey of the Public School System 1946–47* (New Haven, 1947), p. 33.

10. PROFESSIONALISM AND PUBLIC PARTICIPATION IN EDUCATIONAL POLICY-MAKING: NEW YORK CITY, A CASE STUDY

MARILYN GITTELL

Decision-making studies and analyses of local power structure in cities have much to contribute to an understanding of the operation of school systems. More intensive studies of decision-making and the distribution of power in school systems can, in turn, contribute significantly to knowledge of how cities are governed. Almost every study of power in large cities points to functional specialization, dispersion of power to specialists in particular areas, and an increased role of the bureaucracy in decision-making. This study of decision-making in the New York City school system concerns itself with the distribution of power, testing the hypothesis of functional specialization and, hopefully, expanding on its implications.

New York City as a Case Study

The New York City school system is nominally a dependent school district (that is, the school district does not have independent taxing power), and the city schools and school policy have often been described as strongly susceptible to local political influence.[1]

Concern in New York City with the failures of the education system was brought to a head by legislation introduced in the 1964 session of the State Legislature to establish a fiscally independent school system. Mayor Wagner requested the Temporary Commission on City Finances to explore the feasibility of such a plan and to review the general character of the administrative structure in education, with special attention to the role of the Board of Education. An analysis of decision-making in

Reprinted from *Public Administration Review*, XXVII (September, 1967), 237–51. Reprinted by permission of the American Society for Public Administration.

education in New York City was undertaken to determine the impact of fiscal independence on the existing structure. Since no previous study had fully explored the sources and procedures of policy, there was little to go on as to how the school system functioned under its existing structure.

Five areas of decision-making were selected for study, on the basis of diversity in the subject dealt with, the widest possible range of participation by those involved in education, and relevance of the policy selected to the over-all education function. Generally, exploration of a continuum of policy was considered superior to a single policy decision. Historical data and institutional analysis were utilized in all relevant areas.

Selected for intensive study were: (1) selection of the superintendent, (2) increases in teachers' salaries, (3) budgeting, (4) school integration, and (5) curriculum development. Other areas of policy were reviewed in a more cursory way, to broaden the scope of the analysis.[2]

Within any school system, the potential participants in school policy-making are essentially the same, although actual participation may vary according to the relative power of each in given circumstances. Legal power is usually divided between a board of education and the superintendent. As regards the bureaucracy, distinctions must be made among the central administrative bureaucracy and field administrators, top supervisory staff, and middle management. Organizations representing these groups are common in the larger school districts, and their activities can be significant. Teachers and teacher organizations, parents and parent organizations, are potential participants. Specialized education interest groups (ad hoc and permanent) have been active in many communities, and their role can be vital. In the general community there are other potential participants: local, state, and federal officials, civic groups, the press, business organizations, and individual entrepreneurs seeking the rewards of the school system.[3]

The findings of the study emphasize that, in the last two decades, education in New York City has become amazingly insulated from public controls. One could accurately describe the situation as an abandonment of public education by key forces of potential power within the city. Bureaucratization and professionalization are contributing factors. Weber's theory of the emergence of a specialized bureaucracy, monopolizing power through its control of expertise, describes the role of the education bureaucracy in New York City. The claim that only the professionals can make competent judgments has been accepted. Contributing to, and perhaps growing out of, this attitude was the change in the mayor's role to one of noninvolvement. Civic and interest groups (other than the specialized education groups) have responded ambivalently; on the one hand, they accept the notion of the professional competence of the bureaucracy, and, on the other, they accept the need for reform but express a hopelessness regarding their ability to change the system. The result is narrow or closed participation in large areas of decision-making. Effective influence in these areas is restricted to an inside core of top supervisory personnel in the headquarters staff of the Board of Education. Policy alternatives are rarely discussed or offered, and the inclination to support the status quo is reinforced.[4]

The kind of participation in school policy formulation may fall into one of three categories: (1) *closed*—only the professionals in the system participate; (2) *limited*—the Board of Education and/or the mayor and other special interests such as the Public Education Association, United Parents Association, and the United Federation of Teachers participate; or (3) *open*—all kinds of groups not generally involved in school policy are participants. The greater part of school policy-making in New York City falls into the first two categories.

The scope of participation has been widened in some instances because of the interests of participants. The teachers' union, for instance, widened participation on the salary issue to include the mayor because it recognized that it would gain by his participation. The scope of participation was also widened as a result of conflict. The integration issue was not resolved internally in the system, and participation was thrown into the open. In some respects, the issue itself can be said to influence participation. But, when decisions are not visible, those interests that might otherwise become involved do not.

State Participation

State minimum standards for education are not an overriding influence in a large city such as New York, which tends to make even greater demands on itself. What influence the state does have results from the state-aid formula, the regents' policy, and the administrative rulings of the state commissioner of education. Recent studies in other states have emphasized the increasing importance of the state bureaucracy, particularly the commissioner, in local educational policy.[5]

The state commissioner was involved in two major policy decisions affecting New York City in recent years. He was instrumental in the removal of the entire Board of Education in 1961. Subsequently, he recommended a change in procedure for selection of the board. In 1958, his condemnation of *de facto* segregation in New York City was a catalyst to the initiation of board policy on school integration. He continued to influence city policy in this regard by outlining the problems of school segregation in a series of reports.[6] In addition to these more overt actions, the commissioner's influence is manifest in informal contacts with the superintendent and the staff.

City groups have been notably ineffectual as a force in Albany. One study attributes this failure to the splintering of city educational interest groups. The New York State Educational Conference Board is the strongest and most influential coalition of interest groups in the determination of state education policy. City interests are meagerly represented on the conference board, and the state has been able to ignore city education needs without serious political consequences.[7] The general deficiency in leadership in public education in New York is reflected in part in its failure to influence state policy.

City Participation

The most significant trend in education in New York City has been the isolation of school administration from city government. In each city administration since the 1940's, complaints of undue city interference have resulted in the delegation of increased responsibility to the Board of Education.

The National Education Association condemned Mayor LaGuardia for direct interference with the school system, particularly in personnel policy; the institution of a strict merit system and internal controls over promotions and transfers prevented future mayors from engaging in similar practices. In 1951, the Strayer-Yavner Report concluded that education policy was controlled by the Board of Estimate, the mayor, and the budget director of the city because of the line-item budget;[8] subsequently, the lump-sum budget was adopted, giving the professionals complete control over allocation of funds.[9] Complaints about a political board were satisfied by the institution of the civic selection panel.[10]

But it is the increased bureaucratization and overblown professionalization of the school system that has had the greatest impact on school policy-making. The professional bureaucracy has manipulated its resource of expertise to discourage opposition and alternative policies. The acceptance of technical expertise as the most relevant, if not the only, basis for sound judgment furthered the depoliticalization of education policy.

The depoliticalization process has been a two-way street. Contributing significantly to it was Mayor Wagner's stated desire to delegate complete responsibility for the city's schools to the Board of Education.

Detailed review of newspaper items substantiates Wagner's intention to remove himself from educational policy-making.[11] His public statements were always general—in support of more and better schools. On school integration, he repeatedly stated his desire to leave the matter to the Board of Education and the professional staff. "I subscribe without reservation to the goals of quality integrated education in our schools and of equal opportunity for every child. But the plan, the means, the how, where and what—the timetable, the specific approaches and programs—that is for the educators and for the Board to determine."[12] During the most heated periods of controversy, he met with protest groups, but repeatedly refused to intervene.

Requests to Mayor Wagner in 1964 for $45.3 million in additional funds for a More Effective Schools program drew him to the fringe of the integration issue. The proposal called for obtaining additional funds and services for ten More Effective Schools in ghetto areas. Ultimately, his decision favoring a smaller appropriation was reached after consultation with school officials and staff members of educational interest groups.

An aide to Wagner verified that the Mayor had unquestionably shifted responsibility for education policy to the Board of Education. "The Mayor did not want to get involved with school problems," the aide stated, "particularly school integration problems." Wagner became directly involved only in instances where the board and some other city agency came into the type of conflict that had to be reviewed and resolved before the Board of Estimate.

The mayor and the Board of Estimate are major instruments of financial policy, determining over-all budgetary appropriations. Their review of the education budget, however, has been concerned with the total amount to be allotted. Mayor Wagner's continued involvement in fiscal matters was due more to the fact that the board wanted to shift responsibility to him than to his own desire to participate. Although the Board of Education is charged with the legal responsibility for determining salaries and has discretion to increase salaries within the total allotted funds, it has not been adverse to relinquishing responsibility to the mayor for negotiating salaries.[13]

Mayor Wagner, through his negotiators, twice made direct settlements with the union, in 1961 and 1965.[14] Financial commitments were then met by an additional city appropriation and transfers of funds within the education budget. After the 1965 contract settlement, the superintendent expressed dismay at the settlement, which far exceeded his planned budgetary allotment for salary increases.

The union, for its part, sees an obvious advantage in shifting salary decisions to city hall. Albert Shanker, president of the union, stated that the union is in a more viable position in negotiating with the mayor than with the board. In Chicago, which is a fiscally independent district, the union similarly negotiated its new contract directly with the mayor.

Mayor Wagner's policy of noninvolvement was reinforced by two major changes in procedure instituted during his administration: the lump-sum appropriation of school funds and the panel selection of board members. Under a local law first passed in 1962 and re-enacted each year since then, and by way of a memorandum of understanding with the mayor, the Board of Education has the power to determine its own allocation of funds. Budget preparation, the allocation and transfer of funds, and postaudit control are internal operations, controlled largely by the top supervisory staff. The board is the only city agency with such budgetary independence from the municipal government.

Prior to 1961, board appointments were made directly by the mayor. Under the new procedure, the nine members of the board are appointed by the mayor from a screened list of candidates submitted by a selection panel composed of the heads of eleven educational, civic, and professional organizations. The change, made to deter "political" appointments, followed six years of hearings, numerous scandals, and, finally, the removal of the board by the State Legislature.

The mayor is still forced to take part in school policy in two general areas. The first is on issues in which conflict between major participants cannot be compromised without his involvement. Such issues often concern site selection and provoke sharp differences between the Planning Commission and the board. The second area of involvement occurs where key participants decide they have more to gain by the mayor's participation.

One of the obvious questions that arises in connection with the mayor's role is whether the precedents established under the Wagner administration over a twelve-year period have become so integral a part of the structure that they cannot be changed. Mayor Wagner's role conforms to Banfield's portrait of the Mayor of Chicago as mediator of conflicts, rather than as an initiator of policy.[15] A reform mayor who cannot rely on party backing is less likely to accept this role and, in fact, must use his power to initiate policy to gather necessary political support. Mayoral noninvolvement has also been based on public deference to professionalism. Mayor Lindsay has already faced the charge of "political interference" in an attempt to initiate policy in the creation of a civilian police review board and in requiring, or attempting to require, budgeting accountability in education. Other efforts have been similarly criticized by members of the bureaucracy. The emotional commitment to professionalism, although not inviolate, tends to challenge any suggestion of change or alternative course of action as undue "political interference." The effort of Mayor Lindsay to reassert his policy role represents a direct threat to those who have held almost complete power in decision-making in these areas.

The control of policy by the bureaucracy has been considerably enhanced by the self-removal of other potential participants, particularly civic groups. Any mayor who decides to become more directly involved in education policy will face serious criticism, not only from the education establishment, but from other groups as well. Any movement toward an increased policy role for the mayor will also involve structural changes. Possibly, a revitalized interest by the mayor can reactivate civic reformers and public interest sufficiently to expand participation as a basis for reviewing the instruments of policy.

The Board of Education

The nine members of the Board of Education are the official policy-making body for the school system and are responsible for long-range educational planning. Traditionally, the mayor's appointments had reflected careful consideration of balance of interests, as well as of political favor. Catholics, Protestants, and Jews were equally represented, and there was either a Negro or a Puerto Rican, or both. Geographic distribution demanded by the bylaws assured borough representation. The religious and racial balances, interestingly enough, are continued in the current selection process.[16]

COMPOSITION OF THE BOARD OF EDUCATION*

Religion	Old Board		New Board	
	1947	1957	1961	1965
Catholic	2	3	3	3
Protestant	3	3	3	3
Jew	3	3	3	3

* The board was increased to thirteen members in 1968, by order of the State Legislature. The distribution of the enlarged board remained the same.—Ed. note.

There was little question prior to 1961 that the mayor would exercise some measure of control over the board, and the board members, in turn, could use their political influence with the mayor. Strong board presidents who were politically oriented served as the channel for communication with the mayor.[17]

The screening-panel procedure strengthened the role of the civic groups and reduced the discretion of the mayor. Members of the board nominated by civic groups are less likely to be intimates of the mayor and less likely to consult with him on school problems. People outside the formal school structure, interviewed during the study and asked about the new appointment procedure, expressed dissatisfaction with the lack of political "know-how" of board members. They pointed out that board members lack personal influence and can no longer play the political role expected of them by school groups. . . .

The board's role has been largely one of balancing conflicting pressures and interests. It, too, has become a mediator rather than an initiator of policy. As the spokesman for official policy, the board nominally participates in all major decisions. It spends a great deal of its time, however, on sensitive issues where the balance of power in the board has failed to produce consensus. These are not necessarily major areas of policy. For example, site-selection controversies have recently occupied a large amount of board time.

In the areas selected for study, the board's role varied from superficial participation in the budget process, to formulation and promulgation of policy, to failure to achieve implementation in school integration. Selecting a superintendent was the area in which the board has exercised the most direct power. Historically, the selection of the superintendent was a board function, greatly influenced by its president and subject to the support of high-ranking administrators and education groups. In earlier years, the mayor had on occasion controlled the appointment. The selection is influenced by the bureaucratic pressure for appointment of an "insider." Three of the last five superintendents were chosen from the supervisory bureaucracy; the fourth was a former deputy mayor and local college president.[18]

The education interest groups, particularly the Public Education Association, have always been concerned with the choice of the superintendent. Lowi points out that the interest groups in New York City have generally concentrated their attention on appointments, which is confirmed by their involvement in the selection of the superintendent and board members.[19] In the past, the Public Education Association has supported, without too much success, the appointment of "outsiders" with high academic credentials. It has always requested a screening panel of educators to assist the board in the selection process, but in the final analysis the board president has controlled the choice. The Public Education Association has become more influential in the last two appointments than it had been previously. In 1961, the board accepted the recommendations of the professional panel, selecting a highly regarded "outsider." His failure and dismissal resulted in a return to selection of the highest-ranking person from within the system.

In budgeting, the board has tended to rely on the budget presented by the superintendent and his staff. Individual board members have periodically questioned expenditures, but have also made reference to their lack of information in dealing with intricate budget detail. Generally, the board views its role as one of assuring city financial support for the total budget, satisfying staff requests and public pressures.

In school integration policy, the board has exhibited a lack of effective follow-through. In 1957, it set a general policy favoring school integration, utilizing rotation of teachers, rezoning, and site selection as the means for achieving its goals. But the board has failed to effect implementation by the staff. Board members who were questioned noted the practical problems obstructing the implementation of their policy. They also pointed to staff inaction as a cause for delay. A member of the board stated that, were she not on the board, she would probably be out on the picket line, but dealing with the tough problem of ironing out procedures had taken the edge off her dedication to implementation. A detailed case study of school integration in New York City cites the lack of leadership and determination of the board and its equivocation, after the integration policy was established, as key factors in the failure of that policy.[20]

On two major salary increases in recent years, the board has participated in early negotiation, but has been satisfied to shift responsibility to the mayor for final decision-making.

The trend in the board's participation suggests a diminished role in policy formulation under the new board. The board has never fulfilled its obligation for long-range planning, and the new board has not been any more successful in that area. The lack of a strong board staff has greatly limited the level and character of its participation. Without staff, the board cannot realistically challenge or review the programs of the administrative bureaucracy.

It might be more accurate to say that individual members of the board, as it was formerly constituted, were more involved in policy-making as a result of their own political stature and their association with the mayor. As the school system has grown larger and more complex and as policies demand more specialized knowledge, the board has had to withdraw from an effective policy role. The bureaucracy and special interest groups have gained power by means of their expertise, while the board, lacking expertise, has lost power.

Local School Boards

In 1961, the Board of Education was empowered to appoint local school board members for twenty-five district boards.[21] District selection panels submit two or three names for each vacancy to the district superintendents, who pass the list on to the board for appointment. The activation of local school boards was, in part, a recognition of the inadequacy of the city-wide board and a system too overcentralized to respond to local needs. The local boards, however, were given no real authority in the determination of school policy. Generally, they have acted as community buffers, holding hearings and discussing narrow local issues; they have not had the authority to resolve local problems. Local boards view themselves as preservers of narrow local interests, particularly with regard to integration policy. Officially, the boards rarely act as a body; members are more prone to voice personal views on issues. Local boards do not have the information or facility, much less the authority, to follow through on matters.

The Board of Education has been reluctant to delegate powers to local boards for fear that they would encroach upon its own authority. District superintendents are also hesitant to enhance the position of the local boards because they might interfere with local school administration. The compromise was to assign the local boards the power to hold hearings, which is harmless enough.

Under a 1965 reorganization plan, the twenty-five boards were increased to thirty-one to conform with the expanded thirty-one local districts. The new plan was to include greater emphasis on decentralized policy-making, utilizing the district superintendent and the local boards more effectively. There has been no indication, however, that the plan provides for basic prerequisites for redistributing power in the system. Budgeting and personnel policy continue to be centralized, and there is no provision for flexibility in initiating new programs. The superintendent indicated, in an interview, that the budgetary limitations, in themselves, would prevent any effective decentralization of the city school system, and policy formulation will remain a headquarters responsibility so long as these conditions are unchanged.[22]

The Superintendent and the Bureaucracy

One of the most confusing aspects of school administration in New York City is the growth in the power of the administrative staff at the same time that the superintendent has remained a relatively weak chief executive. In part, the strength of the bureaucracy has undermined the role of the superintendent. Several other factors have contributed significantly to this result. The short tenure in office of the last four superintendents has undoubtedly taken its toll. In the last two decades, four superintendents have held the office, none with enough time to enhance that office's powers.[23] Open conflict with the board was evidenced in two of these administrations, one resulting in dismissal. The last two board presidents have proudly claimed that they devoted at least forty-five hours a week to their jobs, indicating their day-to-day involvement in school affairs that properly could be left to the superintendent and their general lack of reliance on the superintendent for policy recommendations. The abandonment of education by civic groups has been another loss to the superintendent, who might otherwise use this outside support for developing his own role.

The superintendent lacks the most essential power of a strong executive, the power of appointment and removal. The supervisory staff is developed completely through inbreeding and promotion from the ranks. Tenured supervisors expect to move to top policy-making jobs, allowing for little flexibility in appointments. No superintendent can rely on his own team of trusted advisers. Appointments from outside the system are almost nonexistent. Loyalties developed within this environment are strong and are based on how one has received appointment. Top-level deputy, associate, and assistant superintendents have moved up in divisions of the system and their loyalties are based on these associations.

A review of the backgrounds of the twenty-five top supervisory staff members showed that they followed a pattern of having served as principals or assistant principals, were brought into the board on special assignment, and/or had served on special committees (usually as a result of contacts already established at headquarters). Assignment to headquarters staff by a school division reinforces the loyalties of staff members to that division and the supervisory staff in that division. In all school reorganization proposals, these loyalties have repeatedly fostered preservation of the status quo.

The superintendent must cope with these potentially competing interests in his own supervisory bureaucracy.[24] He cannot freely develop his own advisory staff and is encumbered by the appointments and promotions made by his predecessors. Any superintendent from outside the system, not himself subject to these loyalties, would find his task all the more difficult. In a magazine article, the author noted, "I am told Calvin Gross could have made a real dent on the New York City schools if only he had a handful of trusted special assistants."[25]

Directives and policy statements issued by the superintendent on key policies have been attacked by his own supervisory staff, both by their professional organizations and, officially, through organized committees on which they sit.[26] In March, 1964, the Council of Supervisory Associations (CSA)—the over-all organization for all of the individual supervisory organizations, such as the High School Principals Association, Superintendents Association, Junior High School Principals Association —issued one of its many reports condemning policies of the superintendent and noting his failure to consult with his professional staff before making decisions. The CSA recently openly opposed the Princeton Plan, school busing, the dropping of IQ examinations, and school pairing, after they were adopted as official policy by the board and the superintendent.

Invariably, policies that require fundamental institutional change are challenged by the supervisory staff.

The inability of superintendents to use basic administrative powers is notable. They have thoroughly neglected the budget as a management tool to shape personnel or organization policy. Several days spent in the budget office at headquarters indicated that the budget office staff did not act in an advisory or policy-making capacity. Budget estimates are based essentially on pre-established ratios of books and teachers to pupils, with slight adjustment according to the category of the school. Budget approvals come from division heads and are reviewed in hearings controlled by these same people. The last superintendent met only once all year with *his* budget director.[27]

In all of the areas studied, the superintendent played a secondary role as an initiator of policy. He had no direct influence on curriculum, with the exception of support by one administration for complete revision of the elementary school curriculum in the 1950's. Curriculum policy has been left largely to the Curriculum Research Bureau and the deputy superintendent.

The superintendent has been most concerned with budget matters and even in that capacity has shown no strong inclination to control the preparation of the budget or to utilize it as a means of controlling his staff. On integration policy, the last two superintendents have virtually delegated their responsibility to the staff, with the result that implementation has not been forthcoming. Although board policy on integration was established in 1957, no superintendent has considered his role one of leadership in forcing implementation. The superintendent, like the major and the board, became a mediator of disputes, rather than an initiator of school policy.

The Administrative Staff

The education bureaucracy in New York City consists of two distinguishable groups, the headquarters staff and the operational field staff. The latter includes some 3,000 principals and assistant principals, 31 district superintendents, and 1,300 department chairmen.

THE SUPERVISORS AT HEADQUARTERS

A precise figure on the size of the headquarters staff is difficult to obtain; it is estimated to be somewhere around 3,000. Close to 800 people at headquarters do not appear on that budget. Although serving as full-time headquarters personnel, they are paid out of local school budgets.

A core supervisory group, which holds much of the decision-making power, includes some thirty headquarters staff members—including the executive deputy superintendent, the deputy superintendent in charge of instruction and curriculum, the Board of Examiners, twenty of the thirty assistant superintendents, and a few of the active directors of special bureaus. With the exception of two assistant superintendents who had earlier experience in school systems outside of New York City, this group was bred in the system, many as principals, almost all with long experience at headquarters.

In each of the decision-making areas analyzed for the study, the supervisory staff at headquarters was a primary participant.

In curriculum planning and development, the headquarters staff, lodged in the Bureau of Curriculum Research, exercises almost complete control over curriculum. The bureau is indirectly influenced by general changes in approach to certain disciplines, that is, the new math, but for the most part it follows a regular routine of three- to five-year review of curriculum bulletins, revisions, and presentation of new guidelines. The actual implementation of curriculum is dependent upon the action of principals and classroom teachers, and this varies considerably from school to school. Although the bureau has curriculum assistants attached to its staff on a part-time basis (40 per cent of their time is spent in the district superintendent's office), there is no planned program for assuring implementation. In fact, the director of the bureau expressed his reservations about their role in implementation.

In budgeting, the distribution and allocation of funds is determined on a division, bureau, and department basis with the staff person in charge the major determinant of his own needs. School appropriations are largely allocated on the basis of pre-established ratios, providing a prescribed number of teachers, specialized personnel, textbooks, and so forth, according to the number of students and the category of school. The district superintendent exercises no discretion in budgeting or in the distribution of personnel. Headquarters personnel monopolize decisions in this area. Old programs are automatically continued, and the adoption of new ones is dependent upon the approval of the superintendent in charge of a division or bureau. The superintendent relies on the judgment of the supervisory bureaucracy for evaluation of programs and needs. There is no internal audit except for a rather cursory and technical review by the small budget office staff. There is no procedure for evaluation of performance or elimination of ineffective programs in conjunction with the budget. Members of the Board of Education have noted their inability to evaluate the complex budget document and make recommendations, and city review of the budget in the past has been extremely limited.

In another major area of policy, school integration, the supervisory staff has been a major participant as a vetoing group. School integration policy was the only area of school policy explored in the study in which there was wide community participation. This was an outcome of the diverse interests and goals of the participants as well as the delicacy of the problem. The supervisory staff, in its inaction and public disapproval of stated board policy, contributed inadvertently to that broadening of participation. The board itself demonstrated its own lack of resolve in promulgating general policy favoring rotation of teachers, school pairing, rezoning, and school reorganization, yet waiting upon the bureaucracy for implementation for eight years. The supervisory staff, for its part, has not only ignored board policy but has disagreed publicly through statements of policy by their own supervisory organizations. Several of these organizations have opposed each of the proposed plans at one time or another. The More Effective Schools program was the only plan they supported fully. It was the only plan that would not have interfered with the existing structure, because it entailed only the expansion of funds and personnel for selected schools.

In the other two areas studied, salary increases and selection of the superintendent, one would assume that the supervisory staff would have no direct influence. Actually, they are inclined to support fully higher salaries for teachers, since their own salaries hinge on an index based on increases proportionate to those received by the teaching staff. The ability of the supervisory staff to gain statutory legislation establishing the index is a significant indication of its strength. As a group, however, they are not direct participants in salary negotiations.

In the selection of the superintendent, members of the supervisory staff are indirectly and directly influential. They represent the most immediate and likely source of supply, since most superintendents are selected from their ranks. They are consulted individually by board members and interest groups for suggestions whenever a superintendent is appointed.

Their own preference for an "inside" appointment has been a major contributing factor in board decisions. The board, of necessity, is concerned with the ability of the staff to relate to the superintendent. The recent unhappy experience with the selection of an "outsider" will more than likely encourage even greater reliance on the supervisory staff in the selection of the superintendent. Board members have indicated their concern with the enormous power of the supervisory staff and the inbred system of selection, but they despair in their inability to change the system.

In other areas studied, tangential to the five decision-making areas, it was evident that the professional headquarters staff, particularly the core of the thirty-odd supervisors, were major policy-makers. Overcentralization has long plagued the school system, and several studies have stressed the need for thorough administrative reorganization, yet board support and efforts by the last two superintendents along these lines have been thwarted by the vested interests of the staff in maintaining the status quo. In school construction and planning, the assistant superintendent in charge has successfully ignored Planning Commission recommendations, as well as integration policy, and is relatively free of other controls. He has become the expeditor of school construction. In the assignment of administrative and teaching staffs to schools, the central headquarters staff has recently increased its prerogatives. Much of the power that has been lodged in the central staff has prevented the expansion of the role of the district superintendents, who, although nominally supervisory, are an anachronism in the system.

DISTRICT SUPERINTENDENTS

Because so much evidence pinpointed power in the professional staff, the author considered it worthwhile to explore more fully the particular role of the supervisors in the field. The district superintendents (thirty-one of them) represent the only means by which the present structure can achieve administrative decentralization and the system's only source of professional liaison with local school needs. A detailed questioning of nine district superintendents suggested that they were not participants in the formulation of school policy. Their ineffectiveness could be attributed to their general lack of budgetary and personnel powers and the inferior caliber of appointments. District superintendents have no discretion in the distribution of funds and the most limited kind of discretion in the assignment of personnel. Their own staffs are small and largely clerical.

The district superintendent acts as a buffer for parent dissatisfaction not resolved by the school principal. Most of the local superintendents interviewed complained that they were not involved significantly in budgeting, curriculum implementation, assignment of personnel, and general formulation of school policy. Very few had meaningful relations with the headquarters staff. Their contact with the schools in the area was limited to periodic school visits and meetings with principals, but rarely with teachers. Even if they could pinpoint special local needs, they felt that there was not much that they could do about dealing with them. The study of the role of the district superintendents verified their dependence on headquarters staff, not only for long-range policy, but in day-to-day decision-making. The variety of directives and forms to be completed for headquarters was a source of severe complaint by the district superintendents. Although a part of the professional bureaucracy, they are probably the least influential as a group. Their lack of participation in policy decisions gives support to the central conclusion of the study: that the central supervisory staff has cornered the power market.

Teacher Participation

Because of the power it wields in collective bargaining, the United Federation of Teachers (UFT) sets major policy. The membership of the union in New York City is over 30,000. It is the official bargaining agent for the city's 50,000 teachers. The union contract determines wide areas of personnel practices, expenditures, and teaching-time allotments. Because salaries and teachers' benefits represent close to half the total education budget, the union is directly involved in matters of finance. The potential power of the union to participate in other policy areas has not been fully realized because of its own choice in concentrating its attention on salary scales and related benefits. Few teachers participate in the most obvious area in which their expertise would be extremely helpful, that is in the development of curriculum. With the exception of a few high school specialists, the Bureau of Curriculum Research has not involved teachers in its programs. There is no evidence to suggest that teachers were consulted on integration policy or the problems of ghetto schools. The union repeatedly voiced its objection to any plan calling for the rotation of teachers, and that has remained a voluntary program. Its only constructive plan was the More Effective Schools proposal. Teachers are not at all involved in budgeting or in selection of the superintendent, either through the union or as individuals.[28]

In 1962, after the first strike in the history of the school system, the UFT negotiated the largest single wage increase ever granted the city's teachers. The UFT gained strength from local union and public support of labor. Its membership expanded considerably as a result of its strike action in 1962, giving it unquestioned priority as collective-bargaining agent for the city's teachers. In its negotiations, the union appealed to the mayor, the Central Labor Council, and the educational interest groups for support. The union has seemingly bypassed the board and the superintendent to use its strength where it is most effective—at city hall.

The union can be viewed as representing another large "professional" group in policy-making in education. Its membership comprises the largest group of professionals in the system. In the few limited areas (outside of salary scale and fringe benefits) on which it has taken a public position, the UFT has largely been motivated by a desire to maintain the status quo. It has supported policies that create rigidities in the system and it can hardly be considered a proponent of change. Board policy on rotation of teachers was met with an appeal by the union to the mayor to prevent implementation. The union has publicly and privately fought transfers of experienced teachers to difficult schools. It also questioned the advisability of 4–4–4 school reorganization because the plan threatened the status of the junior high school teacher.[29] In interviews conducted with union leaders, it was clear that they themselves saw a conflict in objective education and professional goals and the narrow interest of the membership. In some instances, they expressed concern that their own positions of power in the union might be threatened if they violated those narrower interests.

Local Civic and Interest Groups

As has already been demonstrated, education decision-making is closely circumscribed in the functional specialization characteristic of New York City politics. The professional bureaucracy is answerable only to an organized clientele, which reflects the same kind of specialization. Two interest groups in New York City share the responsibility for overseeing education policy: the United Parents Association (UPA) and the Public Education Association (PEA). Board membership in both organizations overlaps, and their professional staffs work closely together. The UPA is a central city-wide organization made up of delegates elected by school parent associations (who have elected membership in the coordinating agency), while the PEA is a composite group, made up of other interest groups in the city. Board members of the PEA represent the major civic groups in New York City.

The UPA, the membership of which is composed largely of middle-class parents, is primarily concerned with local school problems and facilities and has directed much of its attention to these ends.[30] In more recent years, site-selection controversies and school integration problems have occupied much of their time. The UPA speaks for parents and maintains a direct concern with the immediate effects of policy on local school situations. It has, at times, taken general policy positions on "key issues" and, when possible, makes use of direct influence with board members. A current member of the board was an officer of the UPA prior to her appointment and still maintains active communication with the organization. The UPA's executive director was recently appointed staff adviser to the board. The UPA has supported the appointment of supervisory staff in the Board of Education and appears to have viable contacts within the bureaucracy. Although it is unlikely that the UPA could stimulate broad city-wide parent-group support for certain policies, the threat of its large membership has been used effectively to influence board decisions.

The PEA is a composite group representing professional education interests in the city, outside of the school system itself. Its activities have centered on the more long-range educational aspects of school policy. Its strategy has been to study special problems in the system and make public recommendations based on these reports. One PEA report contributed significantly to rethinking and reshaping school policy on vocational schools.[31] In general, the views of UPA and PEA on any issue are never far apart.

In the decisions analyzed for this study, both organizations were participants in selected areas of policy in a most limited way. Their role as overseers of educational policy is generally supportive rather than critical. Their inclination is to work within the structure, never suggesting radical change, and focusing on particular problems. Both groups exercised little influence in the area of curriculum. On occasion, one or both have made general statements regarding the need for inclusion of material in the curriculum, or emphasis in a given field, but neither has indicated special concern with curriculum matters. Both have supported increased school expenditures and larger city and state appropriations. The PEA has tended to support greater independence for the school system in all areas, whereas the UPA seems to prefer continued reliance on city support. Their concern with the board is only in terms of appropriations for particular programs to which they are committed. They also lobby for state and city support for over-all increases in the school budget.

The Citizens Committee for Children, which formerly played a larger role in education affairs, has concentrated its efforts on budget review. Each year it holds hearings in its own offices with the supervisory bureaucracy to review the budget for the next year. Representatives of the UPA and the PEA are usually in attendance. Few changes in the budget result; the exercise serves to solicit interest-group support for programs and findings.

The screening-panel device for selection of the superintendent has given the UPA and the PEA a more direct role in the selection of board members. Both groups are represented on the panel and exercise a notable influence in the selection process.

The PEA has sought a direct role in the selection of the last four superintendents. A change in its influence was discernible when the new board was instituted in 1961. Prior to that time, they had not been successful in their pressure to bring in an "outsider," and their recommendations had been virtually ignored. They were, however, a direct influence in the last two appointments.

Public Participation

Public participation in policy-making can come through two obvious channels: voting and organized interest groups. In New York City, there are no public votes on school issues. The assumption that voting in itself automatically assures meaningful public participation has long been questioned by political scientists. Within the context of a specialized area of decision-making, such as education, the degree of pluralism must be measured in terms of the role and degree of influence of the various public interest groups and elected officials.

As has already been demonstrated, elected officials in New York City play a declining role in education policy-making. Two newspapers in the city report regularly on education matters. Criticism in both has been mild and infrequent. Ethnic and religious groups have been satisfied with adequate representation on the board. Catholic groups intermittently become concerned with textbooks and curriculum, but rely on the Catholic Teachers Association and personal contact with the board to make their minor demands.

Public participation in school policy formulation is circumscribed by the lack of visible decision-making, the shortage of information available to the public on most issues, and a deficiency in the means for participation. Parent associations are active in individual schools, dealing with highly localized and personalized problems. The highly centralized organization of the school system is a deterrent to communication between parents groups and policy-makers. Parents and teachers, the agents closest to the child, are virtually removed from policy decisions.

The school integration issue is the only area in which public response has been vociferous and active. The integration issue has attracted the widest participation of any policy decision explored. Local groups of every shade of opinion have organized to oppose or defend individual plans. Among the most vociferous have been the Parents and Taxpayers Association (PAT) and their opposition, Parents and Neighbors United for Integrated Quality Education (EQUAL). Civil rights groups originally entered the school policy field with the single concern of achieving an integrated system; now they are in the forefront of the demands for decentralization. Local civic groups, chambers of commerce, councilmen, and candidates for public office have voiced strong opinions on proposals. Many of these groups and individuals have never before been involved in school affairs and their current concern has been limited to the integration issue and its ramifications. Public involvement in the integration issue indicated that more widespread participation results when there is no consensus among those with power and when decisions thus become more visible.

Perhaps the most significant development in school decision-making in the last five years has surrounded the integration issue. Aside from its social and human implications, it has had an important political impact. For the past two decades, superintendents, boards, and school bureaucracies have been freewheeling, with little outside pressure. They have successfully closed off school policy formulation from elected local government officials and civic groups. The integration issue has broken open the monopoly of power vested in the small core of school officials. It has raised serious questions regarding the role of professionals, their goals and interests in school policy.

Consensus decision-making, confined to the professionals, limits policy alternatives as well as public participation. A balance between professionalism and public participation is the desired end. Conflict between competing forces and differences in interests and goals guarantee the visibility of policy-making and encourage public participation. These are the characteristics of a system that are most likely to produce change and encourage adaptability.

Lowi points out that changes in New York City have come from three sources: (1) a single unpredictable individual, (2) sources outside the city (the state or federal governments), and (3) a reform or minority party. The last is the most frequent source of innovation.[32] This conclusion would suggest that changes in education will depend on Mayor Lindsay's leadership and perhaps on his ability to enlist greater public support and interest in education policy.

In any policy-making structure, the role of participants and potential participants is relevant. The resources of particular groups or individuals —and the way they are used—are essential factors in evaluating power. The usual assumption that wealth is a primary resource is denied in educational decision-making in New York City. The key resource appears to be professional expertise. The education bureaucracy has become virtually self-contained, sealed off by special training and knowledge. It has expanded its role and limited conflict by manipulation of issues to assert that they are wholly dependent upon expert judgment, which it alone has.

In a rather concise—and, one might say, almost modest—characterization of the educational world in New York City, Sayre and Kaufman noted: "On balance, the school official enjoys an unusual capacity for self-government."[33] In fact, with the exception of the integration issue, there are only three or four areas in which any appreciable outside influence is brought to bear on matters of education policy. Such influence is most direct in regard to the religious and racial balance on the Board of Education and in the distribution of appointments to the supervisory staff. To these items should be added the mayor's role in the determination of teachers' salaries. Some outside influence can also be seen in the negotiations for individual school locations, the bargaining for school construction contracts, and the granting of minor favors by local district superintendents (in their limited sphere of operation). Basically, however, there are no forces acting to broaden education policy and to balance it with other city policy.

As a political subsystem, the New York City school system can only be described as narrow, convergent, and dominated by a consensual elite. This description is in sharp contrast to the usual view of New York City politics as "open"—or to the somewhat typical suggestion, in this instance by Sayre and Kaufman, that "no part of the city's large and varied population is alienated from participation in the system."[34]

For the political scientist, such a disparity poses a basic problem in creating meaningful operational categories by which power can be analyzed. The results of this study indicate the real need to examine how power is exercised in individual areas of activity. Such examinations should explore differences in the distribution of power, the kinds and levels of participation, the degree of integration by city-wide elements, and the role of nonprofessional and nonsupportive interest groups. Working from this type of analysis, the methodological concern with pluralist and power-elite concepts may be shifted to the development of more quantitative measurements of the determinants of open and closed political systems. Such an approach will also provide greater insights into the sources and possibilities for change in a political system.

Notes

1. Wallace S. Sayre and Herbert Kaufman, *Governing New York City* (New York: Russell Sage Foundation, 1960), p. 241.

2. An area omitted which later proved worthy of further exploration was school-site selection and construction. The study reviewed this area only as it related to the integration issue and budgeting.

3. The author analyzed all newspaper items in two daily newspapers for a five-year period, recording all public statements and reports on education policy. These items were categorized by participant and issue, providing a general picture of the public roles and concerns of all participants. A series of detailed, selective interviews with professional staff and board members was conducted. Data were cross-checked in interviews with participants outside the school system, including staff members of the Public Education Association, United Federation of Teachers, and other civic groups. Lawyers and educators knowledgeable in school affairs were also consulted. A special survey questionnaire was developed for longer interviews with the field superintend-

ents. The files of civic groups were researched for relevant data on specific issues. A search was made of all professional and popular literature for accounts of decision-making in other school systems for comparative purposes.

4. Theodore Lowi, *At the Pleasure of the Mayor* (New York: The Free Press of Glencoe, 1965), p. 199, as well as Sayre and Kaufman, *op. cit.*, p. 716, suggested that the system (referring to the city-wide power structure) is more favorable to defenders of the status quo than to those of innovation.

5. Nicholas Masters, Robert H. Salisbury, and Thomas H. Eliot, *State Politics and the Public Schools* (New York: Alfred A. Knopf, 1964), reviews the role of state educational officers in local school policy in Michigan, Illinois, and Missouri. James Conant's concern with the monopoly of the professional educators is particularly relevant. The professionals run the local school systems, control government policy in state administrative posts, and direct the teachers colleges.

6. State Education Commissioner's Advisory Committee on Human Relations and Community Tensions, "Desegregating the Public Schools of New York City," May 12, 1964.

7. Stephen K. Bailey, Richard T. Frost, and Paul E. March, *Schoolmen and Politics* (Syracuse, N.Y.: Syracuse University Press, 1961), and Michael A. Usdan, *The Political Power of Education in New York State* (New York: Institute of Administrative Research, Teachers College, Columbia University, 1963).

8. George D. Strayer and Louis E. Yavner, *Administrative Management of the School System of New York City* (New York: Mayor's Committee on Management Survey, 1951), Vol. I.

9. *Local Law No. 19*, passed by the New York City Council, April 6, 1962.

10. *Education Law*, sec. 2553, subdiv. 1, 2, amended L. 1961.

11. Scanning of five years of school news stories in two prominent New York City papers reveals that Mayor Wagner's public statements were almost always in response to public pressures.

12. *The New York Times*, March 1, 1965.

13. A member of the board disagreed with this interpretation, suggesting that Mayor Wagner had taken the initiative. The same person, however, confirmed the author's view that Wagner did not interfere with the board in education policy. Officers of the United Federation of Teachers confirmed the author's interpretation.

14. In 1961, the press gave credit to the superintendent for his successful negotiation on salaries but neglected to explain why the mayor was involved in the final settlement.

15. Edward C. Banfield, *Political Influence* (New York: The Free Press of Glencoe, 1961).

16. Expectations based on the religious formula were pointed up by an item appearing in the *World Telegram and Sun*, May 29, 1963, reporting criticism expressed by the Catholic Teachers Association of Mayor Wagner's failure to appoint a Catholic to replace a retiring member, Brendan Byrne. Months later, when a Jewish member of the board retired, a Catholic was appointed to replace him, thereby reestablishing the 3–3–3 balance.

17. In the period from 1945 to 1961, the three board Presidents later moved on to political office. Maxmillian Moss was elected Surrogate in Brooklyn, Arthur Levitt was elected State Controller, and Charles Silver became a personal advisor to Mayor Wagner. This would indicate not only their closeness to Mayor Wagner but their active participation in the Democratic Party.

18. The three superintendents chosen from the bureaucracy were John Wade, William Jansen, and Bernard Donovan; the fourth mentioned is John Theobald. Of the five, Calvin Gross was the only "outsider" appointed superintendent. At the time of the Gross appointment, the High School Administrative Assistants Association, the Association of Assistant Superintendents, and the Junior High School Principals Association reminded the board that "home-grown talent should not be overlooked" (*The New York Times*, April 25, 1962; July 2, 1962).

19. Lowi, *op. cit.*, p. 199.

20. David Rogers, Unpublished manuscript on school desegregation. (Center for Urban Education). Sheldon *et al.*, "Administrative Implications of Integration Plans for Schools," in Albert J. Reiss, Jr. (ed.), *Schools in a Changing Society* (New York: The Free Press of Glencoe, 1965).

21. *Education Law*, sec. 2564, amended by L.,1961.

22. The superintendent recently admitted the need for delegating budget and personnel power to local district superintendents (*The New York Times*, February 20, 1966).

23. Allan Talbott, "Needed: A New Breed of School Superintendents," *Harpers Magazine* (February, 1966), pp. 81–87.

24. Personal contact with board members by the staff is not uncommon. Two years ago the situation was so bad that the superintendent issued a statement forbidding memos from the supervisory staff directly to board members (*World Telegram and Sun*, November 15, 1963, p. 47).

25. Talbott, *loc. cit.*

26. Both the High School Principals Association and the Junior High School Principals Association have expressed opposition to the 5–3–4 and 4–4–4 organization plans. Several associations opposed the elimination of the IQ examination, school pairing proposals, and the comprehensive high school plan.

27. The new superintendent appears to be more concerned with administrative matters.

28. In a study of UFT executive board members' perceptions of who makes school policy, most of those questioned attributed little power to the union, except in salary matters. In most areas, they cited the board and the superintendents as wielders of power. Alan Rosenthal, "Pedagogues and Power," *Urban Affairs Quarterly* (September, 1966).

29. Junior high school teachers represent the hard core of union members. The 4–4–4 system represents a reorganization based on a four-year program on three levels: primary school, intermediate school, high school.

30. The UPA is a recent recipient of a New York City Anti-Poverty Operations Board grant to encourage parent participation in schools in underprivileged communities.

31. *Reorganizing Secondary Education in New York City*, Education Guidance and Work Committee of the Public Education Association (October, 1963).

32. Lowi, *op. cit.*

33. Sayre and Kaufman, *op. cit.*, p. 285.

34. *Ibid.*, p. 720.

11. BOSTON: EDUCATION'S LAST HURRAH

PETER SCHRAG

Thirty years ago, in Mayor James Michael Curley's Boston, the Cabots spoke only to the Lowells, and the Irish ran the city; in the "new" Boston of the 1960's, boasting urban progress and redevelopment, any citizen will speak to almost any other, honored political habits are breaking down, and even Scollay Square—the boozy honky-tonk of all-night bars, burlesque houses, and other delights of the flesh—has been razed by the renewers. But at 15 Beacon Street, the headquarters of the Boston School Committee, and in some 200 public elementary and secondary schools—many of them more than a half century old—the Sullivans still speak mostly to the O'Learys, the Caseys, and the McDonoughs! It is their Boston Irishness—political, parochial, and personable—that has given the schools of the city, comprising 93,000 children and 3,800 teachers, problems and qualities that make them distinctive and sometimes notorious in American education.

Boston is every American's Great Historical Site, the city of the Massacre and the Tea Party, of Sam Adams and Paul Revere, of Anne Hutchinson and John Cotton, and of all those proper people who once lived in the Back Bay and on Beacon Hill but who are now as plentiful in exurbs like Marblehead, Milton, and Cohasset. Like many another American metropolis, Boston has been savagely victimized by the flight of the middle class from the central city (although Beacon Hill is still *the* place to live); unlike others it has had—until recently—almost no major development since the Depression. Boston has been hemmed in by jealous suburbs and hobbled by fragmented political control, some of it vested in the Governor of Massachusetts or in special metropolitan districts by people who feared the rising Irish city politicians. Concurrently, Boston has been constricted for more than a half century by financial and social conservatism that preferred a safe 5 per cent and a Friday seat at Symphony (rarely called the Boston Symphony) to anything that smacked too much of risk, adventure, or association with new

Reprinted from *Saturday Review*, May 21, 1966, pp. 56–58 ff. Copyright 1966 Saturday Review, Inc. Reprinted by permission of Saturday Review, Inc. and the author.

groups. Thus, when the Irish and the Italians arrived during the great immigration, they found a city whose main avenues to advancement began with politics and civil service, not with corporate enterprise or industrial growth.

Redevelopment, spurred by two energetic mayors, John B. Hynes and . . . John F. Collins, is now generating new construction and initiative, and even a new urban optimism, but older attitudes and patterns linger. The Irish who live in South Boston, Dorchester, and Charlestown still dominate politics and the civil service—and that includes public education—while the growing Negro population has turned the formerly Jewish Roxbury and North Dorchester area into a black ghetto. Boston's recent school battles—fought mainly on the issue of integration—are in great measure a confrontation of that increasingly militant Negro population (supported by white liberals) with the Irish, Italians, and other lower–middle-class families (and some upper–middle-class homeowners in newer neighborhoods) who comprise the majority of the city's population. Concurrently, they also reflect the struggle of the new and modern against political forces and attitudes that have shaped Boston for more than fifty years.

While Bostonians—and many others—debate the politics of the elected School Committee, speculating whether Mrs. Louise Day Hicks, its most prominent member and leading defender of "neighborhood" schools, will run for mayor,* or perhaps lead a national crusade against school integration, the professional educators at 15 Beacon Street carry on much as they have for thirty years, running a system that displays severe urban problems and decay, that is plagued by the middle-class exodus, and that mirrors, for better or worse, an educational history unmatched in America. Operating alongside a parochial system that educates about one-third of Boston's children, and competing with some of of the most prestigious suburban systems in the country (Newton, Brookline, Wellesley, Lexington), the Boston schools suffer from a tax base that has failed to keep pace with rising educational costs, from a rapidly growing proportion of deprived children (the system is now 25 per cent Negro), and from a constitutional division of power that effectively gives the mayor—not the School Committee—the ultimate authority over school budget increases and new building construction.

Boston ranks low in nationally standardized public achievement tests, in the percentage of students going on to college, and in new school construction, and it is often criticized for an educational conservatism that refuses to keep pace with the academic innovations so visible in the neighboring suburbs and across the country. Like most other major cities, it also has an increasing number of overwhelmingly Negro schools,

* In 1967, she did run and was defeated.—*Ed. note.*

many of them located in aging and substandard buildings. The critics charge that the School Committee's unwillingness to recognize and ameliorate the *de facto* segregation—and the resulting battles—have served to hide the educational shortcomings of the system. And these shortcomings, they feel, are severe.

Attempts are now being made to combat some of the problems. Under Superintendent William H. Ohrenberger, a former football coach and teacher who has headed the system since 1963, Boston is now planning and initiating compensatory programs and experiments to mitigate cultural disadvantages and to provide other special services for deprived children, to increase already competitive teachers' salaries (partly under union pressure), to construct a new campus high school for 5,000 students, and to take other measures to meet its educational problem. Boston is dotted with demonstration projects and special ventures. Yet the system derives its real character not from any program or set of problems, but from the ethnic and political traditions and struggles of the people who have been called the only oppressed majority in the world and who make up two-thirds of the city's population.

If the Irish are dominant in the city, they have practically overwhelmed the schools, taking over from strict Yankee schoolmasters who maintained traditions of quality and order that can be traced back to the beginnings of the Boston Latin School—which still remains the pride of the Boston system—more than three centuries ago. (The history of public education in Boston is inevitably associated with the Latin School and with the students who have attended it since its founding in 1635—Cotton Mather, Sam Adams, John Hancock, Emerson, three presidents of Harvard, Henry Ward Beecher, Santayana . . .) But when the Irish took over—and many have been outstanding teachers and administrators—they seldom brought educational reform or liberalism; more often, they came with attitudes nurtured in a conservative Church and in a parochial establishment as inflexible and repressive as the classic masters of the Yankee tradition. Concurrently, municipal reformers, fearing political shenanigans, enveloped the whole system with rigid civil service routines and at-large School Committee elections, making minority representation and professional deviation almost impossible. Thus, the spirit of John Dewey made few substantial inroads. At the same time, the style of the Church and the parochial schools—which are themselves now changing—was never far away.

The critics of the Boston system like to accuse it of inbreeding and nepotism. They point out that all the members of the board of superintendents—the senior staff of the system—are Catholics, and that all but one or two are graduates of Boston College; that relatives of School Committee members, including a couple of brothers, are teaching in the system; and that Boston, through its attitude and hiring practices, has never encouraged outsiders to apply for jobs. They have pictured the whole establishment, from the School Committee down, as a closed club of unimaginative civil servants lacking interest in outside ideas, lacking contact with the city's great universities, and lacking initiative to innovate. One leading critic—himself a Catholic—has privately called them "real Romans, responsive to authority, and always prepared to take orders." To succeed in Boston, he said, "you have to be a Catholic. It would be unthinkable for Boston to hire a non-Catholic as superintendent. This is a closed system. They never go outside and they never let outsiders in."

In response, members of the administration and the School Committee indignantly rush to defend "our dedicated teachers"—a phrase used constantly—and point to the new ventures with deprived children and to a whole series of budding, though still small, associations with Harvard, Northeastern, Boston University, and other colleges. They also emphasize that in Boston all promotions and appointments are made on the basis of tests and rated lists derived from a point scale not subject to political machinations, that a national campaign is under way to recruit new teachers, and that the Latin School, which still sends every graduate to college (twenty-two to Harvard in 1965), wins far more than its share of national awards.

But the battles about educational quality—about the level and type of vocational training, about administrative conservatism, about the lack of guidance personnel—have been muffled in recent years by the issue of racial imbalance and the personality of School Committee member Louise Day Hicks. For over two years, the School Committee has refused officially to recognize the issue of *de facto* segregation, staring down pickets and boycotts and petitions, and earning itself a national reputation as a popularly elected bastion of resistance to civil rights demands. In the summer of 1965, when Ohrenberger's administration predicted overcrowding in certain Roxbury ghetto schools for September, the School Committee, led by Mrs. Hicks, vetoed the superintendent's apparently innocent plan to bus children to buildings in other neighborhoods, even though these same remedies for overcrowding had been used previously in a similar situation. In response, Negro parents, acting under the system's open enrollment policy, inaugurated their own busing program (Operation Exodus), hauling children to underutilized schools in predominantly white neighborhoods. (Operation Exodus . . . costs $1,200 a week, most of it raised in the ghetto and the suburbs, in "Mothers' Marches," and through charity functions.) And as the busing, dramatizing the racial imbalance controversy, got underway, so did the 1965 School Committee election. For Negro leaders, the issue was the absolute and comparative inadequacy of the ghetto schools—which, they charged, had inferior books and teachers—and the intransigent attitude of the School Committee, which refused even to recognize the existence of *de facto* segregation. For the incumbent majority, the principal plank was preservation of the neighborhood school.

But the campaign made it clear that the more the issues were explained—by either side—the more support Mrs. Hicks received. "People around here are afraid of Negroes," said a South Boston Irish father. "There is no crime, no rapes. They think Mrs. Hicks is keeping them out." Mrs. Hicks, who shudders that she might have received the support of some bigots, nevertheless agrees that it was the matter of racial imbalance and neighborhood schools, nothing else, that decided the election.

And yet, while it is clear that the outcome was largely determined by frightened homeowners in South Boston, Dorchester, and elsewhere who fear the influx of Negroes—and even their presence in the schools—the election was, in some respects, also a rerun of contests and struggles that have taken place in Boston for more than half a century. On the one side were the Irish, the Italians, and others of the middle- and lower-middle classes. On the other were the reform-oriented Citizens for the Boston Schools—young lawyers, League of Women Voters ladies, social workers, academics, as well as a host of individuals that Curley would simply have called "googoos" (after the old Boston Good Government Association)—persons more interested in municipal improvement and abstract political morality than in personal friendships and power, more associated with Beacon Hill, Harvard, the banks, and Yankeedom than with South Boston and the working man. (The Citizens, however, endorsed a slate that included three Irishmen, a Negro, and an Italian woman.) Thus, when Mrs. Hicks's neighbors in Ward 7 spoke about "standing up to *them*"—and many did—they seemed to be thinking not only of the Negro civil rights leaders, but also of all the other unnamed, nebulous devils associated with corporate exploitation, upper-class snobbery, and suburban hypocrisy. For more than forty years the respectable and well-heeled had neglected the inner city and its slums. Now they were in effect telling the Irish and the Italians to atone for their old sins and to balance the schools.

In response, the electorate gave Louise Hicks an overwhelming majority (65 per cent of the votes cast), replaced Arthur Gartland, the only liberal School Committee member, with the otherwise unknown brother of a city councilman, and set the system on a collision course with a new Massachusetts law requiring communities to take steps to eliminate racial imbalance in the schools and to arrange attendance districts and new construction to minimize it. (In April, 1966, $4 million in state funds were withheld from the city pending submission of an acceptable plan of compliance.) In Roxbury, there was even talk about somehow seceding from the Boston system. The vote also seemed to indicate that the quality of education in Boston was not a major issue (someone pointed out that a campaign about crowded classrooms has little appeal to parents of parochial-school children crammed into rooms with fifty others); that it was likely, indeed, that most people hardly cared; and that substantial numbers of school employees, who have traditionally been a political influence, supported the incumbent majority. Arthur Gartland had questioned pay raises for custodians, had challenged special increments for other nonacademic employees, and had never spoken about "our dedicated teachers."

Mrs. Hicks had. The 1965 campaign, and the year of protests and boycotts preceding it, elevated her to the role of prime defender of the teachers and the protector of "our children." A large woman who likes wool suits with fur trim, Mrs. Hicks was, with most of the present School Committee, first elected in 1961, partly on a reform campaign to restore the Latin School to its past glory, partly on the strength of her many contacts and friends in South Boston, and partly on the name of her father, a South Boston judge important enough to have a boulevard named for him. A lawyer, married to an engineer who meticulously avoids the limelight, she has now become a symbol not only of neighborhoodism, but also of resistance to exploitation and oppression, whether they have to do with racial balance or the placement and treatment of teachers. She is proud that she helped initiate a program for returning dropouts, that the city's program for retarded children has been expanded, and that compensatory education for disadvantaged children has been introduced. But her major theme is constantly the protection of the children in their own environment, her concern with the "cultural shock" that busing would produce, and her effort to provide special care where necessary. As she speaks at a gathering or from her seat at the School Committee, she makes it clear that *she* is concerned about all the teachers and all the children. She has become Boston's head mother.

The image is important, and entirely consistent with a system that values obedience and respect for authority as much as intellectual achievement and a questioning temper. Boston was among the last cities in America to permit married women to teach, and it still employs a substantial number of elderly maiden teachers and principals. Graduates of Boston Normal (now Boston State College), or of Regis College or Emmanuel College, they take pride in instilling character and discipline, good conduct and citizenship. For two generations, teachers of this type —as well as the men who came from Boston College during the Depression—set the tone in the Boston schools. And the tone persists.

Neckties are still mandatory dress in most of the public high schools, corporal punishment is still permitted, and cleanliness and order still seem to be among the first things pointed out to a visitor. One hears relatively little about individual development, about teaching children to question or to enjoy, or about anyone moving at his own pace. In the high schools, while a number of teachers are instituting new materials and approaches, especially in the sciences, the older hands are likely to operate from traditional textbooks, and to adhere faithfully to the one they like. "I wish I could get some of them to use more than one book," said a high school department chairman. "But they all want to work with the one they've used." This kind of conservatism is, in some measure, built into the structure of a city and school system as civil service–minded as Boston, for the very procedures preventing political abuses also tend to stamp new personnel with the old image. Boston's teacher examinations, often cited as proof of the city's selectivity, are oriented toward traditional styles, adherence to textbooks, and the conventional wisdom. In American history, for example, applicants are asked:

On an outline map of the United States:
   a) Trace the route of the Erie Canal, naming and locating its terminal cities.
   b) Trace the route of the Santa Fe trail, naming and locating its terminal cities. . . .

Match each of the individuals listed in the first column with the historic incident or book associated with him and listed in the second column:

D. G. Farragut	The Alamo
Davy Crockett	Black Friday
Jim Fiske	Capture of New Orleans
(etc.)	(etc.)

Why is the Senate a much more influential body than the House of Representatives?

What aspect of the make-up of the Senate is open to serious criticism?

Each of these questions can be answered by someone who has studied a high school textbook; none requires genuine historical skills, ability to deal with historical materials, or any real sense of the techniques and limitations of the field. At the same time, the examinations—especially in the primary grades, where they seem more relevant—insure a measure of competence and prevent either political or educational atrocities that might otherwise have taken place.

The gem of the Boston system is the Latin School, which, along with the Girls' Latin School and the Technical High School, draws students from all parts of the city. (All three are academically selective, as compared to the nine district high schools, which must admit all students living in a particular geographical area.) At the Latin School, more than at any other city institution, high standards and quality are associated with rigor and discipline, with carefully structured classes, and with hard work. At Latin *everyone* is prepping for college, not only for the customary suburban status reasons, but because success here means *economic* advancement. The students, many of them from working-class families, report that the pressure is phenomenal, that homework averages about three hours a night, and that genuine deviation is difficult. Overwhelmed by the Emersons, the Brookses, and the Adamses on the one hand and by parental pressure and college ambitions on the other, 2,000 boys at Boston Latin are in many respects far more reminiscent of those at a staid private academy than at a public high school.

And indeed, in its own way, that's what the place is. "The Latin School," said Wilfred L. O'Leary, the present headmaster, "is a state of mind. It's the jewel of education in Boston; if it's nothing, the rest is nothing." Located in a forty-year-old building near the Harvard Medical School and surrounded by other educational and medical institutions, Boston Latin is almost like a separate enclave in the city system—a special ward with a powerful constituency, a scholarship endowment close to $500,000, an uninterrupted relationship with Harvard, and a reputation so weighty that its organized alumni association, with several hundred active members, can still make itself heard downtown. O'Leary —who sometimes speaks of the school like an old New England headmaster, and sometimes like a ward boss—hopes to raise his scholarship endowment to $1 million, to find still better teachers through, among other things, a raiding process he calls "cannibalism"; and to build new classrooms and a new library. "I'm going to see the Mayor," he said, "and I'll tell him that if he gets us the new library I'll name it after him." In the academic realm, he said, "we're willing to try anything. We're using the new mathematics and the new physics. But I think the pendulum is swinging the other way back to the older approach. In math you've got to have answers."

But to O'Leary the most important problem is neither physical nor academic, but moral. "Our biggest job around here is the inculcation of ideals," he said. "We need people who are willing to defend the ramparts, the strong middle-of-the-roaders, who get things done. The people who can confront the tough jobs are the ones who haven't always breezed through everything, who are used to difficulties. They're the ones who are the strength of the society."

Most of the district high schools tend to reflect—though not necessarily to match—Boston Latin School style. They have never really broken from patterns established years ago, have never really undergone a major transformation; until recently, little in the system had. Although the high schools offer programs far more diverse than those of the Latin School—art majors, commercial courses, industrial programs—they also enroll substantial numbers of students in diluted "college" courses sometimes composed of only semirelevant material lifted from the traditional curriculum. In some instances, as at Dorchester High School, while older teachers still look back to the days when students were better motivated, and when they were not two to three years behind in their reading ability, teaching styles seem not to have changed significantly, and the curriculum—with certain major exceptions—still mirrors the Latin School style. (Dorchester, now part Irish, part Italian, and part Negro, was once 65 per cent Jewish.)

Nevertheless—and despite complaints like the *Boston Herald*'s that "rigidity is the rule"—the system has begun to change. In several schools, teachers recalled days not too long ago when children were not allowed to speak in the classroom at all (except in formal recitation), and when "all they ever did in Latin was parse, parse, parse." There are now, side by side with the elderly men and schoolmarms, young faces talking about "teaching processes, not memorizing facts," using the techniques of modern mathematics, discussing the merits of ungraded classes, and instituting the programs of the Biological Sciences Curriculum Study, Chemstudy, and other new courses; student volunteers and practice teachers from the surrounding universities are working in some of the elementary schools; and budding experiments with team teaching, with programed materials, and with new approaches in other areas have been launched.

Most innovation and planning—including a growing federally financed program of compensatory education and experimentation—have been centered in a new Office of Program Development (essentially a research and development staff) directed by an imported outsider named Evans Clinchy. Clinchy, who had been associated with Educational Services, Inc., an independent nonprofit organization of curriculum developers, and with Educational Facilities Laboratory, a Ford Foundation offshoot concerned with academic architecture and equipment, is every inch an Ivy Leaguer—a crew-cut, pipe-smoking, six-foot-four-inch anomaly in a system administered by civil servants who came up through the ranks. So far, according to Ohrenberger, who first proposed the office, the transplant has been successful. Clinchy has begun to build a staff, to plan a saturation project in a ghetto district, and, apparently, to gain the confidence of the administrators. Although it is still far too early to see results, even from the compensatory program, which started long before Clinchy was appointed, he has established himself as a major link with the outside as Boston's Ambassador to Washington and Cambridge. The very fact that he is *there*, and that he is helping to bring in federal funds, practice teachers from the neighboring universities, teaching materials from Educational Services, and specialists and ideas from almost everywhere, indicates that something new is under way.

And yet the city's problems remain immense. Children in the Negro ghetto, where teacher turnover is often high, fall progressively farther behind as they move through the schools. Buildings are substandard. There is little ability-grouping in the elementary schools or in the high schools. The city ranks low in the percentage of high school graduates continuing to higher education (about 25 per cent). Administrators are conservative, and new curricular ideas have thus far had only marginal impact. But the most serious problems are built into the system itself. Although 40 per cent of Boston's pupils attend schools that are more than fifty years old and although funds are available for new construction, no buildings have been started for over two years, partly because final authority rests in a separate commission controlled by the mayor and partly because the School Committee, with its penchant for political and personal grandstanding, has failed to act. (For over a year the School Committee argued about the site for a new 5,000-student campus high school first proposed in 1962. In February, 1966, it passed an order designating the location but—to suit its only Yankee member, a maverick named Joseph Lee—it had to vote that the school must be built with gymnasiums accommodating *all students at once*.) The School Committee's fortnightly deliberations, attended by genial bureaucrats greeting friends, interrupted by irrelevant questions, by lengthy interrogations, and by ex cathedra declarations on everything from urban renewal to the merits of physical exercise, make it clear that the whole system functions as much to impede as to foster change. Although the current chairman, Thomas S. Eisenstadt, a young attorney, has made attempts to keep the discussions moving (he was elected chairman on a promise to be brief), he has had only partial success. And yet, despite the endless discussions —many of which could be handled far better by the staff—many Bostonians agree that this is one of the best School Committees they've had. "This is the first group," someone said, "that I'm convinced is absolutely honest."

And yet, while there has never been evidence of political interference or favoritism, there are employees who believe that "it helps to be known downtown" and that merely being seen at School Committee meetings may facilitate a future promotion. In a system as small as Boston's, where the senior staff knows almost every administrator and many teachers and where one can always find people who once played football together or who were classmates at B.C., it would be surprising if the personal style that pervades much of the city did not occasionally make a difference. At the same time, the cozy criteria of friendship may not necessarily be worse than the mechanical ones of civil service.

Beneath the obvious problems—the smoldering issue of racial imbalance, the inability to start new schools, the budget restrictions (all increases require the mayor's approval)—is the agony of the city itself. Surrounded by jealous suburbs with a large voice in the legislature and suffering from divided authority, Boston, more than most major cities, has been robbed of the talent and the concern it requires. Serving a population of under 700,000 in a metropolitan area exceeding 2,500,000, the city's schools have become politically and socially decimated. The excellent school systems of Newton and Brookline, of Wellesley and Lexington, are the beneficiaries of Boston's departed middle class, of its inadequate tax base, and of its legislative weakness. Without the city's encumbrances, its inherited problems, they drew, and continue to draw, on the best the city had. Not surprisingly, most of them have achieved far more educational recognition. (Recently some of the suburbs offered to bus ghetto children into the predominantly white schools, but it is unlikely that they will ever accept a genuine metropolitan district—as recently proposed—that fully integrates children, taxes, and the concern of the community.)

The Boston schools are a product of this decimation, of the exodus of the middle and upper-middle classes, of the dominant Irish—who, a Negro leader said, "still act like a minority"—and of the civil servants who ran the system for years without a major complaint from anyone. Competing for support with parochial schools (whose patrons have to pay double for their children's education), the schools have been dependent on the interest and commitment of ethnic groups that have had relatively little regard for intellectual achievement, and who have often followed other routes to advancement. These groups may well have associated quality with stern inflexibility and repression (for what models, other than the Latin and the parochial schools, were available?) and have directed their urban radicalism not only against the minions of the First National Bank and Beacon Hill, but also against the cultural standards they represent. "There isn't any Windsor Castle around here," said a person long familiar with Boston. "So where do you direct that hostility?" As a consequence, the schools were only as good as the civil servants, working with an inherited structure, could or would make them, and only as good as their political School Committees would allow.

Now, for the first time in years, other groups—the absent Yankees, the civil rights leaders, the managers and promoters of the New Boston, even, in its own way, the Church—are beginning to take an interest in the affairs at 15 Beacon Street and in the system it controls. The small alliance of old and new Protestants (Yankees and Negroes) is being joined by liberal Catholics who have shed their ethnic politics (Cardinal Cushing, a major Boston influence, has become a vocal critic of segregation) and by others who have heard the message of urban renewal, civil rights, and better education. There is a small but growing understanding that urban redevelopment is useless without good schools and that the problems of the city are equally the problems of the periphery. But while these considerations are applicable to any metropolis, Boston—the Hub —remains in many respects unique, with its own problems, a place shaped by the Irish while the suburban Yankees doodled, a Last Hurrah of education.

12. CHICAGO'S EDUCATIONAL NEEDS—1966

ROBERT J. HAVIGHURST

Most of the big northern industrial cities have very similar educational problems which have grown out of their postwar experience. They are more alike than different if we look at a broad band of cities commencing with Boston and continuing with New Haven, New York, Syracuse, Buffalo, Baltimore, Philadelphia, Pittsburgh, Cleveland, Cincinnati, Columbus, Toledo, Detroit, Chicago, Milwaukee, St. Louis, and Kansas City. These cities all have Negro populations of greater than 10 per cent and this population has approximately doubled between 1950 and 1960. These cities all have seen massive migrations of middle-income people moving out from the central city to the suburbs. The average educational level of the adults in these cities has gone down since 1950 in the face of a rising educational trend in the country as a whole. These cities all have experienced a rapid increase of school enrollment since 1952, which is continuing through the 1960's at a somewhat reduced rate.

To write of Chicago, then, is to write of all the northern industrial cities mentioned above. The common educational problems of these cities are:

1. A relatively low educational background of the majority of parents that is reflected in their children's school achievement

2. A high degree of *de facto* racial segregation in the public schools, amounting to some 70 per cent or more of Negro elementary school pupils attending schools which have a 90 per cent or higher Negro enrollment

3. A high degree of socio-economic segregation in the public schools, with children of low-income families concentrated in certain areas of the city—usually the inner shells of the city

4. A tendency for teachers with experience and seniority to move to the higher-status schools, where discipline is not much of a problem

5. A need for flexible and varied curriculum development suited to the varying achievement levels of the various schools and of the pupils within the schools

"Chicago's Educational Needs" by Robert J. Havighurst is reprinted from *Educating an Urban Population* (Beverly Hills, Calif.: Sage Publications, 1967), pp. 37–59, by permission of the Publisher, Sage Publications, Inc.

6. A need for new high schools located where school population is increasing and also located so as to contribute to social integration of the school population

7. A need for innovation, coupled with responsible experimentation and evaluation of the results of experimentation

8. A great deal of dissension and controversy by the public concerning the policies and practices of the school system.

.   .   .   .

In Chicago, as in several other large northern cities, a continuation of present population trends might result in a growing, segregated Negro population in the city, together with a decrease in the white population, which in turn will grow rapidly in the suburbs. Furthermore, racial segregation may be accompanied by economic segregation, as high-income people continue to move to the suburbs and low-income people cluster in larger groups in the central city.

Both of these forms of segregation would be undesirable from the point of view of one who believes in democracy. They would also be undesirable from the point of view of one who is interested in the public services of the city—the schools, streets, police, fire department, and parks. With a population of reduced income, the city would find it more difficult to support the public services adequately.

Chicago's chief problem is this: how to keep and attract middle-income people to the central city and how to maintain a substantial white majority in the central city. Present trends lead to a decrease of middle-income people and a decrease of whites in the central city. The task is to change these trends.

The cure for the ills of the central city was thought to lie in urban renewal. But, after fifteen years of urban renewal, people have come to believe that the process needs to be revised and reformed if it is to do the job. Some aspects of urban renewal have succeeded, while others have failed. Success has come in certain middle-class areas where the homes were obsolescent and there was danger that these areas would become slums. These areas have been cleared of the poorest housing and large apartment houses or large blocks of single-family dwellings have been built by private enterprise and sold or rented to middle-income residents.

The low-rent public housing has been far less successful. Even though it has improved the sheer physical housing of thousands of low-income families, it has tended to increase economic and racial segregation. The public housing has been so administered that most of the projects are segregated racially. Also, most of the housing projects are either high-rise apartment buildings or blocks of two- or three-storied row houses. The average housing project has over 1,000 residents with 300–400 school-age children. Some housing projects are so large that the children fill up an elementary school. One especially large public-housing project in Chicago has a small high school and three elementary schools serving it alone. In this project, in 1965, were 2,070 children (not all of school age) who received Aid for Dependent Children; 661 families with annual income of less than $2,000; 612 school pupils severely retarded in reading, and 53 per cent of the children in the first grade who tested on a test of reading readiness as not ready to learn to read.

Another subsidized housing project in Chicago, the Robert Taylor Homes, is a series of high-rise apartment buildings stretching for almost two miles along South State Street in Chicago. Not only do the children living in these homes make up most of the enrollment of several elementary schools; at the close of 1964 there were fifty-six elementary school classes meeting in apartments in the housing project due to lack of space in the neighborhood schools. The Robert Taylor Homes has practically all-Negro occupancy. When it was proposed to build these high-rise homes, there was objection from some people on the grounds that it would tend to segregate low-income Negroes, but the city council voted to approve the project. Professor Roald Campbell[1] later commented on this situation as follows:

> In many cases, housing patterns do more to determine the nature of the school than any action of the board of education. One might cite the decision to erect the Robert Taylor Homes, twenty-eight high-rise public housing apartments, down State Street in Chicago as one of the most dramatic examples. Apparently city council members were pleased not to have public housing dispersed over the entire city as had been advocated by Elizabeth Wood, then Director of the Chicago Housing Authority. In any case the two-mile strip of public housing on State Street did more to perpetuate *de facto* segregation in schools than any policy decision by the school board or any other body. But why was there not more collaboration between the board of education, the housing authority, and the city council? This lack of collaboration among agencies at both program and policy levels is a notable problem in our cities.

What has happened in urban renewal in Chicago has happened in practically all of the big cities. From the point of view of those who are interested in social integration, the same mistakes have been made. Yet, it was not necessary to make most mistakes. Subsidized housing in other countries is not generally built so as to entrench economic stratification. It is possible to build small public-housing units spread widely over the city, so that families living in public housing have neighbors with average incomes and send their children to schools of mixed socio-economic status. In fact, the Chicago Committee on Urban Progress, reporting in

1965, went on record as opposed to the kind of public-housing policy which had built these segregated projects. It said: "High density projects should be discontinued as a policy, but subsidized public housing, of appropriate scale and pleasing design, should be blended into normal residential neighborhoods in all parts of the city. . . . Experimentation should be initiated in designing public housing projects for resale to their occupants over a period of time, on a cooperative or condominium basis."[2]

The need is for a concept of urban renewal which may be called *social* urban renewal. This consists in taking advantage of physical urban renewal in a local community area under the leadership of local community organizations to create communities which are attractive to all kinds of people—rich and poor, Negro and white. One sees this concept in action in several areas of Chicago—in the near North Side, in the Hyde Park–Kenwood area, in the area between Congress Circle (the new University of Illinois site) and the Michael Reese–Prairie Shores–Lake Meadows–Illinois Institute of Technology area. These are areas of hope for the future of the central city.

The City and the School System

The program of the schools is the greatest single factor in the decision of middle-income people to live in the central city or to live in the suburbs, and to live in one section of the city or another.

There are two opposite schools of thought among educators concerning the conduct of public schools in the big city. One may be called the "four-walls school." The basic principle is to do the best possible job of educating every boy or girl who comes into the school, whoever he is, whatever his color, nationality, IQ, or handicap. This means building good school buildings, equipping them well, and staffing them with well-trained teachers. At its best, it means being courteous and friendly to parents and to citizens who are interested in the schools, but making it quite clear to them that the schools are run by professionals who know their business and do not need advice from other people. It means making use of the cultural resources of the city—museums, theaters, orchestras, TV programs—under a system which guarantees the safety of the children and meets the convenience of the teachers.

It means keeping the schools "out of local politics." Staff appointments are to be made on the basis of performance. It means a limited cooperation with other social institutions, public and private. The welfare and public aid and public health agencies are asked for help when the schools need it, but they cannot initiate school programs. Youth welfare and delinquency-control agencies have their jobs to do, which meet and overlap the work of the schools. On this common ground, the school's administration must have full control of the use of school personnel and school facilities. In the area of training youth for employment, the school system will use the facilities of local business and industry for on-the-job training according to agreements worked out. Over-all policy for vocational education is the responsibility of the school administration under the board of education, and local business and industry are not closely related to policy determination in this area.

The four-walls type of school system works for efficiency and economy and attempts to free the creative teacher to do the best possible job of teaching under good conditions. The community outside of the school is regarded as a source of complexity and of tension-arousal if the boundary between community and school is not clearly defined and respected.

The other school of thought may be called the "urban community school." The educators who advocate this believe that the big city is in a crisis which has been in force for some years and will last for at least ten years and requires the active participation of schools in the making and practicing of policy for social urban renewal. This big-city crisis is reflected in feelings of uncertainty and anxiety on the part of parents and citizens. There is danger of a collective failure of nerve which saps the vitality and flexibility of the city's efforts at urban renewal. Parents and citizens of middle income are tempted in this situation to escape to the suburbs, where life seems simpler and safer, especially for children.

The urban community school attempts to act constructively in this crisis by involving the parents and citizens in the decisions about school policy and practice. The educator accepts the frustration of working with people who themselves are confused and uncertain about the schools, believing that the only way to solve the problems of the city is to work on a give-and-take basis with citizens and community organizations.

The urban community school includes the intraschool program of the four-walls school, but differs at important points on the relation of the school to the community.

Those who take the urban community school point of view believe there is no viable alternative. They believe that the four-walls school actually causes some of the problems of the community through its rigid rules about attendance districts and about keeping the public away from the classroom. They believe that the schools, by their policies and practices, either attract or repel people in the local community. Under present conditions, the typical school system repels people whom the central city cannot afford to lose as citizens. They believe that the present trend toward economic and racial segregation in the metropolitan area will continue and the central city will lose quality unless the schools take a more active part in social urban renewal.

Civil Rights

The other aspect of Chicago's crisis which especially involves the schools is the civil rights controversy. The public schools are heavily segregated as is shown in Table 12-1. This has come about through the working of the forces that produce residential segregation. In 1963 and 1964, 87 per cent and 89 per cent respectively of elementary school Negro children were in schools with 90 per cent or more Negro enrollment.

TABLE 12-1

EXTENT OF INTEGRATION OF TEACHERS AND STUDENTS IN CHICAGO PUBLIC SCHOOLS
(*in per cent*)

Per Cent of Student Body Negro	STUDENTS							
	Elementary Schools				High Schools			
	Negro 1964	White 1964	Negro 1963	White 1963	Negro 1964	White 1964	Negro 1963	White 1963
99+	66	0.09	64	0.16	39	0	36	0
90–99	23	0.9	23	0.8	23	0.8	24	0.8
50–89	7	3	10	4	17	4	26	4
10–49	3	9	3	8	18	19	12	18
1–9	0.5	14	0.5	12	2	29	2	24
0–1	0.05	73	0.06	75	0.7	47	0	54
Total Number	189,000	175,000	193,000	183,000	48,000	81,000	43,000	82,000

Per Cent of Negro Teachers in School	TEACHERS			
	Elementary Schools		High Schools	
	Negro 1966	White 1966	Negro 1966	White 1966
99+	6	0	0	0
90–99	23	1	0	0
50–89	54	11	58	6
10–49	16	22	37	27
1–9	1	10	5	37
0–1	0	56	0	30
Total Number	5,276	9,068	1,403	4,807

In the judgment of the writer, there was no deliberate attempt by school authorities to segregate Negro pupils. Also, there was not until recently any deliberate attempt by school authorities to promote integration. The school administration officially took the position that it was "color-blind," and would not take color into consideration in its treatment of students or teachers.

The civil rights organizations were not content with this policy and acted through lawsuits and boycotts from 1963 to 1965 to induce the school board to establish a more positive policy toward integration. As a means of settling a lawsuit, the board of education agreed to appoint an Advisory Panel on Integration of the Public Schools, under the chairmanship of Professor Philip Hauser, sociologist at the University of Chicago. In the spring of 1964, this panel reported to the board, recommending a number of practices that it believed would increase the amount of integration in the schools. Chief among these recommendations was a plan for the "clustering" of two or more neighboring schools into a single attendance district, allowing children and their parents to choose which school of the cluster they would attend. It was expected that, by clustering Negro and white schools together, some Negro pupils could attend the predominantly white schools, even though it would mean a longer journey to school. Another recommendation was for a "permissive transfer" policy to allow pupils from crowded schools to transfer to schools that were not crowded. Since most of the Negro schools were crowded, this would presumably have the consequence of placing some Negro students in schools with white majorities.

Although the board of education officially adopted these and other recommendations, not much integration resulted. Opponents of the school administration argued that the superintendent and his staff did not work hard or intelligently to apply the recommendations. . . .

Next Steps for Chicago Schools

The most pressing needs for Chicago schools may be described under the following headings: These were all recommended, along with other recommendations, in a 1964 survey.[3]

1. *New High Schools.* Enrollment projections indicate clearly that there will be further substantial increases in high school enrollment, while the elementary school enrollment will soon stabilize. Already, in 1965, thirty of the forty general high schools were operated at more than 125 per cent of capacity, which means that they were open for twelve or more class periods a day instead of the "regular" nine-period day. The survey recommended the immediate construction of ten new high schools and plans for enough new buildings to serve 30,000 more students as well as to relieve existing overcrowding. By 1966 there were five new

schools or additions with a capacity of 5,280 pupils that could be open within the calendar year. . . .

2. *Compensatory Education.* With federal government funds under the Elementary and Secondary Education Act, the Chicago schools have ample money for a significant program of compensatory education for socially disadvantaged children. A total of $32 million was allocated to Chicago for the school year 1965–66. This was to serve approximately one in five Chicago pupils whose families are below the poverty level.

The money has been used during the first year largely to provide after-school instruction and summer-school instruction, to purchase mobile classrooms, to reduce class size, to provide cultural experiences such as field trips, and to give in-service training to teachers. When linked to a program of preschool classes for disadvantaged children financed under the Economic Opportunity Act, this vast effort may substantially increase the educational achievement of pupils in the inner-city schools. It is important that the elements of this program be fully and objectively evaluated. Unless there is evidence that such programs are effective, the extra funds are not likely to be provided indefinitely.

3. *Curriculum Improvement for All Schools.* For elementary and high schools in all sections of the city there is need of improved curriculum work; that is, better adaptation of textbooks and other instructional materials to the particular children in the schools.

It is a reasonable goal to raise the quality of the work done by pupils to the point where it compares favorably with at least the average suburban schools. This will require improved work by classroom teachers, which in turn will require better assistance and stimluation from principals and curriculum specialists. The expert educators who surveyed classroom teaching found that the *average* classroom was not being taught as well as it should be. They recommended more in-service training for teachers, more time for the department chairman (in the high school) to work with his teachers, more assistance from curriculum specialists, and more attention by school principals to the supervision of their teachers.

4. *Improvement of Teacher Recruitment and Assignment.* In Chicago, as in all the great cities, there is a strong tendency for teachers with greatest seniority to move toward the schools which serve middle- and high-income areas of the city. Table 12-2 shows this tendency in the elementary schools.

The "high status" and "conventional" types of schools serve areas of predominantly upper-middle and lower-middle residents. The "common man" schools are in districts of stable working-class population, while the "inner city" schools serve the lower half of the population in terms of income and education. This table shows that 94 per cent of teachers in high-status schools are "regularly assigned," having passed the Chicago examination for a regularly assigned teacher. These teachers in the high-status schools have a median of nineteen years' experience. On the other hand, 64 per cent of the inner-city teachers are regularly assigned and 36 per cent are full-time substitutes; that is, teachers with a teacher's

TABLE 12-2

TYPE OF SCHOOL AND TYPE OF TEACHER

| | TYPE OF ELEMENTARY SCHOOL | | | | |
	High Status	Conven-tional	Com-mon Man	Inner City	Totals
Number of elementary school pupils	26,500	60,400	68,800	176,000	331,700
Per cent of total enrollment	8	18	21	53	100
Per cent of regularly assigned teachers	94	91	86	64	
Per cent of full-time substitutes	6	9	14	36	
Per cent distribution of regularly assigned teachers	11	23	22	44	100
Per cent distribution of full-time substitute teachers	1	6	11	82	100
Median years experience of regularly assigned teachers	19	15	9	4	

SOURCE: Robert J. Havighurst, *The Public Schools of Chicago: A Survey Report* (Chicago: Board of Education, 1964), p. 170.

certificate who have not passed the Chicago examination. Those who are regularly assigned have a median of four years' experience.

Some way should be worked out to interest the more experienced teachers in teaching inner-city children.

5. *Decentralization of Administration.* It is generally agreed by specialists in school administration that it would be well in the great cities to decentralize some of the administrative authority and responsibility. Such a recommendation has been made for Chicago by Superintendent Willis and also by Professors Morris Janowitz and David Street after their study of the administrative structure of the system.[4] In their report, Janowitz and Street conclude:

> the organizational structure of the public school system can be seen as constituting a significant barrier to continuous and effective innovation. We are dealing with generic characteristics of the school system. While it is essential to increase the amount of decentralization of effective authority, the problem is more complex in that it is necessary simultaneously to increase the articulation and communication among the various elements, both teaching and supervisory, in the school system and the central staff.

They called for strengthening the role of the principal and for creation of four or five regional districts, each with a high degree of autonomy. They said:

> Our central recommendation is that a new level of administration is needed between the central staff and the existing school districts in order to achieve significant decentralization. It is proposed that four or five "super districts" or sector districts be set up in the city of Chicago. These sectors would be geographically defined, each serving a large portion of the city. The school board, the general superintendent and the central staff would be responsible for broad policy, long-range planning, recruitment, fiscal control and relations with state and federal government agencies. The sector districts, operated by sector school superintendents having strong supporting staffs, would be highly autonomous units with power to adapt and develop educational programs for their regions and to develop the types of regional school-community relations which appear necessary. Each district would have an advisory board. The appointment of these boards would go a long way to overcoming the lack of communication that currently exists, especially with the Negro communities. The sector district superintendent, acting on general directives, would have the responsibility for achieving and maintaining racial integration and some of the general principles set forth below. It would be the purpose of the staff of the sector school district to assist teachers and principals in curriculum construction.

Such decentralization would place more authority and responsibility in the hands of regional superintendents, district superintendents, and principals. The survey report paid special attention to the principals. It said:

> Again and again the staff and consultants of the Survey reported that the principal is the key person in the educational system. Sometimes they reported the principal as the source of success in a school, and sometimes as a source of failure. In order to increase the amount of success which comes from the work of principals, certain facts can be pointed out and certain recommendations made.
>
> There are almost 500 principals in the Chicago schools. They range in age from the early 30's to the mid 60's. Their salaries range from $9,500 to $14,500. Some salary increases are automatic, depending on years of service, but others depend on being promoted by the central administration. Most offices in the central administration (assistant and associate superintendents, bureau directors, etc.) are filled from the ranks of principals within the system. Therefore the principalship is a complex hierarchy of positions, not a single position one holds for 10 or 20 years, as is the case in a small city. . . .
>
> The principal in the Chicago schools leads a far different life. Starting at the lowest of the principals' levels, he has eight salary lanes above him to which he can be promoted by action of the administration (not automatically). Above that are four ranks, from district superintendent to assistant, associate, and general superintendent, if he aspires that high. If his job as

principal starts at the young age of 35, he has a 30 year career, and is likely
to be promoted between five and 10 times, which means he will average
three years to six years at a particular school. Thus the Chicago principal is
likely to be a mobile person.

6. *Evaluation and Research.* Chicago and all big-city systems need
innovation and they need changes. But they also need careful evaluation
of their programs. Yet it is difficult to find any school system with an
adequate program of research and evaluation. The Chicago projects for
the socially disadvantaged illustrate the difficulties that big-city systems
face in the conduct of research and development. Several such projects
have been carried on with funds from the Ford Foundation, the Wie-
boldt Foundation, and the U.S. Department of Health, Education, and
Welfare.

Although the projects were set up with enthusiasm and with creative
originality, they were seldom accompanied by a careful design for collecting data on what actually happened to children and teachers before,
during, and after the experiments. If the public is going to be asked to
contribute more millions of dollars to the school budget for new educational practices, it would be wise for the board of education to arrange
for a thorough reporting and evaluation of these innovations so as to
keep the new practices that work and to discard those that are not
successful.

For this function there should be a Division of Educational Research
and Development with responsibility for evaluating the ongoing program
of the school system and for supplying research assistance to people who
are experimenting and innovating in the schools. The cost of such a
division might be about 1 per cent of the operating budget of the schools.

7. *Integration.* In Chicago and other large cities, the Negroes are so
fully segregated by residence that it is impossible to place the majority of
Negro children in integrated schools without a program of mass transportation that would take them to schools far distant from their homes.
Few Negro parents and few of the proponents of integration would support this kind of policy, unless it was tried out experimentally for small
numbers for several years.

In this situation, the tendency for school administrators is to do nothing about integration beyond the policy of permissive transfer that depends upon the initiative of the parents and their ability to provide transportation for their children. The "neighborhood school" tradition is
strong in this country, and it is convenient for nearly everybody—parents,
children, and administrators.

Yet the conviction is growing that integrated schooling is necessary
for good education of Negro children. The strength of this conviction
is illustrated by the following quotation from John H. Fischer, formerly

Superintendent of Schools in Baltimore and now Professor of Education at Columbia University. Professor Fischer at one time believed that a good education could be provided for Negro children in segregated schools. But he has become a strong proponent of integration in New York City. Writing on the problem, he underlines two basic facts—the first is that any school enrolling largely Negro students is almost universally considered of lower status and less desirable than one attended wholly or mainly by white students; and, in his words:

> A second impressive fact, closely related to the first, is the unfortunate psychological effect upon a child of membership in a school where every pupil knows that, regardless of his personal attainments, the group with which he is identified is viewed as less able, less successful, and less acceptable than the majority of the community. The impact upon the self-image and motivation of children of this most tragic outcome of segregated education emphasizes the dual need for immediate steps to achieve a more favorable balance of races in the schools and for every possible effort to upgrade to full respectability and status every school in which enrollment cannot soon be balanced.
>
> The purpose of school integration is not merely, or even primarily, to raise the quantitative indices of scholastic achievement among Negro children, although such gains are obviously to be valued and sought. The main objective is rather to alter the character and quality of their opportunities, to provide the incentive to succeed, and to foster a sense of intergroup acceptance in ways that are impossible where schools or students are racially, socially, and culturally isolated. The simplest statement of the situation to which school policy must respond is that few if any American Negro children can now grow up under conditions comparable to those of white children and that of all the means of improvement subject to public control the most powerful is the school. The Negro child must have a chance to be educated in a school where it is clear to him and to everybody else that he is not segregated and where his undisputed right to membership is acknowledged, publicly and privately, by his peers and his elders of both races. Although his acceptance and his progress may at first be delayed, not even a decent beginning toward comparable circumstances can be made until an integrated setting is actually established.

The strategy of integration should have two principal elements. The first is to stabilize integration in areas where the present population is mixed. This can be done where there is a substantial local community organization which favors integration and where the school administration works effectively with the local community.

Three such areas have been identified in Chicago. Each of these areas has a population of 200,000–400,000. Active programs for community redevelopment and social urban renewal are under way. Commencing with the high schools, integration can be promoted through procedures

worked out by school administrators in close collaboration with community representatives.

A common objection to this proposal is that the area is already
"changing" and nothing can stop it from becoming a segregated Negro
area. This belief is based on experience of the past decade, where the
pressure of Negro in-migrants cooped up in a ghetto often resulted in
rapid segregation of areas on the margins of Negro residence.

The situation in the mid-1960's is quite different from that of the mid-
1950's. Rapid changes of large residential areas are not now in prospect
for two reasons. First, the rate of Negro in-migration is much less than
it was in the 1950's. The demand for unskilled and semiskilled workers
in industry has slackened off, due to the effects of automation in industry. Second, the area of Negro residence is so great, as compared with
that area in 1950, that a given number of Negro residents can be accom-
modated at many points on the perimeter of existing Negro residential
areas without any large increase of segregated residential area. For example, the addition of 50,000 Negroes to the 500,000 who lived in Chicago
in 1950 would cause much more apparent increase of segregated housing
area than would the addition of 50,000 Negroes to the 1 million who
lived in Chicago in 1966.

It is now possible, in Chicago, to maintain large stable areas which are
integrated to the extent of having Negroes and whites living within adjacent blocks, if not within the same block.

With respect to the racial composition of the schools, there is also
some publicly expressed concern over the fact that the public elementary
schools of Chicago have more Negro than white pupils, although Negroes make up only about 27 per cent of the total population. It is feared
that Negro pupils will swamp the public schools.

In this connection, the projections of the Negro school population are
useful. They indicate that the recent rapid increase of Negro pupils in
the schools will soon come to an end . . . there was a wave of high
birthrates between 1951 and 1964 caused largely by in-migration of young
Negro men and women in the early 1950's. This wave is now receding,
and the elementary school population will soon reach a plateau and then
decrease somewhat, reflecting the reduction of births since 1960. Table
12-3 shows census data which lie behind this phenomenon. The numbers
of nonwhite females of childbearing age were relatively higher in 1950
than in 1960 in Chicago. The analogous figures for Kansas City show
that this phenomenon is likely to be common to northern industrial
cities.

Thus, there is no real basis for the idea that the proportion of Negro
pupils in the public schools will continue to increase as rapidly as it has
since 1950.

TABLE 12-3

AGE CHARACTERISTICS OF NONWHITE FEMALES, 1950 AND 1960

Age	CHICAGO (in per cent of total)		KANSAS CITY (in per cent of total)	
	1950	1960	1950	1960
0–4	10.3	15.0	8.5	14.7
5–9	7.4	11.8	6.6	11.0
10–14	6.4	8.4	6.0	8.0
15–19	6.2	6.2	6.0	6.1
20–24	9.7	7.6	8.6	6.5
25–29	11.3	8.0	9.7	6.8
30–34	9.7	8.4	9.0	7.7
35–39	9.2	7.6	9.1	7.3
40–44	7.6	6.2	7.8	6.2
45–64	17.6	16.0	21.8	18.0
65+	4.6	5.0	7.0	7.8
20–44	47.5	37.8	44.2	34.5
Median age	29.4	25.6	32.0	27.7
Total number	265,000	436,000	29,166	43,935

SOURCE: U.S., Bureau of the Census, Vol. I (1950 and 1960).

The second element of integration strategy is to establish and maintain a *special group of integrated elementary schools*, located at places on the margins of Negro-white residence where a considerable group of white children are living. These schools should be operated in addition to the local neighborhood schools. They should be open to voluntary enrollment, with the stipulation that they will have at least 60 per cent white and Oriental pupils and the further stipulation that they are open to every child who is not more than one year below his age level in reading ability. These schools should start at the fourth or fifth grade. Statements of intent by the Board of Education should be made, somewhat as follows:

1. The board will maintain elementary and secondary schools with at least 60 per cent white pupils in sites which are well located for Negro pupils to reach them. However, in many areas these schools will be farther from home than other schools with greater proportions of Negro pupils.

2. In the location of integrated schools (60 per cent or more white pupils), the Board of Education will cooperate with local community organizations to find or choose schools which are approved by the local groups. If there are areas where the consensus is opposed to the location of an integrated school, the board will respect this consensus, though it will also endeavor to help the people of the community meet their responsibilities in a pluralistic society.

3. The Board of Education will provide special remedial teaching

(after school, summer school, tutoring, etc.) available to pupils who are more than one year below their age level in reading ability.

4. Every pupil will have the right to attend the school of his home district or attendance area, regardless of his reading level, unless he is transferred to another school for a special class of some kind that he especially needs.

This program could be started immediately on an experimental basis in one or more areas of the city. Its success would depend on two things: (1) the willingness of large numbers of white parents to send their children to *good* integrated schools; and (2) the willingness of the Board of Education to spend a little extra money to maintain really superior schools.

Integration of faculty is another desirable goal for Chicago. Table 12-1 shows that 56 per cent of white elementary school teachers were teaching in schools without Negro teachers and 30 per cent of white high school teachers were members of all-white faculties in 1966. There were 6 per cent of Negro elementary school teachers who taught in all-Negro faculties.

Probably the normal course of securing seniority and exercising choice will increase the extent of integration of faculties, but this will happen slowly. Some cities are working directly on the matter by promoting a "balanced staff" policy. The aim is to attain within each school a balanced staff based on age, training, race, sex, and experience.

With such a policy stated and worked out with the aid of teacher organizations, the balanced staff would be attained by assignment of new teachers, transfer of young teachers after about three years of experience, and basing promotion partly on the possession of teaching experience in different neighborhoods. The Detroit school system has such a plan in operation.

These recommendations for Chicago schools illustrate the close and essential connection between the narrow educational procedures within the classroom and the broad procedures of social renewal in the great cities.

It is not possible for the public schools to do their task well on the basis of the four-walls philosophy. They must become active and cooperative participants in the remaking of the urban community. When they build new schools, they must locate these schools and determine their size through cooperation with city planning personnel. When they develop new curriculums, they must use the new teaching materials differentially among types of schools and among types of local communities within the city. When they reorganize their administration, they must do so with an eye on the social geography of the city. When they work toward racial and social integration, they must do so as part of a broad program of social urban renewal in which they cooperate with the business men, the church leaders, he labor union officers, and the civil rights workers of the city. They must be attuned to the varied sentiments and aspirations of the common people in the many local communities of which the great city is made.

Notes

1. Roald F. Campbell, "School-Community Collaboration in Our Cities," in *White House Conference on Education: Consultants Papers* (Washington, D.C.: Superintendent of Documents, 1965), pp. 144–51.

2. Chicago Committee on Urban Progress, *A Pattern for Greater Chicago* and *Subcommittee Reports* (1965), pp. 30–31.

3. Robert J. Havighurst, *The Public Schools of Chicago: A Survey Report* (Chicago: Board of Education, 1964).

4. This study has never been published. It appeared in mimeographed form and is presently unavailable to the public.

5. John H. Fischer, "Race and Reconciliation: The Role of the School," *Daedalus*, XCV, No. 1 (Winter, 1966), 29–44.

13. PITTSBURGH:
THE VIRTUES OF CANDOR

PETER SCHRAG

The city of Pittsburgh, until twenty years ago an industrial slum choking on its own smoke and filth, talks urban renewal as if new buildings—not steel or aluminum—were the staples of the city's economy. The local promoters call Pittsburgh the Renaissance City, a phrase that describes a transformation they regard as the next thing to a miracle. *Look at the Golden Triangle and the Gateway Center, the Civic Arena and the Symphony. Look at the sky; it is no longer dark at noon. Look at the public schools. They are going to be so good that middle-class families, who are fleeing every other city, will stay; that people in the suburbs will want to move back.* Pittsburgh, which abolished smog, is now trying to reverse a revolution.

If Pittsburgh's success to date is indeed a Renaissance, then the Mellon family is its Medici, Richard K. Mellon its Lorenzo, and the steel and glass office buildings of the Gateway Center its Sistine Chapel. The Mellons' substantial interests in Alcoa, U.S. Steel, Gulf Oil, the Pennsylvania Railroad, Pittsburgh Plate Glass, the vast Mellon Bank, and several other major corporations make them one of the wealthiest families in America and the most influential in Pittsburgh. In 1943, as the city belched forth the hard goods for the war effort, the Mellons inspired the so-called Allegheny Conference on Community Development, which brought together leaders of industry, labor, and local government and decreed that after the war There Shall Be No More Smoke —and which continues to act as a kind of patriarchal steering committee on urban redevelopment. In the succeeding two decades the city razed the clutter of rotting buildings located at The Point, where the Allegheny and Monongahela rivers meet to form the Ohio; enforced the antipollution laws; and cleared the skies of the smoke that once had hung over the city with a black pall (downtown office workers used to bring an extra shirt to work because the one they wore inevitably became filthy on the way downtown). Pittsburgh has begun to arrest the exodus of people and industry, has reduced unemployment, and has begun to erect the biggest industrial and commercial office buildings (as well as apartment houses and hotels) between New York and Chicago.

In 1958, with the Renaissance well under way, Pittsburgh began to turn its attention to human renewal—and especially to the public schools. These schools, like many of the city's other major enterprises, operate under a benevolent dictatorship headed by a fifteen-member Board of Public Education, appointed by the judges of the Court of Common Pleas. A thoroughly nonpolitical organization composed of businessmen, labor officials, housewives, and people who can only be described as "class," the board directs the operation of eighty-eight elementary schools, twenty-three secondary schools, 2,800 teachers, and the education of 77,000 students. (Some 50,000 other Pittsburgh children attend parochial schools.) Under two dynamic superintendents, Calvin Gross, who was later hired—and fired—as superintendent in New York City, and the incumbent Sidney P. Marland, Jr., the schools broke out of the urban smog and into the broad uplands of foundation grants, compensatory education, team teaching, as well as a Pittsburgh Scholars Program for the advanced 20 per cent, a progressive vocational education program built into comprehensive high schools, and an imaginative campaign of community relations that has brought the city substantial increases in state aid.

What makes Pittsburgh unusual, however, is not the programs, but the fact that the school system, under its benevolent patriarchs, has managed to take the initiative—to lead rather than respond—and to acknowledge its problems with candor. Pittsburgh is perhaps the most pragmatic of American cities; its Republican businessmen accept federal renewal funds with delight, collaborate with the Democratic political machine of former Mayor and Governor David L. Lawrence, and seek all the outside aid they can get. Thus, by the time large sums of federal money became available for education and poverty campaigns, Pittsburgh's schools, aided by Ford and Mellon Foundation grants, had already developed plans for compensatory education, had initiated programs that anticipated Head Start and Upward Bound, and had begun to collaborate with the University of Pittsburgh and Carnegie Tech in writing new courses and curriculums.

New administrators were appointed, salaries were increased, and the entire system was oriented to new approaches and attitudes. At the same time, the board also managed to head off the crippling controversies about segregation, busing, and neighborhood schools that keep other northern school systems on the defensive. With the addition of the federal money —which Pittsburgh quickly received—these innovations have been refined and extended. Team teaching is now standard fare in almost half the elementary schools, the entire vocational program has been revamped, and plans are being drawn for a $100 million program of new school construction that will accommodate every Pittsburgh high school student in one of five Great High Schools by 1975.

"Pittsburgh," said a school administrator, "is trying to stay a jump ahead"—ahead of educational development, of the need for trained personnel, of the civil rights revolution, and of general social and educational problems that are driving middle-class families out of the centers of most other cities. "We're anticipating consequences," said Marland. "I don't know if we can maintain it [the momentum], but we have a chance to make it as a city—a better than fifty-fifty chance. People put down roots where there is quality education. What we want to do is arrest the flight of the whites—to bring them back from the suburbs. The world of the year 2000 is now being cultivated in the cities. This is the place for children to be living together and learning together for the good of the white as well as the Negro child."

Part of the program of staying ahead lies in the administration's willingness to recognize problems and to discuss them with the community. Even its most severe critics—and there are relatively few—usually concede that the board and superintendent are "sincere"—that they are making serious efforts to alleviate segregation, to upgrade ghetto schools, and to plan significant academic programs for all children in all of the city's institutions.

Pittsburgh's schools, now about 38 per cent Negro, are as segregated as those in most other northern communities. Of the city's 600,000 people 17 per cent are Negroes, who live in the ghettos or near-ghettos on the Hill, the Homewood-Brushton district, and the North Side. Because of the city's Appalachian topography—a landscape of hills, deep ravines, and rivers that separate it like so many walls—the ghettos cannot spread as rapidly as they might in other places, but they are ghettos nevertheless.

Two-thirds of Pittsburgh's Negro school children attend elementary schools that are more than 80 per cent Negro; more than half the Negro high school students are enrolled in institutions that are predominantly black. As everywhere else, the Negro schools compile the city's lowest reading scores, its greatest percentage of academic failures, and its most severe social problems. (It should also be said that among the ten schools with the lowest reading scores, one is 85 per cent white.) And yet, the city has faced no major boycotts, no suits, no race riots. Negro leaders have access to the school board and the superintendent, they serve on the school administration's advisory committees, and they are frequently consulted (if not heeded) on policy decisions. What Pittsburgh considers to be Negro militancy would be regarded as Uncle Tomism in New York. ("I call him Pat," said Marland about one NAACP official. "He calls me Sid.")

Part of this situation is the consequence of a history of reasonably good race relations, and of a relatively low immigration of southern Negroes; part is the result of the system's willingness to acknowledge its problems; and part is probably sheer luck. "There is constant potential for deep trouble," said a school official. But so far the potential has not materialized, and the administrators are doing everything they can to head it off. A year ago they made national headlines by devoting their entire annual report to the problems of segregation, and by offering detailed statistics on the relative performance of white and Negro schools.

"This is not a success story," the report said. "It is a statement of the tremendous social demands now directed toward the public schools. . . . We have a serious condition of racial segregation in Pittsburgh, and of de facto segregation in its public schools. Negro boys and girls in large numbers are being educated separately from white children. We also have a serious condition of inferior academic accomplishment among many Negro boys and girls. These conditions are of deep concern to the Board of Education. The swift changes in racial composition during the ten-year period (1955–65) give us little hope for predicting a stable balance [among certain secondary schools] unless, contrary to the prevailing civil rights position, we establish a quota arrangement to prevent resegregation."

None of this, of course, is news in any northern city. What is new, and what drew attention, is the openness with which the school board was prepared to discuss it. Since the publication of the report, the board has appointed an advisory committee on desegregation, which includes Negro community leaders from Homewood-Brushton as well as several civic eminences, and has announced its plans for the five Great High Schools, each of them accommodating about 5,000 students and serving an area sufficiently large to encompass children of all backgrounds. Pittsburgh's entire integration program is keyed to these schools. Since Marland and the board have refused to bus or to rearrange school districts for fear of frightening the whites away, they will use the existing high schools as intermediate institutions, abolish some of the old ghetto schools, and, they hope, rearrange the ethnic composition of the remaining institutions to achieve a somewhat better balance.

But these changes are at least five and perhaps ten years off. ("You put on a pair of pants one leg at a time," Marland said.) Although a bond issue to help support construction of new high schools was authorized by the voters this spring and sites are being acquired, it is unlikely that the majority of the children now in the system will derive much benefit from the new buildings or from the ethnic redistribution that they may permit. The city's controversies—mild by the standards of Chicago or Boston or New York—are therefore centered on what happens in the meantime.

"The board doesn't propose to do anything," said Reverend Leroy Patrick, chairman of the NAACP Education Committee. "The present situation is a nightmare; even the superintendent's own figures show that the Negro child is not getting quality education. Marland has talked such a good line. He has enumerated all the things that the schools have been doing in the ghetto, but now I doubt whether there is any further point of talking. I don't think they're really sincere."

Patrick's major complaint centers on the board's refusal to consider busing or redistricting as interim measures to alleviate segregation and on its unwillingness to press for what one board member privately called "instant integration." To Patrick, all efforts to upgrade segregated schools are futile. "If, after putting massive sums of money into ghetto schools, the children aren't doing any better, then it may not be possible to achieve excellence in segregated classes," he says.

Despite Patrick's accusations of insincerity (a serious charge in Pittsburgh), most of the city's Negro community remains quiescent, if not apathetic. Pittsburgh has no genuinely militant organizations—Negro or white—and there seems to be little enthusiasm for the rowdier style of political action that characterizes more volatile northern cities. The NAACP is controlled by a middle-class element, and its strength rests with a group of Baptist Negro clergymen who are anything but radical, and who recall—for the benefit of the impatient—days when conditions for Negroes in employment, education, and politics were a great deal worse. The city is providing job opportunities for skilled Negroes; it was one of the first to pass a fair-housing ordinance, and it seems to have a capacity for absorbing the Negro leadership in official positions within the Establishment. (They are sometimes called "Dr. Thomases" by the younger people on The Hill.)

Pittsburgh, perhaps still somewhat stunned by the shocks of the Depression and the labor violence of earlier years, now is a relatively docile town. And given the conditions of education, urban development, and cultural change, most Pittsburghers are persuaded that The City Is On the Move. They acknowledge that there is a power structure, directed in some vague way from "the thirty-ninth floor"—the office suite in the Mellon–U.S. Steel Building occupied by T. Mellon and Sons, manager of the Mellon interests. But if the Mellons manage Pittsburgh, few people in the city are complaining. Most residents look at the sky, the new buildings, and the parks, and declare themselves delighted to live in Pittsburgh.

The pride of the Pittsburgh school system is the Taylor-Allderdice High School, a six-year institution with 3,200 students, of whom perhaps 70 per cent come from the predominantly Jewish upper–middle-class area of Squirrel Hill, and who, it is generally acknowledged, help give the school its academic standing, its style, and its twenty-nine National Merit semifinalists (in 1966). With the exception of a handful of Negroes who went there as transfers and who, someone said, "have trouble fitting into a place like this," the remainder are the children of industrial workers from the Greenfield area and other sections, who represent a distinct and alien subculture. "There's Squirrel Hill and there's the Hunkies," said a senior. "There aren't many Hunkies in the Advanced Placement classes or in the Scholars classes, so we don't really see much of each other." At one time the hostility between the groups threatened to become so violent that parents and community leaders stepped in to ease the friction; now the tensions are somewhat more subdued.

Allderdice, like the city's other high schools, is a comprehensive institution offering vocational and technical as well as academic programs —all the city's trade schools are being eliminated—but its reputation rests primarily on its academic standing. "That's a terrific school," a taxi driver volunteered. "They're all brains out there. I hear that 85 per cent of them are A students." Teachers are competent and sometimes outstanding, and the administration strives hard to adopt programs relevant and challenging for any student at any level.

. . . .

Approximately one-fifth of the city's high school students are in the so-called Pittsburgh Scholars Program, a city-wide innovation for the academically talented which began three years ago in the eighth grade and is now being extended to the upper years of the high schools. Students in the program are working with the social studies materials developed under Professor Edwin Fenton at Carnegie Tech and with new curriculums in English, the sciences, and mathematics. Their common approach rests on process-centered, inductive orientation and on an emphasis on structure and technique, with understanding not only of the material but also of how such material can be organized and ordered, of its limitations, of knowing how we know. Some teachers in Pittsburgh, as elsewhere, still treat these new approaches as they do the textbook, focusing on facts rather than method, but more and more are being given some kind of orientation—either within the system or in courses at the city's universities—to enable them to take full advantage of the curriculums now being instituted. Although these programs are tailored for the academically talented, the administrators hope that teachers, who are limited to two classes of Scholars in a five- or six-period day, will carry the approach into their other courses—that the style of the Scholars will become the style of the schools.

Pittsburgh's programs for the academically able have been matched by innovations in technical and vocational education, areas usually relegated to the lower depths of the academic establishment—depths sometimes so low that one can't tell the shops from the boiler room. More than half the city's students do not go on to college; yet, until a few years ago, only 6 per cent were enrolled in vocational courses. "We don't know whatever became of the rest," an administrator said. In 1963, the city conducted a massive survey of the region's occupational outlook and began to replace its trade schools with a three-level system of technical and vocational training within the comprehensive high schools. The product, now called OVT (Occupational-Vocational-Technical) offers training to students at various skill levels within the same trades: auto mechanics, business, food service, merchandising, data-processing, the building trades, textiles, electronics, and other areas. (These courses are not offered at all schools; students who want to work in an area not offered in the home school spend half a day at another school.) In a nursing program, for example, the most able and motivated girls can expect to graduate to further training to become registered nurses; others will become practical nurses, nurses' aides, or hospital assistants. In the courses for laboratory technicians, some students are expected ultimately to qualify for skilled technical occupations; others may not become much more than bottle washers. The major thrust of these programs was to take the stigma out of vocational training and to prepare young men and women for occupations that will not be obsolete on the day they graduate. There are OVT students at Allderdice and Peabody, as well as at the all-Negro Westinghouse and Fifth Avenue high schools.

Thus far, with many of the courses hardly under way, the search for prestige has had only limited success; the stigma is hard to erase. Some of the building trades, moreover, are still closed to Negroes, and there is a fear among members of the Negro community that able students are being shunted away from academic programs to make OVT look good. Yet it is clear that the city—partly because it wants to "keep the derelicts off the streets," partly because it wants to ennoble the service professions, and partly because it must diversify its industrial economy—is putting large sums of money and energy into the project. Ultimately, according to Marland, it will be possible, through summer and night classes, for an OVT student to accumulate a full set of credentials for college admission and thereby to avoid the fatal choice between academic and vocational training that many students must now make by the time they are fifteen years old. "We want to get to the point where half the students are in some kind of OVT program," said Marland.

"We want them to be ready with a marketable skill when they leave school. Even a kid with an 80 IQ can be trained for a useful job. The problem is that American schools have never—never—been relevant for the 10 to 20 per cent of the kids at the bottom."

Despite its penchant for innovation and change, however, Pittsburgh is not a city of demonstration projects—what it tries, it expects to institute across the board. And given the likelihood of continued *de facto* segregation and the pressure of the Negro leadership, however mild, the city is more than ever committed to providing parity education for all children—and to offering compensatory programs for the disadvantaged. Using federal funds, the city is spending an average of $578 per year for each child in disadvantaged areas (compared with the city average of $447), and it is making every effort to recruit and train competent teachers for its inner-city schools. So far, the system has not managed to produce anything like success in its Negro schools, but it may be coming closer than most. The all-Negro Westinghouse High School, for example, has a lot more in common with Allderdice than it does with the image—sometimes more mythical than real—of the blackboard jungle. There are no policemen in the halls, no guards at the doors, and the general atmosphere—despite the misgivings of some teachers and parents —is considerably more relaxed than it is at many of the inner-city schools of Chicago and New York. In recent years, a third of Westinghouse's graduates have gone to college, many to Negro institutions, but some also to Yale, Princeton, Cal Tech, and M.I.T.

"I've felt," said Harry Singer, the principal, "that my job is to so upgrade this school that it provides the best education in the city. We've broken away from the ivory tower concept that if a kid doesn't want to learn, that is his fault. The trouble was that we had no program for them." Singer has instituted a Scholars group, despite the early misgivings of some administrators on the grounds that Westinghouse lacked sufficient academic talent. "I said, 'You try to tell the parents in Homewood-Brushton that their kids aren't good enough,'" Singer reported. "At Allderdice Scholars are born. Here we have to make them." Singer is especially proud of his new OVT educational programs and shops, his garage for auto mechanics, and his child development classes, where the preschool nursery children come from every section—and every race—in the city. The most integrated room at Westinghouse is composed of four-year-olds.

Like most ghetto schools, Westinghouse has its exhausted teachers— people who gave up after their cars were stolen on nearby streets, who have had enough of hostile students, or who have made up their minds that children from the ghetto are culturally incapable of learning. "Some of them tell us in class that they don't care if we learn—they'll get their pay," said a student. "A lot of them aren't trying. But the parents are apathetic, too. If they came in here and complained a little, things might change."

The brighter students feel that there is great teacher turnover (which Singer said is declining) and that the work of the classroom is not rigorous enough. But they also concede that some teachers are good "because they make you work" and because they are clearly concerned about the students. . . .

For anyone trying to assess the schools of Pittsburgh, the central question is whether the biggest problems have been solved, or whether they are still to come—whether the city is ahead of—or behind—the rest of the nation. Pittsburgh's placid history in race relations and its success in taking the initiative in confronting contemporary educational problems have made it a hopeful indicator in the generally bleak picture of urban education.

In 1965, the city won a major victory by persuading Governor William Scranton and the Pennsylvania legislature that the historically inequitable formulas for allocating state funds (which favored the affluent suburbs) needed to be revised. At that time the schools, in collaboration with a citizen organization headed by Edward D. Eddy, the president of Chatham College, mounted a massive campaign to persuade the community—and the state—that the schools were confronting a financial crisis. As a result, the city now expects to derive more than one-fourth of its $41 million budget from the state. Last spring, the system again staged a successful public campaign—this time to gain authorization for a $50 million bond issue to help finance the Great High Schools.

The schools, and Sidney Marland especially, enjoy tremendous support in the community; except for a few civil rights leaders such as Leroy Patrick, they seem to have no critics at all. The chamber of commerce has never questioned a school budget, there are no critical taxpayers associations, no suits, no political battles, not even questions of whether the innovations are necessary—or whether they are significant and effective. Because of this support, the schools have been able to increase salaries—to a starting level of $5,600 and a maximum of $10,000—to open up the administrative staff to new faces and ideas, and to plan the comprehensive high school building program.

Part of the system's strength clearly lies in its leadership. Despite frequent allusions to "the power structure" and to the fact that the whole Renaissance was a product of the happy coincidence of economic and civic interest, it is apparent that nothing could be happening in Pittsburgh without the support of the thirty-ninth floor, and of the industrial and commercial powers of which it is a symbol. The city's appointed Board of Education, only dimly responsive to the immediate wishes of the electorate, has achieved what politically elected school committees in cities such as Boston have not even approached. "The appointed board in Pittsburgh," said Marland, who was a suburban superintendent before he came to the city, "produces the same results as the elected school committee in a place like Darien, Connecticut. You have to appoint people in the city: The individuals on a board such as this would never run for political office." Given such political immunity, the board can make changes, can consult the community, and can listen to citizens' groups with an Olympian security that the politically ambitious could never afford.

And yet, under the cheerful façade, the system still had deep problems. Pittsburgh's compensatory program—based on team teaching and massive expenditures of federal funds—has shown no hard evidence of paying off: There are no validating scores, no data other than the subjective judgments of the teachers and staff. There is, moreover, no hope that there will be any further desegregation for at least five years, and no sign that the exodus of middle-class whites, toward whom so much of the program is directed, has been stopped. At the same time, there is a strong likelihood that urban renewal—despite official concern for the housing problems of the poor—will drive more Negroes into the ghettos and will exacerbate the problems of the slums.

"Given the right conditions—a shooting, for example—we could have a full-scale riot on The Hill or in Homewood-Brushton," said a long-time resident. "We're doing well, but we're not exempt from trouble." On at least one occasion in recent years, a serious attempt was made to burn down one of the ghetto high schools: Only a change in the school's administration forestalled further pyrovandalism.

Perhaps the most serious problem will be simply the maintenance of the initiative and the development of resources—personal and financial— that the schools require. To Marland, finding money (despite the change in the state-aid formula) "is going to be a way of life." Like every other city, Pittsburgh is pressed to maintain urban services—in welfare, health, and safety—and still find the funds to run educational programs as good as those of the suburbs. Recent recruiting activities by the American Federation of Teachers have begun to worry certain members of the board, and it may well be that some of the substantial salary increases granted in the past year reflect the threat of AFT organization.

Both Marland and board president William H. Rea want to maintain —and raise—what Rea calls the "professional status" of the city's teachers and to provide remuneration commensurate to their services. Pittsburgh has already created a "Professional Advisory Committee" of teachers which, Rea hopes, will become the equivalent of a University Senate in shaping the system's policies. Concurrently, the schools are actively recruiting teachers not only from the Pittsburgh area, but throughout the country; they continue to seek foundation support; and they are engaged in a continuing campaign to keep the community informed, and to maintain good relations with it. Marland has a reputation as a great handshaker and as a person who is accessible to all his critics. "Of course he's smooth," someone said. "You have to be smooth to survive."

Pittsburgh is an audacious and ambitious city. It is trying to accomplish—in renewal, in cultural development, in education—what has never been fully achieved in America before. It is attempting to convert what was essentially a one-industry town (sometimes called the northern capital of Appalachia) into a livable, diversified community, to offer equal educational opportunity for all, to arrest the exodus of the white middle class, and to convert the liabilities of urban life into the advantages that cities have always promised. Rea and Marland and their colleagues feel that they have managed to get the people of Pittsburgh—and the state— to recognize the magnitude of the urban problems, and that the tide is beginning to turn. Some families are moving back from the suburbs, and they are not only the old and the childless. Pittsburgh has attracted a new community of intellectuals centered at Carnegie Tech, the University of Pittsburgh, Duquesne, and other area colleges. It now even gets inquiries from people in neighboring Mt. Lebanon and Fox Chapel—two of the more salubrious greenbelts—who would like to get their children into the Scholars Program. (They can, Marland said, if they move back to Pittsburgh.) The many small school systems surrounding the city are simply not large enough to support the diversity of programs that the Pittsburgh schools can offer.

Pittsburgh expects to trade on its size, its reputation, and on the momentum that the Renaissance provides. It still has a great many problems to solve; it has to invent styles of instruction and programs of organization that can provide fully integrated—and significant—education to all its children, advantaged and deprived. It must continue to find money, staff, and good will. It must solve related employment, housing, and transportation problems. And it must find people. But, for the moment, there is a powerful will to succeed. "If we can't do it," Rea said, "then no city can."

14. THE PROCESS OF CHANGE: CASE STUDY OF PHILADELPHIA

MARILYN GITTELL and
T. EDWARD HOLLANDER

The forces that contributed to the decline of the public school system are the same in all large urban systems. Urban schools suffered a long period of neglect and low fiscal priority during and subsequent to World War II. Capital expenditures, curtailed during the war, were insufficient in the late 1940's to replace an old and deteriorating school plant. Teachers' salaries were low, and potentially competent teachers were attracted to other fields and to suburban school systems. Overcentralization and unmanageable school bureaucracies emerged to limit change and to discourage initiative and innovation. The malaise in urban school systems was widespead throughout the 1940's and 1950's, but a cult of "professionalism" insulated the school bureaucracy from outside criticism.

More recently, the insularity of the urban schools has begun to break down. Initially, Russian space successes awakened public interest in education, its goals, and its operation. The growing proportion of Negro pupils in the northern urban ghetto schools made apparent the extent of segregation; the failure of the schools to cope with the changing composition of the cities' pupil population made the school system an obvious target for civil rights groups. The Supreme Court decision of 1954 gave impetus to the demands for quality integrated education. And the civil rights movement, which focused northern protest on the school system, made criticism of the schools respectable again. The thrust of the civil rights groups in the early 1960's may well prove to be the triggering force that will lead to urban school reform in the 1970's.

What differentiates Philadelphia from other large cities is not that reform is needed, but that reform seems to be taking place. More important in some respects than the change itself is the process of change.

Reprinted from Marilyn Gittell and T. Edward Hollander, Six Urban School Districts: A Comparative Study of Institutional Response (New York: Frederick A. Praeger, 1968), pp. 24–49.

An analysis of how and why school reform in Philadelphia was possible can add much to our understanding of large-city school systems.

The Philadelphia school system following World War II offered a paradox in microcosm of big-city school systems. The "credo" called for an apolitical institution devoted to educational needs and governed by a board of notables "above criticism" and above the partisan issues that supposedly corrupt and destroy professionalism in education. In practice, political considerations were paramount in school budget-making and indirectly influenced all educational policy. The schools were governed by a highly political business manager, and the school board served largely to satisfy the public view of the system as apolitical.

Philadelphia's Old Board of Education

The Philadelphia school system was unusual in that its school board was appointed by the Court of Common Pleas. This system was believed to assure recruitment of the most qualified persons on a nonpartisan basis, but quite the opposite effect resulted. The Court of Common Pleas looked to the city's party leaders for recommendations for school board members and the Democratic and Republican Party leadership favored loyal supporters of the political parties.

The influence of party leaders over the Court resulted from the operation of the "sitting judge" procedures used in Philadelphia. Candidates for the Court were selected by agreement between both political parties and the candidates so selected enjoyed the support of both parties. The judges knew the sources of their support and acted accordingly.[1]

The board that emerged from this selection process was comprised of members of the Philadelphia business community, who were less concerned with educational policy than they were with avoiding controversy and limiting school expenditures to acceptable levels. Their avoidance of controversy was dictated both by political and personal reasons. School issues were bound to be highly controversial and embarrassing to political candidates who might be forced into taking a public position. Not only would such a position violate the accepted credo of an apolitical school system, but it also could be politically disastrous. Moreover, it suited the board members to avoid controversy that would inevitably tarnish their reputation and the prestige of a board position as one of bestowed honor. The board was thus conservative and closely aligned with the city's political leadership.

The board was also a venerable one, self-perpetuating both by the selection process and through a tradition of successive reappointments. Although board members were initially appointed to six-year terms, members were generally reappointed until they decided to retire. For example, in 1961, the retiring chairman was seventy-five years old and had served for over twenty years.[2]

Controversy was avoided through a "gentlemen's agreement" to resolve all conflicts in executive session and to present united support of the majority position at public meetings. Board meetings tended to be routine, and public participation was virtually nonexistent. That some conflict did exist is indicated by the large number of executive sessions that were reported in the public records. However, criticism of the board's policies was in bad taste, politically hazardous, and potentially disastrous for anyone with ambitions for leadership in the downtown business community.

The board was successful not only in avoiding controversy over educational issues, but also in limiting school expenditures to levels acceptable to municipal officials. That the board was economy-minded reflected not only the large representation of the business community among its members, but also the power of its business manager and the subtle political relations between the board and city government with respect to tax policy.

The Philadelphia school system was, legally, fiscally independent of the city government—that is, the board had its own taxing and debt-incurring power and did not have to secure municipal approval for its budget. In practice, the school system was heavily dependent on the city's Democratic political leadership, which controlled both the city government and the city's legislative delegation to the State House of Representatives.[3]

Philadelphia's school budget is financed primarily by a tax on real estate, but the board's taxing power was limited to a maximum rate established by the Pennsylvania State Legislature. Since World War II, the board has levied the maximum rate permitted under state law. Periodically, it was required to seek increases in the tax limit, but it did so with great reluctance and as infrequently as possible. The legislature resisted raising the tax limit except in response to considerable local pressure. Such pressure was effective only with substantial support from Philadelphia legislators, which meant that local party leadership approval of the increase was needed. Support was forthcoming only if the requests were modest, politically acceptable, and did not conflict with other municipal needs.

A strong and independent school board would have campaigned hard for public support to obtain needed funds. The Philadelphia School Board, with its conservative orientation, was content to limit its expenditures to amounts that could be financed within existing limits. Only in

1949, 1957, and 1963 was the board successful in raising the tax limit, and then only for modest amounts that did not provide for needed tax leeway. In other years, increases in operating expenditures were modest and resulted from small increases in the values of taxable property.[4]

Similarly, without voter approval, the school debt could not exceed 2 per cent of the value of property taxable for school purposes. Throughout most of this period, capital expenditures were limited to amounts that could be financed within the 2 per cent debt limitation.

The school board, faced with the choice between mobilizing public support for adequate school financing and limiting expenditures to levels acceptable to the local political leadership, chose the latter course of action. The result was austerity capital and operating budgets throughout the postwar period, with a consequent deterioration in school plant and in the quality of school instruction. A second consequence was a continuing dependence by the school board on the city's political leadership and the emergence of the business manager as the most powerful person within the school system.[5]

Legally, the business manager and the superintendent of instruction possessed equal power within the system. Both were appointed by the board, but, while the office of superintendent changed hands over the years, the business manager was in office for over twenty-five years.

As business manager, he controlled school-district contracts and purchased school supplies. He also controlled 200 patronage jobs in the school district and paid the salaries of 260 district employees who worked in other city departments. These latter jobs were major sources of patronage for the party in power. Thus, the business manager had considerable political power. He used that power effectively to enhance his position and to influence party politicians, whose approval was essential for legislative support for school tax increases. He also exercised the power that was legally the school board's. Because board membership was largely honorary and politically dictated, the board was content to permit the business manager (who often had veto power over their appointment) to run the system.[6]

The business manager saw his role both as a custodian of public funds and as an arbiter of internal disputes within the system. He was less concerned with educational policy than with limiting school tax increases to acceptable levels. And, of course, the role he played was consistent with the needs of the groups that ran the city.[7]

The paradox of the Philadelphia school system was that, despite the commitment to the credo and supposed fiscal independence, it was, in fact, deeply involved in local politics in such a way that public review and participation was impossible. For example, until 1960, the board's budget submission was a two-page summary prepared by its business manager and cleared first with "city hall." The detailed report was presumably locked in the business manager's desk and was never made a part of the public record. There is some doubt as to whether it was ever made available to board members.[8]

The supervisory staff carried forth a minimum program for the district. The sanctity of the staff was preserved. Although associate and assistant superintendents were not given tenure and served under one-year contracts, no superintendent was ever replaced. Informal arrangements assured life tenure to every supervisor. Even under a new superintendent, appointed after the business manager's death, few staff changes were made. Philadelphia's inbred bureaucracy, one of the most extreme in the country, continued to function as it had before. Over the years, so little was done beyond the routine minimum operation of the school system that responsibility for policy-making is not difficult to pinpoint. The staff was free to develop curriculum and educational policy. The board was generally cooperative. But the parameters of educational policy were set by control of financial and organizational management exercised by the business manager.[9]

As a result of inadequate spending, insulation from the community, and political control, the Philadelphia public school system in the 1960's was among the poorest urban systems in the country. Elementary and junior high school pupil achievement ranked well below national urban norms in every category tested.[10] Philadelphia was second among large-city school systems in the proportion of pupils attending private schools. With but one exception, its professional staffing ratio was lower than that of every other city in the country.[11] It ranked seventh in current expenditures per pupil among the eleven largest school systems, and its low expenditures reflected below-average teachers' salaries.[12]

Its school plant was obsolete, and overcrowding was widespread throughout the system. In 1965, over 70 per cent of the city's public schools were over thirty years old; sixty-three elementary schools, which provided 15 per cent of the total elementary school capacity, were not of fire-resistant construction and had been built prior to 1907.[13] Nearly 60 per cent of the elementary schools were overcrowded; 83 per cent of the junior high schools and 89 per cent of the high schools were also classified as overcrowded.[14]

The absence of effective criticism limited not only controversy but innovation. A review of school policy over the last decade failed to identify any significant new programs. In 1960, the Great Cities Project and the Educational Improvement Program were adopted, but only in response to pressure from civil rights groups, and then on a pilot basis only.[15]

Reform in the Philadelphia School System

Today, the Philadelphia school system is moving rapidly toward major improvement. That reform has come to Philadelphia's schools is clear; that it is directly identified with Richardson Dilworth, the new board chairman, and his perception of his role as a "change agent" is clearer still. The circumstances leading up to Dilworth's appointment may signify the most dramatic revolution in a city school system in the postwar period.

A major achievement of the reform forces in Philadelphia was the new home-rule powers given the school board by the State Legislature in the summer of 1963. On July 31, 1963, despite opposition from members of the Philadelphia School Board, the teachers' union, the mayor, the city council, and numerous civic associations, the Pennsylvania legislature passed House Bill 367, which transferred taxing power for the city's schools from the state to the city. The law set in motion a series of changes that altered radically the distribution of power within the system and set the potential for widespread school reform.

The law empowered the city council to authorize the school board to levy any tax that the city could levy for general tax purposes, except that no school wage tax could be levied on nonresidents. The transfer of taxing power effectively made the school system fiscally dependent on municipal government.[16] With the transfer of taxing power, a Home Rule Charter Commission was established to recommend procedures for selection of board members and operation of the school board. The resulting recommendations, adopted by referendum, provided for appointment of members of the board by the mayor, using a screening-panel device.[17]

Richardson Dilworth, former mayor of Philadelphia and a leader in the city's reform movement, was persuaded to accept appointment to the board. He did so with the understanding that he would serve as its chairman and would be given veto power over other board appointments.[18] The members of the screening panel were anxious for Dilworth to lead a reform movement within the school system; he was willing to assume this responsibility only if he could be assured of conditions necessary for him to be effective. The new Dilworth board began to function even before it took office.

Shortly after his appointment in September, 1965, Dilworth established three task forces to report to the incoming board on the issues facing the Philadelphia school system. The composition of the task forces was in itself symbolic of the changed attitude toward public education. Rather than rely upon the professional staff for technical expertise, Dilworth chose incoming board members, community leaders, and outside specialists for membership on the task forces. A staff person was assigned to each task force to serve only in a liaison capacity. The choice of task force members and their method of operation was directed at breaking down the insularity of the school system and laying school policy-making open to purposeful public participation.[19]

The task forces began their work by holding a joint public hearing at which close to fifty organizations were represented. All were highly critical of the school system or some aspect of its operation. The hearing pointed the way for the policy recommendations that were to follow.[20]

The task forces recommended far-reaching changes in community relations, curriculum, financing, budgeting, and administration. Recommendations followed a pattern; attacking the insularity of the schools, they included open school board meetings, recruitment of noninstructional professionals from outside the educational establishment, recruitment of teachers and administrators from outside the system, involvement of community leaders and parents in school policy-making, and the use of volunteer instructional and noninstructional help. School reorganization on a 4–4–4 basis was urged.[21]

In the same spirit, the new board continued to involve community leaders in school issues through open meetings, responsiveness to studies by community groups, and periodic consultation among board, staff, and community groups. For example, in January, 1966, Dilworth appointed a thirteen-man committee, including executives of leading Philadelphia banks and businesses, to study financial needs.[22] The board also sponsored a three-day seminar to provide an opportunity for community groups and the professional staff to interact on a variety of school problems.[23]

THE NEW SYSTEM IN OPERATION

One of the most controversial areas of new board policy has been its aggressive recruitment of outsiders for the system. The supervisory staff is being reorganized and thirty-five top-level appointments have been made, with the promise of more to come. Many of the new staff appointees are not professional educators and have no experience in the system. A new superintendent was appointed from a suburban district in New Jersey. He has indicated his desire to bring in people from around the country to stimulate change and assure its implementation. Those who are his immediate assistants are talking about the coming school revolution. Some of the outsiders recruited to the system are replacing administrative personnel, graduates of Pennsylvania normal schools, who rose through the ranks from teacher to principal to professional administrator. The effort to bring in fresh thinking has been extended down to the teacher level through an ambitious nationwide teacher recruitment program.[24]

The thoroughgoing revision of financial management will provide the groundwork for planned revitalization of the system. Building on task force recommendations on budgeting, the school district is in the midst of implementing a "planning, performance, budgeting" system (PPB). A consultant to the task force from a national certified public-accounting firm has been retained as the new director of finance. He is adjusting the system to long-range planning based on demonstrated priorities that will be determined in precise program evaluation. The goal of the system is both to assure program evaluation and to measure individual school needs. Adjustments have required new staffing, retraining of old staff, and, most important, top-level policy acceptance of the new technology and its potential role in school policy-making. The board and the new superintendent have given complete support to the implementation of the new budget and accounting procedures. It is likely that PPB will be one of the built-in mechanisms for change that traditional school system management now lacks.[25]

A second mechanism for change is the establishment of long-range planning for school organization, program, and curriculum. The planning program, supported by a federal grant and directed by a former business executive, will provide for a continuing review of educational innovation and its adaptation for implementation in the Philadelphia school system.[26]

An obvious and dramatic demonstration of the board's public support has been the significant increase in school spending. While fiscally independent, the school district's capital and operating-budget increases were minimal, largely determined by its business manager and the political leadership with whom he was aligned. During the past two years, school spending has increased 50 per cent—a record increase for the district and equal to half the increase in the preceding ten years.[27] The school district has undertaken a massive $450 million rebuilding program that will replace or renovate virtually every school building in the system. In May, 1966, voters approved the first phase of the program by authorizing a $60 million increase in the school debt. Further requests for increases are planned for each of the years through 1972.[28]

Though the extent of actual change thus far has been relatively limited—the new board has been in office for a relatively short period—the nature of accomplished change is highly significant. By moving outside the community for new and needed expertise, by seeking out and providing mechanisms for encouraging community involvement, and by pioneering in long-range planning and evaluation, the Philadelphia board has set the stage for changes yet to come. That so much has been accomplished in so short a time is a remarkable feat for a school board whose heritage had been one of the most backward large-city school systems in the country.

THE PROCESS OF CHANGE

The organizational changes that have taken place in the Philadelphia school system are more widespread and far-reaching than have been experienced in any large-city school system in the country. There has been a complete redistribution of power—from an insulated bureaucracy supported by local politicians to a strong reform board supported by a broad community power base.

The direct cause of the redistribution of power was the shift in taxing power from state to city and appointment of the board from the Court of Common Pleas to the mayor. But these legal changes were the results of a struggle for control of the school system that was waged during the 1962–64 period. The environment for reform was established by the city-wide reform movement that was active in Philadelphia in the 1940's and the 1950's and by the complete deterioration of the schools, which made the need for reform apparent to all. The initial pressure for reform arose within the board, in the person of Mrs. Albert M. Greenfield, who pressed hard for increased financial support. As a dissident voice within the board, she broke its seeming unity and encouraged outside criticism. Subsequently, the civil rights groups found in the overcrowded schools an issue to which the board was forced to respond. Its response took the form of the appointment of a broad community Special Committee on Nondiscrimination, which provided a forum for voicing discontent and served to mobilize the disorganized and weak community groups concerned with schools.

When the pressure for additional financing met the strong opposition of party leaders, a crisis developed that brought into being a coalition of the reform members of the business community, civic groups, and civil rights groups. The reform members of the business community played a key role, through the Greater Philadelphia Movement (GPM), in giving power to the growing revolt and transforming the issue from increased financing to reorganization of the school system. The issue, thus joined, was fought in the State Legislature. There, a Republican governor with the support of a Republican legislature was unwilling to bear the onus for raising Philadelphia's school taxes. Philadelphia's Democratic legislative delegation could not be united in support of a comprehensive tax program. The governor, with widespread support from Democratic reform elements in Philadelphia and from community groups in the city, was able to shift taxing powers from the state to the city despite equally widespread opposition from the school board, the school bureaucracy, the city council, the mayor, and the local Democratic Party leadership. Subsequently, the Philadelphia reform movement, with broad community support, was able to install Richardson Dilworth as chairman of a newly constituted board appointed by the mayor. Dilworth and the new board, with no commitments to the city's party leadership, the city council, or the school bureaucracy, and with community support, were able to move rapidly and effectively to use their power to achieve sweeping organizational changes.

.   .   .   .

THE ROLE OF THE CIVIL RIGHTS GROUPS

The civil rights movement, though relatively weak in Philadelphia, played a significant role in achieving school reform—initially, by pointing to the overcrowded conditions in the Philadelphia schools and, subsequently, by joining with other groups to achieve school reform.

Philadelphia schools were hardly pioneers in pressing for integrated education. As late as 1935, Philadelphia's schools were segregated, a factor explaining the high proportion of Negro administrators in the school system.[29] Following residential patterns in all northern cities, the school system remained *de facto* segregated, as it still is today. The Supreme Court decision in *Brown v. Board of Education* was hardly noticed in Philadelphia. It was not until 1959, five years later, at the urging of the Education Equality League, that the board expressed a firm belief in nondiscrimination. Their statement simply affirmed "that there shall be no discrimination because of race, color, religion, or national origin in the placement, instruction, and guidance of pupils."[30]

Two years later, dissatisfied with a policy without a program and lacking wide support for community action, the NAACP provided counsel in a suit against the Board of Education brought by several parents (the Chisholm suit). The suit asserted that the board, in providing portable classrooms at a crowded school that was 98 per cent Negro rather than providing transfer to an underutilized school, had committed an act of purposeful segregation. The suit, along with other civil rights activity, aroused concern over the overcrowding of public schools in the Negro sections of the city.[31]

At budget hearings in the fall of 1962, various school and community representatives protested overcrowding, inadequate facilities, poor student achievement, and teacher shortages—primarily in schools in Negro neighborhoods. A new board president had recently been elected and he responded to community criticism in early 1963 by setting up a Special Committee on Nondiscrimination; three board members and 100 others, including school officials, community leaders, and interested persons, were appointed to it. The committee was the first instance of open policy-making in the Philadelphia school system. It brought together a wide variety of persons concerned with schools, thereby mobilizing community interest and participation, which continued throughout the period during which major changes were made in the fiscal and political structure of the school system.[32]

THE ROLE OF THE GREATER PHILADELPHIA MOVEMENT

The GPM is the instrument of reform for the business community in Philadelphia. Organized in 1948, it has less than fifty members, mostly corporation lawyers and bankers. Although others are co-opted into membership (for example, from labor and the Jewish community), control is firmly in the hands of the Main Line families.[33] It has the support of the press and exercises control over a number of nonprofit corporations—in this sense, it is the closest thing to a nonprofit holding company. GPM supported reform mayors Dilworth and Clark.

The reform movement had ignored the education issue throughout the 1950's. Dilworth, himself, had said: "We had so many other things that we had to do and nobody worried much about the schools. . . . We just figured they were all right. . . . We just didn't realize how neglected they were becoming."[34]

In September, 1960, GPM undertook a study of the Philadelphia school system. Initially, the study was to focus on the school teachers, examining teacher recruitment and personnel problems. During this period, the schools were confronted with major personnel shortages, primarily the result of low starting salaries and the more attractive suburban school settings. In making its 1960 study, GPM was determined to use its own field researchers, relying upon the school staff only for specific information. Midway through the study—sometime in late 1961 or early 1962—objectives were shifted away from personnel policies to the much more significant and sensitive issue of financial administration and selection of school board members.[35] The reasons for the shift are hard to discern, but they seem to be related to both the growing anxiety over overcrowded facilities brought to the public's attention by the Chisholm suit and the growing pressure from Mrs. Greenfield and other board members for increased financing. John Patterson, who now holds a key policy-making position in the schools, played a major role in the shift in emphasis of the study. He had ties to GPM (through the business community) and also to the Citizens' Committee for Public Education, which was then the only effective independent civic group concerned with education issues.[36]

The GPM report was a direct attack on the school board. It was a vote of no confidence, not only in the board, but also in the fiscal and administrative structure of its schools. The report was issued in two parts. The first part was transmitted on May 17, 1962, to General J. Harry LaBrum, who was then chairman of the school board; it covered administrative problems. The second part, which dealt with personnel problems, was issued six months later. The first part had great impact on the community, not only because its recommendations suggested the need for a major redistribution of power in the system, but also because it was a GPM document: GPM has always pressed hard for any recommendations it made and has usually been successful in securing their adoption.[37]

The study's principal recommendations were its call for mayoral appointment of a new school board, using a screening-panel device, transfer of power to set the maximum tax rate from state to city, establishment of unit control by downgrading the business manager's position to associate superintendent, and, as a continuing policy, board authorization of independent study of school-district problems.[38] All of the report's major recommendations were ultimately implemented.

THE SCHOOL BOARD

Although civil rights group pressure and the GPM study were vital to school reform, the timing of reform—delayed as it was until 1962—was tied to the power distribution within the school system. Until 1962, Louis Obermeyer served as chairman of the school board, a member of long standing and a respected and powerful member of the downtown business community. Obermeyer gave the school board the full prestige of his presence and effectively set it above criticism. Under Obermeyer, the board's actions were private; public participation was actively discouraged. Obermeyer could count on the business manager to manage the school system's finances with restraint, and modest financial needs could be met through personal negotiations with local political leaders.

The business manager's control over school system finances was not seriously challenged until 1958, when newly appointed board member Mrs. Albert M. Greenfield pressed successfully for a board study of the schools' "current needs." Mrs. Greenfield is a prominent civic leader and the wife of one of Philadelphia's most successful financiers. The Greenfield report recommended increases in teachers' salaries and more funds for textbooks, thus shaking the otherwise constrained financial balance achieved by the conservative board and the business manager.

Mrs. Greenfield independently developed public support and succeeded in obtaining an increase in the real estate tax limit. The Democratic county chairman had pressed for increased state aid, but the legislature had rejected this in favor of the tax-limit increase.[39]

In 1961, the business manager suffered a serious heart attack and was placed on a rigid medical regimen, which reduced his effectiveness. His illness, coupled with Mrs. Greenfield's presence as a proponent of increased spending, and the growing activity in the Negro community for school integration changed the character of school board membership from one of bestowed honor to one of political sensitivity. In 1962, while the business manager was ill, the chairman retired from the school board. Shortly thereafter, the business manager died, ending twenty-five years of unparalleled power in the school system.[40] The power gap left by the death of the business manager and the retirement of the chairman opened the way for reform.

A new school board chairman was appointed. Whereas the former chairman's presence on the board placed it above criticism, the new chairman invited criticism. He has been described as "overbearing, a veritable bull in a china shop." Prior to his board role, he had been in a controversy with a leading business executive, the husband of a board member, and had succeeded in ousting him from his position of power in the Chamber of Commerce. His position was vulnerable, and criticism of the school system became fashionable.[41] The new chairman's response to criticism was the appointment of the Special Committee on Nondiscrimination. This further opened school policy-making to public participation.

During this period, the Citizens' Committee for Public Education was rejuvenated and it joined in the growing controversy over the schools. Mrs. Greenfield had been supported in her crusade for better financing by the committee. Though relatively small and without a broad base of support, it comprised a core of knowledgeable and hard-working persons concerned with quality education. Its membership was drawn from local parent groups, whose interests had broadened from local concern to overall school problems. With the schools facing growing financial crises and mounting civil rights pressure, the committee began to stimulate interest in school reform through criticism of school board policy. The participation of its members as disinterested persons concerned with quality schools encouraged wider participation by noneducation interest groups.[42]

THE FISCAL CRISIS

With the death of the business manager in 1962 and the retirement of Obermeyer, power on the board shifted to those persons pressing for increased expenditures and financing. A 1961 deficit had been covered by the discovery of a "camouflaged reserve" accumulated by the business manager.[43] But, in late 1962, the board faced a major financial crisis requiring an increase in taxes. The president of the board, General La-Brum, stated that the school system needed $50 million over the next five years.

At that time, the Pennsylvania legislature was Republican-controlled and a Republican governor (Scranton) was in office in Harrisburg; the city was controlled by the Democrats, who faced an election in 1963. The board sought the governor's help in securing a tax increase proposing a surcharge on the federal income tax and a penny-a-pack cigarette tax. The governor did not support the cigarette tax and the Democratic mayor of Philadelphia opposed the income tax. The Republican majority in the legislature stipulated that, as a condition of any comprehensive tax increase, every member of the Philadelphia delegation in the legislature (all but two of thirty-nine were Democrats) would have to support the program. Early in 1963, the board president wrote to every legislator, appealing for support for the tax program. The Democratic county chairman proposed a bipartisan move for a tax increase. However, when specific programs were proposed, they were opposed by one or another of the participants.

Finally, on February 9, 1963, Governor Scranton came out in support of the GPM recommendation and suggested a shift of taxing power from the state to the city. The shift was opposed by most members of the school board (except Mrs. Greenfield), who feared "political interference," and by the mayor and the city council, who did not want responsibility for levying increased taxes. The move was also opposed by the Democratic county chairman. GPM took the initiative, forming the Educational Home Rule Assembly (EHRA) to press for implementation of its recommendation. EHRA added the prestige of a number of civic groups, including the Citizens' Committee for Public Education, to the power of GPM and mobilized support for home-rule power.

A bill to effect the shift in taxing powers was introduced in the State House of Representatives by Republican Representative Austin Lee, who had close ties with GPM. The Democratic city committee immediately circulated a petition opposing the shift. As a result of a meeting with LaBrum, Scranton agreed to shelve temporarily the shift proposal, while the board and city officials attempted to develop a tax program with broad city support. The Democratic county chairman brought together sixty community leaders (excluding the Citizens' Committee for Public Education and GPM) to develop a program. They agreed on nine separate taxing powers, which would have netted a sum $9 million short of the board's requirements. The proposal had broad community support.

As a result of pressure from the Philadelphia Teachers' Union, the governor supported the proposal and convinced the Ways and Means Committee to report all nine measures to the floor. The Philadelphia Democratic delegation supported three of these measures and left the assembly when the other six came up for a vote. The three measures that passed were a 1 per cent tax on ground rents, a 2 per cent tax on pari-mutuel betting, and an increase in the real estate tax rate.

Scranton then announced that he would sign no tax bills unless the home-rule bill was also passed. Opposition to the home-rule bill was developing because of concern that it would provide for an elective board. Scranton conferred with William H. Wilcox, executive director of GPM, who opposed an elective board. Out of this meeting came a proposal for the establishment of a Home Rule Charter Commission to determine the method of board selection; its proposals were to be submitted to referendum. Opposition by LaBrum and city council members was of no avail. The bills shifting taxing power and establishing the charter commission were both passed.[44]

During the course of the meeting of the legislature, GPM led the coalition of groups that supported fiscal home rule. It provided widespread community support for the governor, which was necessary to counteract the opposition of the board and the city's political leadership to the transfer of taxing power. GPM and EHRA played the determining role in the transfer of taxing power and assured the reform movement a major role in control over the city school system. Though their role was a necessary condition for reform, it was not a sufficient one. They needed, and obtained, the support of the Citizens' Committee for Public Education and other civic groups.

THE HOME RULE CHARTER COMMISSION

The shift in taxing power from the State Legislature to the city was an interim measure subject to final resolution by referendum. The Charter Commission was empowered to prepare a home-rule charter for the schools, including recommendations for the method of board selection and its taxing power.[45] These issues were widely debated throughout 1964. Some supported an elected board that would have its own taxing power and, hence, would be fiscally independent. GPM campaigned hard for its recommendations for an appointed board to be selected by the mayor, using the screening-panel device. They also favored giving the city council the right to establish tax limits, while retaining in the board complete power over budget preparation and administration.

The Citizens' Committee for Public Education played a significant role in the debate, both by providing a forum for discussion and by its support of the GPM recommendations. GPM and its director, William H. Wilcox, retained their influence, and it was GPM's recommendation that was adopted in the charter commission report.[46] The report was submitted to referendum on May 18, 1965, and was easily carried.

THE ROLE OF THE MAYOR

Mayor Tate was an unwilling recipient of his newly received powers over the city's schools. In past years, no mayor of Philadelphia would openly indicate a policy position on education matters. To do so would expose him to accusations of political interference. There was also recognition by Philadelphia's mayors that there was little to be gained and much to be lost from involvement in school policy.[47] Under the old structure, the mayor had no formal procedural role. Under the home-rule charter, the mayor had the responsibility for appointment of the Board of Education and was directly concerned with the allocation of financial resources for the city's school system. Mayor Tate has, thus far, continued the tradition of noninvolvement despite his formal power. He has been able to do so—forced to do so—because of the screening panel's recommendation of Richardson Dilworth as school board chairman.

As a former mayor of the city and a popular and powerful political figure in his own right, Richardson Dilworth has been able to function independently of city hall. It seems, also, that Dilworth was the personal choice of the reform movement and GPM for school board chairman. When his name was first suggested and he expressed interest in the position, the screening panel would consider no other person. That Mayor Tate agreed to both his appointment and his condition of acceptance (that he have veto power over all other appointments) testifies to the strength of his support in the city.

Reform in Philadelphia was achieved through a coalition of the reform movement, education interest groups, and civil rights groups. The civil rights groups, though politically weak and generally ineffective at the time, drew public attention to the sad state of the city's schools. They served as a catalyst for growing community concern, which activated existing civic groups and helped mobilize public support for reform. In other cities, these pressures have led only to increased spending in an effort to satisfy civil rights groups. In Philadelphia, because of the combination of circumstances described, fundamental reform was achieved.

Change has occurred in Philadelphia primarily because the reform movement was willing to accept political responsibility for school policies. Representing the economic power establishment in the city, they saw in the dilapidated state of the city's schools a serious threat to the economic future of the downtown business community. They were not willing to accept school reform solely in terms of increased expenditures. They sought, through administrative reform, to establish control over the system, open it wide to public scrutiny, and, thus, achieve basic and meaningful changes in program and direction.

The radical changes that have occurred in Philadelphia are the direct result of the involvement of the members of the downtown business community who saw in school reform a first step in alleviating the social and ethnic problems that face the city. The involvement of GPM differentiates Philadelphia from other large cities in the nature of the changes that have been effected.

Prior to 1964, the Philadelphia schools were, legally, fiscally independent of municipal government, but heavily dependent—fiscally, politically, and academically—on the city's political leadership. Public participation was nonexistent and the school system was a closed system. Today, Philadelphia's schools are legally fiscally dependent on the city government, but they operate with maximum fiscal freedom and with no significant interference from city hall. The system is more open, with responsibility clearly defined in the board chairman, Richardson Dilworth. Public participation at this policy-making level is widespread, with major interest groups such as the Urban League, the Citizens' Committee for Public Education, the Equal Opportunity League, the Pennsylvania Federation of Teachers, and others actively studying school problems and influencing school policy.

It is not fiscal status that explains the district's independence from, or dependence upon, municipal government. It is the strength of the school board and its political leadership and the character of public support that are important. A weak or apolitical board can become dependent upon political leadership in seeking a necessary share of public resources for its support, whether it is by law dependent or independent fiscally. A strong board, one that is able to develop its own independent political power base, with strong political leadership is able to function with maximum freedom both from city and state governments and from its own administrative staff no matter what its fiscal status.

Notes

1. Robert L. Freedman, A *Report on Politics in Philadelphia* (Cambridge, Mass.: The Joint Center for Urban Studies of the Massachusetts Institute of Technology and Harvard University, 1963), II, 18–19, and VI, 1; and William R. Odell, *Educational Survey Report for the Philadelphia Board of Public Education* (Philadelphia:

Board of Public Education, 1965), p. 16. Excerpts from the Odell Report appear in Chapter IV, below; citations to this work, however, refer to the original.

2. Greater Philadelphia Movement, A *Citizens' Study of Public Education in Philadelphia* (Philadelphia: Greater Philadelphia Movement, 1962), pp. 9 and 12; Odell, *op. cit.*, p. 15.

3. Freedman, *op. cit.*, VI, 6. The preshift taxing limits were set forth in state statutes: Sec. 652 of the Public School Code; Act of May 23, 1949, P.L. 1661, as amended (24 *P.S.* 583.1); Act of November 19, 1959, P.L. 1552 (24 *P.S.* 583.10); Act of July 8, 1957, P.L. 548 (24 *P.S.* 583.6); Act of May 10, 1951, P.L. 237, as amended (24 *P.S.* 581.32); Act of May 23, 1949, P.L. 1669, as amended (24 *P.S.* 584.1–584.3)—from William B. Castetter *et al.*, *Guide to Apportionment of and Controls Governing Pennsylvania Public School Funds* (Philadelphia: Philadelphia Suburban School Study Council Group E, 1966), pp. 33–34.

4. Odell, *op. cit.*, p. 360; and Freedman, *op. cit.*, VI, 6.

5. Freedman, *op. cit.*

6. *Ibid.*, VI, 2–5.

7. Interviews with community leaders, January, 1967.

8. Greater Philadelphia Movement, *op. cit.*, Part A, p. 17; Odell, *op. cit.*, p. 360; and interview with local education reporter, January, 1967.

9. Odell, *op. cit.*, pp. 19–22; and interviews with community leaders, January, 1967.

10. Odell, *op. cit.*, p. 60.

11. *Ibid.*, p. 344.

12. *Ibid.*, p. 343; and Philadelphia Public Education Board, *Journal of the Public Education Board* (1958).

13. Odell, *op. cit.*, p. 337.

14. School Program Review Committee, *An Analysis of the Proposed 1966–1971 Capital Program and 1966 Capital Budget of the School District of Philadelphia* (Philadelphia: Citizens' Council on City Planning, 1966), p. 7.

15. *Report of the Special Committee on Nondiscrimination of the Board of Public Education of Philadelphia, Pennsylvania* (July, 1964), p. 29. The lack of innovation in the past decade was determined from Odell, *op. cit.*, ix; from interviews; and from the failure of the research staff to uncover any innovative programs.

16. Act of August 9, 1963, P.L. 640—from Castetter *et al.*, *op. cit.*, pp. 33–34.

17. Act of August 9, 1963, P.L. 643; and Educational Home Rule Charter Commission, *Proposed Supplement to the Philadelphia Home Rule Charter* (Philadelphia, 1962).

18. Interview with local education reporter, January, 1967.

19. Eight of the nine incoming board members (Dilworth excepted) participated in the formulation of the task force reports—*Reports of the Task Forces to the Incoming Board of Education* (Philadelphia, 1965).

20. "Report of Task Force on Manpower and Programs to Richardson Dilworth," in *ibid.*, pp. 5–6.

21. See "Report of Task Force on Manpower and Management," "Report of Task Force on Capital Program and Physical Plant," and "Report of Task Force on Budget Analysis and Procedures," in *ibid.*

22. *The Evening Bulletin*, March 4, 1966.

23. See School District of Philadelphia, *Current School District Activities: Background Material Prepared for School District Workshop* (Philadelphia, 1966).

24. Interviews with local education reporter and school officials, January, 1967.

25. Interviews with school officials, January, 1967.

26. School District of Philadelphia, *A Comprehensive Program for Innovation: Underlying Premises and Planning Approaches to Force Title III Operational Requests* (Philadelphia, 1966), pp. 36–45.

27. *The Proposed Operating Budget of the School District of Philadelphia, The Fiscal Year Beginning July 1, 1966*, p. 6; and Board of Education, *Annual Financial Report* (Philadelphia, 1965), p. 2.

28. *The Evening Bulletin*, May 17, 1966.

29. Interview with local education reporter, January, 1967.

30. Philadelphia Public Education Board, *Journal of the Public Education Board* (1959); *Report of the Special Committee on Nondiscrimination* . . . , pp. 6–7; and Odell, *op. cit.*, p. 29.

31. *Report of the Special Committee on Nondiscrimination* . . . , pp. 37–38.

32. The committee made numerous recommendations as it proceeded in its work, many of which were adopted as board policy in 1963 and 1964. The committee ceased to be active as a community force after its formal report was issued in July, 1964.

33. Freedman, *op. cit.*, VI, 2–3, 6, and 8.

34. Quoted in Bernard McCormick, "The Man in the Double-breasted Suit," *Greater Philadelphia Magazine*, LVIII (January, 1967), 150 and 152.

35. Greater Philadelphia Movement, *op. cit.*, Part A, p. 2.

36. Interviews with community leaders, January, 1967.

37. Freedman, *op. cit.*, V, 3.

38. Greater Philadelphia Movement, *op. cit.*, Part A, pp. 5–7 and 32–34, and Part B, pp. 1–12.

39. Freedman, *op. cit.*, VI, 7–8.

40. *Ibid.*, VI, 12; and interviews with community leaders, January, 1967.

41. Interviews with community leaders, January, 1967.

42. Freedman, *op. cit.*, VI, 6 and 11–13; and Greater Philadelphia Movement, *op. cit.*, Part A, pp. 23 and 25.

43. Freedman, *op. cit.*, VI, 9.

44. This account taken from *The Philadelphia Inquirer*, January–August, 1963.

45. Act of August 9, 1963, P.L. 643.

46. Educational Home Rule Charter Commission, *op. cit.*

47. Freedman, *op. cit.*, VI, 1.

IV

School Governance and Reform

The varied failures of school systems in America's urban communities have led to the call for studies that would pinpoint the roots of failure and lead, eventually, to the formulation of proposals capable of rectifying conditions. Several major studies of large-city systems have been made in recent years, and this chapter offers highlights from three of the more important ones. The chapter also presents relevant commentaries on the studies.

The preliminary concern of each study was the detailed evaluation of urban school conditions. Generally, the researchers were able to determine with precision the specific failures. The dominant themes in these studies—all of which related to reforms within the system—involve concern with administrative reorganization and with the provision of more resources to support and expand existing programs. Thus, the emphasis is placed on preserving the basic outlines of the system while, in terms of quantity and efficiency, reforming certain aspects of it.

Commentaries on these studies indicate support for their approach by professional educators already operative within the system and criticism by spokesmen for the groups and ideologies newly interested in education. The latter group of commentators is concerned with revision of the existing power structure, as well as with the techniques for perfecting teaching; they feel that educational innovation is vital and, at the same time, impossible unless a basic restructuring of existing systems occurs. The professional educators believe in the soundness of existing methods and administrative techniques and argue that additional resources and support are all that is needed to correct present inadequacies.

In the sense that it describes in great detail the operation of the Philadelphia school system and offers a set of recommendations for improvement that are geared toward administrative reorganization, structural change, more money, and expanded capital plant and staff, the Odell study of Philadelphia is traditional. The Passow study of the Washington, D. C., school system breaks from the same general pattern only in its call for a form of decentralization geared to eight large districts. In dealing with a school system that is overwhelmingly composed of black children, it presents both a set of unique problems and a picture of black dominance—the potential wave of the future in our urban school systems. Commenting on the Passow study, Paul Lauter and Florence Howe are considerably more vehement in their condemnation of existing conditions. They call for political as well as administrative reforms.

The Bundy proposals for the New York City school system are radically different in approach from the recommendations of Odell and Passow. The Bundy panel calls for improving educational services through political change: the restructuring of the present school system into a decentralized system in which there would be between thirty to sixty separate school districts governed, to a large extent, by community representatives and parents in the local districts. The Bundy Plan set the context for a political argument that is still being disputed in New York City. Countering the Bundy proposals is the interim report of the Council of Supervisory Associations of New York. This organization represents the administrators and bureaucrats who now govern the city's schools. In the last selection in this chapter, Jason Epstein evaluates the Bundy Plan in terms of the general problem of the alienation of the poor, who, in our urban areas, are predominantly black. Epstein suggests that, if today's poor are to have the same opportunities that other ethnic groups enjoyed once they had amassed sufficient political power to restructure the institutions they felt were failing them, urban institutions such as the schools will have to undergo major change.

15. EDUCATIONAL SURVEY REPORT FOR THE PHILADELPHIA BOARD OF PUBLIC EDUCATION

WILLIAM R. ODELL

The Philadelphia Board of Public Education entered into a contract in June, 1963, with Dr. William R. Odell of the Stanford University School of Education to serve as director of an educational survey of the Philadelphia public schools. The survey period was to cover approximately eighteen months, with the findings and recommendations of the survey to be submitted to the Board of Public Education on or about December 31, 1964.

The director was authorized to select all persons connected with the survey because of their special competence in the various areas of investigation comprehended by the survey, but persons presently residing in the Philadelphia metropolitan area were not to be included on the survey staff. The Board of Public Education's desire was to have an independent, outside viewpoint brought to bear upon current local school problems.

The scope of the study was comprehensive with respect to the educational program. It included an appraisal of preschool and elementary programs, secondary school programs, adult education programs, student services and pupil guidance programs, selected phases of the physical plant program, financial resources, school-community relationships, patterns of organization, administrative operations, and the professional staff personnel program. Also included were responsibility for consultation with the Board of Public Education concerning recommendations of the recently completed Worden and Risberg *Survey of Operations* (a report on school business operations) and continuing contact with the Shils study of classified staff personnel problems.

.   .   .   .

Reprinted from William R. Odell, *Educational Survey Report for the Philadelphia School Board of Public Education* (Philadelphia: Board of Public Education, 1965).

Two central conclusions emerge from the findings of the educational survey of the Philadelphia public schools. First, the school system includes a large number of able and dedicated staff members and offers an array of excellent programs. Second, there are a number of critical organizational, curricular, and instructional improvements needed at all levels of the school system. Our focal concern with the problems we have identified and with the development of recommendations for the solution of these problems should be interpreted with due regard to the first of these two basic conclusions.

Evidence from the testing programs conducted by the Division of Educational Research in Philadelphia and by the Educational Testing Service of Princeton, New Jersey (supported by the Report of the Special Committee on Nondiscrimination of the Board of Public Education and by the Fels Institute Report on Special Education and Fiscal Requirements of Urban School Districts in Pennsylvania), reveals that the average achievement in basic skill subjects at the elementary school level for the Philadelphia system, taken as a whole, falls approximately one-half year below achievement levels for comparable pupils in other school systems. One-third of the Philadelphia pupils are in schools where averages in the skill subjects are from 1¼–2¼ years below grade norms at the end of the sixth grade. Achievement in the areas of science and social studies is comparably unsatisfactory at the sixth-grade level, and presumably in other, earlier grades as well.

The general ninth-grade level achievement falls well below expectancy in most areas sampled by the Educational Testing Service survey, and especially in science and social studies. Senior high school achievement is generally unsatisfactory for the least able quarter of the pupils. These same pupils, according to our analysis sample, participate very little in extracurricular activities. The pattern of curriculum choices for senior high schools is undesirably elaborate and opportunities to elect courses to achieve a balanced education are difficult or impossible in several of the curriculums. Boys in particular have a difficult time throughout their school careers.

The school day for pupils and teachers is uneven in length among school levels. It is badly planned at the elementary school level, with an overlong lunch hour; much too short at the senior high school level; and irrationally unequal in length for junior high, senior high, and technical high schools. The work of the school system is not well distributed among the three levels—central office, district offices, and individual school units.

The following is a summary of the main ideas and recommendations drawn from preceding chapters of the survey report:

1. Any final solution to genuine improvement of the public school

program in Philadelphia depends upon broad community acceptance of the fact that past educational programs and financial-support levels are not adequate to meet the accumulated tasks of the local public schools. If problems that exist are to be solved, additional funds equal to, or greater in amount than, those spent in surrounding suburban school systems (where in many ways school problems are simpler) must be made available. This is a problem for the local community of Philadelphia, the state of Pennsylvania, and the federal government to solve together.

Our recommendation is that the Philadelphia per pupil expenditure goal be set at $650 for 1966, and at higher levels in succeeding years, as it becomes financially possible to do so. The recommended figure will equal the school-support levels of some Philadelphia suburban communities and make possible immediate and continuing improvements in the Philadelphia public school program. Any lesser financial-support program than the foregoing one will not make possible the improvements now obviously needed. This matter is of primary urgency in Philadelphia.

2. A major bottleneck checking the improvement of the educational program in Philadelphia is the shortage of classroom, library, elementary cafeteria, and other educational spaces. A city-wide long-range master plan for physical facilities must be adopted and implemented before substantial kindergarten expansion, class size reduction, lengthened high school day, improved socio-economic and racial integration school attendance patterns, etc., can be achieved. This matter is of second-ranking urgency in Philadelphia.

3. The central administrative organization should be reconstituted to make functions of individual staff members clearer and more unitary. Basically, the responsibilities of the central administrative staff are system-wide *planning, control,* and *evaluation*. Only programs that are necessarily or more effectively implemented when centralized for the entire system should be *operated* from this top level.

A revised administrative organization plan to achieve these purposes is presented in this survey report, and its adoption was recommended. The essential features of this plan are:

A. The Board of Public Education should continue, as it has increasingly been attempting to do in recent months, to become more of a deliberative, policy-making body concerned with the development of long-range improved educational and capital programs for the school district of Philadelphia. The board should engage less in administrative acts, and it should improve its methods of communication in all constructive ways with community and staff in order to raise its public image. An improved image is essential for the proper performance of the board's highly important role in the city of Philadelphia.

B. The main central-office administrative positions, all responsible to the superintendent of schools/secretary of the board, are:

   1. Deputy Superintendent of Schools*
   2. Associate Superintendent for Research and Development**
   3. Associate Superintendent for Special Education and Pupil Personnel Services**
   4. Associate Superintendent for Curriculum Planning**
   5. Associate Superintendent for Area Schools**
   6. Associate Superintendent for Personnel*
   7. Associate Superintendent for Physical Facilities**
   8. Business Manager
   9. Director of Informational Services**
  10. Coordinator of Intergroup Education**
  11. General Counsel
  12. Director Financial Planning

4. The scope of responsibility and the size of the staff of the district superintendents of schools should be steadily expanded: first, experimentally in one or two districts and, ultimately, in all districts as conditions warrant. The chief function of the district administrative level should be the operation and supervision of the instructional programs of schools, recognizing the responsibility of each school principal to be the leader in his school. Two new district offices should be established immediately to help equalize the sizes of the existing eight districts.

5. Both the conception and the implementation of the instructional program of the schools call for significant improvement in many particulars. Briefly, these are as follows:

A. *The Elementary Schools.* It is necessary first to develop a more adequate over-all curriculum for these schools at the system level, while accepting and encouraging adaptations of the basic curriculum in schools across the city, in the light of the vast differences in the total pupil population. At the same time, more systematic arrangements must be made for the installation of new and revised curriculums and organizational schemes in schools, and for the career development of teachers and principals from the time they enter the system throughout their years of service. Extension of the kindergarten program—and, ultimately, of the prekindergarten program to selected pupils—must receive a high priority in future planning.

B. *The Junior High Schools.* The recruitment, induction, retention, and career development of teacher personnel is the singular problem at this school level. To cope with this problem, it is recom-

---

* New positions recommended by survey.
** Reconstituted positions under proposed organization.

mended that the Philadelphia public schools create a number of "portal schools" for the induction of new teachers and also establish in each subject field in each junior high school a formally differentiated position of head of department or supervisor of instruction. With respect to the program of studies, it is recommended that the formal distinctions between the several curriculums in Grade 9 be sharply reduced or abolished and that a course in science be made available to all pupils in Grade 9.

C. *The Senior High Schools.* A longer school day and the redesigning of several curriculum patterns are required to permit and encourage pupils of all ability levels to achieve a more desirable balance in their general, specialized, and extraclass educational programs. Existing policies for staff allocation and utilization reveal the need for precise separation of allocation for administrative and supervisory tasks from provision of personnel for instruction. There is also need for exploring dramatically new teacher and pupil assignment patterns, such as team teaching, large- and small-group instruction, and independent study. The strong department head structure of the senior high schools should be expanded to all subject fields, with provision for combining groups of teachers in blocks of junior and senior high schools when the total number of teachers in a given subject field in any one school appears too small to justify assignment of a department head.

D. *Occupational and Vocational Programs.* The coordination of the program of occupational education should be unified under one administrative head within the Philadelphia public school system, with assistant directors ultimately heading the separate divisions. Adaptation of the existing programs to rapidly changing job needs, new work conditions, and federal programs for youths and adults is highly essential. Special concern should be devoted to the possibility of developing post–high school technical institutes and to modified programs of extension and TV education.

6. A revised plan of ability and achievement testing for Philadelphia schools needs to be developed to include the use of tests from outside sources. The results should be used for immediate instructional program improvement within the system.

7. The working relationships among special education programs, pupil personnel and counseling services, and psychologists need to be re-examined and the roles of psychologists, counselors, social workers, school psychiatrists, attendance officers, nurses, etc., realigned into a more comprehensive team enterprise. Possible increased emphasis upon preventive

and group techniques at the local school level to balance case work on the present pattern of referrals requires careful examination.

8. Curriculum planning should be considered as a separate function from, though closely related to, instructional improvement. There needs to be a better total system of curriculum planning for the Philadelphia public schools to include all subject areas on a cyclical basis. Subject matter experts and other specialists need to be continuously and systematically involved in order to provide the technical competencies required. Experimentation is functionally a part of curriculum development; demonstration is an integral part of instructional improvement.

9. There is need in the personnel office for specialized personnel to deal continuously with staff groups, both professional and classified, concerning a wide range of problems related to compensation and general working conditions. Revision of professional salary schedules and adjustments in length of teachers' days at all school levels needs careful study and prompt board decision.

16. TOWARD CREATING A MODEL URBAN SCHOOL SYSTEM: A STUDY OF THE WASHINGTON, D.C., PUBLIC SCHOOLS

A . HARRY PASSOW

Teachers College, Columbia University, undertook a comprehensive fifteen-month study of the District of Columbia public schools to assess current programs and practices and to make recommendations which, if implemented, would insure education of good quality for Washington's population. In contracting for the study, the Board of Education opened the Washington schools and themselves to the critical inquiries of outside observers who were deliberately seeking weaknesses which would account for the educational inadequacies of the system. In detailing contractual relationships, it was agreed that "the entire school system, including personnel, records and facilities [was] to be opened to the consultants, limited only to the extent necessary to maintain the confidentiality of records of individual pupils and staff members." The board, the school system, and the community are to be commended for joining with study personnel in seeking ways of strengthening education in the District of Columbia.

The study was conducted by thirty-three task forces, each dealing with a specified problem area. Eighty-one task force chairmen and consultants, ninety-seven graduate assistants and students, and a resident staff of six research assistants probed all aspects of education in Washington. They visited schools and classes; interviewed students, staffs, parents, community members, and school and community leaders; administered questionnaires and inventories to pupils and staff members; examined pertinent pupil records and other school data; studied reports and records from other agencies, governmental and private; and drew on appropriate data sources wherever they could be found. The thousands of pages of reports which they submitted, together with basic documents and data analyses, constitute a reservoir which can now be tapped for further study and planning.

Reprinted from A. Harry Passow, *Summary of a Report on the Washington, D.C. Public Schools* (New York: Teachers College, Columbia University, mimeo., 1967).

The study was carried on in the middle of a year of significant educational, social, and political upheaval. As professional educators, study personnel were impressed with the way various segments of the community and the school system were responding to the need for educational change.

.   .   .   .

With its poverty, slums, and obsolete schools and schooling, the District of Columbia is presently exemplary only of the worst of urbanized settings. Congress and the nation cannot continue to tolerate nor even contribute to such a situation. Congress can help in at least two ways: (1) It can strengthen Washington's financial position with respect to present budgetary arrangements and (2) it can legislate special categorical grants for the next five to ten years to create the laboratory model demonstrating that city schools can provide full and equal opportunities to develop the talent potential of its entire population.

Washington is not just another troubled large city; it is the nation's capital and its international center. The District of Columbia schools cannot be treated as just another school system, different only in that its patrons are without vote and in that it is subjected to greater "federal control." America's cities are in crisis and turmoil, and Washington is one of those cities, but it is much more to the nation. Schools alone cannot resolve the problem of the cities, but, without adequate education, there is little hope of alleviating the difficulties that metropolitan areas face. What better place is there for the nation to tackle its urban problems than in the city which houses its national and international leadership?

.   .   .   .

Despite some examples of good quality education, of dedicated and creative professionals at all levels, of a pattern of improving financial support, and of efforts to initiate new programs, education in the District of Columbia is in deep and probably worsening trouble. Unlike most large-city systems, which have a core of "slum" schools surrounded by a more affluent ring, the District of Columbia has a predominance of so-called inner-city schools. These schools include large concentrations of economically disadvantaged children, a largely resegregated pupil population, a predominantly Negro staff, a number of overaged and inadequate school buildings, and inappropriate materials and programs. The consequence—as the Panel on Educational Research and Development, President's Science Advisory Committee, noted of such schools across the nation—is that "adolescents depart . . . ill-prepared to lead a satisfying, useful life or to participate successfully in the community." The panel concluded its judgment of such schools by observing that "by all known criteria, the majority of urban and rural schools are failures."

Applying the usual criteria of scholastic achievement as measured by standardized tests, by holding power of the school, by college-oriented and further education, by post–secondary school employment status, by performance on Armed Forces induction tests, the Washington schools do not measure up well. Like most school systems, the District of Columbia has no measures on the extent to which schools are helping students attain other educational objectives, for there are no data on self-concepts, ego-development, values, attitudes, aspirations, citizenship, and other "nonacademic" but important aspects of personal growth. However, the inability of large numbers of children to reverse the spiral of futility and break out of the poverty-stricken ghettos suggests that the schools are no more successful in attaining these goals than they are in the more traditional academic objectives.

The study findings confirm the general impressions that many professionals and lay citizens have about education in the District of Columbia as presently organized and operated: The schools are not adequate to the task of providing quality education for Washington's children. The generalized findings, documented in the report, point to a school system which reveals:

A low level of scholastic achievement, as measured by performance on standardized tests

Grouping procedures which have been honored in the breach as often as they have been observed in practice

A curriculum which, with certain exceptions, has not been especially developed for, or adapted to, an urban population

A holding power or dropout rate which reflects a large number of youths leaving school before earning a diploma

An increasing *de facto* residential segregation for the District of Columbia as a whole, which has resulted in a largely resegregated school system

Staffing patterns which have left the schools with large numbers of "temporary" teachers and heightened Washington's vulnerability at a time of national teacher shortage

Guidance services which are unable to reach the heart of the personnel welfare needs of the pupil population

Inadequate evaluation and assessment procedures, together with limited use of test data for diagnosis and counseling

In-service teacher education programs which fall far short of providing adequately for the continuing education essential for professional growth

A promotion system which has lacked the basic ingredients of career development and training for supervisory and administrative leadership

Patterns of deployment of specialists, such as supervisors and psychologists, which tend to limit their effectiveness

A "reacting school system," rather than an initiating one, insofar as innovation, long-range planning, and program development are concerned

A central administrative organization which combines overconcentration of responsibilities in some areas and proliferation and overlap in others

Budgetary and business procedures which are needlessly complicated and cumbersome

Substantial numbers of school buildings which are less than adequate for conducting a full educational program and in which the maintenance program lags badly

Poor communication between the schools and the communities they serve

A board of education whose operating procedures appear to be unusually cumbersome so that an inordinate amount of time is spent on repetitive debate and on administrative detail rather than policy leadership

Relationships with other youth-serving agencies which are less than optimal.

.   .   .   .

To a greater or lesser extent, many of these same findings exist in other large cities. But the fact that they are found elsewhere in no way mitigates their impact on Washington's population. Thus, the District of Columbia faces a two-pronged challenge: providing massive remediation of existing learning difficulties for those new in school and designing developmental and compensatory programs for thousands of children who will be entering school in the years ahead.

17. THE SCHOOL MESS

PAUL LAUTER and FLORENCE HOWE

A white school administrator in the District of Columbia unwittingly provided a clue to the pathology of urban education. She was talking frankly about the "two language" problem of a school population that is 91 per cent Negro. Yes, she agreed, Negro children speak a dialect whose consistency we ought, in some measure, to respect. "But then," she said, warming to her subject, "there is the problem of getting jobs. For example, take the young man who goes to the store for a job. A lady comes out of the store with a package, and he goes up to her and says, 'Lady kin ah kerryer packsh furya?' Well, she isn't quite sure what he has said, and his tone has put her off as well, and so she says, 'No, thank you.' And the boy doesn't get the job." The sight of black children educated to haul packages for ladies is a common and haunting one: You see them at Washington's supermarkets any day in the week. Nothing so shapes the education these children are given as the ideas people hold about the purposes of that education.

No more extensive catalogue of the failure of urban education has been provided than a recent study of the Washington, D.C., public schools. The Passow Report grew out of pressure from citizens' groups in the District of Columbia for a plan to change the faltering school system. The former Superintendent of Schools Carl Hansen was under considerable personal attack by some members of the school board and by civil rights groups; and, with the Board of Education, he was the defendant in a federal suit, brought by a Negro, Julius Hobson, attacking discrimination against Negro children in general and, in particular, the "track system," a rigid form of ability-grouping instituted by the superintendent. Hansen agreed to a study, at least in part it would seem, as a delaying tactic, and proposed for the job the National Education Association (NEA), a group often accused of being a company union, since its huge membership includes school administrators as well as teachers. But liberal groups did not trust the notion of educators passing judgment on their local colleagues—the NEA's national office is in Washington. Through the efforts primarily of the Washington, D.C., Citizens for Better Public Education, whose current chairman is Mrs. Gilbert A. Harrison, they sought out Columbia University's Teachers College and, in June, 1966, helped to arrange a $250,000 contract for the year's study.

Those forces working to reform the schools clearly wanted the prestige of Columbia and of "research findings" to substantiate the patent defects that everyone had long observed in the system. White parents had been fleeing Washington since World War II—only 55 per cent of the children in Washington's schools were white when desegregation was ordered. Negro parents able to afford it had been sending their children to private schools in increasing numbers. It was only a matter of time before Washington's schools "served" only those, black and poor, who could not escape them.

Meanwhile, however, Julius Hobson's federal suit against the school system was heard before Judge J. Skelly Wright, the architect of desegregation in New Orleans. In June, 1967, on the day before Passow's preliminary findings were released, Judge Wright handed down his ruling —and thoroughly upstaged the report. Judge Wright found that the superintendent and the board "unconstitutionally deprive the District's Negro and poor public school children of their right to equal educational opportunity with the District's white and more affluent public school children." He attacked segregation of students and faculty, unequal distribution of funds among predominantly white and black schools, and the "track" system. Tracking, said Wright, condemned black and poor children, on the basis of inappropriate aptitude tests, to a blue-collar education in lower tracks distinctly unequal to that provided white children in upper tracks. Many Negro schools had no honors track and few white schools had the "basic," or lowest, track. Wright ordered an end to tracking, decreed that children be transferred to relieve overcrowding and to achieve maximum desegregation, and asked the schools to prepare a plan for integrating their faculties and instituting equal services for Negro and white students. Hansen, faced with a sharp judicial condemnation of his regime and forbidden by the board to appeal in his capacity as superintendent, resigned; Congressmen talked about providing for election of the school board, instead of having it appointed by the federal district court judges. It appeared that a new educational day might be dawning in Washington, what with the force of the Wright decision, the possibility of local democracy, and the details and proposals of the Passow Report.

As Judge Wright's decision delighted the militants who had brought suit, so the Passow Report has pleased its liberal sponsors. Its pages, however unreadable for the most part, honestly document enormous failure at all levels by all participants in the system. Thirty-three task force chairmen and a staff of more than one hundred reported to Passow their observations of the schools and the communities around them, the administrative offices, even their interviews with congressional committeemen. With professional shrewdness, they examined the administrative hierarchy, the curriculum, books and equipment, population shifts, attendance, teachers' education and background, and more besides. The endlessly detailed report, probably put together too hastily by Passow, is a disorganized compendium of all findings: The divisions are arbitrary and everything is given equal importance; there is no real direction—only a hope that Washington will become a model to the nation.

But from the mass of statistics, surveys, and observations, two images emerge. First, an image of administrative quagmire: The system is an irrational accretion of conflicting provinces and traditional loyalties, too understaffed in most areas to do a job well, yet too large to be responsive to classroom needs. Passow charts the breakdown of communication between lower echelons and policy-makers: Principals, for example, are almost never consulted about staff appointments to their schools, nor teachers about curriculum materials and aids they need in class. On the other hand, curriculum policy is handed down in bare outline and without real guidance for teachers, with the result that they generally offer to students the shell of a program: Reading, for instance, is taught as if it were a matter of breaking some mysterious code, rather than as a useful tool for gaining understanding and enjoyment; and unused and misunderstood science and mathematics equipment lines the bookshelves.

Beyond the bureaucracy's bungling—indeed, seemingly remote from it —one sees a second image, that of students who are not learning. Passow's statistics bear out what everyone already knew from experience: that segregated Negro children in Washington, as in every city, perform abysmally by all "achievement" measures. Of eleven high schools in the District of Columbia that Passow examined, one is 93 per cent white, another 60 per cent black, the rest between 84 per cent and 100 per cent black. Test scores for the white school show its students performing among the top 10 per cent in the country. Scores in the predominantly black schools are generally in the lowest third—with the integrated school always ahead of the segregated ones—and, in math, mostly in the lowest *tenth*. Achievement tests are, indeed, misleading in many respects, organized so that middle-class students will normally do better; but the fact remains that most of the students in the nation's capital do not perform in reading, writing, and arithmetic at anything close to national norms, grade levels, or any standards that can get them good jobs. One-third cannot really read well enough to pass civil service examinations. As a result, Passow tells us, private employers in the District of

Columbia and federal personnel officials accuse one another of having skimmed the cream of the high school graduates. Meanwhile, knowing how dull and useless school is for them, between 40 per cent and 50 per cent of the students drop out.

The reaction of these dropouts is probably healthy and appropriate. Passow's analysis of administrative breakdown, of an inept curriculum and low morale, would, no doubt, be enough, were the Washington schools guilty merely of failing to teach skills or encourage curiosity, adventure, enthusiasm, pride. But, in fact, occasionally the impression is of a school system only too successful. "Children in the elementary schools visited by this task force," says the report, "were having abundant opportunities to *overlearn passive conformity*." Students who drop out may well be rejecting not only the failure of the schools to teach them skills; they may be rejecting what the schools *do* teach. The report is worth quoting in this regard, though it is well to note that these quotations appear only in the sections describing instruction in the elementary schools and in English [classes].

> When the teacher has all the ideas, gives all the directions, handles all the materials, and admonishes the children to sit still and not talk—if they do not rebel or withdraw completely—most children respond with an unquestioning acceptance of the teacher's rulings on all matters. For instance, "a child was not allowed to color his Halloween pumpkin green, even though the teacher had just read a poem referring to the green of a pumpkin when it was small."
>
> The child spent most of his day paying the closest possible attention to his teacher, following her directions, responding to her questions, and obeying her rules. The children were not encouraged to talk to one another, either formally or informally—indeed, the principal technical criticism the observers had of the language program was that it did not seem to deal with speech. And the sad fact is that, in spite of all this, the children don't really learn to read. . . .
>
> The children sang when instructed to do so, chorused responses when given recognized signals, and worked on written assignments, copying exercises from the chalkboard. The children spent most of the day writing at their desks, rarely speaking except in chorus. No one argued, disagreed, or questioned anything. At no time when I was in the room did any child ask a question.

It is entirely in keeping with the elementary program just described that almost every Negro boy in Washington's high schools must participate in a "cadet corps" whose first objective is "to inculcate habits of orderliness and precision, to instill discipline and thereby respect for constituted authority." It is no accident that in high schools with large white enrollments the voluntary nature of the cadet program is explained to students, and one-quarter or fewer of the students join—while five of the predominantly black high schools have 100 per cent enrollment. Only a rare statistic like this one, or an occasional comment, catches the inner character of the Washington school system: "The teachers act as if warmth and sensitivity to individual feelings were somehow in conflict with the intellectual purposes of school instruction." What is taught in a school, after all, cannot be fully expressed in administrative or even academic language. It is conveyed by the nature and atmosphere of its classrooms, the attitudes of teachers and students toward one another and toward learning. Washington's school system ignores the lives of its students, offers them an irrelevant curriculum, emphasizes correcting their speech, appearance, habits, personalities—from kindergarten on—works mostly by close-order drill, permits students to spend more time on cadet corps than on English or math, guards instructional materials from student use. It is a system that treats "the child as a 'piece of children' rather than as an individual human being." It teaches him that he is unimportant, stupid, dirty; it teaches him to despair and hate; it teaches him to quit. It does not teach him to function with intelligence and power.

Why is this so? How has Passow explained the fact that Washington's schools have become instruments for pacifying and degrading students rather than inspiring and educating them? Since Washington (with 91 per cent or more of its 150,000 schoolchildren black and more than 50 per cent of them poor) is only a more advanced and obvious case of urban education, a diagnosis of its disease can serve, with minor modifications, for Chicago or Gary or Los Angeles.

Passow finds every part of the system contributing to the confusion and degeneration of the schools, but he emphasizes first the responsibility of the administrators and the board, then the inadequate preparation of teachers. He charts the almost total lack of articulation among parts of the system. Parents cannot find anyone to respond to their complaints, administrators are forever involved in petty details instead of leadership, experimental and research projects come and go without much relation to the system and with indifferent support and less evaluation, and teachers are left prey to their fears for their safety and advancement, and without a sense of freedom to follow their own best instincts should they ever feel the inclination to do so.

They seldom do, Passow suggests. Most Washington teachers—78 per cent of whom are Negroes and 80 per cent women—have been poorly trained in the District of Columbia or in similarly weak, segregated systems. For the most part, they know only the "say and listen" method and they do what has been done to them. Trained as passive students in authoritarian classrooms, they are really more comfortable in them. An open classroom with active, inquisitive youngsters is worrisome. Unanswerable questions might be asked; a teacher might be "wrong," get out of her depth, be embarrassed. Noise might attract the unfavorable eye of principal or supervisor. Better to establish uniform *control*, set the dimensions of the class at the limits of one's own knowledge and personality. Then nothing unknown or threatening can come up—except, of course, "unruly" children, who can be sent to the principal. Besides, whole-group instruction, which is what Hansen's instructional program mostly called for, demands total control, or so the teachers believe. Thus, as a product of a repressive system, Passow makes clear, the typical Washington teacher has internalized its main value—control—and elevated it into an educational idol.

There are further problems of race, status, and attitudes toward students that Passow does not sufficiently examine. His questionnaires on teachers' attitudes do not probe far and their interpretation is disputable. For instance, Passow finds that Washington teachers score high on an "assurance" scale and are not notably "authoritarian," but he fails to account for their admitted hostility to experiments which upset the routine or the authoritarian character of their classrooms. Again, among a list of "factors which interfere with teaching and learning" presented for teachers' reaction, Passow includes only two—class size and faculty turnover—that concern the character of the school and classroom or the teachers themselves. Predictably, most teachers blame parental indifference or students' recalcitrance and poor training. Depending on the grade they teach, 34–41 per cent of the teachers cite low level of student intelligence as a factor—one wonders how many more believe that but will not admit it; 50–72 per cent cite poor student training in basic skills. Passow's conclusion that "teacher evaluations of the quality of education seemed to be an assessment of school offerings and practices, not of the educational potential of the children," seems, therefore, a bit simple. Indeed, Passow's view of the instructional program, as well as our own experience in Washington, suggests that teachers' views of their students *and* themselves are both more ambiguous and more central to the problem than Passow allows.

During the summer, in a preservice institute with a group of Washington teachers theoretically committed to participating in an experimental program, a dispute about hair revealed a great deal about the teachers' self-images and their attitudes toward being Negroes. A film had shown a little Negro girl stroking the long, straight hair of her white teacher. "Why," a staff member, a Negro woman from Detroit, asked, "hadn't the teacher reciprocated? Why didn't she make the child feel that she was beautiful, too?" After a certain amount of hedging, a Negro teacher said, "But how could she reciprocate? She couldn't say the child's hair was beautiful—it isn't. It's all kinky and nappy, bad hair."

When the term began, the same teacher was one of the first to insist that experiments were all right for suburban children, but "these children" needed something different—discipline, control, a tight hand. Thus it is not surprising that District of Columbia teachers—Negro and white—while favorable, in one Passow survey, toward Peace Corps volunteers, college professors, Jews, and even Negroes (could they have anticipated, with long classroom skill, what was expected of them?) are coolest toward John Birchers, Communists, the Ku Klux Klan, and Black Power. The fact of the matter is that most teachers are of low social and economic origins, barely "escaped," as some perceive it, from the ghetto. They have ambivalent, often strongly hostile, feelings toward the ghetto children they teach; and the system, with its tracks, its decrepit schools, its lack of suitable and plentiful material, confirms their low expectations of the students, and, in effect, gives them a mechanism for acting out their hostility without ever being aware of it.

A third party responsible for conditions in the Washington schools, Passow mildly suggests, is Congress, which has been unwilling to provide adequate funds, especially for new construction. Passow accepts the universal groan about the District of Columbia's peculiarly tedious budgetary process: School board requests are first cut by the D.C. government, then by congressional committees. But the fact is that Congress functions not very differently from local white power structures in other cities. For political and racial reasons, the Congress (through the conservative House and Senate District committees) continues to insist on controlling the D.C. school budget, although it contributes only 15 per cent of the District of Columbia's funds. (Passow says that 25 per cent is a reasonable minimum contribution.) Budgetary control permits Congress to make political and educational policy for the schools, as Senator Byrd recently made clear when he forbade the use of regular school funds for "busing"—though the busing complies with Judge Wright's orders to relieve overcrowding and promote further desegregation. Moreover, budgetary control has permitted Congress, acting the role of absentee landlord, to reduce steadily the percentage of Board of Education requests granted. In the past thirteen years, Congress has cut almost $150 million from requests. Similarly, although Washington enjoys a relatively strong real property tax base, it shields property owners through sharply declining assessment ratios and low tax levels, while its sales tax, even on food, falls disproportionately on the poor, whose children are thus doubly robbed. As a result, over the last ten years, Washington's per pupil expenditure has risen only 63 per cent, as compared with a national average of 81 per cent—and this despite the increasing desperation of school problems in the District of Columbia.

Passow is remarkably restrained in his comments about congressional responsibility for the degeneration of the District of Columbia's schools. His strategy is not to harp on past failures, but to hold out a vision of Washington as "the nation's laboratory for the creation of a model for urban school systems and its showplace to other countries of how America's goals and values for equal opportunity can be attained in the metropolitan setting." As an eductional and administrative reformer, Passow provides a compendium of currently acceptable ideas for improving urban education—ranging from total administrative reorganization to new ambitious programs, like regular classes for four- and some three-year-olds. Most useful are his ideas about the re-education of teachers. Passow suggests that teachers should spend between 15 per cent and 20 per cent of their regular working day in "continuing education" if such study is to be really useful and not simply a sporadic activity, motivated primarily by desire for higher wages. He recommends establishing with the help of universities, Staff Development Centers for teacher education and curriculum development. He would have the curriculum developed flexibly—by teachers, principals, specialists, working together in an individual school building. He understands that teachers need support, encouragement, and the chance to grow—even as their students do: "Only as teachers come to believe in themselves and in the children they teach and are provided with the assistance in diagnosing and planning required for individualizing instruction, can the education program advance." It is a fine sentiment, but the record Passow provides of past studies ignored, present plans undermined, as well as the magnitude of the changes he recommends, suggests that his vision is suspended somewhere in political limbo.

Any proposal to change urban education must contend with problems fundamentally political rather than educational. The failure of integration, acknowledged in Passow's scant twelve pages on the subject, is a case in point. Only thirteen years ago, integration was seen both as an educational goal and a political strategy, but urban schools today are more thoroughly segregated than they were in 1954. There is, as Passow points out, no greater proportion of Negroes in the Washington area than there was 100 years ago, and thus no greater population barrier to integration. Certainly we know how to integrate the schools: Feasible plans already exist for educational parks, busing, pairing of schools, reorganizing school-district lines; and we know the further changes in metropolitan planning, housing, governmental structures, and so forth, needed to develop integrated communities. But, as Passow says, "none of this is likely to happen—indeed all of it is certain not to happen—until Marylanders, Virginians, Washingtonians, and Americans are convinced that their interests will be better served by making the national capital area a well-integrated metropolitan community than by keeping it the white-encircled black ghetto that it is now." Precisely—white Americans do not consider it in their interest to invest heavily in integration. It is not merely a question of money; it is also a matter of pledging white children to such integration. Thus, however reasonable its educational goals (the Coleman Report has shown, for example, that Negro students perform better in *comfortably* integrated schools), however essential its social goals (in a multiracial society, separate education can only perpetuate racism), as a political strategy, integration now appeals neither to reformers and liberals like Passow nor to black militants who have waited for it too long and in vain.

With integration sidetracked, the political questions then become: First, will white Americans pay the costs of the "unequal" education needed to provide equal opportunity to black children and, then, what kind of education will such "compensation" be? The cost of reconstructing urban school systems—which is what Passow is asking Washington to do—will approach, if it does not exceed, the cost of constructing almost wholly new integrated systems. To cut class size from forty to ten, to build new classrooms, to re-educate teachers, to provide both special services (medical, social, academic) for students and new books and materials will cost at least five times the present national per pupil cost, probably as much as $180 billion for the next ten years. Where is the political power to pry that kind of money loose from the Congress—or, for that matter, from any source for any urban system? Who is to guarantee, moreover, that such programs will not, like present Title I dollars from the Office of Education, become a kind of rivers and harbors bill, with each part of the educational establishment getting its bit to continue doing what it has been persistently failing at all these years? But again, money is not the only issue: Black militants and others are questioning the credibility of "compensatory" education, at least in the hands of those currently in power.

The controlling idea of compensatory education is that black and poor children are "culturally deprived" by their immediate family and slum environment. Hence, what they need is an extra dose of what middle-class children get. Educators locate the problem in the child himself and ask how the child can be changed to fit the schools' definition of achievement, instead of asking how the schools must change to serve the child. Thus, Head Start must be used to "prepare" the children of the poor for obedience and cleanliness in kindergarten. The idea of school as a "civilizing" or socializing agent is not in itself necessarily objectionable; rather, it is that no matter how carefully one defines "deprivation," its connotations include, as Dan Dodson of the New York University School of Education has suggested, the latest version of notions about original sin and natural inferiority. Where then, militants ask, is the evidence that compensatory programs won't become a more elaborate way of pushing kids around, strait-jacketing them to fit the system—all in the name of "saving" them from the damnation of deprived (read inferior) backgrounds?

The political reality that Passow does not see is expressed in the indignation of Judge Wright: "The Washington school system is a monument to the cynicism of the power structure which governs the voteless Capital of the greatest country on earth." Such monuments to cynicism exist, like giant Victorian prisons, in every city of this land. Public education, once a means for integrating and elevating American society, has become a source and carrier of the society's pathology, its teachers and administrators virtually unconscious of their own illness. The superintendent of one of the largest school systems remarked casually to us a few months ago that it will be years before people regain confidence in the schools. In the meantime, students and dropouts educated to carry packages, or guns, hang on street corners, waiting to turn the fires in themselves against the cities. Why then, the current desperation urges, trust the school system at all? Why not tear those prisons down, break the system's monopoly?

Passow's firm commitment to public education—his belief that it can, with help, cure itself—is what separates his recommendations, finally, from those more recently proposed by Kenneth Clark, James S. Coleman, and McGeorge Bundy. Though there are differences among them, the three are united in their skepticism about the system's ability to change. Coleman's idea—already under study by the U.S. Commissioner of Education—is that schools contract the teaching of basic skills to entrepreneurs like IBM and the General Learning Corporation, who would be paid on the basis of results—measured according to standard "achievement" in reading and arithmetic. Kenneth Clark, seeing public education as captive of a white middle class intent on retaining its own power and privilege, suggests the establishment of separate schools to compete with the urban systems. These might be run by states or the federal government, by colleges, industry, labor unions, or the army. Unlike Clark and Coleman, who propose goading the system with new, competing institutions (or allowing it to wither away), Bundy and other proponents of "decentralization" would break the system by diffusing its authority, especially among parents elected to local school boards which would serve limited school populations. Fred Hechinger of *The New York Times* analyzes Bundy's proposal as "an effort at both radical change and pacification of a strife-torn city. . . . It aims . . . to put an end to the feeling, now prevalent in the ghetto, that many of the district superintendents . . . are colonizers sent 'down' by the outside power structure [and] to defuse the present guerilla warfare by giving elected parents—and only parents, not outside agitators—the kind of power and responsibilities normally enjoyed by suburban school board members." Whatever their dangers, such proposals* respond to the distrust of urban systems and appeal to the interests of potentially powerful groups: the growing "welfare-industrial complex," ghetto parents and black militants, and the politicians and foundations anxious to provide the latter with "creative" channels for their anger. If they are bound to meet opposition from the educational bureaucracy and teacher groups, among other powerful forces, these ideas still have built-in political clout, which Passow's recommendations generally lack.

Passow, repeating again and again that Washington should and must become a model system, has only his moral fervor and an appeal to conscience to energize his plans. Given his loyalty to the system, the eclectic character of his suggestions, and his air of agreeing with all critics, even his proposal for some form of administrative decentralization has little political bite. Passow recommends dividing the system into six or eight community school districts of perhaps 20,000 students. Each would have a locally elected school board which would choose a district superintendent from a centrally approved list. Within the rules established by the central District of Columbia board, the local boards would establish or consult on curriculum, personnel, and budget—though it remains unclear how they might do this and what power they would really have. Bundy's proposals are not essentially different. But it is a measure of the political gulf between New York and Washington that his have received much attention, fierce attack, and some significant support, whereas Passow's, like most of the report, have been received with little fervor, especially in the ghetto. This is not, finally, so much a consequence of his ideas, but of the Washington Judge Wright so bitterly described. At a recent conference held by Passow for college, school, and community representatives, 80 per cent of those present were white. Most "community representatives"—that is, Negroes—had not bothered to attend. As one Negro who did come explained, "they don't believe much is going

---

* Coleman and Clark assume the virtues of competition, using as their model the somewhat dubious history of American industrial development. Competition in automobiles and cigarettes has produced results, in the form of profits, for companies, but it has hardly produced products that are healthy and inexpensive for the consumer. As a matter of fact, it is often the case not that competition leads to superior results, but that well-advertised shabby goods drive better ones off the market. No doubt, too, the military gets certain results with men under its control (though it would be well to look more closely at just what their results are)—Mussolini made the trains run on time. But it is not, as Clark suggests, simply antimilitary rhetoric to ask what other values and objectives are served by an education in the hands of industry or the military. To say that urban systems now block the economic mobility of black children and intensify class distinctions is not to say that education in the hands of the military-industrial complex will not remove black children from the frying pan of the ghetto to the fire of the battlefield.

to happen." In New York, where there have been demonstrations and other successful actions by parents against the school system, decentralization is a live issue, perhaps because it offers a means to activate the ghetto politically. In Washington, the largely quiescent Negro community has been promised so much so often and disappointed so persistently that it views any set of proposals with suspicion, if not contempt. The attitude toward the Passow Report ranges between "tell me when they really change anything" and "that's another quarter of a million dollars Whitey has spent on himself and not on our kids."

If adopted, the decentralization Passow suggests may help to awaken the political consciousness of Washington, whether or not Congress decides to provide for the election of a city-wide board. That proposal has verbal support from nearly everyone in Washington, and probably will be enacted during the coming year. But the lack of any sense of urgency is reflected by the fact that it is now stalled in the Senate because of a trivial political hassle as to whether elections should be held in the spring or fall. In any case, an awakened consciousness is only one step toward meaningful education for the children of Washington. One often forgotten correlation of the Coleman Report suggests that students do better when they sense that the school is relevant and responsive to *them*; that it is in some sense theirs; that, in short, they have power in it—even, if they will, Black Power. There is a lesson to be learned from that correlation, a lesson proved every day by the banality and intellectual brutality of *sub*urban education: Only so long as schools honestly serve the interests of the students can they succeed. Whether schools are responsive to boards, administrators, teachers, or parents will not finally ensure that they are responsive to children. And while they are instruments to pacify or control children, to produce manpower or package carriers, they will continue to fail.

18. RECONNECTION FOR LEARNING
(THE BUNDY REPORT)

MAYOR'S ADVISORY PANEL
ON DECENTRALIZATION OF THE
NEW YORK CITY SCHOOLS

Preface

This panel was created by Mayor John V. Lindsay under an Act of the 1967 State Legislature (Chapter 484 of the Session Laws of 1967). The Act directs the mayor to

> prepare a comprehensive study and report and formulate a plan for the creation and redevelopment of educational policy and administrative units within the city school district of the City of New York with adequate authority to foster greater community initiative and participation in the development of education policy for the public schools . . . and to achieve greater flexibility in the administration of such schools,

and to submit the report and plan, together with legislative recommendations, to the governor, the Board of Regents, and the legislature, not later than December 1, 1967. The mayor announced the creation and composition of this advisory panel on April 30, 1967.

He gave the panel its formal charge at a meeting on May 11. Thereafter, the panel appointed a staff director, who assembled a staff of full-time assistants and *ad hoc* and special consultants. The City of New York appropriated $50,000 for the study.

The panel made extensive efforts to elicit information and ideas. Through the press and through formal invitations to civic, community, and professional organizations, it solicited plans for decentralization. Through a field staff it sought information and searched out attitudes throughout the city.

In addition to a series of meetings of its own throughout the summer and fall, the panel conducted formal discussions with hundreds of repre-

Mayor's Advisory Panel on Decentralization of the New York City Schools, *Reconnection for Learning: A Community School System for New York City* (New York, 1967).

sentatives of communities throughout the city, including local school board members and members of the Education Committee of the Council Against Poverty; teachers and supervisory personnel; deans and presidents of public and private colleges and universities in the city; and civic and political leaders. It held informal discussions with many others. Through questionnaires and interviews, the views of teachers and supervisors were solicited. A feasibility study on school boundaries was commissioned on contract. To the hundreds of men and women who generously shared their experience, insights, and time with us, the panel and its staff are deeply grateful.

Summary of Recommendations

In order to:

increase community awareness and participation in the development of educational policy closely related to the diverse needs and aspirations of the city's population,

open new channels and incentives to educational innovation and excellence,

achieve greater flexibility in the administration of the schools,

afford the children, parents, teachers, other educators, and the city-at-large a single school system that combines the advantages of big-city education with the opportunities of the finest small-city and suburban educational systems, and

strengthen the individual school as an urban institution that enhances a sense of community and encourages close coordination and cooperation with other governmental and private efforts to advance the well-being of children and all others,

all with the central purpose of advancing the educational achievement and opportunities of the children in the public schools of New York City,

the Mayor's Advisory Panel on Decentralization of the New York City Schools recommends:*

1. The New York City public schools should be reorganized into a community school system, consisting of a federation of largely autonomous school districts and a central education agency (sec. 2).

2. From thirty to no more than sixty community school districts should be created, ranging in size from about 12,000 to 40,000 pupils—large enough to offer a full range of educational services and yet small enough to promote administrative flexibility and proximity to community needs and diversity (sec. 3).

* Numbers in parentheses refer to sections of the draft legislation.

3. The community school districts should have authority for all regular elementary and secondary education within their boundaries and responsibility for adhering to state education standards (sec. 6).

4. A central education agency, together with a superintendent of schools and his staff, should have operating responsibility for special educational functions and city-wide educational policies. It should also provide certain centralized services to the community school districts and others on the districts' request (sec. 8).

5. The state commissioner of education and the city's central educational agency shall retain their responsibilities for the maintenance of educational standards in all public schools in the city (secs. 8 and 19).

6. The community school districts should be governed by boards of education selected in part by parents and in part by the mayor from lists of candidates maintained by the central education agency, and membership on the boards should be open to parents and nonparent residents of a district (sec. 5).

7. The central education agency should consist of one or the other of the following governing bodies: (1) A commission of three full-time members appointed by the mayor, or (2) A Board of Education that includes a majority of members nominated by the community school districts. The mayor should select these members from a list submitted by an assembly of chairmen of community school boards. The others should be chosen by the mayor from nominations by a screening panel somewhat broader than the current panel (sec. 7).

8. Community school districts should receive a total annual allocation of operating funds, determined by an objective and equitable formula, which they should be permitted to use with the widest possible discretion within educational standards and goals and union contract obligations (sec. 15).

9. Community school districts should have broad personnel powers, including the hiring of a community superintendent on a contract basis (secs. 6a and 9).

10. All existing tenure rights of teachers and supervisory personnel should be preserved as the reorganized system goes into effect. Thereafter, tenure of new personnel employed in a particular district should be awarded by the district (sec. 11).

11. The process of qualification for appointment and promotion in the system should be so revised that community school districts will be free to hire teachers and other professional staff from the widest possible sources so long as hiring is competitive and applicants meet state qualifications (sec. 11).

12. Community school boards should establish procedures and channels for the closest possible consultation with parents, community resi-

dents, teachers, and supervisory personnel at the individual-school level and with associations of parents, teachers, and supervisors.

13. The central education agency should have authority and responsibility for advancing racial integration by all practicable means (sec. 8v). The state commissioner of education should have authority, himself or through delegation to the central education agency under guidelines, to overrule measures that support segregation or other practices inimical to an open society (sec. 19).

14. The community school system should go into effect for the school year beginning September, 1969, assuming passage of legislation in the 1968 legislature (sec. 5).

15. The main responsibility for supervising and monitoring the transition from the existing system to the community school system should rest with the state commissioner of education. The principal planning and operational functions should be assigned to a Temporary Commission on Transition that should work closely with the current Board of Education, the superintendent of schools, and his staff (sec. 20).

16. The transition period should include extensive programs of discussion and orientation on operations and responsibilities under the community school system and on educational goals generally. School board members should be afforded opportunities for training and provided with technical assistance on budgeting, curriculum, and other school functions.

Problems and Principles

THE GOALS OF CHANGE

The New York City school system, which once ranked at the summit of American public education, is caught in a spiral of decline.

The true measure of a structure of formal education is its effect on individual children. By this standard, the system of public education in New York City is failing, because vast numbers, if not the majority of the pupils, are not learning adequately.

The city as a whole is paying a heavy price for the decline. Here and there, in an individual school, pupils receive excellent preparation. But even in prosperous neighborhoods, parents' confidence in the public school system is diminishing. Their doubts are based not so much on such quantitative measures as achievement scores as on less measurable deficiencies—ranging from a lack of innovative content and teaching methods to a uniformity in program offerings that fails to respond to the varied capacities, talents, and needs of individual pupils. Day in and day out, and at impassioned annual budget hearings, come complaints about facilities and materials, varying from triple shifts in some schools and the lack of library, lunchroom, and gymnasium facilities in others, to delays in obtaining modern textbooks.

But the most evident and tragic failures are occurring in those parts of the city that need education most desperately—the low-income neighborhoods.

The city's poor, as a rule, have little choice but the public schools for their children's education. Others can choose, and many do. New York City is not only losing a large share of its younger middle-income (predominantly white) families to suburbs,[1] but a large portion of the children of those remaining are not attending public schools. From 1957 to 1966, the enrollment of "others" (the designation by the Board of Education for those who are not Negroes or Puerto Ricans) decreased 15 per cent.[2] However, the number of white school-age children (aged five to nineteen) living in New York City remained roughly the same—about 1,195,000 in 1965.[3] In Queens and Richmond, the fast-growing predominantly middle-class boroughs, the number of students enrolling in parochial and other private schools between 1955 and 1966 increased at a much greater rate than public school enrollment.[4]

No school system is free of shortcomings, but in New York the malaise of parents is heightened by their increasing inability to obtain redress or response to their concerns. Teachers and administrators, too, are caught in a system that has grown so complex and stiff as to overwhelm its human and social purpose.

Whether the reaction is quiet frustration or vocal protest, the result throughout the city is disillusionment with an institution that should be offering hope and promise. No parent, no teacher, no school administrator, no citizen, no business or industry should rest easy while this erosion continues.

The causes of the decline are as diverse and complex as the school system itself and the city that created it. But one critical fact is that the bulk and complexity of the system have gravely weakened the ability to act of all concerned—teachers, parents, supervisors, the Board of Education, and local school boards.

The result is that these parties, all of whom have legitimate concerns of their own as well as the common concern for the welfare and opportunity of the 1.1 million public school pupils,[5] are heavily occupied—sometimes preoccupied—in preserving a partial and largely negative power against a faceless system and nameless dangers. And efforts to attack the causes of decline are overshadowed by the energy consumed in assessing the blame.

The first step toward renewing the system is to provide a means of reconnecting the parties at interest so they can work in concert. After that will come the even more difficult task of renewing the New York City public school system so that it can play its part in the larger effort toward social renewal to meet drastically changed times and conditions.

Dr. Bernard E. Donovan, the Superintendent of Schools, said in June that "fundamentally the public schools have not changed to meet this rapidly changing society." He continued:

> This is particularly true of public school systems in large cities. I say this with full knowledge of the many, many innovative devices, procedures and concepts which have been introduced into the public schools of large cities by forward-looking and dedicated staff members. But I repeat, the general pattern of the public school has not changed to meet a vastly changing society.[6]

While the task has hardly been done elsewhere in urban America, the challenge now is for New York to return to the habit of being first in public education.

.   .   .   .

THE CONDITION OF EDUCATION IN NEW YORK CITY

The panel was not charged with re-examining the performance of the New York City schools. The shelves are full of thorough studies of the system's strengths and weaknesses, and the written and face-to-face advice and testimony the panel received from hundreds of parents, other citizens, teachers, and other professionals gave witness to the decline of educational effectiveness. Although, as noted, many are quick to point the finger of blame at someone else, few are proud of the over-all performance of the schools.

Some of the gross indicators of shortcomings in the performance of the school system stand in contrast to the attempts made to improve the system.

Efforts

In the last decade, funds for the New York City public schools have more than doubled—from $457 million in 1956–57 to $1.168 billion in 1966–67[7]—while enrollment increased one-fifth.[8] The per pupil expenditure—some $1,000[9]—stands above [that of] such other large cities as Chicago, Detroit, St. Louis, and Philadelphia and many suburban school districts.[10] Median elementary class size has been reduced by 8 per cent,[11] and the classroom teaching staff has increased by 37.6 per cent.[12]

Nor has the system been without experimentation and innovation. The Higher Horizons (earlier, Demonstration Guidance) program, though no longer operating, was an important attempt to compensate for the deprivation of pupils in low-income areas. The school system has introduced teacher aides and a volunteer program to free teachers from nonprofessional duties in some schools. After-school study centers and all-day neighborhood schools have been established. Experiments in team teaching, work-study programs, computerized instruction, and other methods are under way. In an effort to improve the organization and effectiveness of secondary education and particularly the vocational high schools, the Board of Education is considering the conversion of all high schools to comprehensive high schools. It has given some support to the More Effective Schools program put forward by the teachers' union. The board has also sought to decentralize the administration of the system.

The Record

The following information and data relate to pupil performance and various shortcomings in the New York City public schools. The panel recognizes that one of the most difficult and controversial questions in educational analysis is that of the causal relations between the schools and pupil performance. Furthermore, we are convinced that responsibility for what the student achieves is shared jointly by parents, the community-at-large, and the school system, to say nothing of other agencies that influence the urban environment. Our purpose in noting the educational shortfall in New York City, therefore, is to indicate that all parties must recognize the gravity of the education crisis. And while the school system is not solely responsible for academic failures, it certainly is the principal agency to which New Yorkers must look for a reversal of the trends.

In a 1965 state-wide pupil evaluation conducted by the New York State Education Department, 55 per cent of the students found to be below levels that the State Testing Service defined as "minimum competence" were New York City public school students, although the city's enrollment comprises only 35 per cent of the state's total. The tests covered reading and arithmetic in the elementary and ninth grades.[13]

In November, [1967,] shortly before this report was scheduled for publication, the Board of Education announced city-wide reading and arithmetic scores for the 1966–67 school year. The data indicated that one out of three pupils in the city's schools was a year or more behind youngsters in the nation as a whole in reading and arithmetic. Except in the ninth grade, where New York City scores were 0.3 per cent better than the national norms, the gaps ranged from 1.0 per cent behind the national level (eighth-grade reading) to 17.0 per cent behind (sixth-grade mathematics).[14] The per cent of New York students behind national norms has increased in all but one grade (the eighth) since May, 1966.

Another measure of the fact that performance is declining comes from state-wide tests. The proportion of sixth-grade pupils in the city scoring below state-defined minimum competence increased from 31 to 45 per cent between 1965 and 1966, compared to the state-wide increase from 20 to 23 per cent.[15]

These data, however, do not indicate the degree of retardation relative to other children across the country, with whom New York City children ultimately must compete for higher education and jobs. Data provided to the panel by the Board of Education indicate, for example, that 25.6 per cent of the city's fifth-grade pupils are one year and eight months behind national performance norms in reading, as against 16.0 per cent for the country as a whole. The proportion of reading-retarded pupils increases to 42 per cent for seventh graders, and changes to 36 per cent (as against 30 per cent nationally) among eighth-grade pupils. . . .

Of the 64,117 students admitted to the city's high schools and scheduled to graduate in the class of 1967, only 43,864 graduated. Of those graduating in 1967, 21,364 received academic diplomas; in other words, only one-third of the students admitted to high schools in New York City receive the minimum preparation for college entrance.[16] Nationally, over 43 per cent of the students admitted to high school go to college.[17]

Of the ten nonspecialized and predominantly (over 85 per cent) white high schools in New York City, six graduate less than 43 per cent of their admissions with academic diplomas.

A borough breakdown on high school graduates reveals that Queens had 44 per cent and Staten Island 34 per cent academic diplomas as compared to original admissions. Manhattan, the Bronx, and Brooklyn graduated 25, 30, and 35 per cent respectively, including graduates of the specialized academic high schools.[18]

The last specialized high school was established in the city in 1938 (the Bronx High School of Science). None exists in Richmond or Queens, the city's fastest-growing boroughs.

In 1966–67, 89,227 pupils were in facilities classified by the Board of Education as overcrowded; at the same time, 99,872 were in schools listed as underutilized.[19]

Some 12,000 students, according to a report in April by fourteen civic groups, were suspended during the last school year. They included mentally retarded or emotionally disturbed children—many of whom were then left to their own devices. The report also said that many students are suspended without being given a fair hearing, on charges ranging from failure to do homework to fighting with other children.[20]

Thirty per cent of the school system's teachers are "permanent substitutes," who do not have standard licenses.[21]

Since 1955, following a Public Education Association finding that 78.2 per cent of the faculty in mainly white New York City schools were tenured, compared to 50.3 per cent in predominantly Negro and Puerto Rican schools, the Board of Education has succeeded in raising the proportion of tenured teachers in the latter schools to about that of the former.[22] However, in terms of years of faculty experience (including tenured and regular substitute teachers), the Special Service Schools, those populated with pupils with the most severe learning problems, have fewer experienced teachers than the city as a whole[23]—57 per cent with three or more years of experience, compared to 70 per cent for all other schools.

Last year, there were 500 classes to which no teacher was assigned on a permanent basis, and teacher absences accounted for an additional 1,500 uncovered classes daily, or the equivalent of some 30 schools or one average school district.[24]

RESPONSIBILITY

The Relation of the Public to Public Institutions

Nothing is more difficult—or more important—in our modern urban society than the re-establishment of clearly understood and effective lines of responsibility. The presumed advantage of large institutions and systems, public and private, is that they serve more people more efficiently and economically, but in the process many have become ends in themselves and fortresses of impersonality. In institutions directly responsible for serving human needs, the consequences of overweening size and sheltered bureaucracy can be profoundly destructive.

The responsibility of public officials to the public is fundamental in a democratic society. Officials are required to account publicly for their past actions. The public is assumed to have the right to act against officials with whose performance it is dissatisfied. The customary channel for such action is the vote, and even appointed officials should be responsible to some elected official so that attention is paid to the public's concerns with their performance. And large, complex public systems, even if ultimately subject to the judgment of the polling place, should provide other channels to and from the public, in order to render an account of their activities and to sense the needs and concerns of the communities they serve.

The developing crisis of impotence and voicelessness was eloquently described recently by J. Irwin Miller, a leading American businessman who is also a former president of the National Council of Churches:

> In the Thirties you had the poor or the disadvantaged merely wanting welfare. You get a new voice today which rejects the welfare state unless you have a say in the part that affects you. I think that a great deal of the unrest that you find in business is a feeling on the part of people that they want a say. You have the students who want a say in the university. You have the poor who want a say in their programs. All of us feel maybe we want a say in foreign policy, which is a little more difficult. You have developing nations who want a say in what happens to them. This is a new kind of thing. . . .

> I think we're suffering some of the pangs of bigness, and growth, and impersonality, but you can't avoid being big. So many of the undertakings you want to accomplish in this society can't be accomplished except by very large groups. Even the New Left wants the things made by the assembly line or the education at a large university. You've got to solve the problem of how you take on a big activity, but make bigness your servant, not your master.[25]

Responsibility in Education

The concept of local control of education is at the heart of the American public school system. Laymen determine the goals of public education and the policies calculated to achieve them. Professional educators are the chosen instrument for implementing policies determined by laymen. They should also advise on goals and policies, but the public's right to evaluate and to hold publicly employed officials responsible is fundamental.

When the educational enterprise is going smoothly, the public does not often exercise its right to evaluate. It is after the system begins to break down and the public finds itself inadequately served that the issue comes to the fore. Often the right of the layman to an account of professional performance, while given lip service, is in effect nullified by challenges to his competence to inquire into what are considered basically professional affairs. But education is public business as well as professional business. Public education in the United States was never intended to be a professional monopoly. Through many just struggles, educators have achieved professional status and protections against political and sectarian domination. But the scales must not tip toward a technocracy in which the public cannot exercise its right to scrutinize the professional process in education. As Superintendent Donovan has said: "The staff of large city public school systems can no longer feel that the educational programs in the schools must be left solely to the professional educators who are accountable to nobody but themselves. The children belong to the parents. The parents pay taxes to support the schools. The parents have a right to know what is going on in the schools."[26]

This concept of responsibility can easily be misunderstood, as the panel learned in some of its discussions with both citizens and teachers. It cannot imply the surrender of professional standards and integrity; it must not imply the loss of initiative; and it should not subject the professional to harassment or capricious or arbitrary domination. In a properly balanced distribution of responsibilities, there should be no contradiction whatever between the professional obligations of the teachers and the ultimate responsibility of public officials. On the contrary, that latter obligation is itself a part of the professional duty of the teacher or supervisor in a system of public education.

Nor does the concept confer upon elective authority the right to suppose that merely to state a requirement creates a binding obligation upon the teacher. There is such a thing as asking too much, and it is a truism that in a complex system no one element can be responsible for everything that happens. The occasional parent who supposes that all that is needed is to give the teacher orders is as wrong as the occasional teacher who supposes that no one has a right to give him any guidance at all.

.   .   .   .

PHASES OF DECENTRALIZATION

A 1961 legislative act empowered the Board of Education to "revitalize local boards."[27] The number of districts was reduced from fifty-four to twenty-five. The system of appointment of local board members was removed from the hands of borough presidents and placed with the central Board of Education. The board was required to seek the advice of local screening panels (chosen by the presidents of parent associations in each district) in appointing local school board members, and therefore the local units now rested on a somewhat stronger community base. Nonetheless, the districts remained "largely paper organizations, with little administrative power."[28]

A 1965 reorganization increased the number of districts to thirty-one,[29] and placed high schools as well as junior high and elementary schools under jurisdiction of district superintendents. Although it purported to promote greater emphasis on district policy-making, the plan left the critical areas of budgeting and personnel policy centralized. The local boards remained, under law, "advisory only."[30]

In April, 1967, the Board of Education issued a statement of policy to further facilitate decentralization in the districts.[31] District superintendents were given control over a lump sum (from $40,000 to $60,-000)[32] for minor maintenance and supplies for all the schools in their district, authority over the utilization of teaching and nonteaching positions, and a potentially greater degree of flexibility with curriculum innovations and experiment. The local boards for the first time were provided with office space but no professional or supporting services. In October, the board issued guidelines for stronger consultation with local school boards in its appointments of principals and district superintendents.[33]

These steps have not given the local boards actual decision-making authority, although district superintendents are now required to consult them on a variety of matters. The only formal channel of communication remains that between the local boards and the central Board of Education.

At the same time the board reiterated a desire "to experiment with varying forms of decentralization and community involvement in several experimental districts of varying size," and asked the superintendent of schools to submit specific proposals for experimental districts as soon as possible.[34]

In May, 1967, the board approved a plan for the establishment of seven demonstration projects designed to "improve the instructional programs for the children in the schools concerned by bringing the parents and community into a more meaningful participation with the schools."[35] Two have been activated in part: (a) an experiment in a single school, P.S. 129 in Brooklyn, in which planning, operation, and evaluation are to be undertaken jointly by parents and staff with assistance from a university (four or five more such individual-school experiments were envisioned); and (b) creation of two multischool units consisting of an intermediate school and its feeder primary schools, supervised by a board elected by the community and administered by a coordinator selected by the board in consultation with the superintendent of schools. Two communities were invited to submit such proposals; one, a community planning group around I.S. 201 in Harlem, has done so, while the other, around Joan of Arc Junior High School on Manhattan's West Side, has not yet. In the meantime, however, two other community proposals for experimental districts—in the Ocean Hill–Brownsville section of Brooklyn and the Two Bridges section of the Lower East Side—were approved by the Board of Education, along with the I.S. 201 proposal, in July.

In the summer following the appointment of the mayor's panel, the board established its own advisory committee on school decentralization, headed by Dr. John Niemeyer, president of the Bank Street College of Education.

Effectiveness

The New York City schools, it is clear, while more *administratively* decentralized in form in the last few years, are not *effectively* decentralized in practice. While local school boards provide a useful forum for discussing school-site selection and other subjects, and sometimes exert decisive influence on less-than-routine matters, they lack effective decision-making power and they cannot hold anyone *responsible*—not the district administrator, nor the central authority—for the performance of the schools in their district. The responsibility which the central authority has delegated to the district superintendent is more than before, but his basic orientation is still upward to administrative superiors, not across to the level of the district school board and to the community it is designed to serve.

The energies of the 270 men and women who serve on the local school boards have been worn down by a school system structure that prevents them from turning their judgment and their special knowledge of local needs into decisions that matter.

Assessing their own effectiveness, a representative committee of current local school board members, in a series of recommendations to the panel, declared: "much of the enthusiasm, dedication and potential of these boards for significant contributions to public education has been blunted by an unresponsive and resisting school bureaucracy, buttressed by archaic legalistic concepts as to the 'advisory only' nature of local school boards."[36]

Some school board members have resigned in frustration, and at the time of writing one board that resigned en masse last spring has not yet been replaced.

Martin Mayer, a former school board member of five years' service, has described the dead end to which many such men and women have come under the present structure: "there was almost nothing I could do for the people who called me, and little of substance that could come out of our meetings. . . . This giant empire is almost completely insulated from public control."[37]

Leading civic organizations concerned with the schools believe the Board of Education's April, 1967, decentralization policy still lacks essential elements of administrative decentralization or community participation.

The Public Education Association, in a statement generally approving the policy, said:

> If it has one weakness, it is its lack of emphasis on the fullest possible participation of community groups working with the local school board and the district superintendent and his staff in a cooperative effort to improve education.
>
> . . . The consultative role which you have set out for these boards in the selection of the district superintendent, in our judgment, is not enough to give them a sense of responsibility for school affairs in their district.[38]

The United Parents Association, which has for several years urged decentralization, said with reference to the latest phase: "We view decentralization as a means of providing greater authority and flexibility to the professional staff at the district level. Superintendents and principals who are closest to the problems should be permitted to get things done without constantly referring to higher headquarters."[39]

The Women's City Club said that the force of local school board participation in personnel and budget matters still rested on "what are essentially subjective judgments." It continued: "[Local school boards cannot] enforce a claim to full participation on a district superintendent who is not really responsible to the local school boards. The personnel procedures should be extended to include the appointment of the district superintendent."[40]

In short, despite important steps since 1961 in reactivating and reconstituting local school boards and in improving their consultative role, they operate within the constraints of a law that prevents them from serving as effective organs of local participation and responsibility in educational policy.

Notes

1. Between 1950 and 1960, New York City lost a net of 1.2 million whites, while the white populations of suburban counties increased in large amounts. For example, 441,000 whites moved into Nassau County and 90,000 moved to Westchester. In New Jersey, 147,000 whites moved to Bergen County, 105,000 moved to Middlesex, and 67,000 moved to Morris County.—Regional Plan Association, *The Region's Growth* (New York, May, 1967), Table A-23, p. 141.

2. The "other" public school enrollment decreased from 650,080 in 1957 to 551,-927 in 1965.—Jacob Landers, *Improving Ethnic Distribution of New York City Pupils: An Analysis of Programs Approved by the Board of Education and the Superintendent of Schools* (New York: City School District of New York City, May, 1966), p. 47.

3. In 1960, the number of white school-age persons (5–19 years old) in New York City was 1,175,000. A 1965 estimate showed about 1,195,000 individuals in this category.—U.S. Department of Commerce, Bureau of the Census, *Census of*

Population, 1960; Regional Plan Association estimates and adjustments from Chester Rapkin, *The Private Rental Housing Market in New York City, 1965* (New York: The City Rent and Rehabilitation Administration, December, 1966).

The predominantly white parochial and private school registers within the city stood at 427,845 in 1964–65. (The final 100,000 whites who are unaccounted for by the combined public and private school enrollments in 1965 may be assumed to be those who have graduated from high school before the age of 19, or who have dropped out, as well as those who are bused to parochial and private schools outside the city.)—Board of Education of the City of New York, Bureau of Attendance.

4. Between 1955 and 1966, the total public school enrollment increased 18.6 per cent (170,537) and that of the nonpublic schools 17.4 per cent (64,551). In Queens, the total public school enrollment increased 21.2 per cent (43,797), while the nonpublic school enrollment increased 38 per cent (31,001). In Staten Island, the increase in the public schools was 46.7 per cent (12,886) and in the nonpublic schools 60.7 per cent (8,822).—Board of Education of the City of New York, Bureau of Attendance. (Recently, this growth in nonpublic school enrollment, it should be noted, is not attributable to a rise in the Roman Catholic school population in Queens. In fact, their Catholic parochial school enrollments have decreased over the last two years.—Data supplied by the Rev. Franklin F. Fitzpatrick, Catholic Schools Office, Diocese of Brooklyn, October 20, 1967.)

5. Board of Education of the City of New York, *Facts & Figures—1966–1967* (New York: Office of Education Information Services and Public Relations, 1967), p. 51; hereafter cited as *Facts & Figures.*

6. Bernard E. Donovan, Superintendent of Schools, City of New York, "The Role of a School System in a Changing Society," Address Delivered to Invitation Conference on "The Process of Change in Education," Lincoln Center, New York City, June 15, 1967, p. 1.

7. Marilyn Gittell, T. Edward Hollander, and William S. Vincent, *Investigation of Fiscally Independent and Dependent City School Districts* ("Cooperative Research Project No. 3,237" [New York: The City University Research Foundation with Subcontract to Teachers College, Columbia University, 1967]), Appendix A, Table V, p. 220; and *Facts & Figures,* p. 1.

8. Gittell *et al., op. cit.,* Appendix A, Table XVIII, p. 233.

9. *Facts & Figures,* pp. 6 and 51.

10. Gittell *et al., op. cit.,* Appendix A, Table XI, p. 226. Additional data provided by National Education Association, Research Department, October 18, 1967.

11. Gittell *et al., op. cit.,* Appendix A, Table XIII, p. 228.

12. *Ibid.,* Appendix A, Table XIV, p. 229.

13. Regents Examination and Scholarship Center, Division of Educational Testing, *Test Results of the 1965 Pupil Evaluation Program in New York State* (January, 1967).

14. *The New York Times,* November 2, 1967, p. 50.

15. Data provided by Regents Examination and Scholarship Center, Division of Educational Testing, Pupil Evaluation Program, August, 1967.

16. Board of Education of the City of New York, Office of Academic High Schools, *Report on Graduates* ("AHS 50" [January and June, 1967]).

17. Data provided by U.S. Department of Health, Education, and Welfare, Office of Education, *Biennial Survey of Education in the United States.*

18. Board of Education of the City of New York, Office of Academic High Schools, *op. cit.*

19. Board of Education, *Utilization of School Buildings 1966–67,* prepared under the direction of Bernard E. Donovan, Superintendent of Schools, School Planning and Research Division, October 31, 1966.

20. ASPIRA, *et al., Preserving the Right to an Education for all Children: Recommendations to the New York City Board of Education Regarding School Suspensions.* April 5, 1967 (developed by ASPIRA, Inc., Citizens Committee for Children of New York, Inc., Congress of Racial Equality, Inc., Congress of Racial Equality,

Inc.–Brooklyn Chapter, EQUAL, HARYOU-Act, Inc., Massive Economic Neighborhood Development, Inc., Mobilization for Youth, Inc., New York Civil Liberties Union, Public Education Association, Puerto Rican Association for Community Affairs, Inc., United Neighborhood Houses of New York, Inc., United Parents Association, Urban League of Greater New York).

21. Data provided by Board of Education of the City of New York, Bureau of Personnel.

22. Board of Education of the City of New York, Bureau of Educational Program Research and Statistics, School Experience Index, *Teachers with More Than Five Years Teaching Experience in Elementary and Junior High Schools, School Year 1966–67*, Report prepared by Madeline Morrissey.

23. *Ibid.*

24. United Federation of Teachers, *United Teacher* (November, 1966).

25. Steven V. Robert, "Is It Too Late for a Man of Honesty, High Purpose and Intelligence To Be Elected President of the United States in 1968," *Esquire* (October, 1967), p. 181.

26. Bernard E. Donovan, address, *op. cit.*

27. *McKinney's 1961 Session Laws of New York*, ch. 971 (1961).

28. Fred Hechinger, in *The New York Times*, May 14, 1965, p. 1.

29. One, which exists on paper only, awaits the further growth of population in Staten Island.

30. *McKinney's 1961 Session Laws of New York*, ch. 971 (1961).

31. Board of Education, City School District of the City of New York, *Decentralization; Statement of Policy*, April 19, 1967, p. 1; hereafter cited as *Decentralization; Statement of Policy.*

32. Data provided by the Director, Division of Maintenance and Operation, Office of School Buildings, Board of Education of the City of New York, August 22, 1967.

33. *The New York Times*, October 20, 1967.

34. *Decentralization; Statement of Policy*, p. 5.

35. Bernard E. Donovan, Superintendent of Schools, *Decentralization Demonstration Projects*, Proposal submitted to the Board of Education, April 12, 1967, p. 1.

36. Local School Boards, Committee on Decentralization, J. Robert Pigott, Chairman, *Proposal, New York*, August 4, 1967.

37. Martin Mayer, "What's Wrong With Our Big-City Schools," *Saturday Evening Post*, September 9, 1967, pp. 21 and 22.

38. Public Education Association, *Statement of the Public Education Association on the Decentralization of Authority and Responsibility in the New York City School System*, presented by Mrs. J. Lawrence Pool, Vice-President, March 8, 1967, pp. 2 and 4.

39. United Parents Association of New York City, Inc., *Statement by Mrs. Florence Flast, President of The United Parents Association Before the Board of Education in Regard to Draft Proposal on Decentralization*, March 7, 1967, p. 1.

40. Women's City Club of New York, Inc. *Statement of the Women's City Club on Proposals for Decentralization Before the Board of Education Hearing*, presented by Mrs. Alexander A. Katz, Chairman, Education Committee, March 7, 1967, p. 1.

19. INTERIM REPORT NO. 2, JANUARY, 1968: THE BUNDY PLAN

COUNCIL OF SUPERVISORY ASSOCIATIONS

Foreword

The New York City school system has achieved demonstrably excellent results over the years and continues to achieve superior educational results in most respects. It has not been successful in its efforts to solve one major problem—coping effectively with the educational needs of disadvantaged children. So, too, have other institutions that share the responsibility for this problem failed, among them the federal government, organized labor, business and industry, the churches, and the social agencies. The failure is not confined to New York City, but is characteristic of urban centers throughout the nation.

As a consequence, there is a growing public dissatisfaction with our schools, especially on the part of those whose children are most affected. While the dissatisfaction embraces many areas other than education, such as housing, employment, and health, the schools must face their particular responsibility and do their best to meet it.

COMMON AIMS

In the attempt to help the educationally disadvantaged and to improve public education in general, various plans have been promulgated. They differ in their approaches and recommendations, but all of them include three common aims: to provide better educational services, to facilitate greater participation of parents and community in school affairs, and to make the schools an agent of social progress. The latest plan is that of the Mayor's Advisory Panel on Decentralization, known as the Bundy Plan.

Reprinted from The Council of Supervisory Associations of the Public Schools of New York City, *Response to the Lindsay-Bundy Proposals*, "Interim Report No. 2" (New York City, January, 1968).

The Council of Supervisory Associations (CSA) has stated that the Bundy Plan neither achieves the desired aims nor supplies feasible solutions. In fact, its adoption would do irreparable harm to the schools and thus to the pupils. At the same time, we recognize the necessity for constructive steps that *will* lead us toward the goals of better education, increased parent and community involvement, and social progress. Therefore, we present for consideration (1) an evaluation of the Bundy Plan and its proposals and (2) guiding principles of a program to achieve the ends we all seek, plus specific suggestions for implementation.

We hope in this way to prevent hasty acceptance of ill-conceived and damaging proposals and to encourage instead concerted action in directions that will bring real and lasting benefits to the children in our schools.

Defects in the Lindsay-Bundy Plan

In the letter of transmittal to Mayor Lindsay preceding its report, the Advisory Panel states: "The first premise of this report is that the test of a school is what it does for the children in it." The test of a plan to improve the schools should also be what it does for the children. Yet nowhere does the Bundy Plan advance a concrete proposal to give direct help to pupils.

Its entire rationale is founded rather on the questionable assumption that smaller, autonomous school districts in New York City would function like school districts of similar size in suburban communities, such as Scarsdale or Great Neck. This analogy is highly inaccurate. School boards in areas such as these are responsible for the collection and expenditure of tax funds and account to the voters of the community for their fiscal policy. The proposed thirty to sixty districts in the Bundy Plan are artificially created areas and in few cases have the characteristics of true communities. It is easy to envision the squabbles that will arise among them over what they consider their fair share of educational funds. As the Public Education Association asks: "In other words, in what ways will this plan make it likely that the education of children, particularly in poverty areas, will be more effective?" Unfortunately, there is no answer. Changes in organizational structure, as such, do not produce improved pupil achievement.

POOR USE OF FUNDS

Actually the plan is inimical to pupil welfare because it diverts funds to administrative positions that could otherwise be used for the children and for educational services. The unwarranted duplication and over-lapping of functions of the central board of education and all the sup-posedly autonomous school districts—in curriculum, personnel, budget, supplies, special services—would involve tremendous increase in cost. An estimate of $300–$400 million per year may be a conservative one. The Bundy Report, on page 43, notes that "dollar cost . . . is not a major question." We would agree if the money were applied to the children's benefit instead of to structural changes and administration.

INEFFICIENCIES UNDER BUNDY PLAN

The Bundy Plan impedes the education of children in other ways. Each community school district will have its own curriculum. The pen-alties imposed on New York City children, with their high mobility rate, are evident. Pupils transferring from one district to another will have to adjust to different subject offerings, different curricular requirements, and different standards. Also, with each district operating independ-ently, there will be fragmentation of many supporting services, such as mental health and textbook selection. Educational resources which can now be furnished efficiently because of large-scale management will be provided by thirty to sixty organizations rather than one. Aside from the increase in overhead and expense, the services themselves will, of necessity, be weakened. A further disservice is the diffusion of fiscal re-sponsibility with each district receiving its total annual allocation of operating funds. The cases, under such a system, of mismanagement and misuse in some districts will serve to hamper the effective functioning of the schools.

END OF MERIT SYSTEM

However, the most serious harm to education is wrought by the pro-posals relating to personnel. The Bundy recommendations abolish com-petitive merit examinations and return to a selection process which can only introduce such considerations as political influence, race, and re-ligion. The doors will be opened to various pressure groups who see thousands of jobs available on the basis of politics and favoritism rather than competence and merit. The chief sufferers will be the children.

COMPETITION FOR TEACHERS

In addition, individual community school districts will compete for teachers. It is inevitable that more favored districts will siphon off a disproportionate number of able teachers and supervisors, leaving fewer applicants for the disadvantaged districts. At present, assignments are made to all districts, including those in poverty areas, from city-wide competitive lists. Although there are still difficulties in recruitment, practically all positions are being filled by professionals who have met the standards of a merit examination. Under the Bundy Plan, communities with large numbers of disadvantaged children will tend to get the poorer teachers, and even these will be in short supply. The tragedy of the report is that despite its professed efforts to aid disadvantaged children, especially those of Negro and Puerto Rican origin, its effect will be to deprive them of increased funds, supportive services, and qualified personnel, and to depress them further.

The major emphasis of the Bundy Plan is indicated by its title: *Reconnection for Learning.* Its first stated purpose is to "increase community awareness and participation in the development of educational policy." An examination of the proposals will show that this purpose is not fulfilled and, to some extent, is even circumvented.

BASIC CONTRADICTIONS

The report concedes, on page 18, that "most local school boards, including those in sixteen of the country's twenty-five largest cities, are elected by popular vote." Then it proceeds to argue against direct elections: domination by political clubs, expense of campaigning, distastefulness of election campaigns, domination by sectarian interests. In short, the framers of the report trust local "communities" to control personnel selection, curriculum, educational policy, and budget but not to elect their own representatives.

As a substitute, the report offers an eleven-man school community board, six of whom would be selected through parent assemblies and *five directly by the mayor.* Which would be the dominant group: the six members with individual ideas chosen by the parents or the five members chosen by the Mayor and answerable to him? Multiply this by the number of school community boards in the whole city and ask whether educational matters would be decided by local communities or centrally by the mayor's office. The answer is manifest.

ACCOUNTABILITY OF SCHOOL BOARDS?

It is odd, too, that this plan which tries to be so thorough has made no provision for accountability of school board members to the parents and community. Once a member has been selected—by the parents or by the Mayor—regardless of his deficiencies, there is no machinery for his removal during his term of office. There is also no definite design for any more voice by parents in individual schools than they now have. Statements are made on pages 30 and 31: "Community boards should guarantee a full flow of information and consultation." "The Community Superintendent of Schools should consult with parents." "Parent groups should be consulted by principals." These are expressions of good wishes but not genuine aspects of a plan with clear provisos.

We have, therefore, in the Bundy proposals a replacement of central bureaucracy by local bureaucracies and by centralized domination of city hall. We do not have provision for greater parent and community influence either at the district level or within the individual school. There is no "reconnection for learning."

IGNORES SOCIAL PROGRESS

Finally, any plan for our schools must be judged by its potential for social progress. We are in the midst of a great progressive social revolution, and changes in public education must be part of that revolution. The approach of the Bundy Report is a superficial one in that it focuses on the schools alone without regard, except for incidental references, to other institutions or forces. It assumes that current social unrest can be appeased by an administrative restructuring of the school system. The needs of our youngsters for better housing, improved recreational facilities, higher education, job training and placement, medical care and social services, all in an interrelated framework, are largely ignored.

PROMOTES SEGREGATION

In actuality, the report takes a giant step backward in the direction of ethnic segregation. For a long time, integration has been one of our prime goals. We achieved a substantial degree of integration in New York City despite great difficulties. The U.S. Civil Rights Commission, among others, affirms that New York City has been in the vanguard of major cities in achieving some measure of integration in its school system. The establishment of thirty to sixty enclaves, as recommended in the Bundy Plan, will give each community board the right to determine how many pupils it will take from other districts. This is a blueprint for segregation.

To compound the confusion, the Bundy Report stresses haste in the extreme. It envisions the radical reorganization of a school system which services more than a million children in a period of two years. This may well be one of the largest gambles in history. A generation of children may be the unfortunate victims of this plan.

In sum, the Council of Supervisory Associations cannot accept the Bundy Plan. As knowledgeable educators and as forward looking citizens, we must express our utmost opposition. The plan gives structural change priority over pupil progress and welfare. It presumes to increase public and parent involvement in the schools but operates so as to vitiate such involvement. It not only neglects present-day social forces within which the schools must function but even operates so as to obstruct social progress. Thus, the report, while it claims to be an attack on the problems of public education, is really an attack on public education itself.

The CSA Program

It is not our purpose—and cannot be—to offer a complete and comprehensive scheme for instant or total improvement of public education in New York City. This is something that even the Bundy Plan does not purport to do. We believe, however, that specific and significant steps can be taken, in terms of fundamental aims and clear guiding principles, toward amelioration of the main problem—the unmet needs of the educationally disadvantaged child—and other problems that are closely related. The first aim, as we have indicated, is to provide better educational services for the disadvantaged pupil in particular and for all pupils in general. We recommend the following principles of action:

1. *Any additional funds—for instance, the hundreds of millions of dollars that would be spent on changes in administrative structure, as described in the Bundy proposals—must be used directly for classroom instruction and pupil services.* There must be a massive increase in funds for New York City public schools through revised allocations by the city, the state, and the federal government. These moneys would be employed in the intensification and expansion of services to pupils, especially those who are educationally disadvantaged, in such ways as the following:

(i) Prekindergarten and early childhood programs
(ii) Corrective and remedial help as part of a skills development program
(iii) Identification, counseling, and guidance
(iv) After-school and community services
(v) Extended summer programs to overcome the educational lag between May and September

(vi) Thorough-going orientation and training of parents in methods of helping their children at home

(vii) Extended use of auxiliary personnel and establishment of career ladders, so as to provide more resource persons to work with the children

(viii) Coordinated assistance of community groups and agencies

(ix) Development of more functional measures of pupil progress in reading and other basic skills in place of the culture-biased standardized tests now being used.

(x) Intensive preservice and in-service teacher training

(xi) Smaller pupil-teacher ratio

While many of the programs have already been initiated, they have been limited by uncertainties and inconsistencies in funding. We require a guarantee of ample and continuous financing for these educational services and for accompanying social services. The key to public confidence in the schools is not a diagram of shifts in organizational structure but a full application of measures that will expedite pupil progress and achievement.

2. *The schools should operate within a structural framework that best serves the educational process and the children.* It is as easy to be in favor of decentralization as it is to be against sin. The question is one of definition. A decentralization plan negating central authority, setting up independent and competitive districts, and unnecessarily duplicating many services will create confusion and waste. On the other hand, a form of decentralization, increasing autonomy and flexibility in specified activities for individual schools and their districts but retaining central coordination and support, is highly desirable. The difference is not merely in degree but in kind. New York City is a single administrative unit in which all communities are interdependent. Only a relative decentralization—actually a reduction in centralized functions rather than decentralization as such—is feasible. What we should do, therefore, is decentralize control in all educational areas which can be better handled on a local basis and retain central control where not to do so would lead to harmful consequences.

MANAGING FUNDS

Once this frame of reference has been established, lines of demarcation become clearer. In the case of budgetary matters, the central board should continue to manage funds for such mandated purposes as salaries, pensions, and major aspects of construction and repair. The schools, through the local board, should have money immediately available for direct purchase of supplies and texts (with the central agency establishing the price where possible), minor building maintenance and repair, and educational services. Curriculum should be a city-wide function along with all the curricular resources that can be furnished, but schools and local districts should be free to adapt and modify curriculum in accordance with pupil needs or aspirations. There should also be centralized responsibility for pupil personnel services and special education, with facilities and personnel deployed to provide strength at the local level.

SELECTING PERSONNEL

For the adequate staffing of the schools, both qualitatively and quantitatively, especially in poverty areas, it is essential that personnel selection be handled centrally by a Board of Examiners; also, that recruitment, assignment, and transfer of personnel be coordinated by a central agency. Arrangements can be made for some geographical decentralization of personnel selection, as needed, under the auspices of the Board of Examiners. In communities where staffing is difficult, officially designated representatives may be used, temporarily or permanently, to assist in implementation of procedures.

ASSIGNING STAFF

Insofar as is feasible, principals and district superintendents should have a say in the local assignment of teachers and other staff members, with allowance for contractual agreements and the needs of other schools and districts. The local school board should have a voice in the choosing of a district superintendent, but the minimum qualifications and the final decision should be within the province of the superintendent of schools. In the assignment of principals, the final decision must be a professional one made by the superintendent of schools, after conference with the district superintendent, with regard for rights of transferees and the choice of one out of three from competitive lists.

CENTRALIZING SECONDARY SCHOOLS

Another advantageous move would be to place all secondary schools under the control of the central Board of Education with provision for a central planning agency for vocational education. So many of the students in senior high schools come from various districts that they do not properly belong within a single district. Without the senior high schools to administer, district superintendents and school boards would have more time for their primary function: services for the school children residing within the district. By the same token, a careful look should be taken at the intermediate and junior high schools. Some multidistrict or regional design for these middle schools might be developed.

These recommendations, if carried out, would give local schools and districts greater autonomy and flexibility in significant areas and still preserve the advantages and safeguards of central responsibility.

3. *For the sake of the pupils, implementation of change should take place in planned, systematic, and orderly fashion, with due consideration for experimental controls and economic efficiency.* The Bundy Plan proposes many changes simply in the name of change. Whether they will be costly or wasteful or deleterious seems less important than iconoclasm per se. One example is the alteration in the number of districts and their boundaries. If the system can function with thirty to sixty districts, why not keep the present thirty? In the normal course of events, new local school board members would be selected and other district superintendents would take office as vacancies arose, but in the meantime, the schools and the pupils would have the benefit of stability of leadership. An arbitrary shift in district lines creating fresh districts could cause the departure of every current district superintendent and local school board member at one time. The result would be chaos. It is vital, therefore, that the present thirty districts be substantially retained as a working basis for orderly transition.

4. *Since the pupils are entitled to the best teachers and supervisors available, members of the professional staff should be chosen on the basis of competence and merit, without regard to race, color, or creed.* We have already reviewed the consequences of foregoing a merit system of personnel selection built around competitive examinations. We recognize, however, that methods of selection must be constantly improved and extended. With this precept in mind, we make the following recommendations:

(i) The continuation of competitive examinations and other necessary selection procedures under the auspices and protection of the Board of Examiners. Every school system in the state uses other criteria beside mere certification.

(ii) More effective utilization of the probationary period for members of the school staff, with more efficient and workable procedures for dealing with unsatisfactory personnel.

(iii) Major efforts to train and evaluate teachers and supervisors through the development of internships, the use of teacher trainers, extension of professional promotional seminars, intensive help for newly appointed teachers and supervisors, and coordination with colleges and graduate schools of education in their preparation programs.

(iv) Continued adherence to standards of performance and experience, based on job analysis and requirements, for teachers, supervisors, and principals.

(v) Establishment of official performance and experience requirements for district superintendents, including a specified number of years as a principal in a large urban school.

(vi) Filling of vacancies for supervisory positions with candidates from existing eligible lists, all of whom have demonstrated their fitness and their right to the position in a challenging battery of written and personal tests and evaluation of previous experience.

New York City must continue to insist that its teachers meet requirements above the minimum. It must then institute or improve and strengthen pretraining and in-service training.

5. *There should be a close working partnership between parents and the professional staff based on a clear understanding of their respective roles.* Through meetings, agreements by committees, joint publications, and other means of communication, guidelines such as the following should be established as the basis for parent-professional relationships, whether on a local or city-wide level:

(i) A community sponsors and supports public schools to achieve an educational program for the children. The public schools, by their very nature, belong to the community. The professional staff must necessarily be the agents of the community in helping to reach the goals of the educational program.

(ii) The functions of the professional staff include performance of the services they have been trained to provide, such as determination of classroom teaching practices, curriculum development and improvement, pupil placement in classes or groups, and selection of materials of instruction. Although the community can challenge the professional staff on questions of pupil progress and achievement, the methods of effecting such progress and achievement must be left to the professionals and their expertise.

(iii) The professional staff is fully accountable in general to parents and community for the success of the educational program. However, individual professionals can be held specifically accountable for their effectiveness and their performance only to the fellow professionals and experts who supervise and rate them.

(iv) Parents have the responsibility of supporting the school and its endeavors through their share in the community program for the schools, their active interest, their participation in auxiliary services and activities, and the attitudes they inculcate in their children. Professionals have the responsibilities of doing their job well and interpreting the educational program, in an effective and consistent manner, to the parents and to the public, and in helping parents to play their parts in the joint endeavor of educating children.

The foregoing guidelines are instances of agreements that should be formulated between teachers and supervisors on the one hand and parents and community members on the other, so as to resolve current differences of view and enable all parties to work harmoniously for the welfare of the children.

(v) Do we know what the parents and public really want? Is local control their major concern or the education of their children? Is there really a crisis in public confidence in the schools? The Bundy Report and comments of some journalists supply one picture. Visits to the many schools with successful ongoing programs supply a different picture altogether. Also, there seems to be considerable variation between opinions of parents and claims of pressure groups that obtain wide publicity.

Essential to any plan for improving public education is that our schools become agents of social progress. The schools have a prime responsibility for the welfare and progress of children, but they cannot do the job alone. There must be an expansion of services on all fronts, particularly in poverty areas. This over-all need is recognized by the federal government and the state Board of Regents.

This multiservice approach, within which the schools would play a major, but not a sole, part would include health, welfare, housing, employment, recreation, education, and other socio-economic factors. It would be a joint endeavor of community members and professionals from various disciplines, including school personnel. Within this comprehensive rationale, a viable and lasting school-community program could be developed.

20. THE POLITICS OF SCHOOL DECENTRALIZATION

JASON EPSTEIN

Public hearings on questions of school policy in New York are typically ritualistic and empty, the issues being either trivial or decided in advance by the interested parties. Lately, however, Negroes and Puerto Ricans have begun to come to these hearings and the tone, as a result, has considerably sharpened and become bitter, so that the Board of Education, which usually sends a representative, now occasionally stays away. Last summer [1967], for instance, the board decided not to attend a hearing held by the Mayor's Council Against Poverty to consider whether the Board of Education of the ghetto communities themselves should have charge of some $69 million in federal funds intended for the improvement of ghetto schools. Dozens of Negro and Puerto Rican leaders testified at this hearing, and one after another of them urged that, sooner than give this money over to the board which, they argued, would inevitably use it against the interests of the ghettos, the city should give it back to Washington.

Most of these speakers represented community organizations within the ghettos; many of them were parents, and some were black schoolteachers. Nearly all of them described the public school system as a racist conspiracy to deny the children of the ghetto an education, and themselves, if they happened to be teachers, advancement. Their complaint was not that the schools had tried and failed, nor even that they hadn't bothered to try, but that they had deliberately or reflexively blocked and stupefied the children. Some of the speakers wanted the federal money spent on an alternative school system, run by the local communities within the city, responsible not to a distant and authoritarian central Board of Education, but to the parents themselves. What they wanted, in effect, was to get rid of the central school administration, with its complacent bureaus, its record of failure, and its insularity, and to take charge of the ghetto schools themselves.

Last fall these desperate and angry voices were joined by that of the formidable McGeorge Bundy, who, having left the War Room of the White House, has been for the past year and a half head of the Ford Foundation. The so-called Bundy Report, which appeared in November, 1967, became the first of several plans for decentralizing the New York City public school system by proposing to turn its powers over to the various communities within the city. Mr. Bundy's proposal was to break the system into between thirty and sixty largely autonomous community subsystems, each with substantial control over its own budget, personnel, and curriculums. Soon after the Bundy Report appeared, Mayor Lindsay presented a modified school decentralization plan of his own which was more nearly calculated to appeal to the state legislators whose approval is required before any substantial changes can be made in the city system.

When the legislature ignored Mr. Lindsay's modifications, the New York State Board of Regents, which is ultimately responsible for the city schools, offered still another plan. The Regents' proposal would create somewhat fewer autonomous school districts, thus limiting the extent of decentralization, but it went beyond both the Bundy Plan and the mayor's modification by offering to do away immediately with the present nine-member Board of Education and replacing it as of June 30, 1968 with a new, five-man board, appointed by the mayor. Last month, at the urging of James Allen, the State Commissioner of Education, and with the support of a group of business leaders, the several plans were coordinated and presented to the legislature in Albany. Though the current proposal closely follows the Regents Plan, Commissioner Allen had no difficulty in getting the mayor and Mr. Bundy to go along, for both the city administration and the Ford Foundation apparently share with the Regents and the state commissioner the belief that the city schools are at the edge of chaos.

Whether the system should be broken down into thirty or sixty districts, as the Bundy Plan suggests, or into twenty districts, as the Regents have advised, the urgent matter is to wrench the school system away from the bureaucrats who are now running it and whose failure now threatens the stability of the city itself. As a practical matter, the children of the ghetto, who now comprise nearly half the total public school enrollment, are largely without a functioning educational system at all, and the present school administration has shown that it is incapable of supplying them with one.

Mr. Bundy's report represents his debut in urban affairs, but for the former White House official the political crisis which his report hoped to settle is nothing new. In the ghettos of New York as, a decade ago, in the Mekong Delta, an angry and insurgent population feels that it has exhausted its last political options and is now ready for violence, even if violence means suicide. For the parents of the ghetto the schools are the only means by which their children can escape, but each year, as the failure of the schools becomes more apparent, the grip of the city's discredited education officials grows tighter. The city is thus faced with a classic revolutionary situation. The problem for Mayor Lindsay and Mr. Bundy is to keep the peace, but the present strategy is the opposite of what it had been in Vietnam. There we strengthened the mandarins. The plan now is to weaken them and to offer a form of self-government to the indigenous population. At the heart of the various decentralization programs is the dispersal of New York City's central educational bureaucracy, a pyramid of some 3,000 officials, so firmly impacted at its base and so remote at its summit that it promises to survive (unless it is destroyed by its angry clientele) longer than the pyramids of Egypt.

The proposed New York City school budget for next year is nearly $1.33 billion. The strategy of decentralization is to turn much of this money, and thus much of the power to run the schools, over to local boards of education, a majority of whose members will be chosen by the parents within the individual communities, while the rest will be appointed by the mayor from lists supplied by the central board in consultation with representatives of the various neighborhoods. Thus, in theory, the central board will be reduced largely to looking after labor relations, the protection of the children's constitutional rights, maintaining educational standards, data-processing, city-wide testing, and so forth. The real power—that is, the power to give out the 60,000 jobs within the system—will reside with the politically chosen local boards.

Though it is unclear from the report whether these local boards will, in fact, reflect the interests of their communities, or will accommodate themselves, as the central board itself does, to city-wide interests and pressures, resulting in the same inertia from which the system suffers now, it is clear that the proponents of decentralization are less concerned with what is taught in the schools than with who runs them. In this they share the attitude of the present school administration, as well as that of the school administration a century ago, before civil service reforms replaced a political spoils system in which school jobs were given out by local leaders in consultation with city hall. The main assumption of the proposed new legislation is that, since the city's demographic center has begun to shift toward the ghetto, the distribution of power within the school system should now begin to shift accordingly.

As the Bundy Report itself acknowledged, the case for restricting the power of the central board is hardly original. A study issued in 1933 urged a form of decentralization, and there have been others in 1940,

1942, 1949, 1962, and 1965. But the current proposals are unique in their urgency and aggressiveness, partly because their sponsors feel that it is no longer a matter merely of improving the schools but of saving the city, and perhaps, since the case of New York is typical of all large-city systems, of saving the entire country. The proposed legislation asks for immediate and specific reform to take effect as soon as next month. Mr. Bundy, Mr. Lindsay, and Commissioner Allen are offering New York's educational mandarins hardly more time to pack their bags than the Diem family got.

There are, however, a number of difficulties with the plan, the most serious of which is that the board and its professional staff, supported in the present case by the powerful United Federation of Teachers, are unlikely to give up without a fight. Their political resources are formidable and, given what they stand to lose—that is, their jobs—they are likely to fight bitterly. To the administrators and teachers, as well as to their representatives in Albany, decentralization means that a largely Jewish bureaucracy, with a strong residue of Irish flavoring, must now begin to make way, at least in the ghetto schools, for a largely Negro insurgency. White candidates for principal ($18,970–$25,795) or assistant superintendent ($30,000), who have served their time in the schools, passed their examinations, waited in line, attended the banquets, made the friends, and done whatever else the system expects of its future leaders, will, if the new legislation is enacted, have to stand by while Negroes and Puerto Ricans, appointed by community boards of education, take the jobs which these candidates have been waiting for and which they feel they have earned. In Negro and Puerto Rican districts even the incumbent principals and superintendents, to say nothing of the individual teachers, will not be safe from the local boards, for while the proposed new legislation promises to maintain the tenure of these people, it does not guarantee to keep them in their present jobs. The local boards, under decentralization, will have the power to pluck the present staff members from wherever in the hierarchy they may now be perched and throw them, tenured but jobless, into cold storage until they resign or can be retired.

According to the Board of Examiners which administers the so-called merit system by which teachers and principals are advanced to higher positions (and which the new legislation proposes to abolish), the Bundy Report was "terrifying in its implications" for "white teachers." Privately, the report has been called anti-Semitic. Recently it was attacked by the Board of Rabbis. Last month Herman Mantell, president of the Council of Jewish Organizations in Civil Service, which represents 26,000 members of the Jewish Teachers Association, promised that his organization will campaign against persons who are implicated in "creating political chaos" in the school system, by which he presumably meant not only the mayor, the state commissioner, the Board of Regents, and the Ford Foundation, but also whichever state legislators are so bold as to vote for decentralization.

Though the language of the Bundy Report was conciliatory, as when its authors insisted that they had been "deeply impressed by the honesty, the intelligence and the essential good will" of the same educational leaders whom they intended to rusticate, the report's message was clear to the bureaucrats even before it was published. Their response was predictably critical, occasionally agitated, as in the case of the Board of Examiners, but reassured by the knowledge that the system has survived plenty of trouble so far, including its conspicuous and admitted failure to educate the children of the ghettos, and it will probably survive this crisis, too. Though the present school administration has tried to refute the report on such grounds as its implied attack on "professionalism," its main strategy has been to keep cool, avoid public arguments, and support the idea of decentralization in principle, though only in principle, while counting on representatives of the city's ethnic majorities, prodded by such statesmen as Mr. Mantell, to kill the proposal in the legislature. As if anticipating such a response, the Bundy Report chastised the board for its characteristic inertia, what the report calls its "negative power," the power to thwart its critics by ignoring them, on the proven assumption that sooner or later the critics will grow tired and quit.

To experience this negative power directly, as anyone does who becomes entangled with New York City's educational bureaucracy, is often bewildering and usually infuriating. No doubt the authors of the Bundy Report, as they made their way through the enervated corridors of New York's school headquarters, past the bland or sullen officials, had plenty of chances to see this system at work and to conclude, quite apart from the larger political considerations which prompted the report in the first place, that whatever is wrong with the schools must begin with its central administrative staff. It is easy to see how the authors of the report may have felt that the first step toward reconstructing public education in New York must be to get rid of this frustrating organization, or at least to circumvent it, as the prosperous middle class had done years ago when it built its own system of independent schools, and as the population of the ghetto now wants to do when it insists upon running the ghetto schools itself.[1]

Yet, for all the anguish which the school bureaucracy inspires, it would be naive to assume that its negative power can easily be manipulated or sidestepped through institutional reforms, or that these reforms, assuming they can ever be legislated, can then, in fact, be implemented. One might have thought that Mr. Bundy had learned from his experiences in Saigon how stubborn an established hierarchy can be in the face of even the most zealous attempts to change it. But, even if he had never heard of General Ky, he had only to consider the miserable history of school desegregation in New York to know the many ways in which such bureaucracies protect themselves from the moral and political assaults of the outside world.

Though school desegregation had been ordered, in effect, by the Supreme Court in 1954 and mandated, in turn, by the Board of Education, as well as by the state commissioner, it became clear by the end of the 1950's that the schools in New York were going to remain largely segregated, not, as some sociologists have said, because there were not enough white children to go around, but because a number of principals and other administrators, fearful of the white parents and often because of their own prejudices, decided to ignore or subvert orders from the central board to integrate their schools. It would be unfair, however, to blame this failure solely on the headquarters officials who were charged with desegregation. A bureaucrat's power over his subordinates, and thus his strength within the hierarchy, is partly determined by whether these subordinates will carry out his orders. If enough of them resist or passively ignore what they are told to do, and if they are supported by forces —in this case the white parents—over whom the system has no control, then the responsible officials are likely to retreat, as in fact they did. That neither the superintendent nor the central board, armed with the authority of the Supreme Court, offered to discipline the rebellious principals suggests how stubborn the negative power of such a bureaucracy can be.

In this sense, the problem in New York is not that there is too much central authority, as the various decentralization plans seem to imply, but that there is not enough, and that, what central authority there is, is ineffective. In its resistance to integration the system showed that it was already "decentralized" to the point of anarchy. Aware that their power depended upon the compliance of a tenured field staff, the administrators at headquarters, when events required that they assert the authority of their offices, typically replied that "it is not our job to tell the principals how to run their schools," as if the responsibilities of leadership were somehow a violation of democratic procedure.[2]

Faced with this collapse of central authority, the leaders of the ghetto communities, who had been promised integrated schools, and who had conveyed these promises to the credulous, if restless, parents, correctly decided that they had been betrayed and that to depend any longer upon the board was useless. What they discovered was that for many school officials public education was not mainly a matter of teaching the children but of maintaining stable terms of employment for teachers, and, of course, administrators themselves. If these ghetto parents needed to be convinced further that negotiations with the system were a waste of time they had only to await the plans for Harlem's I.S. 201 to be announced.

The story of I.S. 201 is somewhat complex, but since it relates directly to the present move toward decentralization, and since it foreshadows the increasingly violent confrontations that can be expected between the community and the school authorities if decentralization is not enacted, it is worth outlining here. The initials I.S. stand for intermediate school, an institution which includes grades six through eight and is intended eventually to replace the present junior high schools, which include grades seven through nine. The point is to get the children out of their local elementary schools a year earlier and into the larger intermediate schools, which are supposed to draw their students from a wider community and thus, through this purely technical means, enforce a kind of integration. To do this the intermediate schools must be built in what the board calls "fringe areas," that is, between white and black neighborhoods. They must also be big enough to draw children from a number of elementary schools. At first, I.S. 201 was to have been simply another mid-Harlem junior high school, built to relieve overcrowding in two adjacent junior high schools, and the Negro borough president of Manhattan approved the site accordingly. At this point, however, an officious administrator at headquarters decided, ostensibly in the interest of integration, to make the new school an intermediate school. But he neglected to change either the mid-Harlem site or the capacity of the building, with the result that Harlem's first intermediate school would inevitably be as segregated as a school in New York could possibly be. Probably this administrative decision resulted from nothing more sinister than the disingenuousness, together with the insensitivity, of the official who made it and from the tendency of the system to deal with its problems by changing their labels. Nevertheless, the Harlem leaders who had agreed to continue working with the board were enraged.

A new and tougher leadership emerged whose alliances, insofar as they felt they needed any with the white community, were not with the Board of Education but with the foundations, the mayor's office, and the various antipoverty programs; the forces, in other words, which generated the Bundy Report. Meanwhile, some of the disenchanted parents whose children were enrolled in I.S. 201 decided that, since they were stuck with the school, they might as well run it themselves. The famous disorders followed in which the white principal was forced to leave and the board, since it was no longer a matter of offending the white parents and in order to avoid any further trouble in the ghetto, more or less capitulated to the militant Negroes. Shortly thereafter, the Ford Foundation proposed that I.S. 201 become the pivot of a partly autonomous Harlem school district whose budget would be augmented by Ford. Ford also decided to finance two other "demonstration" districts, one in lower Manhattan and the other in Brooklyn, as further experiments in local autonomy. The school administration accepted these plans, partly in the spirit that, for the time being at least, it was getting rid of a headache, and perhaps also on the assumption that these "demonstration" districts would, like most other attempts at reconstruction within the system, come to nothing. Furthermore, the board had no choice. The alternative to capitulation was open warfare. The Bundy Report soon followed, with its proposal that the authority of the central board be severely reduced throughout the city.[3]

The question remains, however, whether the report and its subsequent modifications make sense in themselves: whether local autonomy offers a real solution to the crisis in public education. The answer goes beyond the question of who runs the school system, for the ultimate problem is not whether black officials replace white ones but whether the children will learn more in a system administered by several black school boards than in one dominated by a single, impotent white board. Unfortunately, neither the Bundy Report nor the Regents Plan gives us much to go on, for they neglect to show how the inertia at headquarters leads to the disasters in the classrooms, or whether there are any meaningful links between the two phenomena at all.

As a result, it is unclear how a formally decentralized system, replacing the present anarchy, based upon decaying, but still potent, traditions of mutual self-interest, will stimulate the 60,000 teachers, 30 per cent of whom are substitutes, to outdo their present performances. Both the Bundy Plan and the Regents' proposal are content to assume that, once the present bureaucracy is out of the way, talents and energies which heretofore have languished will awaken and find their way, through the presumably enlightened local boards, into the schools. That the various plans fail to show how decentralization might actually affect the children and their teachers in the classrooms is perhaps understandable, since their aims are largely political: to avert a revolution by redistributing political power and jobs. But the pedagogical question remains, for it would be foolish to reorganize the system only to discover that this sort of tinkering made no difference at all; that, no matter how the system were organized and no matter who got the jobs, the problems in the classrooms would remain; that the real difficulty had lain in a different direction all along.

To raise such questions, however, suggests the complexity of the intersecting puzzles which the authors of the decentralization plans must have faced as they did their work; for not only had it been a matter for them of forestalling a revolution in the ghetto, but of simultaneously proposing solutions to pedagogical problems which have so far perplexed nearly everyone who has tried to think about them. To have had to face these dilemmas within the sharply foreshortened perspective of America's racial agony compounds the puzzle, so that one is amazed to consider that Mr. Bundy and his colleagues agreed to undertake their work at all. That they had also to state their conclusions in the form of legislative proposals elevates their task to a truly metaphysical level of difficulty, made still worse by the gloomy presence of an educational bureaucracy which all the forces of history, concentrated as they are on the ghettos of New York, have been powerless to budge. It may nevertheless be possible, by ignoring the legislative consequences of one's speculations, to begin to sort out at least some of the threads in this tangled web. Perhaps the place to begin is where the board itself feels it has failed most conspicuously: teaching the children to read.

In New York City, nearly 50,000 children in the third grade, about 60 per cent of the total, read so poorly that, according to the Board of Education, "their success in the higher grades is highly unlikely." For thousands of New York City children, particularly in the ghetto, their failure to learn to read marks the first of a series of failures whose cumulative effect must be devastating and permanent.[4] Yet, until recently, it had seemed that learning to read was a process which, despite all the fussing in the classroom over curriculum and materials, was for most children more or less automatic, like learning to walk or talk. In her recent book,[5] however, Jeanne Chall, the reading specialist at the Harvard Graduate School of Education, has shown that this process has not been nearly so self-evident as one might have assumed. Debates over how to teach the children to read have been going on for decades, but she also shows, despite her own preference for a particular set of pedagogical tactics, that the terms of the debate have now become somewhat obscure: that on the level of theory, at least, no one really knows much about how children learn or how they should be taught.

In her useful book, Professor Chall approaches the question pedagogically—whether to teach the children phonetically, linguistically, or by the method based on the recognition of whole words, or by various combinations of the three. But her book also implies an underlying cultural question which, unfortunately for our understanding, she never adequately explores. The question which haunts Professor Chall's book and which haunts the decentralization controversy, too, is whether a common language can be taught or learned at all, no matter what the pedagogical tactics and no matter how the schools are administered, once the children sense the hostility to their style of life and their color of an alien and overpowering environment; once they discover, in other words, that no matter how hard they try, they are unlikely ever to be accepted as genuine participants in American society.

For middle-class children of no matter what color, the impulse to learn to read has usually been strong enough to prevail over even the whimsical pedagogy which Professor Chall so scrupulously describes. For these children the classrooms seem not so much the place where they are taught as where they teach themselves, through their intrinsic curiosity and ambition, while their teachers stimulate and direct the process. It is only later, when some of these middle-class children grow unsure of the goals and values of their schools, that their enthusiasm for the classroom diminishes and they no longer respond to the curriculum and the teachers. As Edgar Friedenberg, among others, has shown, these middle-class adolescents, when they become disaffected with schools, grow irritable or aggressively conform, depending on their individual characters, or they drop out. Extreme cases withdraw, or become violent or assertively break the law.

For many ghetto children, versions of these pathologies seem to occur almost from the beginning of school and, though it would be wrong to press the analogy, it may not be unreasonable to suspect that these elementary school "dropouts," like their counterparts among the middle-class adolescents, are rejecting, in ways that hardly suggest a failure of intelligence or sensitivity on their part, a culture which refuses to take them or their parents seriously as human beings and as citizens. For many of these children, the recognition that they represent an arbitrarily diminished category within the life of the city may occur for the first time in the classroom, where they begin to encounter the rituals and temptations, but also the rigors, of middle-class life, and where they discover—no matter what color their teachers or principals may be—the discouraging truth of their special status.

In suggesting that the ghettos now run their own schools, the advocates of decentralization seem to acknowledge this problem and to suggest that, if the children cannot learn from a dominant and hostile white culture, perhaps they can learn from a specialized and more congenial culture of their own. Yet there is something disingenuous or romantic about this idea, for in its struggles with white prejudice the racial underclass in America has produced not an assured and functioning alternative to the dominant culture, but a depleted and anguished version of it, whose corrosive effects on the parents are often pathetically reflected in the confused and alienated children. It is unclear from the decentralization proposals how, under such social circumstances, a formally decentralized school system will generate among the children of the ghetto the faith that their efforts in the classroom will be rewarded by a chance to take part as responsible citizens in a country which welcomes and will reward their loyalty and trust.

It is not, after all, as if the residents of the ghetto were, like the Algerians or Cubans, the rightful owners of their own country who had only to get rid of their foreign exploiters to return to their own culture and develop their own economy. For all the talk about racial separatism and Black Power, the Negroes are inevitably trapped in America, so intricately caught in the tragedy of its racist history that there seems literally no way for them to disentangle themselves. Unlike the other ethnic minorities, the Negroes are without even the dubious resource of cosmopolitanism. They may learn to speak Swahili and think of themselves as Yorubas or Muslims, but culturally the majority remains quintessentially American—the one ingredient in the melting pot which seems actually to have melted—and their special characteristics are largely those of the urban American underclass, alienated now even from the remnants of the plantation culture which they knew in the South.

Though the teachers may evade this lesson in their classrooms—indeed, the curriculum requires them to, with its talk of brotherhood and the achievements of those Negroes who have managed to transcend the system—there is no evading the fact, for the truth is as plain as the streets of Harlem and as crushing. Though Negro principals responsible to Negro boards of education may in some way mitigate or postpone the discovery, they can hardly invalidate it, for the brutal poverty of the American ghettos must be obvious to the children and profoundly degrading. No matter who runs the schools, the most poignant lesson to be learned in the ghetto is despair, which, as it deepens, paralyzes the mind and will. It is a process which seems for thousands of children already to be well advanced by the third grade.

Yet to leave the question at this point is to abandon not only the ghetto, but the city itself, to catastrophe, for the fate of the one is inextricably bound to that of the other. Whatever Black Power may mean in a positive sense, its negative meaning is clear enough, for the ghettos by their very presence—quite apart from the possibilities of violence—imply the end of urban society. The 50,000 third-graders now languishing in their classrooms are a burden which the next generation of taxpayers can hardly support, not only in the form of increased welfare costs, police protection, and other social services, but in the loss to the city's economy of much of its future working and taxpaying population. Businesses which depend upon a predictable supply of trained personnel have already begun to leave the city, and though new office buildings continue to go up, the moneylenders have become apprehensive. Yet, it is astonishing that most of the city's commercial and financial leadership remains so indifferent to this impending threat to its own interests, for it takes no great sophistication to project the future cost to the city's economy of the failure of its public school system. At the rate of $3,000 a year in direct and indirect costs to support a person on welfare, the 50,000 third-graders whose failure the board has predicted will, when they come of age, cost the public $150 million a year, assuming that for every child who grows up to escape the ghetto there is another who has escaped the board's statistical estimate. To this annual sum must be added the cost of the second grade, the first, and the grades yet to come, to say nothing of the loss to the city of the productive capacity of such vast numbers of its citizens.

Perhaps the city will survive the summers that are immediately ahead, but it is unlikely to survive an economy that seems about to go into reverse, as the city's faltering revenues are increasingly absorbed by a largely unproductive population. Last year the city's budget for social services was $1.07 billion. This year the budget will be $1.390 billion, an increase of nearly 30 per cent. Under such pressure the city's tax base is certain to erode as middle-class taxpayers, unable to support such rapidly accumulating burdens, move out, and as businesses, unable to staff their offices, follow them to the suburbs. In such circumstances it makes no difference that much of the city's welfare budget will eventually be supported by federal funds. The fact is that such costs are, in themselves, unsupportable. The failure of the third grade obviously is a disaster to which the proprietors of the city should quickly turn their attention, for if the children of the ghettos are trapped in a dance of death, their dancing partners are the holders of the city's mortgages, the owners of its utilities, the beneficiaries of its bridges and tunnels, and the rulers of its commerce. For the ideologists of Black Power to talk of coalitions with the working class seems beside the point. Their appropriate allies are the city's power elite.

Yet, when one searches for the flesh and blood which constitutes such an elite, one finds instead a sociological abstraction much as one finds, in searching for the true manipulators of Black Power, a political abstraction. It is not simply the Board of Education whose power now seems to have become fragmented and its authority hollow, but the city itself which no longer appears capable of protecting its own interests.

The advocates of decentralization are obviously correct to assume that the pedagogical problems which afflict the schools are ultimately political problems; that the children will not learn to read, will not accept the confinements of civilization and the responsibilities of citizenship, until a substantial shift of power has taken place within the city. But the proposal that power be shifted from a moribund Board of Education to the political leaders of the ghetto is a pale and inadequate imitation of the kinds of bargains that have to be struck and the amounts of power that have to be exchanged. The children will hardly accept the rules of civilization so long as they know that there are no places for them in it, that they must therefore live outside the culture of the city not only as its victims but, actively or passively, as its antagonists. One has only to visit a middle-class schoolroom to sense the strength of will required of the children to sit in their chairs day after day, year after year, and pay attention to the largely trivial curriculum, nor is it conceivable that such powerful restraints can be imposed for long by the authority of the teachers and the institution. It is only the child himself, sensing that failure in school implies failure in life, who can set such rules and find the interior strength to obey them. Now and then it is superficially charming, amid the anguished poverty of a ghetto school, to find this restraint occasionally missing and the children apparently gayer, more spontaneous—one would have to say brighter—than their middle-class counterparts. Yet the charm fades, as one bitterly wonders whether the source of this gaiety may not lie in the recognition by the children— often reinforced by their teachers—that, because they are black, they have failed already and further effort is useless; that the systematic re- straints by which, for better or worse, middle-class character is formed, are for them irrelevant. Obviously it will take more than a few black elementary school principals to offset the despair which now encloses these children. It will take something as powerful as the knowledge that they will one day come of age and inherit the society in their own right, a recognition which most white children have never lacked, yet which may, at last, turn out to have been a delusion unless their black neigh- bors come to share it with them.

In such circumstances it is disappointing that the legislature has so far greeted decentralization so diffidently, for, whatever its pedagogical inadequacies, it supplies a beginning and a model which, with vigorous leadership, might be exploited further. Perhaps one day it might be possible to turn other city institutions over to black leadership—the ghetto police precincts, for example, or the public utilities or the enor- mously powerful Transit Authority, even the bridges and tunnels and the housing and redevelopment agencies, which imply control of the city's construction industries and therefore of its traditionally segregated trade unions and their rich pension funds.

Recently, the State of New York established a Metropolitan Com- muter Transport Authority to bring the metropolitan area's several transport facilities together within a single agency. A generation ago such an agency would probably have been put in the hands of that con- summate power broker, Robert Moses, who would have known exactly how to distribute its incidental blessings—in the form of jobs, contracts, and accumulated cash reserves for further investment—among the job-lot power brokers who have for years dominated the city's political and institutional life. It would, of course, be naive to assume that Governor Rockefeller had much freedom to decide who was to run the new Transport Authority, particularly the freedom to cross the city's well-defended ethnic barriers. Yet, what might have happened had this powerful public trust been given to the authentic black leaders of the ghettos instead of to the white politicians to whom the governor, as a matter of course, has handed it over?

That black leadership may have little experience in planning public transportation is beside the point. Moses didn't know much about it himself, as anyone knows who has tried to negotiate the Long Island Expressway at rush hour or has waited in traffic on the Triboro Bridge while his plane takes off from Kennedy Airport without him. Mass transportation in New York could hardly be worse, and the proposals offered by the new Transport Authority don't promise any improvement. Yet, just as the school system may be seen as primarily a source of employment for a certain class of citizens rather than mainly as a means of educating children, so the transport network may be seen as primarily a means of enfranchising and stabilizing another substantial element of the population rather than mainly a means of moving people from one place to another. As for where and how the new roads and subway tunnels are to be built, black leadership can hire the same planners and engineers that white administrators can hire, while, from the point of view of achieving political stability, the blacks have an incalculable advantage. By distributing the power of such an agency among their own constituencies, these black leaders can generate the positive meanings which Black Power now lacks and which it can never achieve through violence alone.

At first glance, the political costs to the governor of such a radical transfer of power might seem suicidal, as it might have seemed suicidal for the *ancien régime* to invite the leaders of the Jacobins to supervise the treasury at Versailles. Had he issued such an invitation, however, Louis XVI and his friends and relatives might have died with their heads on, while the history of France would probably have turned out no differently had the spectacular violence of the Revolution been avoided. The present monarchy, based on an enfranchised bourgeoisie, would most likely have to come to pass in any event.

If such proposals might have seemed whimsical in 1798 and only slightly less whimsical in 1917, perhaps we have by now lived with revolutions long enough to find them no longer really whimsical at all. It was not, after all, such a disaster for the Yankee proprietors of Boston to turn their public institutions over—no matter how reluctantly—to the relatively uncultivated heirs of Ireland's great hunger. Mr. Bundy's own rise to power is itself an incidental consequence of his ancestor's foresight in this regard. Clearly, the question of race presents special difficulties foreshadowed by the indifference of the ghetto children to the future of our common society. Nor does it make sense to say that the black communities in New York lack the political power that the Irish once had in Boston, for the blacks, in their despair and abdication, can, through their accumulating pressure on the public treasury, bring the city down. In this sense, the blacks have won their revolution already. The violence which the city also faces is, from a political point of view, anticlimactic. The alternative left to the white majority is capitulation or genocide.

The discouraging obstinacy of New York's educational bureaucracy hardly suggests that the police department, the transportation bureaucracies, or the other city agencies will prove any less reluctant to turn their powers over to the black community. Yet, in the severity of the crisis there may be some hope. If there is, in fact, an American power elite, clearly the time has come for it to defend its interests against its own bureaucracies, and to exploit, in ways that have nothing to do with generosity, the residual middle-class impulses which one continues to find amid the social wreckage of the ghetto. It was not, after all, Malcolm X's plan to destroy the American middle class, but to build a black version of it from the proceeds of black dry-cleaning stores and service stations. The flaw in Malcolm's vision was its modesty. The necessary goals of Black Power are the fundamental institutions of the city itself.[6] If these goals are not met, it is impossible to see how the schools can transmit their language and their culture to tens of thousands of ghetto children, and then what will be left of the city?

Notes

1. As it is already doing in a small way through its street academies and Harlem Prep, privately supported ghetto schools whose enrollment consists mainly of public school dropouts and whose aims are to send most of these students on to college.

2. No reform is possible in New York City until the headquarters staff and the principals are made directly accountable for their performances. Neither the Bundy Plan nor the Regents' proposal specifically provides for such direct accountability, though both imply it. Middle-class parents who send their children to private schools take such accountability for granted. The headmaster's job depends directly upon the approval of the parents represented by their trustees. The five-man board proposed by the Regents will be effective only if it can find ways to hold the professional staff personally responsible for their performances. Under the system of tenured civil service it is hard to see how such a program of direct accountability can be implemented. Nevertheless, it should be the primary duty of any new board to assess the work of its professional staff and, in consultation with local boards, replace incompetent personnel as circumstances require.

3. Though *The New York Times* supports decentralization editorially, its coverage of the experiment in decentralization at I.S. 201 has been superficial and inflammatory. By exaggerating the difficulties that the school has experienced, and continues to experience, Leonard Buder, who covers I.S. 201 for *The New York Times*, has given the impression that the community is incapable of running the school. According to Buder, the legislature has been diffident toward decentralization partly because of what it has read about I.S. 201, most of which Buder has written himself. Part of the trouble, however, comes from the equivocal relationship between the local community and the central bureaucracy. Though the board agreed to support the experiment in local control of I.S. 201, it has done little to help and much to hinder not only I.S. 201 but the two other "demonstration" districts as well. Buder's reports emphasize the chaotic results while ignoring the board's obstructive tactics. I.S. 201 has thus become the exemplary victim of a system in which the central staff refuses to relinquish its powers and may even have attempted to subvert the experiments in local autonomy, as it had earlier subverted desegregation. Fred Hechinger, the education editor of *The New York Times*, also supports decentralization in his articles, but warns against "extremists" who might take over if the professional staff should be removed. It is unclear, however, what Hechinger means by "extremists."

4. Of nearly 30,000 academic diplomas awarded to graduates of the city high schools in 1967 only 700, according to the Urban League, went to Negroes.

5. Jeanne S. Chall, *Learning to Read: The Great Debate* (New York: McGraw-Hill Book Co., 1967).

6. Some black leaders argue impressively that the white bureaucracies will never turn their city-wide powers over to blacks. They propose, instead, that black leadership concentrate on taking power within the ghettos themselves and running them, in effect, as separate cities. There is much to be said for this idea, but how will the autonomous ghettos finance their independent economies without external support? There are few public institutions within the ghettos capable of producing investment capital, whereas such city-wide or metropolitan institutions as mass transport typically generate quantities of new capital for further development. No wonder their proprietors hang on to them so jealously. It will not be enough for blacks to control their essentially dependent ghettos if whites do not recognize their self-interest in capitalizing black communities through public or semipublic institutions.

V

Community Control
of the Schools

The logical result of the political struggle for school reform—which has passed through stages of concern with administrative reorganization, new educational techniques, integration, and the like—is the present call, voiced most strongly in the ghetto communities of our cities, for decentralization of school systems and community control of the schools. Some ghetto dwellers are now so disillusioned with the existing system of education that they call for complete separation in the form of totally independent districts; most, however, still desire only to share power. Many of the latest studies of urban school systems and educational politics conclude that decentralization and community control are not only logical but also desirable. As many of the previous selections in this volume indicate, there is strong evidence of the need for extensive changes. There are those who argue that, if such changes take the form of community control and decentralization, they would be well within the constructive traditions of the American democratic system. In short, the dramatic shifts in power that would result from the implementation of programs of community control are not as radical as opponents purport. Significant change in political and social institutions in response to popular outcry is one of the great characteristics of the American experience. Demands for community control of schools by low-income deprived groups who happen to be predominantly nonwhite do not differ to any large extent from the profound struggles for change that have been initiated by the deprived groups throughout our history. One need only to recall how local political machines and local governments were captured by Irish-Americans to find a relevant example. The power of the labor movement today is itself testimony to the success of a working class, composed primarily of European immigrant groups, in its attempts to restructure political institutions in order to assure for itself access to the fruits of America's economic treasures. The conflicts surrounding such changes were often very violent and bloody, and, indeed, violence was an integral part of the labor movement's attempts to wrench rights and benefits from a built-in and powerful establishment. The parallels between such events and the present struggle by the urban poor are clear.

Community control is suggested as a mechanism for bringing the poor into an active partnership with the professionals who dominate policy-making in city schools. There is no guarantee that it will cure all the ills of deprivation, but a dramatic change seems to be needed—particularly in the area of education—and community control has sufficient merit to warrant, at the very least, a lengthy and meaningful testing.

The selections in this chapter, reaching beyond the failure of urban school systems, explore these two significant avenues for reform. Peter Schrag's analysis of the general failure of school systems concludes with a statement of support for school reform; at the same time, Schrag questions whether decentralization, in and of itself, is necessarily the answer. In the analysis that follows, Mario Fantini explores various mechanisms for reform and, weighing all possibilities, comes out strongly in support of community participation in the decision-making process.

In New York City, the controversy over community control has been particularly explosive, reaching a critical pitch in the autumn of 1968, when the United Federation of Teachers and the Council of Supervisory Associations struck the schools on a city-wide basis. For what it has to say about the interests and participants in the community control debate, the New York City situation is especially illuminating. At issue in the strike was the extent of powers granted to the three experimental decentralized school districts set up in the spring of 1967. The immediate cause of the strike was the action, taken in May, 1968, of the elected local school board of the Ocean Hill–Brownsville experimental school district in ordering the transfer of nineteen administrators and teachers from the district. The UFT, attacking the method of transfer as a violation of due process, struck the district that spring. After a summer of investigation and negotiation, the issues remained: Was the method of transfer a violation of due process? Did the local school board have the power to hire and fire administrators and teachers in the district? With both sides stalemated, the teachers struck the entire city school system, carrying with them the support of the CSA.

The two articles that follow present contrasting views on these questions. On the one side, the report of the New York Civil Liberties

Union concludes that the due process issue was a smokescreen set up to obscure the UFT's real purpose: to prevent community control from being instituted throughout the city. On the other side, Adolph Stone, an official of the CSA, attacks the report, arguing that the union's position was both justified and proper in light of conditions in the experimental district.

Marilyn Gittell concludes this section with an overview of decentralization and community control. In her article, she states her support for community control and decentralization both in terms of the need for a restructuring of our fundamental concepts about democracy and in terms of the actual New York City experience with the experimental school districts.

21. WHY OUR SCHOOLS HAVE FAILED

PETER SCHRAG

In the context of traditional American belief, Section 402 of the Civil Rights Act of 1964 is one of the simplest, most unambiguous directives ever issued to a government agency. It instructs the U.S. Commissioner of Education to carry out a survey "concerning the lack of availability of equal educational opportunities for individuals by reason of race, color, religion, or national origin in educational institutions" in the United States and its possessions. Presumably, the wording of Section 402 merely pointed toward an examination of the effects of overt racial discrimination in American schools. What it produced instead was a 737-page document that demonstrated not only the ineffectiveness of schools in overcoming the handicaps of poverty and deprivation, but also the fact that no one knows what the phrase "equal educational opportunities" means and that, given the conditions of contemporary American society, it can have no meaning. Education in America is patently unequal, it is structured to be unequal, and it can only define its successes by its failures. On the dark side of every conception of "opportunity" lies an equal measure of exclusion and rejection.

No one needs another set of statistics to prove that American Negro children—and many others—are being miseducated, that they are behind in the elementary grades, and that they fall further behind as they move through school. In the twelfth grade more than 85 per cent of Negro children score below the average white on standardized tests of achievement, their dropout rates are higher, and their self-esteem is lower. We can dispute the validity of the tests as indicators of intelligence, but there is not the slightest doubt that, if they measure educational achievement and if they predict future success in school and college (as they do), then the children of the poor minorities in America perform well below average. What the new statistics do provide is solid evidence for the repeated assertion by civil rights leaders and others that what chil-

Reprinted from *Commentary*, XLV (March, 1968), 31–38, by permission. Copyright © 1968 by the American Jewish Committee. Used by permission of the author and the publisher.

dren learn in school are the rules and attitudes of second-class citizenship, and that the school is a highly effective mechanism not only for advancement but for selecting people out.

Historically, "equality of educational opportunity" simply demanded that all individuals were to have access to similar resources in similar public schools; where children failed, it was because of their own limitations, their lack of ambition and intelligence, not because of the inadequacies of the schools or the society. If the schools were found to favor a particular race or economic group (as they were in many of the desegregation cases), one could rectify the inequities through application of relatively simple standards: the appropriation of equal resources to the education of children of all races, the integration of schools, or the reassignment of teachers. The definition never contemplated the difficulties children might bring from home or the fact that even the best teachers and resources, according to the conventional standards, were keyed to middle-class experience, motivation, and attitude. More important, it never contemplated genuine integration. What it presumed was that only the white middle-class society offered ideals and standards of value and that whatever the ghetto offered, or what minority children brought with them, was to be disregarded, deflated, or denied. The traditional melting pot was stirred by Protestant hands with a white ladle.

It will be years before the sociologists and statisticians get through with the data in the government's report, *Equality of Educational Opportunity*, that was prompted by Section 402. The study, headed by Professor James S. Coleman, of The Johns Hopkins University, was eighteen months in the making, cost $2 million to produce, and included data on 600,000 children and 60,000 teachers in 4,000 schools. It is written, as Christopher Jencks said, "in the workmanlike prose of an Agriculture Department bulletin on fertilizer," and it is so thoroughly crammed with tables, regression coefficients, and standard deviations as to make all but the most passionate statisticians shudder. (Ultimately, it turned out, even some of the statisticians began to shudder.) Nonetheless, the Coleman Report has probably become the most influential educational study of the decade. It formed the basis of the recent report of the U.S. Civil Rights Commission, *Racial Isolation in the Public Schools*, it provided ammunition for a federal-court opinion on segregation in the Washington schools, it is the topic of conferences and seminars, it is endlessly quoted at meetings, and it became the subject of a year-long study at Harvard under the direction of Daniel P. Moynihan and Thomas Pettigrew (who also wrote the Civil Rights Commission Report). It may be a measure of the times that, where forty years ago we produced educational philosophy and ideology, we are now producing statistics.

The Coleman Report comes to two central conclusions:

1. That the most significant determinant of educational success (as measured by standardized tests of mathematical and verbal performance) is the social and economic background of the individual student, that formal instructional inputs—which are not as unequally distributed between races as supposed—make relatively little difference, and that the social and economic composition of fellow students, not materials or libraries, is the most important in-school resource.

2. That children from disadvantaged backgrounds (regardless of race) benefit from integration with advantaged kids (regardless of race), but that the latter are not harmed by such integration. Proper integration mixes rich and poor and produces a general social gain: The poor learn more; the performance of the rich does not go down.

The Coleman conclusions substantiate propositions that have been gaining currency in the last few years. If racial integration is pedagogically desirable, then clearly social and economic integration, and the interplay of cultural styles, are even more important. Poor blacks and whites can learn from each other, but rich and poor—under the proper conditions—can benefit even more. The report's conclusions on the impact of teachers are not entirely clear, but they do indicate that good teachers and effective educational environments are more important to the disadvantaged than to those who have access (in the home, for example) to other resources. Even so, teachers, libraries, laboratories, and other formal inputs are not as important as fellow students.

Carried to its ultimate, the Coleman Report seems to indicate that schools make relatively little difference, except as a place where kids learn from each other, and that money spent in improving them is likely, at best, to yield marginal results. The first temptation, of course, is to dismiss that assertion as an absurdity: We take it as an article of faith that the public school has always been the great American social instrument, the device that converted the raw material of immigration into an endless stream of social success. Now, oddly enough, the school seems to be failing in the very functions on which its reputation has always been based. It does not seem to be able to bring the most indigenous and American of all "immigrants" into the mainstream or even to give them the educational qualifications that life in the mainstream requires. Given the insights of recent experience, we might now properly ask whether the school was ever as successful or important in the process of Americanization and education as the history textbooks sentimentally picture it. With the possible exception of the Jews, did the school ever become a major avenue of entry for the ethnic minorities of the urban centers? How effective was it for the Irish, the Italians, the Poles? Was it the school or the street that acculturated our immigrants? What about such Americanizing institutions as the political ward, the shop, and the small town? A half century ago American society provided alternatives to formal education, and no one became officially distressed about dropouts and slow readers. Now the school has become *the* gatekeeper to advancement, and, while it is being blamed for obvious failures, it may actually be doing better than it ever did before.

And yet, despite the accumulation of studies and statistics, we still don't know how much difference formal instruction makes, except to amplify characteristics that have already been determined somewhere else. The Coleman *conclusions* indicate that it doesn't make much difference, but here semantic problems and statistical difficulties begin to get in the way. What the Coleman group did was, in essence, to take schools with students of similar backgrounds and try to determine how much difference varying inputs seemed to make. (E.g., given two all-Negro schools, did children in the school where teachers had better training, higher degrees, for example, perform better than those in the other school?) In controlling for student background, however, Coleman and his colleagues may have underestimated the crucial fact that almost all schools are internally harmonious systems and that, where children come from disadvantaged backgrounds, their teachers are also likely, in some respects, to be disadvantaged. Two economists, Samuel Bowles of Harvard and Henry M. Levin of The Brookings Institution, point out in the *Journal of Human Resources*[1] that if the methodology of the study had been reversed, so would the conclusions; that is, if Coleman had controlled for such educational inputs as teacher training, the social background of the students would have appeared to make little difference. They point out, moreover, that the Coleman Report, despite the vast sample, was unavoidably biased through the refusal of many school systems to furnish data; suburban systems were statistically overrepresented while big cities, which have the most severe problems, were underrepresented. The most vicious attribute of urban school systems, until recently, has not been their consistent failure with the disadvantaged, but their refusal to produce honest data on that failure. In case after case, they pretended (perhaps because of the historical definition of "equality") that, despite statistical evidence to the contrary, it was individual children, not schools, that failed. Bowles and Levin contend, moreover, that the Coleman Report's conclusion that teachers' traits (verbal facility, educational level, etc.) are relatively unimportant is not supported by the data, which suggest exactly the opposite; that the report's data on the importance of class size are useless; and that its conclusions about the effect of integration are questionable, since "the processes of residential and academic selection imply that those Negroes who attend predominantly white schools are drawn largely from higher social strata." In brief, integration is educationally effective among those who are already educationally and socially "advantaged."

The most significant difficulty, however, is one that the Coleman Report did not create and cannot solve. What does equality mean in education? Does it mean that the average Negro should be doing as well as the average white, and that the resources devoted to his education should be improved until he does? Or does it point to some sort of parity in resources? Or to something else? Coleman himself said that the focus of his report was not on "what resources go into education, but on what product comes out." He then goes on to say (in an article in *The Public Interest*[2]) that "equality of educational opportunity implies not merely 'equal' schools but equally effective schools, whose influences will overcome the differences in starting point of children from different social groups."

Pedagogically and politically, Coleman's suggestion is pleasant, impossible, and probably undesirable—pleasant because it has a nice democratic ring; impossible because the haves in the society won't allow it to happen; undesirable because it assumes that all social and cultural differences should be equalized away, that Negro children (or Chinese or Jews) have nothing to offer *as Negroes* except problems and disadvantage, and that their culture (or perhaps even their genes) gives them nothing special that might be socially, educationally, or personally valuable. A Negro in this context is nothing but a disadvantaged white.

Since we are now beginning to discover the crucial importance of the very early years of childhood, it is likely that we can achieve a greater measure of equality—to narrow the gap between the advantaged and the disadvantaged. More effective preschool programs, and a general extension of the social responsibility of the school for children from deprived homes, may make the classroom more effective. But the matter of achieving genuine equality is another question.

As to the politics: the most effective way that a middle-class parent can endow his children is by buying them a superior education—by giving them the head start his advantages can provide—and he is not likely to run slower to let the poor catch up. Given Coleman's standards, the only way to determine whether schools "overcome the differences in starting point of children from different social groups" is when Negro children from Harlem do as well in College Board scores or reading achievement as do whites from Scarsdale. Yet, when that happens, Scarsdale will have lost its reason to exist. Is the average white afraid of integration or "equality" only because the Negroes would, as he often says, "drag down the standards" or also because, ultimately, they might succeed? What would happen if the prep schools and suburban high schools, let alone the Ivy League universities, were no longer a guarantee of advantage and ultimate success? What if the game were genuinely open? It has often been said that American economic viability depended in part on the existence of a class of individuals who were available for the dirty jobs that the society requires (try the suggestion that we guarantee everyone a living wage, and listen to the prophecies of economic doom), but is it not equally conceivable that, for many, self-esteem and success are themselves defined by the failures of others? We can assert that technology is taking us to some sort of economic nirvana in which menial work is superfluous and we will no longer require Negroes to do it. And yet, doesn't the psychology of success always require a class of failures, and aren't the black, by virtue of their cultural inheritance, always the best candidates? Can we ever maintain a middle class without a lower class, or does it thrive, like Alcoholics Anonymous, on the continued presence of a group of people who, it is assumed, need reform and from whose failures the successful can draw esteem? Even if we dismiss that as the bleakest kind of cynicism, we are still confronted by the difficulty of a system where cash and power are convertible into educational assets; where educational assets are, in turn, the major qualifications for entry into the life and prerogatives of the middle class; and where the poor have neither. No governmental program is likely to alleviate the inequities.

As to the pedagogy: Coleman's assumption in talking about the different starting points of children "from different social groups" is that all talent is equally distributed through the population, and that inequities are generated only by social, rather than ethnic or cultural, characteristics. The current evidence seems to make the assumption doubtful; it points, indeed, to a very different course of action from the one Coleman advocates. For years there was a lot of condescending talk about the attributes and activities of different ethnic groups (all Jews were tailors, the Chinese ran laundries, the Negro had "rhythm"), and we properly reacted with egalitarian indignity when we decided how silly and pernicious that talk had become. Are we now going overboard the other way by suggesting that all talents and interests, of whatever kind, are distributed absolutely equally through the different ethnic sectors of the population? In establishing criteria for academic success—indeed, for social success generally—are we emphasizing certain skills and measures at the expense of others that may be equally valuable not only to the individual's personality and self-esteem but to the society generally? In a recent article in the *Harvard Educational Review*,[3] Susan S. Stodolsky and Gerald Lesser report on research that indicates that the relative strengths and weaknesses in different attributes remain constant for various ethnic groups, regardless of whether they are middle or lower class. Jews, for example, score higher, relative to the general population, in verbal ability than they do in space conceptualization. For Chinese children, the relative strengths and weaknesses in verbal ability and space conceptualization are reversed. (Similarly, Negroes seem to perform somewhat better in arithmetic skills and space conceptualization than they do in verbal tests; for Puerto Ricans, the pattern is almost the reverse.) Although middle-class children score higher in *all categories*, the relative ethnic differences are not eliminated. To Lesser and Stodolsky, these findings suggest new distinctions, definitions, and a new course of action. To Coleman's call for equalization, they want to add what they consider the equally important objective of diversification, of trading on the strengths of different ethnic groups and helping them to develop those strengths to the maximum. "Beyond deploying all necessary resources to achieve minimal equality in essential goals, further development of students may well be diverse," they write. "Following our principle of matching instruction and ability we incidentally may enhance the initial strengths which each group possesses. For example, through the incidental enhancement of the space-conceptualization skills of the Chinese children, we may produce proportionally more Chinese than Jewish architects and engineers. Conversely, through incidental enhancement of verbal skills of the Jewish children, we may produce proportionally more Jewish than Chinese authors or lawyers." There is no suggestion here about producing a Jewish or a Chinese curriculum; what they do propose is tailoring the mode and techniques of instruction to the strengths of particular children.

Studies like this are a long way from producing comprehensive solutions, but they demonstrate how complex the problem has become, how little we know about learning, and how ineffective most current remedial programs seem to be. One of the difficulties, indeed, is determining just what the problem really is. The Coleman Report, whatever its weaknesses, has made the definitional problem painfully clear. When we talk about the education of Negroes, or urban schools, or the ghetto, are we talking about ethnic minorities, a social class, or simply the universal difficulties of operating effective schools, no matter who their pupils happen to be? Clearly, there is validity in the charge that some teachers are racially and socially biased, and that the phrase "cultural disadvantage" can be used, like assertions about Negro inferiority, as an excuse for failure, a cop-out for bad teachers. The psychologist Kenneth B. Clark has often pointed out that statements about uneducable children tend to become self-fulfilling prophecies, and that teachers who talk this way don't belong in the classroom. At the same time, it's hard to believe that the same attitudes don't operate in classrooms full of lower-class Italians or Appalachian mountaineers, or that the Protestant school-marms of the year 1900 were altogether open-minded about the Jews and the Catholics.

Before anyone comes back with the declaration that "we made it on our own, why can't they?" let's quickly add that the economy that permitted "making it" on one's own is dead and gone, and that, when it comes to many contemporary school systems, *all children* tend to be disadvantaged. What I'm suggesting is that many schools are not educational but sociological devices which destroy learning and curiosity and deny differences as often as they encourage them, and which value managerial order above initiative, good behavior above originality, and mediocrity above engagement. (Yes, of course, there are exceptions.) All too often, they demand styles of behavior antithetical not only to social and ethnic minorities but also to most other original or "difficult" children, no matter what their background. They are instruments of social selection and, as such, they screen out misfits for the middle class, regardless of race, color, or national origin. In performing this function, every guidance counselor becomes an immigration officer and every examination a petition for a passport. Lower-class youngsters, wrote Edgar Z. Friedenberg in *The Vanishing Adolescent*, "are handy with their fists and worse; but they are helpless in the meshes of middle-class administrative procedure and are rapidly neutralized and eliminated by it. . . . They quickly learn that the most terrifying creatures are those whose bite passes unnoticed at the time and later swells, festers, and paralyzes; they cannot defend themselves against the covert, lingering hostility of teachers and school administrators." This hostility, says Friedenberg, is generated by a reaction to the personal intensity of young men and women who resist personal repression offered in the name of adjustment. "Any individual through whom subjective intensity may intrude into the processes of bureaucratic equilibrium is extremely threatening to our society." The school, in short, is not an instrument of pluralism, but of conformity. It turns out shoddy goods for the dime-store trade; its teachers are not professionals but petty civil servants who teach children to deny their own instincts and honesty, teach them little tricks of evasion, and reject those who are not acceptable for the mold. While the deviants of the upper class may have access to special schools in the suburbs or the hills of New England, the poor have no choice: The law *requires* them to go to one particular school in one community which, as often as not, treats them as inmates. The school in this instance becomes a sort of colonial outpost manned by a collection of sahibs from downtown. Their idea of community relations is telling parents to encourage their kids to stay in school, help them with their homework, and live the life of Dick and Jane. As a result, the neighborhood school is in, but not of or by, the neighborhood.

Given these conditions and the failures of the ghetto schools, the current demands for decentralization and community control are hardly surprising. There is nothing radical about them, except in the view of school personnel who have been trained to suspect community pressure and who regard any overt mixture of politics and education as the ultimate evil. The advocates of decentralization, who feel that ghetto parents should have as much control over the education of their children as the parents of the small suburb, see political action as the only way to make the school effective and responsible: The issue is not a black principal or a black curriculum for their own sake, but making the schools accountable, and developing the sense of participation that is expected to come with it. If parents are involved, they may provide the interest and support that the education of their children requires. The schools will then become *their* schools, the teachers *their* teachers. A principal working for parents is going to try harder than one who is responsible only to bureaucrats downtown.

For many militants, the appeal of decentralization—as an essential component of community power (read Black Power, if preferred)—is extremely powerful. At the same time, the concept of decentralization suffers from some serious ambiguities. There are people like Roy Innis, a leader in CORE, who favor a single Negro school district in Harlem, a system as distinct from that of New York City as the schools of Buffalo. For most others, including white liberals, the model is a collection of small districts, each hopefully resembling those of the suburbs or the small town, each immediately accessible to the parents and the community. The difference between the two is as large as the difference between Thomas Jefferson and John C. Calhoun: One visualizes a thoroughgoing decentralization—educational federalism; the other calls forth the ghost of the doctrine of the concurrent majority. It is based on the presumption that the Negro community is as distinct from the mainstream as the peculiar institution which helped give it birth and on which Calhoun founded his brand of separatism more than a century ago. Both suffer from what may be an excessive belief in the power of formal education and a conviction that racism and bad intentions, rather than educational incompetence, are the major sources of educational inadequacy.

Yet if this were the whole problem—if teachers and schools were guilty of nothing more than middle-class bias or political irresponsibility toward the poor—the situation would not be as difficult as it is. Even if one grants the possibility of effective decentralization as a *political* solution (assuming that parents can run schools without turning them into political battlegrounds or hothouses of nepotism), what of the educational solutions? The pressure for decentralization does not stem from some specific educational program that large systems refuse to adopt and which the militants consider appropriate to the problems of their neighborhoods and children. Indeed, if the Coleman Report has any validity—and there is little reason to doubt that children from different social backgrounds do learn from each other—then decentralization, which will help institutionalize segregation, is a step backward. Thus, the Bundy Report, which outlines a plan of decentralization for New York City, and the Coleman Report, one might think, were composed on different planets.

The great possibility of decentralization (in New York, the proposal is to establish between thirty and sixty semi-autonomous districts) is not some large educational breakthrough, but no more, and no less, than the immediate objective itself: giving the community a greater sense of participation and voice in the management of one of its institutions. (In this respect, it is no different from increasing community control over planning, street-cleaning, or the administration of the local precinct of the police.) It is thus a revolt against the "professionals"—the people who took charge, in the name of reform and good government, and apparently failed to deliver the goods. In its unwillingness to trust the experts, the demand for decentralization is frontier populism come to the city, a rejection of outside planning and expertise. Parents whose children attend decentralized schools may (with luck) learn more about political action and school management than their children learn about reading or mathematics; so far, at any rate, the chances for the first outweigh those of the second. The mystery of power is, for the moment, more fascinating than the problems of instruction.

The fact is that no one, in the ghetto or out, has yet developed a vision of what the ghetto schools ought to do, how they should operate, or what an educated Negro child ought to be if he is to be something different from a dark-skinned middle-class white. The existing ghetto schools fail Negroes not so much because they are different from all other schools—as the integrationists once assumed—but because they are too much like them. Local control may introduce diversity and new ideas, but those changes are far from clear. At this point there are few alternative models to the existing public school program. The current talk about relevance in Negro education—about more Afro-Americanism in the curriculum, about Negro history, about urban problems—and the peripheral efforts to use the arts (painting, the dance, music) as ways of engaging children's interests have not taken us very far toward genuine educational integration, toward the point, that is, where ghetto children have the skills to compete effectively in the larger world. It has been said again and again that conventional instruction in formalized academic skills is difficult for children whose lives provide few examples of the value of formal education and little reinforcement for work that might pay off in some vague abstract future. Middle-class kids are, in some measure, to the manner born, and they find plenty of reinforcement around them: They often succeed regardless of school. For many ghetto children, instruction, to be successful, has to be immediately attractive or interesting. (There are, to be sure, many ghetto children from families whose ambitions are identical to those of the middle class.) Whether or not "enjoyment," as someone said, "is a prerequisite to competence," it is plain that skills for the larger world may appear only remotely valuable in the immediate life of a child. The humanity of children may be very distant from the problems of negotiating the economy. The problem is how to get from one to the other.

The proposals for solving the problem are endless and, as might be expected, they are often contradictory. There is no consistent Negro demand in education, any more than there is a white one. Some Negro parents are as committed to authoritarian teachers and rote learning as the village schoolmarm; others regard them as racially repressive and pedagogically useless. (Most Negro parents are probably as conservative about education as any others.) I suspect that part of the anger and frustration in all racial school disputes stems from the inability of the parties to be entirely clear about what they want. Should the schools be more middle class, more white than white, turning out suburban doctors and lawyers, or should they be training men and women who can cope with the outside world but whose energies are directed to the black community and whose loyalties remain in the ghetto? (The controversy is similar to a conventional school debate between advocates of vocational training and college preparation, but the race aspect charges it with explosive overtones.) Whatever the position, the issue is clear: Almost inevitably it revolves around the problem of moving the child from where he is to the larger world—resolving the inconsistencies between the attitudes and experience of poverty and the formalized skills and motivation that the world demands.

There is no disagreement anywhere that there is a common culture that demands certain levels of verbal and social ability. The question slowly emerging from the current debates, however, is whether that ability must become a universal virtue. Should we be concerned only with the preparation of economic functionaries and the development of conventional academic skills, or also with the growth of human beings whose dignity is not necessarily dependent on middle-class standards of success? Is an understanding of algebraic functions any more desirable than the ability to paint or dance? (The mandated requirements for many jobs—nursing, for example—include verbal abilities that are higher than those the jobs actually require; the stipulated credentials are not necessarily related to the characteristics the jobs demand.) Are we establishing norms that tend to undervalue characteristics that all of society could well use, and for which certain children might be especially well prepared, or do we have to make *all* children into replicas of the middle class?

For the next several years we are likely to hear more and more along this line. In its most extreme form, the argument says that not only is the American school an instrument of the white middle class, but that the overriding emphasis—in school and out—on high verbal and cognitive skills is itself a form of racial and social bias. The rational mind, with its emphasis on a high degree of verbal and analytical facility, is, in a manner of speaking, our thing. We invented and perfected it, and for the last fifteen years most curricular reform has been directed to the task of putting a larger and more powerful dose of it into the classroom. Thus we have, even more thoroughly than before, arranged education to separate the sheep of privilege from the goats of deprivation. Increasingly, we will now have to confront questions about what has been excluded. Are we missing something more intuitive, personal, and intangible? Is it possible to extend the Lesser-Stodolsky kind of analysis to include—along with assessments of verbal and mathematical characteristics and the ability to conceptualize space—things like affective and intuitive qualities, creativity, and some general feeling for the poetic, the visual, the musical?

Because these things are difficult to test, and because their cash value has usually been remote, the schools tend to disregard them, or to assign them to a secondary level of importance. Of all the things that make life rich—the arts, the various elements of literary and personal sensitivity, social and political involvement, philosophy, religion—very few have even a minimal place (except as lip service) in the public school program. One may not be able to mandate such activities in a large compulsory school system, but it is possible to offer them as alternatives to the public school, and one can conceive of all sorts of programs for doing so. The issue here is not to turn every ghetto school into an academy of the arts, but to offer diversity—teaching the skills of a trade or of an art with as much of a sense of importance as we teach mathematics or history. The objective, in each instance, is to draw upon the experiences and interests of the kids, to give them a sense of motion and relevance, and to provide choices, not only as to school and school control, but also as to style of learning. We have, with the single public system, and the instruction it offers, created a single standard of success and failure (and the large hippie element seems to indicate that the standard is not acceptable even to some of those who might meet it). Perhaps we have to recognize the principle of pluralism not only in a cultural context but in an educational one as well. A few years ago such suggestions would have been regarded as racist slurs, but it is now the black militant who regards Swahili as desirable for Negroes as Latin.

Carried to its extreme, the argument leads to a romantic trap, a wishful attempt to arm the weakest members of a technological society with the least effective weapons for dealing with it. It may be nice to think that there are dishwashers with the souls of poets (or even with the skills of poets), but that thought provides no foundation on which to base an educational system. There are, in our culture, a variety of important and rewarding functions that require no extensive verbal or mathematical skills (despite the exclusionist tendency of certain trades and professions to impose arbitrary educational standards for membership). Nonetheless, there remain certain levels of verbal ability without which few people can survive, except in the most menial situations. In our ambiguity and guilt about middle-class life, many of us hold a corresponding ambiguity about those who are left outside the mainstream: the happy hillbilly, the engagement and passion of the ghetto, the uninhibited poor. What we disregard is that, given the choice, most of them would elect to live like us; because of educational deficiencies, they do not have the choice. There is, said a Negro sociologist, only one way out of the ghetto, "and that's out." The reason, finally, that so few of them make it has little to do with differences in culture, or the fact that teachers and administrators are ignorant about the lives of the children assigned to them; it is because they still don't know how to teach. Negro schools are bad because all schools are bad. We simply don't know very much about how children learn. This is, in the end, what the Coleman Report proved. It may also be the greatest single contribution of the civil rights movement.

But to say that greater diversity, the provision of educational options, and a new emphasis on intuitive learning can be carried to extremes is not to deny the validity of the idea, either in the ghetto or anywhere else. For the past decade we masculinized the schools with mathematics, physics, and with a variety of new tough-minded curriculums. Educational criticism in the next decade may well concern itself more with the soft side of things—with noncognitive approaches, and with a reaffirmation of Deweyan ideas. There are a number of people who are talking seriously about a "curriculum of concerns," educational programs that begin with the interests and experience of kids, not with predetermined sets of skills to be learned. Most of the ghetto experiments that seem to have potential are pure Dewey: letting children talk their own stories and developing vocabulary and writing skills from them; trips to factories, galleries, and museums; stories and poems about the streets of the city and even about addicts and junkies. These things, too, can be carried to undisciplined extremes. None is a cure-all, but nothing in education ever is. The very nature of the enterprise is unsettling and troublesome. Education and maturation mean change, and that, in turn, means dealing with new problems, new elements every day. Equality is relatively easy to define in employment, in housing, or in medicine. It is impossible to define in education because the very nature of the enterprise demands distinctions and produces diversity.

Are we then to abandon integration and concentrate exclusively on the problems of the classroom? Plainly, the answer is no—no, because it still seems, at least to some of us, morally important; no, because, lacking better tools, it still appears to be an effective technique for education; no, because any alternative to integration is, despite immediate attractions to the contrary, unthinkable. Yet, if integration is to have any meaning, it must be a two-way street—integration not only *between* races, going both ways, but also between the school and the community, school and job, culture and culture. If equality of educational opportunity means merely an effort to improve the chances of the disadvantaged to run the race on our terms, things will never be equal and whatever they have to offer will be lost. Are we really courageous enough to provide a broad range of educational options and not to worry about who's at what level in which track? Are we really interested in education or merely in grades, credits, and diplomas? In the structure of the existing school system, segregation, repression, competition, and failure are all essential parts. Every class has a bottom half, and it tends to include, numerically, as many whites as blacks. Until we are ready to stop selecting people out, almost any conception of education is going to involve some sort of segregation. Our democratic professions might be vindicated if the ranks of the successful were as well integrated as the ranks of the failures, but would that solve the problem of education? What would we do with the failures if they were a statistically average shade of tan? The fundamental issue is not the equality of Negro schools, but the lives of all young men and women, no matter what their category or stigma. "If urban educators are failing," says Robert Dentler, the director of the Center for Urban Education, "they are failing where the newly emergent culture of the urban society itself has failed to specify either ends or means for the educator or his clientele. . . . We are in a period when the place of all children in this culture is in transition." What the problem of Negro education has done, or should be doing, is to alert us to a far larger range of social and educational questions, and to the fact that the goal of maximizing human potential is still a long way off.

Notes

1. Samuel Bowles and Henry M. Levin, "The Determinants of Scholastic Achievement—An Appraisal of Some Recent Evidence," *Journal of Human Resources* (Winter, 1968).

2. James S. Coleman, "Toward Open Schools," *The Public Interest* (Fall, 1968).

3. Susan S. Stodolsky and Gerald Lesser, "Learning Patterns in the Disadvantaged," *Harvard Educational Review* (Fall, 1967).

22. COMMUNITY PARTICIPATION

MARIO FANTINI

A vision that arouses both fears and hope is emerging from the crisis in public education, especially in our cities. That prospect is that public education will return to the direct control of the public—but not just a traditionally "prepared" public; not simply the civic leaders who serve on city-wide school boards, or parent-association leaders who are endowed with verbal and organizational skills and college degrees; not just the enlightened business leaders who recognize good schools as a drawing card to local economic development (or a dampener on racial unrest). The murmurs now being heard in two or three large cities are coming from the "garden variety" of parent and community resident —including ghetto parents with little formal education—calling for a say in the operation of public schools.

The prospect is frightening to many because it rises from the soil of civil strife and growing racial hostility, assertiveness, and even hatred. But even without these factors, the prospect would alarm the majority of professional educators (and many sympathetic laymen), who fear the dismemberment of complex systems of education by the hand of people said to be incompetent. For, after all, we are not talking about a plaything. We are discussing a vaunted American institution, which is credited with advancing democratic practices and with opening the doors of opportunity to millions of immigrants for more than a century. Moreover, it is an institution with an enormous and growing capital plant and annual operating budget.

The positive aspects of this kind of public control are more difficult to perceive. One possibility is that, under the right conditions, real public control of public education could provide more effective education. It could also foster the revitalization of one of the most revered canons of American society, citizen participation in democratic processes. And,

Reprinted from the *Harvard Educational Review*, XXXVIII (Winter, 1968), 160–75, Harvard University Press. Copyright © 1968 by the President and Fellows of Harvard College. This article will appear in the forthcoming expanded edition of *Equal Educational Opportunity*, to be published by Harvard University Press, 1969. Used by permission of the author and the *Harvard Educational Review*.

on the most profound level, perhaps intimate public engagement in public education could lead to realization of one of the most fundamental goals of education: to make better citizens, all along the age spectrum. Merely to suggest these prospects is to invite accusations of romanticism or naïve idealism. But an examination of more hard-headed approaches to modern public education suggests that this idealistic path may turn out to be the most practical and efficient.

Some Premises

Before examining past and future approaches to the solution of the educational crisis, it would be well to make explicit the premises of my argument:

1. That public education is failing generally. The most visible failure is in the urban, low-income, racial-minority ghettos. But if one holds education responsible in part for shortcomings throughout American society, education has failed more widely. The shortcomings include such features of contemporary life as the alienation and withdrawal of many economically and culturally advantaged college-age youth and the impotence of social consciousness in mobilizing an adequate response to the nation's domestic crises. Public education's precise share of the blame for these shortcomings need not be calculated in order to assert that it bears *some* share, even a substantial one.

2. That public education is a governmental function. It is supported by the public at large, not simply by the immediate users, and it is subject at least to review, if not to close accountability, by elected public representatives somewhere along the line.

3. That while the goals of American public education are not confined to skill development, the present operational definition of quality education is performance in basic skills at or above grade level, as measured by standardized tests.

4. That the growing complexity of the education process is no cause for attrition of the concept of public control of public education.

5. That public education is a universal right. Therefore it cannot, even *de facto*, be limited to those who are responsive and congenial to whatever the prevailing mode of public education happens to be. Public education has an affirmative obligation to meet the needs not only of the "normal" but also of the physically and otherwise handicapped, and of those who are unresponsive or hostile to the prevailing process.

6. That the public has a right to determine educational policy and to hold professionals accountable for implementing policy. Thus, when 70

per cent of ghetto children are not reading at grade level, their parents have a right to question professional performance since the schools are supposed to educate everyone.

7. That urban education is synonymous with the education of low-income racial minorities whose growing despair is both a threat and a challenge to America's great cities. The general urban crisis is inextricably linked to the crisis of urban education.

The Nature of the Crisis

In the last twenty years, the nation has overcome with reasonable success what were regarded as "crises" in public education. The first was a deficit in facilities and personnel, due mainly to deferred spending during World War II and to a rise in the birth rate. We still have not caught up, but the capital investment has been truly impressive, and progress on the number and salaries of personnel has been almost as significant.

The second "crisis," escalated to a national emergency by Sputnik, was the inadequacy of training in science and mathematics. Sputnik led to additional offerings in these fields, and large-scale curriculum experimentation has resulted in more and better-prepared students in these fields.

But all these improvements in public education have left the basic system unchanged. They have strengthened the status quo, enabling the system to serve better those it has always served best. The heart of the present crisis in public education is the realization that the system has failed a major segment of the population. This failure was the most intractable crisis all along, but it did not come to full public awareness until the nation took official cognizance of poverty amidst affluence and until the nonwhite one-fourth of society's economic underclass began to assert its civil rights and demand a full share in political and economic opportunity.

Our present preoccupation with the disadvantaged, however, has not diverted critics from concluding that the total system of education is incapable of addressing the challenge of providing excellent education for a diverse student population. Consequently, the mission of fundamental educational reform is not for the poor alone, but for all.

There is little agreement regarding the locus of the problem of school failure. At one extreme is the assumption that the failure of any child to learn lies primarily with the learner—in his physical, economic, cultural, or environmental deficits. At the other pole is the notion that, if pupils are failing, the school system itself needs basic rehabilitation.

Under this assumption, the school's obligation is to diagnose the learner's needs, concerns, and cognitive and affective style, and adjust its program accordingly. In the early stages of concern about the learning problems of the disadvantaged, the searchlight played almost entirely on the shortcomings of the learners. A salutary shift toward a more comprehensive diagnosis of the teaching and learning system, as well as the problems of the learner himself, seems now to be developing. Emerging with the shift is a set of prescriptions—alternatives for intervention designed to reform the process and practice of public education.

Intervention Alternatives

A continuum of five basic approaches to intervention may be identified: compensatory education, desegregation, model subsystems, parallel systems, and total system reform. With the exception of compensatory education, these are largely untried concepts, but in some cases— model subsystems, for example—the few existing examples are sufficient to provide a basis for examining the likelihood of success or failure.

COMPENSATORY INTERVENTION

Compensatory education—attempts to overcome shortcomings in the learner—is the most prevalent form of intervention designed to raise pupils' academic achievement. It characterizes such efforts as the Ford Foundation–supported Great Cities School Improvement programs, Title I of the Elementary and Secondary Education Act, and New York City's early Higher Horizons program and recent More Effective Schools program. Compensatory education seeks to attack a spectrum of defects in the learner—verbal retardation, lack of motivation, and experiential and sensory deprivation—that presumably prevent his participation in the learning process. In addition to grafting extra education onto the regular school experience, proponents of compensation have attempted to nip deficiencies in the bud through preschool programs like Project Head Start.

For the most part, however, compensatory education is a prescription that deals with *symptoms*, with strengthened doses that have been ineffective before—more trips, more remedial reading, etc.—without real differences in kind. It is essentially an additive, or "band-aid," approach that works by augmenting and strengthening existing programs. It builds layers onto the standard educational process in order to bring the strays into the fold and to fit them into the existing school mold. The assumption is that the schools need to do somewhat more for disadvantaged pupils, but it does not presume that the school itself is in need of wholesale re-examination.

Enormous effort, ingenuity, and funds have been invested in compensatory education, but the evidence gathered from even the best efforts indicates that they are having little significant impact on the problem of low achievement among disadvantaged children. The proponents of continued compensatory intervention argue either that not enough effort and resources have yet been applied or that greater attacks must be made on factors external to the schools (typically, family stability, housing, and income), or both.

But the compensatory approach is viewed with increasing distrust by the parents of academic failures both because the techniques are not achieving their goals and because these parents are rejecting the premise that the fault lies in their children. Doubts are also beginning to arise among educational strategists disappointed by the failure of incremental inputs to the existing system to make a substantial difference.

DESEGREGATION

Since the 1954 Supreme Court decision, a principal motivating factor in efforts toward integration has been the assumption that Negro pupils' achievement improves in an integrated school environment. The Coleman Report tends to support this view, and the U.S. Commission on Civil Rights is unequivocal in stating: "Negro children suffer serious harm when their education takes place in public schools which are racially segregated, whatever the source of such segregation may be. Negro children who attend predominantly Negro schools do not achieve as well as other children, Negro and white."[1]

In most urban settings, integration has proved elusive, if not impossible. The failure to achieve integration to any significant extent was due first to massive white resistance. Now it is even less likely to occur in our lifetime because of the growing concentration in the inner city of Negro and other nonwhite minorities. The only possible plan for achieving integration in many large cities, metropolitan integration across present school-district boundaries, seems politically unfeasible.

Moreover, minority-group members themselves show a growing shift away from integration at the option of the white majority. The new focus of Negro and other racial-minority parents is on power and control over the schools their children attend. The changing mood springs not only from the poor record of integration efforts, but also from a revolt against the condescension perceived by minority-group members in the school desegregation efforts of the post–1954 decade. First, many of them resent the fact that integration is, under current power arrangements, an option of the white community. Second, they believe that the dependent status of the Negro in American society is perpetuated by the notion that the only way to help the black child is to seat him alongside white children. Beneath this mood is a quest for stronger racial identity and pride, and a desire to gain more control of their own destiny. The initial desire for integration was based, say many Negro spokesmen, on the belief that parents in predominantly white schools exercised enough power to insure that the school offered quality education, in which Negro pupils should share. The converse is powerlessness, further destruction of identity, and increasing disconnection from the larger society.

The implication for public education is greater participation by Negroes in control over predominantly Negro schools. This is rather different from the "separate but equal" doctrine, since some Black Power philosophers reason that, when Negroes achieve quality education under their own aegis, they will then be prepared to connect (integrate) with the white society on a groundwork of parity instead of deficiency. A good school then would be defined not by the kind of children who attend it, but by the quality of the education offered by the school. In short, they seek connection as equals.

The goals of integration, therefore, must be broadened to restore a quality that has been sidetracked in the emphasis on the educational achievement goal of desegregation. That is, we must reaffirm our commitment to connect with one another as human beings. We must recognize that viewing diversity and differences as assets rather than unfortunate barriers to homogeneity has as positive an effect on human growth and development as the teaching of academic skills. All of which is to suggest that militant Negro demands for participation in control of public education is actually a means of greater *connection* to society, precisely opposite from the connotations of separatism usually associated with Black Power.

MODEL SUBSYSTEMS

In an effort to explore new and improved learning strategies and techniques, experimental units are being created in which educators hope to develop improved training, retraining, curriculum, and methodology patterns—and, lately, greater community participation—that may be demonstrated and disseminated throughout entire school systems. Within a school system, a subunit may consist of one or a cluster of schools. Projects under Titles III and IV of the Elementary and Secondary Education Act are seeking to create subsystems on a regional basis, through consortia of institutions.

Although some colleges and universities have for many years maintained experimental undergraduate subsystems (honors colleges, for example), the trend toward this mode of intervention in public schools may have started with a progress report (by a panel headed by Jerrold Zacharias) to the U.S. Commissioner of Education in March, 1964. The report led to the creation of a model subdivision in the Washington, D.C., public schools. At about the same time, the Syracuse, N.Y., public schools (in the Madison Area Project), and later the Boston public schools, created subsystems in a deliberate attempt to provide the total system with a development and training conduit for successful innovative practices. The most recent, and most visible, instances of model subsystems in a large urban establishment are three experimental school clusters in Manhattan and Brooklyn, including the intermediate school 201 complex. These differ from earlier subsystems in that they are governed by community-based boards, although they must still seek ultimate approval on any number of basic decisions from the central Board of Education.

Many see the subsystem as a means for involving new institutions and persons outside the educational establishment with the urban schools. In New York City, for example, New York University, Teachers College, and Yeshiva University have "adopted" single schools or clusters of schools. Antioch College has assisted an experimental subsystem school in Washington, the Adams-Morgan School, and is seeking to adopt schools in Philadelphia and Dayton, Ohio. In addition to colleges and universities, community agencies, research and development centers, Peace Corps and VISTA veterans, private industry, and the professions are seen as possible sources of new talent and ideas introduced through model subsystems.

Intervention through model subsystems represents substantial progress toward a realization that "more-of-the-same" approaches have limited utility. It represents a refreshing intellectual concession that the educational process and system may share responsibility with the learner for his failure to achieve. It also borrows a leaf from scientific, technological, and industrial enterprises in its commitment to research and development.

The vogue for subsystems is developing rapidly, despite scant experience with them and even scantier evidence of success. There are intrinsic constraints in the organizational framework within which dependent subsystems seek to explore the avenues of change. First, experience suggests that the model subsystem may lack the autonomy and freedom it needs to follow findings through to their ultimate conclusion. More likely than not, explorations into new school patterns call for breaking the rules, and the mother system is frequently unwilling to give her precocious, adventurous children much latitude. Furthermore, subunits too often depend for their new energies and resources on imported consultants who do not become integral members of the existing structure. And, as a practical matter, the educators selected to head subunits are often irreversibly captive to bureaucratic rigidity; their underlying identification is likely to be with the large system that sanctioned the experiment (that is, with the status quo) rather than with the new territory the experimental subunit seeks to explore. The experimental systems also are under pressure to produce results quickly. The mother system, which itself may be in disarray due to years or decades of decline, nonetheless is impatient to evaluate the subsystem, and perhaps vested interests are only too ready to label it a failure if it does not turn out a shining record of extraordinary achievement in a year or two. Whether the subsystem is dependent or largely autonomous, it is not likely to affect an entire system that is governed by an adept and hierarchy-hardened bureaucracy and conditioned by fixed patterns of behavior. Moreover, the educational substance of subsystems has, up to this point, been fragmented. The experiments tend to concentrate on one or another piece of improved instructional practice—team teaching, new careers for the poor, role-playing, teacher training, or reading, for example —but seldom with the form and structure of the total system.

PARALLEL SYSTEMS

One set of approaches to quality education does not take the form of intervention in public education; rather, it calls for opportunities for students to escape into a parallel system. Such approaches assume that if the poor (or others) cannot reform public education, they should be afforded options to it.

A few privately managed schools have been established in urban ghettos, and several others are in the planning stage. Precedents for such schools exist in southern Freedom Schools (notably Neil Sullivan's school for Negro pupils deprived of educational opportunity when the Prince Edward County, Virginia, public schools closed to avoid integration). Some northern counterparts include Harlem's Academies of Transition and the New School for Children in Boston's Roxbury section. The Urban League–sponsored street academies are sending more than 75 per cent of their students—hard-core rejects from the public school system—to college.

Of considerable potential significance to urban education is an act approved by the Massachusetts State Legislature late in 1967 which enables the state Department of Education to assist and sponsor experimental school systems operated by private nonprofit corporations.

Assuming a greater role in education and urban problems, states could establish yardsticks, "educational TVA's," by which to measure the effectiveness of different forms of educational innovation.

Project Head Start schools are also "private" in the sense that they exist apart from the public school system and are not subject to its rules and regulations governing personnel, curriculum, and other matters. Some of these schools are financed under federal tuition grants and foundation funds, and efforts are being made to obtain support for others from business and industry. A special hybrid, a publicly financed but totally independent school system (an enclave apart from the regular New York City system) with a per capita budget received directly from the state, was proposed in 1967 by the Harlem chapter of CORE, though it failed in the New York State Legislature.

Nonpublic schools have advantages; they do not have to deal with distant and entrenched bureaucracies, with school boards unfamiliar with their particular needs, or with teachers' unions. They are free to hire teachers from a variety of personnel pools and to sidestep rigid credential-granting procedures. They may even abandon such practices as tenure and retain, promote, or discharge teachers purely on the grounds of merit and performance. If the schools are governed by boards with a substantial representation from the pupils' parents, they are likely to be more responsive to the children's needs and thereby encourage better rapport and partnership between the home and the school. In the most general sense, they afford the poor the choice that is open to many middle-class parents: to educate their children elsewhere if they are dissatisfied with the performance of the public schools. And if enough private schools are available, the pattern ushers in an entrepreneurial system in which parents can choose, cafeteria-style, from a range of styles of education—Montessori, prep school, Summerhill, and others.

Carried to its logical conclusion, however, the parallel-school approach would reduce the scope of public education, if not dispense with it altogether. The establishment of private schools sufficient to handle significant numbers of poor children would require public support and, in effect, establish a private system of publicly supported schools. Middle-income parents would demand similar privileges. For financial reasons alone, the parallel-school approach is hardly likely to become widespread in the foreseeable future; moreover, the scheme would founder on political, if not constitutional, grounds. Finally, since private schools are not subject to public control, there would be no guarantee against the organization of programs by special interest groups for ends inimical to a free and open society. Support of such enterprises at public expense would be intolerable.

These arguments are, of course, no reason to discourage programs that enable more low-income pupils to attend private schools. Private schools could serve a valuable yardstick function if they were run under conditions that simulated the resources and inputs of public education —particularly comparable per capita expenditures, and admission policies that would embrace a range of low-income pupils, including the "disruptive." But that is the limit of their usefulness as an alternative to improved public education, for they could never serve the majority of the children of the poor.

TOTAL SYSTEM REFORM

Since the compensatory approach has apparently failed, since desegregation is not a realistic short-range prospect, since model subsystems do not give much evidence yet of realizing their promise, and since parallel systems are basically an avoidance of the challenge to reform the schools where most children will continue to be educated, the latest —and, in my view, most promising—approach to intervention is reform of total school systems, structurally and otherwise. There are several approaches to total system intervention.

One approach is to provide new leadership for the system as a whole, while leaving the system's form and structure basically intact. This approach is exemplified by trends in Philadelphia, where a reform-minded central school board, including former Mayor Richardson Dilworth, and a new superintendent of schools with a record of innovation are attempting to strengthen the effectiveness of the old system with the infusion of new staff and new styles. Pittsburgh, too, is improving the efficiency of the existing system, within the operational definition of quality education as achievement according to norms.

Another approach consists of reorganization of the system into quasi-autonomous districts—i.e., decentralization. Washington, D.C., has begun moving in this direction, beginning with single model schools. The Passow Report on the District of Columbia schools recommends a total system reform by decentralizing the system into eight subsystems of approximately equal size.[2]

Still another form is the proposed merger of the school systems of two entire political jurisdictions—the city of Louisville and Jefferson County. The Louisville–Jefferson County merger differs markedly from the piecemeal metropolitan experiments noted earlier. In this case, the new metropolitan system is to consist of a number of subdistricts, each with considerable autonomy yet federated into a single system to preserve the best of the worlds of bigness and smallness.

In the subsystems, models of excellence must swim against the tide of the status quo system. The total approach has no such constraint; there is no boring from within, for everyone starts at the reform gate at the same time. In a federation of autonomous subsystems, each with an equitable share of resources, instructional practices would operate in an open, competitive market. The most successful models would be on display as a challenge to other school systems to adopt their approaches or surpass them in performance.

New Energy Sources

The intervention proposed in November, 1967, by the Mayor's Advisory Panel on Decentralization of the New York City Schools—the Bundy Report—adds a crucial new energy source to the total system pattern.[3] Administrative decentralization of large school systems had been in the wind. (New York City itself had for the last six years begun loosening the reins of a highly centralized system.) But the Bundy Report's proposals go well beyond administrative arrangements into a form of public engagement in the process of education that is without precedent in large urban systems and, in a sense, without much real precedent even in many suburbs and small cities.

The Bundy Report was significantly titled *Reconnection for Learning*. The plan calls for more than a redistribution of power; it also provides new means of energizing school reform. Reform requires fuel. Sustained school reform needs not only ideas, but human resources and dynamic support from the public and the profession. All too often, the energy for educational reform consists only of a few professionals, practitioners or veterans who have shifted their struggle from the front lines to universities or the author's desk. The Bundy Plan expands the base of energy to include the most numerous, and possibly the most powerful, energy source: parents and the community-at-large.

It offers the professional who is working for improvement within the system a powerful ally who is also highly motivated to reform the system. Ghetto parents, especially, have come to the same verdict as the most astute students and practitioners of education: that urban education is failing and desperately in need of reform.

But professional recognition of this energy concept is slow to come, for it assumes an altogether different professional-lay relationship from what now prevails. In the last several decades, education—in self-defense and for other reasons—has rapidly become professionalized. There has been an inverse correlation between professionalization and parents' involvement. Two other forces have tended to keep parents from participating in the education process. One, earlier in the cycle, though persisting in the urban ghetto, was the low level of the parents' own education relative to the teachers'. The immigrant, regardless of his desire for education for his children, was hardly likely to challenge the assigned authority represented by a native-speaking, better-educated teacher. The other factor, of course, is the growing size and impersonality of public school systems in large cities.

Even well-educated, middle-class parents who seek to engage in *meaningful* school decisions are deterred short of effectiveness by the inertial mass of the system or by the aura of professional exclusivity. Even the atmosphere in school buildings discourages parental presence (parent visiting days two or three times a year are prime evidence) and most parents visit school only in response to trouble. Thus, we have carefully drawn boundaries for how far parents, singly or in parent-teacher associations, may go, even in asking questions of professionals. A sophisticated PTA member may nag at a school board that does not offer French in elementary school, but she will rarely ask for research results (or for research to be initiated) on the effectiveness of the school's language instruction. Still less is she apt to ask for such information as the school system's criteria for teacher selection or for evidence of its aggressiveness and imagination in recruiting teachers. Even when probing questions are asked, information is often safeguarded as being in the professional domain alone. Only now are some school systems beginning to accumulate and release performance data on a school-by-school basis.

But perhaps the role of the parent should go far beyond asking pointed questions. Should parents have a voice—preferential if not determinative—regarding school curriculum? Should parents have a say in the kind of teacher they feel is best suited to the needs of their children? These are questions to which most professionals—and, indeed, many parents—would offer a reflex negative. Yet, within the framework of basic standards and goals, there are many options. Mathematics may be taught in any number of ways, and there are a variety of approaches to foreign languages. If the school is dedicated to instilling learning *skills*, content is as much a means as an end, and one choice will often serve as well as another. Why then should not the choice represent what is most meaningful to a particular community? Very often the professional choice is only one of several objectively reasonable choices; his word is final because he has a monopoly on the authority. If community involvement is to be real, if parent-teacher partnership is to have any meaning beyond lip service, the proper role for the professional would be to outline the educationally sound alternatives and to afford the parents and the community a choice among them. Parallels may also be found in such other aspects as selection of materials, personnel policies, and allocation of resources.

Although, as suggested, the parent has never been a true partner in the education process, at least the concept of lay and local control of public education has a long historical tradition. But the tradition has been diluted and is largely impotent against the force of a professional monopoly.

Professional educators have not ignored parents or the community. Elaborate structures and devices have been fashioned—parent-teacher associations, visiting days, American Education Week, parent education programs, dissemination of information—ostensibly to "inform" the parent. The administrator who seeks a "happy" school (or "tight ship," as the case may be) will see that his parents are paid some attention or even a degree of deference. He will be patient in explaining homework policies. Schools of education include community relations in their curriculums, and, in many systems, advancement through the administrative ranks requires a certain number of credits in community relations.

.   .   .   .

What would be the purpose of real parent and community participation? We begin from the position that when people have a part in their institutions, they share responsibility for them and are more likely to pay close attention to the stated mission and actual performance of the institution.

Thus, participation has a positive effect on the participants as well as the system. For example, as parents in East Harlem became more engaged in the education process, "quality education" replaced "Black Power" as the slogan. Responsibility comes with the power of an effective voice. In the train of responsibility, judgment, stability, and dedication to constructive purpose are likely to follow. The pattern of the revolutionary is that, upon assumption of power, he shifts from destroying institutions to building order and new institutions (of his own kind, to be sure).

Participatory democracy in education should also give parents and community a tangible respect for the intricacy and complexity of the professional problems in urban education. It is not likely that parents who have gained admission as true partners in the process will oversimplify and lay the blame for educational failures solely on the professional. As things stand now, low-income communities *outside* the system understandably lay the blame squarely on the assigned professionals: "You are paid to teach, to deliver a certain product. When overwhelming numbers of our children fail to learn, you are not delivering. You are not meeting your professional obligation." The syllogism is simplistic: It ignores the fact that professional talent can be thwarted by a system, and it does not take into account extra-school factors in teaching and learning. But it is an altogether natural response from parents to whom the system provides no access and offers but two alternatives: total resignation and apathy; or anger, protest, and, sooner or later, some form of retaliation.

Skeptics who concede the right of parents to participate in the education process, nevertheless question their technical qualifications to engage in educational decisions; the question is raised particularly (though not exclusively) in relation to low-income, poorly educated parents. But the question should be not what parents know now, but what they can come to know about the technicalities of education. That they want to know is suggested by the few instances in which they have become more or less equal partners in the process. Their concerns soon broaden; they begin to ask, for example, who are the most talented reading specialists in the country, because we want them to help us. In qualifying for school board membership, too, they seek training for themselves—something rare among would-be school board members even in wealthier communities.

Admitting the public to the education process, therefore, should result in the addition of many new hands and minds to the tasks. These would be true partners, who participate in the enterprise and know it from their own experience, who do not simply take the established goals and procedures of the enterprise as virtues because its professional managers say so.

The school, after all, is only one site of the total curriculum to which children are exposed. Considerable learning takes place at home and in all manner of community institutions including the street corner, the church, the press and other mass media, and neighborhood organizations. As parents are admitted to participation in the schools' education process, they will become better equipped "teachers" of that part of the "curriculum" in which they are the prime agents—rearing in the home. Studies under Basil Bernstein of the University of London's Sociological Research Unit have illuminated discontinuities of socialization among the home, the child's peer group, and the schools.[4] Continuity could be restored if parents participated in the formal education process.

Greater public engagement in the public education process should also add political strength to pressures for increased financial support for education; a "parents' lobby" with unprecedented motivation and commitment might arise. Nor should the possible effects on parents in their own right be overlooked. Few people can engage in a social cause and not themselves be transformed. Relevant education in an institutional setting that is willing to experiment in the art—and yes, the mysteries—of learning and teaching is such a cause. It could bring into the lives of men and women working at tedious jobs or leading lives of boredom (factors by no means peculiar to low-income groups), a new *spirit* in an activity with immediate relevance to their own families. This is to say nothing of the possible chain reaction that meaningful engagement in the education process could have in stimulating parents to enlarge their own education.

Thus, the realignment of the participants in public education could produce rich yields for all the main participants:

—for the parents, a tangible grasp on the destiny of their children and opening to richer meaning for their own lives.

—for professionals, surcease from an increasingly negative community climate and, more positively, new allies in their task.

—for the children, a school system responsive to their needs, resonant with their personal style, and affirmative in its expectations of them.

And finally there is the goal of participation for its own sake, an intrinsic concomitant—and test—of democracy. Education could no doubt be conducted efficiently if it were contracted out as a technical service, without the furniture of lay boards, community relations, and so on, especially if quality is defined strictly in terms of grade level achievement. But in an open society, the process of participation itself is a social and educational value, despite the inefficiencies it may entail.

This is more than an alternative approach to halting the spiral of public education's failure. It is a design for social reconstruction.

Notes

1. U.S. Commission on Civil Rights, *Racial Isolation in the Public Schools* (Washington, D.C.: Government Printing Office, 1967), Vol. I.

2. A. Harry Passow, *Summary of a Report on the Washington, D.C. Public Schools* (New York: Teachers College, Columbia University, mimeo., 1967).

3. Mayor's Advisory Panel on Decentralization in the New York City Schools, *Reconnection for Learning: A Community School System for New York City*, in Chapter IV, above.

4. See, for example, Basil Bernstein, "A Socio-linguistic Approach to Social Learning," in J. Gould (ed.), *Social Science Survey* (New York: Pelican Books, 1965).

23. THE BURDEN OF BLAME: A REPORT ON THE OCEAN HILL–BROWNSVILLE SCHOOL CONTROVERSY

NEW YORK CIVIL LIBERTIES UNION

Reflect how you are to govern a people who think they ought to be free, and think they are not. Your scheme yields no revenue; it yields nothing but discontent, disorder, disobedience; and such is the state of America that, after wading up to your eyes in blood, you could only end just where you began . . .

> Edmund Burke, speaking in the
> House of Commons, April 19, 1774

The current school dispute in New York City has yielded no revenue; it has yielded nothing but discontent, disorder, disobedience. It has been a dispute with no heroes, and many villains.

Summary of Conclusions

The New York Civil Liberties Union (NYCLU) supports school decentralization as a means of giving ghetto communities equal access to the process of making decisions vitally affecting the education of their children. We are also deeply committed to due process of law and academic freedom. We do not find any inconsistency in our support for decentralization and our commitment to due process and academic freedom. Indeed, we find the charge that existing standards of due process are seriously threatened by community control unfounded, both in theory and fact.

The NYCLU is issuing this statement at this time because we believe that it is crucial to set the record straight regarding the causes of the chaos in Ocean Hill–Brownsville. Our examination of the record

Reprinted in full with the permission of the New York Civil Liberties Union.

has persuaded us that *the chaos was not a result of local community control*. On the contrary, we are persuaded that *the chaos resulted from efforts to undermine local community control* of the schools.

Specifically, our research leads us to the following basic conclusions:

1. That from the beginning, *the central Board of Education attempted to scuttle the experiment in Ocean Hill–Brownsville* by consistently refusing to define the authority of the Local Governing Board.

2. *That the United Federation of Teachers has used "due process" as a smokescreen* to obscure its real goal, which is to discredit decentralization and sabotage community control.

3. That there are serious shortcomings in existing Board of Education standards of due process, which have long permeated the entire school system; and that to the degree that the Ocean Hill–Brownsville board violated due process, it did so only by following normal standards and procedures of the Board of Education.

4. That the major burden of blame for the chaos in Ocean Hill–Brownsville must fall on the central Board of Education and, lamentably, on the United Federation of Teachers (UFT).

These conclusions are entirely supported by public documents that have been generally available but largely ignored or distorted. These include the Niemeyer Commission's report to the Board of Education; the report and recommendations of Special Trial Examiner Francis E. Rivers after the administrative hearing of charges brought by Rhody McCoy against ten Ocean Hill–Brownsville teachers; a special pamphlet on decentralization published by the UFT; the contract between the UFT and the central board; and the official bylaws of the Board of Education.

The Role of the Board of Education

Ironically, the demand for decentralization or, more properly, community control of the schools began with the failure of the central board to implement integration effectively. In explaining their failure, Board of Education administrators often said that they could not and would not "tell the principals how to run their schools."[1] Integration failed at least partly because it was resisted by many principals and because the system was already administratively decentralized to the point where recalcitrant principals were not forced to comply with board policy on integration.[2]

The growing sense of betrayal among ghetto leaders, who had been repeatedly promised integrated schools, came to a head during the I.S. 201 controversy. Intermediate schools, embracing grades five or six through eight, were specifically designed to further integration by getting children out of elementary schools a year or two earlier and into intermediate schools which would draw their students from a wider community to produce a greater racial mixture. To do this, the intermediate schools were supposed to have been built in areas that bordered on both black and white communities, and built to accommodate large numbers of children.

I.S. 201 fulfilled neither condition. It was built in the middle of Harlem and its capacity was no larger than a normal junior high school. As a UFT pamphlet published early in 1968 said: "Having been promised by the Board of Education that the school would be integrated, parents of children there soon found they had been betrayed, and that the school would remain segregated. Mounting frustration coupled with the increasingly obvious fact that children were not learning soon led to a translation of the original demand for integration into one for 'local control.' "[3]

Disenchanted black parents decided that, since they were once again stuck with a segregated school, they might at least run it themselves. Thus was born the movement for community control of black schools. It is crucial to remember that integration was not abandoned by black parents but by the Board of Education, which consistently failed to deliver on the promise of integrated schools. It is also crucial to remember that the demand for community control was a direct response by ghetto residents to the lack of access to decision-making processes that vitally affected the lives of their children. In that respect, "community control" came to symbolize the struggle for democratic power just as "no taxation without representation" symbolized a similar struggle by the founders of the American republic.

In the wake of the disorders that followed, the Board of Education, with financial assistance from the Ford Foundation, established I.S. 201 as part of a somewhat autonomous experimental school district in Harlem. At the same time, two additional "somewhat autonomous" experimental districts were launched, one in lower Manhattan and the other in Brooklyn in an area known as Ocean Hill–Brownsville. From the start, no one knew what "somewhat autonomous" meant. Certainly the board never said. For whatever reason, the board simply never defined the powers of the local governing boards of the experimental districts.

According to the Niemeyer Report,[4] a broad spectrum of the Ocean Hill–Brownsville community began to meet in February, 1967, to plan "for some means to participate more directly in school affairs."[5] For five months, the group continued to meet, was in contact with the mayor's office, and held exploratory discussions with the Board of Education's administrative staff.[6]

In early July, 1967, the Ford Foundation gave the local planning group $44,000 for the specific purpose of completing the planning phase of the experiment according to a twenty-six-day timetable.[7] On July 29, 1967, at the end of the twenty-six days, the Planning Council produced a written set of proposals which was submitted to the Board of Education in August.[8] These proposals clearly defined specific powers, responsibilities, and functions of the Local Governing Board. Among other things, the proposals provided that the Local Governing Board would be directly responsible and answerable to the New York City Superintendent of Schools and the New York State Commissioner of Education.[9]

Thus, it is clear that, although the Planning Council was asking for effective community control, it was by no means demanding complete independence. Indeed, it was merely seeking powers already possessed by every suburban or rural township in New York State.

The Planning Council's proposals also included the following provision:

> 8. The [local] Board shall make provisions for periodic evaluation of the total program. Such evaluations will include the project administrator, principals, teachers, community workers, etc. *This is not to be construed as meaning the [local] Board will do the evaluating. Existing Board of Education procedures for evaluating teachers will remain intact.* [Emphasis added.][10]

This provision makes it clear that the Planning Council did *not* contemplate bypassing existing procedures and substituting for those procedures arbitrary standards of its own. Indeed, at this point, the Planning Council did not see any conflict between existing standards of due process and effective community control. But as events would soon make clear, the Board of Education had little intention of going through with a genuine experiment in community control. The first indication of this came when the Planning Council attempted to elect parent representatives to the Local Governing Board. According to a recent study of the Ocean Hill–Brownsville dispute,[11] the Planning Council needed the names and addresses of students in order to register the parents who were eligible to vote. The Planning Council asked the Board of Education for help; but the board refused.

> The Board told them the community groups could get the necessary names and addresses only by hiring two Board of Education secretaries to go into the files. When the community leaders agreed to do this they were informed that the two secretaries had gone on vacation and that no one else was available. The Ocean Hill leaders were dismayed, but they got sympathetic teachers to canvass students for their addresses. Then, by going from door to door, they finally got 2,000 parents registered by August.[12]

Although this patchwork approach produced several unorthodox practices in the election which followed, the Niemeyer Report concluded that "no charges were made or misdeeds observed" and that "there was no evidence of coercion during the nominating process or during the election period itself."[13] By August, 1967, the Local Governing Board had been elected and, in addition, Rhody McCoy, an acting principal with seventeen years of experience in the New York City school system, had been selected as the project administrator.

As the opening of school approached, the Board of Education had still not acted on the Planning Council's proposed delineation of the specific powers, responsibilities, and functions of the Local Governing Board. As September grew closer, no one yet knew who was going to run the schools, who had the power to do what, and exactly what the content of the experiment was supposed to be. Despite repeated urgings by the Local Governing Board that it simply could not operate, much less conduct, a valid experiment unless it knew what its powers and responsibilities were, the central Board of Education consistently refused to define those powers. In fact, according to the Niemeyer Report, "both parties [were] still awaiting the specific delineation of powers and authority to be granted" as of July 30, 1968, when the Niemeyer Commission concluded its work.[14]

Apparently, *once the Board of Education understood that what Ocean Hill–Brownsville really wanted was an experiment in genuine community control, it backed off even before it had begun.* Almost immediately, the board began to talk about community *involvement* as opposed to community *control*.[15] And then, in January, 1968, more than five months after the Planning Council had submitted its proposals, and four months after the "experiment" had "begun," the central board suggested its own guidelines.[16] These guidelines completely emasculated the experiment in community control by stripping the Local Governing Board of virtually all of its substantive powers. Moreover, it left blurry and vague the lines of authority between the Local Governing Board and the central board. The Local Governing Board met with the central board and again asked for more specific delineation of authority and for the restoration of significant powers. But the central board refused to act.[17]

Thus, as the school year passed its mid-point, it became clear that the Board of Education had, in effect, scuttled the experiment. It had refused to delegate significant powers and it had refused to specifically define administrative authority. *It is an abiding mystery how an experiment in community control is supposed to proceed when no control is given and no authority is defined.* As the Niemeyer Report noted, the ambiguity about operational powers raised the critical question of who has authority to run the schools.[18] It is a question the Board of Education has never answered.

Vacuums created by the absence of clearly defined lines of authority are usually filled by individual discretion, arbitrary action, and administrative abuse. Only chaos can then result, as it has in Ocean Hill–Brownsville. The burden of blame for that chaos must fall on the Board of Education for leaving lines of authority undrawn and governing power undefined. If the central board deliberately set out to discredit decentralization by insuring chaos, it could not have done so more effectively. It freely predicted that decentralization would be chaotic and by its actions it made certain that its predictions came true.

The Role of the United Federation of Teachers

In the beginning, teachers were involved cooperatively with the Planning Council. At the time of the Ford Foundation grant, teachers were participants in the planning of the Ocean Hill–Brownsville experiment and, according to a statement by the teachers quoted in the Niemeyer Report, they were quite happy with the Planning Council.[19] At some point in September, 1967, the teacher representatives began to complain that they had been bypassed in the planning stage and no one was listening to them.[20] At first, the teachers' annoyance seemed to be directed primarily at the Ford Foundation and the central board for having initiated the planning phase in early July when most teachers would have left for summer vacation.[21] Soon, however, the focus of teacher complaints was the Planning Council itself for having "begun expanding on the plan without our presence."[22] As disagreements grew between the teachers and the Planning Council, open, bitter, and hostile exchanges apparently took place. In the context of previous grievances between the teachers and the community, it did not take much to develop the disagreements into hostile mistrust on the one side and mounting fear on the other.

On September 2, 1967, the new Local Governing Board held its third meeting and appointed five new principals for their schools. The appointments were made necessary when five incumbent principals left the district at the beginning of the experiment. Although the five new principals all had state certification, they were not chosen from the approved "waiting list." As Richard Karp put it: "What irked [the teachers], and what frightened a large number of union members was the fact that the principals chosen by the community were not on the approved Civil Service list. No one denied the merit of the elected principals, but the sight of educators chosen with no regard for bureaucratic procedures seemed to strike symbolically at every teacher's job security."[23]

The next week, the UFT called a city-wide strike. Although the union claimed that the strike was designed to extract city-wide pay increases and smaller classes, the Local Governing Board perceived the strike as a show of power aimed against Ocean Hill–Brownsville and specifically, in reaction to its hiring of the five principals. The UFT asked the Local Governing Board to support the strike, but was refused. At this point, the teacher representatives resigned from the local board, never to return. It was this incident which marked the beginning of the escalation of rhetoric between the Ocean Hill–Brownsville board and the UFT, and exposed the deep fears and hostility that existed between the white, middle-class educational establishment and the black community.[24] The community began to accuse the teachers of scuttling the experiment, and the teachers, having resigned from the Local Governing Board, began to talk about black extremists and black racism.

Given the enormous social and psychological pressures inherent in the situation and given also the Board of Education's refusal to define clearly the powers of the Local Governing Board, it is difficult to sort out the equities in the dispute between the teachers and the Local Governing Board up to the September, 1967, strike. It is enough for the purposes of this report to note that, at some point in late September, 1967, the UFT grew very fearful of community control and determined to block it, discredit it, and, if need be, defeat it.

In the months that followed, the UFT began to fan the flames of racial fears as it increasingly harped on "extremism," "the militants," and "Black Power." This much is a matter of public record.[25] The UFT was soon joined by the Council of Supervisory Associations, which sued to remove the five principals appointed in September, and which encouraged its members to abandon the experiment. To be sure, on November 1, 1967, all eighteen assistant principals left Ocean Hill–Brownsville.

Then, in the December 20, 1967, issue of the *United Teacher*, a periodical publication of the UFT, it was announced in an article on Ocean Hill–Brownsville that "The UFT has been negotiating with the [central] Board of Education for a transfer plan which will enable teachers to leave, although the union has encouraged them not to leave their schools. . . . The transfer plan being settled upon would give teachers the option of transferring at two points during each school year for as long as the experiment continues."[26]

It must be pointed out that transfers are not ordinarily available to teachers on such an easy basis. The procedures and regulations are complicated and require twelve pages of the contract between the UFT and the board to explain.[27] In general, the normal contractual procedures are designed to discourage teachers from fleeing ghetto schools. According to the Board of Education, "the present contract with the UFT provides that teachers must serve five years on regular appointment before being eligible for transfer; after this, their names are listed in order of seniority."[28] There are other limits as well, including an absolute prohibition against transfers at teacher initiative of more than 5 per cent of the teachers at any one school during any one year.[29]

Yet, in Ocean Hill–Brownsville, the UFT sought to ignore all these procedures and gained the right for unlimited numbers of teachers to transfer out at will for the duration of the experiment, to abandon the experiment for as long as it continued, and then to be free to return, presumably when "normal" conditions had been reinstated. Apparently, the UFT was not very concerned about the disastrous consequences to the experiment that might occur if large numbers of teachers were allowed to leave. Significant numbers of teachers did leave, sometimes in groups large enough to cause serious shortages.

Months later, when the Ocean Hill–Brownsville Local Governing Board attempted to exercise a similar unilateral right of transfer, the UFT cried foul. Yet, quite apart from the issues of due process raised by the manner in which the Local Governing Board attempted to transfer nineteen teachers and administrators, the UFT appeared to take a position of startling inconsistency. On the one hand, the UFT claimed that, due to special conditions in Ocean Hill–Brownsville, teachers should be allowed to bypass all the contractual procedures and transfer out at will. On the other hand, when the Local Governing Board made the same claim (that, due to the special conditions of the experiment, it should be allowed to transfer teachers to another district), the UFT expressed indignation and pleaded for strict fidelity to established procedures.

In trying to appear to the public as if it was only seeking fair procedures for teachers, the UFT has consistently claimed that it is in favor of decentralization. Yet it is a matter of public record that, during the last session of the State Legislature, the UFT carried on intensive lobbying activities against the Board of Regents Plan to implement decentralization and institute community control.

When school opened on September 9, 1968, the UFT went out on strike. The NYCLU supports the right of teachers to strike. Unfortunately, the UFT chose to use the strike not only to demand the reinstatement of the transferred teachers, but also as an extension of its lobbying efforts to defeat decentralization. By this time, the UFT was predicting that local community control would lead to chaos. By striking, the UFT proved its point by creating chaos.

The Due Process Issue

By early spring, 1968, the following was clear:

1. The Board of Education, by refusing to delegate power or define authority to the Local Governing Board, had ruined the experiment and set itself squarely against community control.

2. The UFT, by its special agreements involving transfers and by its emerging lobbying position against the various proposed plans, had set itself squarely against community control.

3. The Council of Supervisory Associations, by its suit challenging the appointment of non–civil service principals and by encouraging assistant principals to leave Ocean Hill–Brownsville, had set itself squarely against community control.

4. The $44,000 of Ford Foundation planning money, which had run out in the fall of 1967, was not going to be followed up by the previously promised $250,000 to fund substantive programs until the Local Governing Board was formally recognized by the central board.

Thus, by spring, 1968, without funds, without power, without authority, and with serious opposition in the ranks of its teachers, the Ocean Hill–Brownsville board was virtually unable to run its schools or conduct its experiment. It is against this background that, in April, the Ocean Hill–Brownsville board decided to transfer nineteen of what it called the "most uncooperative" teachers and administrators.

At first—and this appears to be a fact that is not generally known— McCoy tried to reassign the nineteen *within* the experimental district. According to the Niemeyer Report, McCoy had the authority to do that based on oral information he had received.[30] Yet, when some of the teachers refused to be transferred, the Board of Education refused to back up McCoy's authority.[31] Apparently, it was clearly within McCoy's authority to transfer personnel *within* his district until he actually tried to exercise it.

Next, McCoy requested that the nineteen be transferred to another district entirely. This request was denied by Superintendent Donovan.[32] Finally, in early May, 1968, the Local Governing Board sent notices of transfer to the nineteen, referring them to Board of Education headquarters for reassignment.[33] This transfer was interpreted by the professional staff, the community-at-large, and the press as dismissal.[34]

In attempting to understand why the attempted transfer was so widely perceived as an attempted firing, it is important to examine the distinction between transfer and dismissal in the Board of Education bylaws.[35] Dismissals must be accompanied by the requirements of due process, including written notice of charges, right to a hearing, right to confront witnesses, right to call witnesses, right to introduce evidence, right to receive transcript, right to appeal, etc.[36] The bylaws mandate these requirements for regular teachers and the UFT contract extends the requirements to substitute teachers.[37] *But neither the bylaws nor the contract mandate the requirements of due process for mere transfers.* Article II, Section 101.1, of the bylaws says:

> Transfers of members of the teaching and supervising staff from one school to another shall be made by the Superintendent of Schools, who shall report immediately such transfers to the Board of Education for its consideration and action.[38]

The purpose of this provision is apparently to allow the superintendent maximum flexibility to move teachers around for a variety of reasons.

Implicit in the provision is the assumption that the right to a job does not include the right to choose your assignment within the system. In fact, many hundreds of such transfers take place during every school year, apparently without the UFT's objection. Why, then, did the UFT make such a fuss in this case and insist on due process when it knew that due process was not required under existing procedures? The answer is clear: The UFT demanded due process because it wished to create the impression that the teachers had been fired and because it wished to discredit the Local Governing Board. This conclusion is hardly speculative. In many of its advertisements, the UFT has used the word "fired." Furthermore, the Niemeyer Report bluntly states the UFT motive: "the UFT demanded written charges, thus placing the request for transfers [for which no charges are required] into the realm of dismissal."[39]

Thus, at least by existing standards, the entire due process issue has been, from the beginning, a myth created by the UFT and swallowed whole by practically everyone. Eventually, McCoy yielded to the pressure to bring charges. As a final irony, it must be noted that, in exonerating the teachers of the charges, Trial Examiner Francis E. Rivers noted in his opinion that "Perhaps if the Unit Administrator [McCoy] had sent to the Superintendent of Schools a simple request to transfer the teachers, without assigning any supporting charges, he [the Superintendent] may have been able to do so without a hearing by virtue of Article II, Section 101.1 of the By-Laws of the Board of Education."[40] Which is, of course, precisely what McCoy had done.

It is by now not difficult to guess what the motives were behind the game being played by the central board and by the UFT. The Niemeyer Report makes it clear: "Under normal circumstances the Demonstration Project might have been able to accomplish the transfer of 'unsatisfactory' personnel informally, but a larger struggle was being waged in the New York State Legislature over a general proposal to decentralize the entire school system."[41] For, almost precisely at the time that the UFT decided to create the due process myth, UFT representatives were in Albany lobbying against community control. It certainly seems abundantly clear that the due process issue, as used by the UFT, was nothing but a smokescreen behind which the effort to discredit and destroy community control could go on.

The Future

It is clear that under present standards, the superintendent of schools has the power to transfer teachers without due process. If the superintendent's powers are transferred to unit administrators under decentralization, as they should have been in the experimental districts, then the unit administrator would have the power to transfer teachers without due process. *There is no question that under present standards, the UFT created the due process issue out of thin air.*

But, in looking toward the future, the NYCLU urges the adoption of stricter standards than those that exist today. We admit that whoever the administrator is, he ought to have the flexibility to transfer personnel administratively. But we also know that in many instances this power is used punitively. And since the Ocean Hill–Brownsville board admits that at least four of the teachers it wished transferred were guilty of "opposing openly the Demonstration Project,"[42] the power to transfer appears to have been used punitively in Ocean Hill–Brownsville.

We cannot condone such action. We insist that those who exercise power do so with full respect for due process of law and the right to dissent. "Due process of law" is not a mere technicality unrelated to the substance of power. On the contrary, it goes to the very heart of the procedures by which free men regulate their affairs. Freedom is truly indivisible; if the Ocean Hill–Brownsville dispute proves anything, it proves that, unless decisions are made and disputes resolved through fair, honest, and equitable procedures which respect individual rights, everyone will suffer. We are firmly and unbendingly committed to this view. But we are also committed to the view that, while fair procedures are necessary, they are not sufficient. The main goals of decentralization must be to provide black and Puerto Rican children with equal access to quality education and black and Puerto Rican parents with equal access to the process of making decisions that affect their children's lives.

As of now, the Board of Education's decentralization plan makes no mention at all of specific grounds for transfer. Standards for evaluating teacher performance in ghetto schools must be spelled out specifically and known in advance by administrators, teachers, and parents. If such standards are not set, we can expect to see charges made against teachers by local boards, which, even if substantiated, will be considered illegitimate by the central board on appeal. Fair procedures will be useless if what those procedures are supposed to determine is irrelevant.

The achievement of those goals may well inconvenience many of us. Teachers and administrators may have to be transferred for reasons that seem to them improper or unusual. Yet it is entirely possible that a teacher may be competent to teach in a white, middle-class school and incompetent to teach in a black or Puerto Rican ghetto school. Recent studies have clearly shown, for example, that a student's achievement is directly related to his teacher's expectations. The effect of teacher expectations of the academic achievement of black and Puerto Rican children thus appears to be a crucial factor in assessing the effectiveness of ghetto schools.[43] It may be necessary, therefore, to reevaluate the criteria for transfers to include the legitimate grievances of ghetto communities. If teachers who are otherwise competent are ineffective with black or Puerto Rican children, then perhaps such ineffectiveness should be seen as a legitimate reason for transfer to another school.

In order to avoid chaos in the future of the sort that we have suffered in the recent past while proceeding with decentralization, the NYCLU calls upon the Board of Education to take the following steps:

1. Make the adoption of a plan for effective community control its first priority. Such a plan should precisely set forth the powers and responsibilities of local governing boards and the rights of administrators, teachers, and students.

2. Spell out the criteria for transfer, expand such criteria to include standards of effectiveness, and establish, for the first time, standards of due process for punitive transfers.

3. Appoint an educational ombudsman to serve as an independent office of review of all local and central board decisions under decentralization. The ombudsman, who must have impeccable credentials of integrity and impartiality, should have the power to receive complaints from students, teachers, administrators, or parents. He should have the power to subpoena witnesses, inspect records, and hold hearings. His powers of action, however, should be limited to recommendation and publicity. In view of the dishonesty and duplicity that characterized the recent dispute, an office of ombudsman would seem to be a useful mechanism to provide the public with independent information and analysis.

If the due process standards suggested above are clearly spelled out for the future, all legitimate fears of the UFT should be ended. If the powers and responsibilities of local boards are clearly spelled out for the future, then all legitimate fears of the local communities should be ended.

Finally, we suggest that intensive meetings be held with representatives of the three local experimental districts, the UFT, the central board, and such civic organizations as the NAACP, the United Parents Association, the Citizens Committee for Children, and the NYCLU to work out standards for due process *and* community control. We need a massive act of good faith on the part of all parties to the dispute. Certainly we have had enough bad faith to last a century. How long must we continue to "wade up to our eyes in blood?"

Notes

1. Jason Epstein, "The Politics of School Decentralization," in Chapter IV, above, p. 293.

2. See generally, David Rogers, *110 Livingston Street* (New York: Random House, 1968).

3. Eugenia Kemble, *New York's Experiments in School Decentralization: A Look at Three Projects* (New York: United Federation of Teachers, 1968).

4. The Niemeyer Report was the final report of an advisory commission appointed on July 1, 1967, by the Board of Education to study school decentralization with particular emphasis on the three experimental districts. The commission's full title was the Advisory and Evaluation Committee on Decentralization to the Board of Education of the City of New York. It functioned from July 1, 1967, to June 30, 1968. Its final report, entitled *An Evaluative Study of the Process of School Decentralization in New York City*, was submitted to the board on July 30, 1968, and was released in September, 1968. Its chairman was John H. Niemeyer, President of Bank Street College of Education, and its other members were Mrs. Lillian Ashe, former President of the United Parents Association; Dr. Charles R. DeCarlo, Director of Automation Research for I.B.M., James Marshall, former President of the New York City Board of Education; Frederick O'Neal, President of Actors Equity; and Mrs. Celia Vice, Chairman of Local School Board #14, Brooklyn. The staff executive director was Dr. Bert Swanson, Director of the Institute for Community Studies at Sarah Lawrence College. Hereafter cited as Niemeyer Report.

5. Niemeyer Report, p. 72.

6. *Ibid.*

7. *Ibid.*

8. *Ibid.*, p. 74.

9. *Ibid.*

10. *Ibid.*, p. 75.

11. Richard Karp, "School Decentralization in New York: A Case Study," *Interplay* (August–September, 1968).

12. *Ibid.*

13. Niemeyer Report, p. 77.

14. *Ibid.*, p. 91.

15. Karp, *op. cit.*

16. Niemeyer Report, p. 91.

17. *Ibid.*, pp. 93–94.

18. *Ibid.*

19. *Ibid.*, p. 73.

20. *Ibid.*

21. Kemble, *op. cit.*

22. *Ibid.*

23. Karp, *op. cit.*

24. *Ibid.*

25. Kemble, *op. cit.* See also, generally, *The New York Times*, from September, 1967, to the present.

26. Kemble, *op. cit.*

27. Agreement between the Board of Education of the City of New York and United Federation of Teachers, Local 2, American Federation of Teachers, AFL–CIO, pp. 20–32; hereafter cited as UFT Contract.

28. Board of Education, *Tentative Proposals for Decentralization* (August, 1968), p. 2.

29. UFT Contract.

30. Niemeyer Report, p. 96.

31. *Ibid.*

32. *Ibid.*, p. 94.

33. *Ibid.*

34. *Ibid.*

35. Bylaws of the Board of Education of the City of New York; hereafter cited as Bylaws.

36. *Ibid.*, sec. 105a.1.

37. UFT Contract, Art. IV, sec. F, para. 15b and 15c.

38. Bylaws, Art. II, sec. 101.1.

39. Niemeyer Report, p. 94.

40. Report and Recommendations of Special Trial Examiner, Board of Education, City of New York, Administrative Hearing into Complaints of Rhody A. McCoy, p. 5; hereafter cited as Trial Examiner's Report.

41. Niemeyer Report, p. 95.

42. Trial Examiner's Report, p. 4.

43. Robert Rosenthal and Lenore F. Jacobson, "Teacher Expectations for the Disadvantaged," *Scientific American* (April, 1968).

24. A CRITICISM OF THE NEW YORK CIVIL LIBERTIES UNION REPORT ON THE OCEAN HILL–BROWNSVILLE SCHOOL CONTROVERSY

ADOLPH STONE

The report of the New York Civil Liberties Union (NYCLU) on the Ocean Hill–Brownsville school controversy is superficial, inaccurate, and biased. It does a great disservice to education, race relations, and civil liberties.

It does a disservice to education because it obscures and falsifies the nature of the problem, discussing the "demand for decentralization or, more properly, community control," as though the two terms were synonymous. McGeorge Bundy, who headed the group which put forth the Bundy Report on school decentralization, is quoted in *The New York Times* of October 27, 1968, as deploring "some simplistic views of community control"; he also said that "perhaps we failed in not making the point more sharply that you need a strong central agency, with public confidence, as well as decentralization."

The NYCLU Report states that those who want community control are "merely seeking powers already possessed by every suburban or rural township in New York State." This is not true. Educational districts outside of the city have independent taxing power; local school boards are responsible to the voters for how they spend the money. The New York State Education Department exercises considerable supervisory power over the educational structure outside of the city. It has traditionally left this power within the city to the Board of Education.

The degree of decentralization deemed desirable and the extent of the powers which should be exercised by any community board are certainly questions on which reasonable men may differ. To suggest, as the NYCLU does, that anyone who does not support the definition of "community control" propounded by the Ocean Hill board must accept

Used by permission of the author and the Combined Action Committee, CSA–UFT, District I, November, 1968.

the "burden of blame" limits the kind of discussion needed to find the solution for our city's educational problems.

It does a disservice to education also by subordinating the due process issue to that of community control and by presenting excuses for those violations which it does not "condone" but does not condemn. Due process is the heart of academic freedom. Teachers who are not free to develop their own answers and to disagree with authority cannot be expected to develop qualities of freedom and independence in their students.

The report does a disservice to race relations by apparently supporting the position that the conflict is essentially racial. It places a black community on one side and a white power structure on the other. While racial extremists have undoubtedly played a part in fomenting the difficulties, the problem of due process can arise in any community, and the attempt to present it as a racial conflict falsifies the basic issue and helps intensify racial feelings.

The report does a disservice to civil liberties by obscuring the centrality of the due process issue and by establishing "community control" as a new civil liberty. Community control can extend freedoms; it can also limit them. Most of the incidents of censorship, discharge of teachers for political and social opinions, and attempts to stifle freedom of discussion have taken place in areas with strong community control. The precise mechanism by which a school system can best operate is not properly an area in which the Civil Liberties Union should hold a position. By so doing, it makes the Civil Liberties Union into another partisan political group and destroys its usefulness as a defender of civil liberties.

A Biased Report

One might expect that a document of the Civil Liberties Union would have a calm and judicious tone and would examine the facts impartially and in detail. This report, unfortunately, is full of propaganda devices and of loaded language. Thus, it states of the 1967 strike: "Although the union *claimed* that the strike was designed to *extract* city-wide pay increases and smaller classes, the Local Governing Board *perceived* the strike as a show of power. . . ." (Emphasis added.)

It quotes a journalist unfriendly to the United Federation of Teachers (UFT), Richard Karp, on the teachers' reaction to the selection of principals who had not passed competitive examinations: "No one denied the merit of the elected principals, but the sight of educators chosen with no regard for bureaucratic procedures seemed to strike symbolically at every teacher's job security." "Bureaucratic procedures" are, of course, civil service examinations and the merit system.

It brings in the patriotic motif: " 'community control' came to symbolize the struggle for democratic power just as 'no taxation without representation' symbolized a similar struggle by the founders of the American republic." Those who want segregation in the South have a fine democratic slogan also, "freedom of choice"!

Nor are the facts examined carefully or impartially. The report states that "We find the charge that existing standards of due process are seriously threatened by community control unfounded, both in theory and in fact." The theory of community control is never examined; one never knows what the NYCLU means by community control. The facts selected are only those which fit the conclusion that right is on the side of those who seek to establish this undefined "community control."

The bias of the report is perhaps most clearly established in its efforts to suggest motives behind the UFT's fight for the reinstatement of the teachers in the Ocean Hill–Brownsville district. The report charges that the due process "myth" was nothing but a "smokescreen behind which the effort to discredit and destroy community control could go on," and that the strike which started this September [1968] not only was for reinstatement of the teachers but also was an "extension of its lobbying efforts to defeat decentralization."

No effort is devoted to determining the motives of the Local Governing Board. Indeed, the report spends considerable time in indicating that the tentative plan of the Local Planning Board, in July, 1967, accepted the position of the Local Governing Board as responsible and answerable to the New York City Superintendent of Schools, but does not indicate that, when in operation, the Local Governing Board claimed the right to complete authority, independent of the central board. What could have been the motive of the Local Governing Board for suddenly, early in May, 1968, attempting to put out of their positions in the district nineteen teachers and supervisors except the desire to assert openly and bring about a confrontation of its power to control completely its district, regardless of the law and of the union contract?

The Role of the Board of Education

One of the conclusions of the NYCLU is that "from the beginning, the central Board of Education attempted to scuttle the experiment in Ocean Hill–Brownsville by consistently refusing to define the authority of the Local Governing Board." The NYCLU Report omits entirely the explanation of the board's position. The board began by approving of local planning boards financed by the Ford Foundation; these were to develop plans for experimental districts. The plans presumably would then be discussed and some type of experiment in local control would emerge. According to the Niemeyer Report: "the central cause of the difficulty is the fact that from the inception of the Demonstration projects, the Board of Education and the Superintendent had one set of purposes and expectations, while groups seeking and wielding local power have had a different and incompatible set." The Board of Education wanted planned experiments, but the local groups had no interest in serving experimental ends. Apparently, the original action came from the existing Council Against Poverty groups in each community, supported by a representative of the Ford Foundation and individuals from two universities.

Running through all the differences between the Ocean Hill–Brownsville board and the central board is the demand of the Ocean Hill–Brownsville board for complete community control and the desire of the central board to find a way of combining a measure of decentralization with retention of considerable central authority. Furthermore, the central board stated that it had no legal authority to turn over to any local board the powers demanded by the Ocean Hill–Brownsville board. When the Ocean Hill–Brownsville Planning Board completed its plans and presented them in August, 1967, it speedily made its own arrangements for election of a Local Governing Board, and the local board wanted to have the power to govern. While the central board agreed to the selection of a unit administrator and permitted the local board to select its own principals (not from the approved lists, an action to which the supervisors' association took strong exception), it was not ready to determine just how much authority local boards should have. Perhaps the central board should have acted more quickly, but in September there was a city-wide strike in the schools, and it took several months of discussion (with open hearings) for the board to work out its own guidelines on decentralization. These guidelines were issued in January, 1968, gave only limited powers to local boards, and were completely unacceptable to Ocean Hill–Brownsville and the other two demonstration districts. The Niemeyer Report states, "In March, 1968, the three Demonstration Projects agreed upon a 'consensus' document which demanded full authority, although the Board of Education could not go beyond the legal limits placed upon it by the State Education Law."

The Ocean Hill–Brownsville board asked for complete control of its own budget, with its own bank account; the right to hire and fire; and the right to make its own contracts for building maintenance and repair, according to the Niemeyer Report. The Board of Education, the

Niemeyer Report went on to say, "has not yet granted *formal* approval to the Project Boards because they were constrained by the State Education Law and Union contracts not to accede to the demands of the Project Boards."

The Board of Education, the legally constituted authority in charge of the New York City schools, was required to run the schools in conformity with the State Education Law, and it could not legally delegate its authority elsewhere in the absence of legislative enactments giving it this right. The NYCLU may wish to look upon its actions as inept, confused, timid, and terribly slow, and it may consider that the members of the board were opposed to what it considered meaningful decentralization, but to suggest it had the right and the duty immediately to give the Ocean Hill–Brownsville board all the powers it sought, and, failing this, was guilty of "scuttling the experiment," is a distortion of the facts. It is interesting to note that the chairman of the Board of Education in the period in which its actions are so harshly criticized by the NYCLU was Lloyd Garrison, member of the board of the American Civil Liberties Union (ACLU). The Board of Education was not guilty of "consistently refusing to define the authority of the Local Governing Board," but, rather, guilty of disagreeing with it as to how much authority it should have. The report of the NYCLU draws abundantly upon the Niemeyer Report, but it does not quote or discuss this conclusion of the Niemeyer Committee: "Two major lessons are to be learned from this confrontation: one is the need for a legal base or legislation to transfer sufficient authority for an adequate decentralization program; the other is the fact that in some local communities militant groups may be expected to continue to demand powers for which no one yet has proposed legislation."

The Role of the UFT and the Due Process Issue

The defense of due process is one of the principal reasons for the existence of the ACLU. It is especially regrettable that the NYCLU misstates both the facts about the nineteen teachers and supervisors who became the focus of the due process struggle and the policy of the Board of Education on transfers. The NYCLU Report states that, at first, McCoy tried to reassign them within the district, but was prevented from doing so by the Board of Education; then, he asked that they be transferred to another district, but the request was refused by Superintendent Donovan; and, finally, "The Local Governing Board sent notices of transfer to the nineteen, referring them to the Board of Education headquarters for reassignment."

As to reassigning the teachers within the district: Mr. McCoy stated at a meeting on October 22, 1968, that the teachers he wished to re-assign within the district were five others, not the nineteen later involved; that these five objected to a transfer to the new I.S. 55, apparently because Homer Ferguson had been assigned as principal. (Mr. Neier, who was at the dinner meeting, denies the accuracy of the statement, but it is supported both by others at the meeting and by the fact that at least one other teacher in the district was so transferred.) As to requesting the assignment of the teachers to another district, Superintendent Donovan stated on a television program("The Way It Is," Sunday, October 27, 1968, Channel 7) that, although he had earlier told Mr. McCoy that if Mr. McCoy had any special difficulties with teachers who opposed the program, he should inform Donovan and Donovan would try to get them transferred; nevertheless, McCoy had never made any such request. Dr. Donovan said that the first time he, Donovan, heard about the nineteen was when he read it in the newspaper. The Niemeyer Report states that the nineteen received notices of "termination of services," not transfers. In fact, they received the notices by registered letter, in school, in the middle of the teaching day on May 9, with seven weeks of the term left.

The NYCLU quotes the bylaw of the Board of Education which gives the superintendent of schools power to transfer teachers, and states that "many hundreds of such transfers take place during every school year, apparently without the UFT's objection." These hundreds of transfers are those made at the requests of teachers, those necessitated by new buildings, by drops in registers, and similar reasons. It is *not* the practice of the board to make disciplinary transfers without a statement of charges and the right to a hearing. Supervisors are required to show that they have conferred with teachers about alleged weaknesses, have made suggestions for improvement, have informed the teacher in writing of shortcomings, have given the teacher the opportunity to file written answers; a whole series of hearings at several levels under the grievance procedures in the UFT contract is available to the teacher who feels he has been treated unjustly. Judge Rivers's findings showed that none of these conditions were maintained in the case of the teachers in the Ocean Hill–Brownsville district.

When a conflict arises between a teacher and a supervisor, sometimes the best solution is a transfer. Mr. Niemeyer, chairman of the board's Committee on Decentralization, stated (in *The New York Times*, September 14, 1968) that "the board had promised to transfer quietly teachers who were unacceptable to the Ocean Hill–Brownsville Demonstration School District, but the district's governing board would not go along." He further said that the UFT would not have objected to the transfers if they had been made routinely. "It would have worked out; it's done all the time." This does not mean that teachers in such circumstances are transferred arbitrarily, without charges or a hearing; as Mr. Niemeyer says, "It is worked out." Discussions are held with the principal and with the district superintendent; the teacher can have a union representative present. The transfer, when it is made, is by agreement.

Judge Rivers, in his statement exonerating the teachers of the charges, noted that "Perhaps if the Unit Administrator had sent to the Superintendent of Schools a simple request to transfer the teachers, without assigning any supporting charges, he [the Superintendent] may have been able to do so without a hearing . . ." This, the NYCLU stated, was "precisely what McCoy had done." But he had not sent such a request, though apparently he had been invited to do so. Instead, he announced that he had "terminated the services" of the teachers. Had he sent such a request, there need not have been formal hearings of the kind Judge Rivers mentioned, but the superintendent and the teachers and the UFT representatives would have met and perhaps "it would have been worked out."

The NYCLU calls upon the Board of Education to "establish, for the first time, standards of due process for punitive transfers." It is certainly desirable that such regulations be written out, but such standards have been, in effect, in practice for many years. It is the NYCLU and the Ocean Hill–Brownsville board that are attempting to destroy due process. It must be remembered that Mr. McCoy gave as the reason for the transfer of the teachers the charge that they were "out of tune with the political atmosphere in the community," and that four of the teachers were accused of "opposing openly the Demonstration Project." The NYCLU Report says that "at least by existing standards, the entire due process issue has been, from the beginning, a myth created by the UFT." If arbitrary "termination of services" on the basis of such charges, without any specifics or hearings is not a violation of due process and civil liberties, one wonders what the NYCLU definition of these terms might be.

Another charge of the NYCLU is that the UFT "demanded due process because it wished to create the impression that the teachers had been fired." But the NYCLU Report also states that "if the superintendent's powers are transferred to unit administrators under decentralization, . . . then the unit administrator would have the power to transfer teachers without due process." But where would they send transferred teachers if each district has the right to hire and fire? The statements and actions of the Ocean Hill–Brownsville board clearly indicated that, in taking the action they did, they were claiming the right to get rid of all teachers who dared exercise any independence of thought and not just to establish some right of transfer.

In September, 1966, with the opening of I.S. 201, a series of incidents developed in various parts of the city in which militant groups attempted (and often succeeded) in forcing out principals, and in which teachers were insulted and harassed. The atmosphere created by these incidents had a great bearing on subsequent developments, *and the failure of the NYCLU Report to include mention of them makes impossible a full understanding of the situation.* The NYCLU says blandly that "It is enough for the purposes of this report to note that, at some point in late September, 1967, the UFT grew very fearful of community control. . . . In the months that followed, the UFT began to fan the flames of racial fears as it increasingly harped on 'extremism,' 'the militants,' and 'Black Power.'" This seems to imply that some sinister purpose, unrelated to actual events, lay behind the use of such phrases. This period witnessed picketing of schools by militant groups, sit-ins in principals' offices, displacement of principals, and verbal and even physical attacks upon teachers.

Much attention is given to an effort of the UFT to negotiate for the right of teachers to transfer out of the experimental school districts if they so wished. This, the NYCLU asserted, showed that the UFT was not concerned about shortages this would cause in the district and that, if the UFT claimed this right for teachers, it was only fair that the local board should have a similar right to transfer teachers out of the district. But the UFT's action can only be understood against the background of incidents created by such groups as Brooklyn CORE. The UFT was beseiged by teachers who were worried by the demonstrations and threats; it urged them to remain in the district, but tried to arrange the right of transfer for those who felt it urgent. Unlike the action of the Ocean Hill–Brownsville Governing Board, this agreement was negotiated; transfers were to be made only at the end of the term and not (as in the case of the nineteen) in the middle of the term. To parallel the action of the governing board, the UFT would have sent a group of teachers to Livingston Street, without previous notice to their schools or to the central board, to demand immediate reassignment to other districts.

Another charge of the NYCLU against the UFT is this: "In trying to appear to the public as if it was only seeking fair procedures for teachers, the UFT has consistently claimed that it is in favor of decentralization. Yet it is a matter of public record that, during the last session of the State Legislature, the UFT carried on intensive lobbying activities against the Board of Regents Plan to implement decentralization and institute community control."

The UFT had its own decentralization plan. Indeed, it had participated in the early planning in the Ocean Hill–Brownsville district. However, as the Niemeyer Report states:

> Later, toward the end of September, the teacher respresentatives were to complain bitterly that they had been bypassed in the planning phase and in fact they were seldom listened to. They described the general atmosphere of the planning meetings as . . . "extremely hostile and negative. There was a constant stream of remarks to teachers which stated that teachers were bigoted, incompetent, disinterested, obstructive, and were attempting to sabotage the plan.
>
> "The atmosphere became so hostile that teachers hesitated even to ask a question or express an opinion. Any attempt at teacher comment was met with insults and charges of obstruction."

The UFT teachers ultimately left the local board.

The UFT decentralization plan called for larger districts than those proposed in the Regents Plan, to prevent fragmentation of the city into enclaves controlled by a particular racial or ethnic group. The UFT felt that the Regents' bill did not offer adequate protection for teachers' rights. As noted on the first page of this report, McGeorge Bundy now sees the defects of the similar Bundy Plan. As for the NYCLU judgment of UFT motives, is it hypocritical to favor one kind of decentralization but be against another kind? Is it improper to lobby against a bill if the union considers it a bad bill? How can the right to favor one measure and oppose another be considered a violation of civil liberties?

The Merit System

The NYCLU makes several oblique and hostile references to the merit system, though no specific recommendations on the matter of selection of teachers and supervisors are made. Referring to the appointment of new principals by the Ocean Hill–Brownsville board, the report states that they were not chosen from the approved "waiting list"; that this list is made up of individuals who have passed a competitive examination is not mentioned. Richard Karp's comment, quoted earlier, about "educators chosen with no regard for bureaucratic procedures" is cited and then the statement is made that the Ocean Hill–Brownsville board perceived the September, 1967, strike as a reaction to its hiring of the five principals. Subsequently, the report lists as one of the conditions in spring, 1968, which brought on the "transfer" of the nineteen: "The Council of Supervisory Associations, by its suit challenging the appointment of non–civil service principals and by encouraging assistant principals to leave Ocean Hill–Brownsville, had set itself squarely against community control."

The appointment of principals who had not passed competitive examinations was a violation of the law. The CSA won the suit mentioned above; it is now on appeal. No evidence is presented to show that the CSA encouraged assistant principals to leave Ocean Hill–Brownsville. Obviously, the Ocean Hill–Brownsville board had the right to ask that the law which regulated the appointment of principals and other personnel be changed. Obviously, those who opposed a change and regarded the appointments as illegal had the right to bring suit to prevent the appointments. Apparently, the NYCLU regards an attempt to enforce existing civil service laws as a violation of "community control" and, therefore, a violation of civil liberties. To most teachers it seems that open competitive examinations, with standards the same for all and with appointments from a ranked list, are more in harmony with concepts of civil liberties than are appointments made at the will of any one local board.

The Election of the Local Governing Board

The report states that the first indication of the fact that "the Board of Education had little intention of going through with a genuine experiment in community control" came with the election of parent representatives to the Local Governing Board. The proposals of the Local Planning Board were not presented to the board until the beginning of August, 1967. When the Planning Board asked the central Board of Education to give them, or help them get, the names and addresses of parents of pupils in the local schools, they were unable to get them and had to resort to local canvassing to get the names. That the schools are shut down in August and that the board always moves slowly are more likely explanations for lack of cooperation than sabotage. In addition, it seems a procedure of dubious merit to run an election before there had been an opportunity to survey and discuss the plans of the Planning Board and for parents to hear the views of various candidates. These are among the factors which led the Appellate Division of the New York State Supreme Court to declare on October 24: "Whether in view of the facts stated with respect to the lack of statutory authority for the election, or the manner of their 'election,' [that] this Governing Board may be deemed to be a duly elected body is subject to serious doubt."

Intransigency of the UFT

The UFT is presented as intransigent and uncooperative. According to the Niemeyer Report, the Board of Education and the UFT were willing to accept binding arbitration to settle the dispute about the nineteen teachers and supervisors; the Ocean Hill–Brownsville board refused. Then, Dr. Allen suggested Mr. Kheel as mediator; both sides agreed. (This occurred in spring, 1968.) The UFT was ready to accept his recommendations; the Ocean Hill–Brownsville board refused. It also refused to accept the findings of Judge Rivers, who heard the charges against the teachers.

Conclusions

1. The due process issue was the basic issue in the controversy. It was especially important because the precedent set would be most significant for the continued existence of due process in a decentralized school system.

2. Although the ACLU has always defended due process, the NYCLU not only did not defend it in this situation, but in fact defended those who violated due process.

3. The report of the NYCLU on the Ocean Hill–Brownsville situation is a one-sided polemic, with all data not in agreement with apparently preconceived conclusions omitted.

4. Community control in education is an educational and political rather than a civil liberties question.

5. If it follows this precedent, the NYCLU can just as reasonably take a stand on any other social and political issue. When it does so, it will be just another political body; its role as defender of civil liberties and uniter of all those who defend civil liberties will disappear.

6. The ACLU should examine the actions of the NYCLU in the Ocean Hill–Brownsville school situation and take such action as is necessary to prevent distortion of the function of the ACLU and its affiliates.

25. COMMUNITY CONTROL
OF EDUCATION

MARILYN GITTELL

While political scientists and sociologists research who has power, we tend to ignore the powerless. While we study decision-making, we are reluctant to expose nondecision-making. Satisfied to rationalize a multiple-elite structure as pluralism,[1] we depreciate the relevance of public participation in the political process.[2] The scope of our research and concerns is reflected in our limited views of institutional and social change in the cities.[3]

The ghetto community, in the meantime, has exposed the insulation of the political system and challenged its irrelevance to their demands for "a piece of the action." These communities are struggling daily with a political structure in the cities that combines two oppressive elements: bureaucratic centralization and specialization, and professionalism. In the face of these obstacles, ghetto leaders are necessarily concerned with restructuring to form a participatory system. They are forced to consider, and force all of us to consider, new mechanisms for increasing public participation. Unless they and we can find the channels for such participation, our political system may be in serious difficulty. The city school system is one of the battlegrounds and, in many respects, it reflects the larger problem in microcosm.

City Schools and Public Education

There are those who suggest that educational institutions cannot correct the maladies of the society that reflect larger social problems. In the 1930's, when educators similarly rejected George Counts's plea for using education as a vehicle for social change, they presaged a period of thirty years of insulation of the school system from social needs.[4] It

This is a revised and expanded version of "Community Control of Education," and is reprinted with permission from *Urban Riots: Violence and Social Change, Proceedings* of The Academy of Political Science, Vol. XXIX, No. 1 (1968).

should by now be evident that educational systems are a vital component of the constructive adjustment of urban institutions to the changing needs of our society.

The public education systems in our large cities are paralyzed. Their failure is political as well as educational. The educational failure is relatively easy to substantiate: There is sufficient hard data in test scores, dropout rates, the number of academic diplomas produced, and so forth, to establish the nature of that failure. Rationales developed to relate the cause of this failure to the problems of a disadvantaged community, while they may be valid, do not in any way negate the responsibility of the school system to educate its clientele. The inability of school professionals to cope with this problem must still be labeled an educational failure.[5]

It is unfortunate that we do not have enough reliable information to measure comparatively the success or failure of the school systems in meeting the needs of immigrant populations over the years. Too often it is assumed that the education of the disadvantaged in previous decades was somehow successful. Nonetheless, while the data are limited, there is some evidence to suggest that educational institutions in large cities have traditionally been unable to meet the needs of the ghetto community. The difference in the current problem is that dropouts in the black community are unemployable because of racial barriers and automation, whereas earlier dropouts were hidden in an expanding work force.

The Political Failure of City School Systems

The political failure of the school system cannot be measured quantitatively except in the sense that educational failings can be traced to the environment of the total system. From my own research, I am convinced that the political failure of the school system is fundamental.[6] It can best be described in terms of the development within the city of a political subsystem whose policy process is wholly controlled by a small professional elite at headquarters. The policies emanating from this elite support an educational establishment that maintains a status quo orientation in all areas of education policy.

The lack of innovation in city school systems, except as periodically stimulated by outside funding, is indicative of this status quo orientation. Over the last sixty years, city school systems have experienced a high degree of professionalization combined with extensive centralization of the educational bureaucracy. In every large city, an inbred bureaucratic supervisory staff sits at headquarters offices holding a tight rein on educational policy. Their vested interests are clear: Any major shift in educational policy might well challenge their control of the system. Perhaps the only new agent to enter the domain of school affairs in recent years is the teacher organization or union. Unfortunately, these groups have concentrated their attention on salary and related issues; on all other questions, they have supported establishment policies.[7] Additionally, we have seen the abdication of responsibility for education by civic groups, businessmen, labor unions, and parents. The result is a closed political system, which, if measured against our ideological commitments to public participation, falls far short of any standards for a pluralistic society.

The Rationale for Community Control

The initial thrust that followed on the *Brown v. Board of Education* decision in 1954 was directed at achieving quality integrated education. It met not only with public opposition to change but also with bureaucratic inaction. In every large city, school segregation has increased in the last decade. Residential patterns explain part of the problem, but, beyond this, many plans for integration have simply been sidetracked. The integration movement, however, provided the ghetto community with insights into their exclusion from the school decision-making process. It was the struggle for integration that spotlighted the political failure of large-city school systems. How could the ghetto communities be assured of quality education and a participatory role in the system? The response has been clear. Those who now control the schools have been unable to produce results; they have excluded the public from its rightful role in the policy process; the structure, therefore, must be adjusted to give the community a measure of control over educational institutions. Participation in itself provides an involvement with the system that can not only diminish attitudes of alienation but also serve to stimulate educational change. This new role for the community is not conceived of as an abandonment of professionalism but, rather, as an effort to achieve a proper balance between professionalism and public involvement in the policy process. The definition of community includes parents of school children, as well as those segments of the public that have been excluded from a role in public education. Hence, community control implies a redistribution of power within the educational subsystem.[8] It is directed toward achieving a modern mechanism for participatory democracy. It attempts to answer the political failure in education systems, and, as regards the educational failure, community control is intended to create an environment in which more meaningful educational policies can be developed and a wide variety of alternative solutions and techniques can be tested. It seems plausible to assume that a school system devoted to community needs and serving as an agent of community interests will provide an environment more conducive to learning.

Community Control as an Instrument for Social Change

Support for community participation is voiced by the educational establishment and the professionals, but their concept of community participation is more closely related to the traditional parent-association concept and has nothing to do with community control of decision-making. It is essential that community control be defined in clear and precise terms. As one critic has noted, "participation without power is a ritual." Community control of the schools must involve local control over key policy decisions in four critical areas: (1) personnel, (2) budget, (3) curriculum, and (4) pupil policy. Local governing bodies must be locally selected, and mechanisms for encouraging broader community participation must be thoughtfully developed.

Properly instituted, community control is an instrument of social change. The redistribution of power is in itself an aspect of that change. If adequate provision is made for giving the community the technical resources to carry out this new role, community control has the potential for offering new insights into our concept of professionalism and our general theories of educational expertise. If community boards have the resources to engage a variety of professionals and nonprofessionals in the policy process, institutional changes of all kinds can be anticipated. The business community as well as university faculties and research centers may become more actively involved in the schools. Flexible staffing policies and innovative institutional arrangements are more likely to be developed. The scope of other community resources will be greatly expanded as well.

Demonstration School Projects in New York City

The three demonstration projects established in New York City, in July, 1967, to experiment with community participation offer some experience on which to base predictions. Although these three demonstration districts (Ocean Hill–Brownsville, Two Bridges, and the 201 complex) suffer from an almost total lack of delegated power and resources, they have already proved that community involvement can and does expand the scope of professional and public participation. Teacher and administrative recruitment in these districts has been innovative even within the constraints of established central procedures and the union contract. In Ocean Hill–Brownsville, seven new principals were appointed by the Local Governing Board, drawing on people from outside the regular bureaucratic hierarchy. For the first time, a Puerto Rican and a Chinese principal were appointed to head local schools.[9] A unit administrator (equivalent to a district superintendent) appointed by another of the local boards is trained in public administration rather than in the traditional professional education area. His insights and approach differ markedly from the usual school administrator. Another district, in the process of recruiting a unit administrator, established community orientation as a *sine qua non* for the candidates. Each of the districts is seriously discussing teacher-training programs to be developed jointly with universities; it is hoped that such programs will be more realistic and more constructive in recruiting and preparing teachers for ghetto schools. The districts have, in their short history, drawn on the expertise of professionals in fields not previously involved in the schools; anthropologists, political scientists, and sociologists have been used. In addition, community people have been viewed as a new and special kind of resource.

The implications of community control as an instrument of social change are reflected in the obvious threat they present to the holders of power in the system and to the public in general. The press and propaganda reports describe only the difficulties that these communities have encountered. Charges of racism have been played up, but no effort has been made to discuss constructive changes in the districts. The United Federation of Teachers (UFT) and the Council of Supervisory Associations (CSA) regularly proclaim the extremist character of governing-board members or those who control them. Actually, the governing boards include a representative cross-section of ethnic groups in the communities, and these attacks are often motivated by a refusal to accept the political and educational goals and interests of the boards. Members of the local boards are, largely, parents of school children in the district; many are from lower-income groups and their involvement in community affairs began in poverty programs; several had never been involved in school affairs prior to the creation of the demonstration districts.

Unfortunately, the three districts have been spending a great deal of their time and effort struggling with the Board of Education to secure the powers that would justify labeling them experiments in community control; a more reliable test of their viability awaits the conclusion of that negotiation.

The Bundy Plan

The most significant general proposal for community control to date is the Bundy Plan, presented to the mayor of New York City in the autumn of 1967.[10] The plan calls for city-wide decentralization and rather extensive community control. It suggests a city-wide education structure for special schools, for establishing minimum standards, for control of capital construction, and for provision of voluntary services at the request of local districts. By its provision for local selection of a majority of the members of local school boards and for community control of the expense budget, student policy, curriculum, and personnel, the Bundy Plan meets the test of redistributing power in the system. Perhaps the plan's obvious commitment to community control explains the opposition to it. The outcry surrounding the Bundy Plan suggests the general alignment of forces to be faced by any proposal for decentralization and increased community control in cities throughout the country. It also reflects the current education power structure and its failure to respond to the pressing demands of the community.

Those who, for a decade, have resisted school integration and eschewed the plight of the ghetto schools now draw on these very arguments to denigrate the Bundy Plan. Local school board members who have resisted efforts at integration in their own areas for over a decade are now defenders of city-wide integration—or, at least, they oppose plans for decentralization and community control because such plans presumably would deny the possibility of achieving integration. The UFT, which, in the last decade, successfully staved off several mandatory teacher transfer plans (designed to ensure adequate staffing for ghetto schools), now expresses great concern with the effect that the Bundy Plan might have on integrated staffing of ghetto schools. The CSA, which has regularly impeded the progress of plans developed to effect integration and, over the years, has shown minimum interest in programs to improve ghetto schools (in one effort, it acted as plaintiff in a court action—which is rumored to have cost $1 million—against the three ghetto school demonstration projects and the Bundy Plan) now rationalizes its opposition to the Bundy Plan by arguing that the ghetto areas will suffer if decentralization is implemented. Political leaders who, in the past, have ignored school issues—except to support local community efforts to resist the various integration plans that have periodically been mounted, announced, and cancelled—are now also champions of integration for the ghetto community.

Viewing the decentralization controversy as it has developed around the Bundy Plan and the experimental demonstration districts, it is possible to mark out three phases. In the first phase, a rhetoric related to the concept of community control was developed to defeat the Bundy Plan. The Board of Education, initially reticent about the development of the three school demonstration projects (in effect, they were charmed by Ford Foundation funding into accepting them), began to claim the projects as proof of their own commitment to evolutionary decentralization and as evidence of their faith in community participation. Apparently, however, their faith fell short of giving those districts control of budget and personnel, the essential elements of local power. The UFT, in order to maintain a proper image, indicated its strong support for community control while simultaneously waging a continuing struggle against ghetto parents. It supported the court action of the CSA against the demonstration projects and directed that its members boycott local school board elections. (It should be noted that the directive was ignored by a sizable group of teachers in elections in the I.S. 201 and Two Bridges projects.) The UFT has, at different times, been on both sides of the demonstration project issue. It originally participated in the creation of the projects and insisted on representation in their planning and governance. In fact, each of the project plans embodied requirements for teacher representation on local boards. The UFT supported representation by chapter chairmen to assure UFT, as distinguished from teacher, involvement. Almost as soon as the UFT recognized that it could not control the enterprise, it withdrew support and prepared to battle community interests. The UFT leadership reinforced their opposition to the projects after their September, 1967, strike action. They could not forgive the ghetto parents who had violated their picket lines. The growing conflict between the UFT and ghetto parents was reflected in the fact that, in the demonstration project areas, all schools remained opened during that strike. (Ghetto parents, particularly in the project areas, see the UFT's contract as a major restriction on their power to engage in the development of educational policy; accordingly, if the More Effective Schools program pushed by the union were to be expanded, they believe that it should be a policy decision made by the community or, minimally, with the community.)

The CSA apparently never had any conflict about community control; they have consistently opposed it and they readily defend unadulterated professionalism as a primary need of any school system. Parent and community control, they continue to suggest, will result only in a return to corruption, patronage, and chaos. Either they have no compunction in shedding the Deweyan theories and ideology of education in a democracy or they have become far more concerned with power than with ideology. The CSA battle is not one of rhetoric alone. They have lobbied local and state legislators and party leaders and they have mustered all their strength for what they consider a life and death battle. They feel themselves deeply threatened by parent and community power.

An evaluation of the first phase of the school-reform movement and the attempt to secure community control in New York City cannot ignore the role of the mayor and the white community. The Bundy Plan was developed by a mayor's panel and, although the mayor's revised plan reduced community control somewhat, his general support of the concept has been a source of its strength. Professionals in the system and in the Board of Education have not been reluctant to label the mayor's interest and involvement as "political interference." The white community, on the other hand, has been decidedly split on the Bundy Plan. Large segments of the educated middle class are so committed to professionalism that they vigorously reject community control by questioning their own qualifications to participate in school decision-making. While the adage of "let George do it" aroused the ire of the old-style reformer, the new reform movement has to face a tougher trend of "let George, the professional, do it."

The first phase in the controversy culminated in the spring of 1968 in a concerted attempt by opponents of decentralization to prevent legislative action. The thrust of the attempt was directed against the Regents' bill that had been introduced into the State Legislature during that spring. Neither the union nor its new-found ally, the CSA, spared any expense in trying to defeat the passage of this decentralization bill, which had been based on the Bundy Plan. The UFT reportedly spent upward of $500,000 in a public relations campaign that included hundreds of school meetings, newspaper ads, and radio spots; the CSA assessed its members nearly $1 million for a war chest, though it actually spent less money and expended less effort than did the UFT.

The pro-decentralization forces, lacking tight organizational direction and unlimited funds, were hampered in their attempts to press for a meaningful bill. The two most influential civic educational organizations, for example, the United Parents Association and the Public Education Association, in presenting their own drafts of a decentralization bill, departed significantly from the Bundy model. The net effect of the various ideological differences among black and reform white groups was to enfeeble their collective strength. A loose umbrella coalition was finally formed in the early spring of 1968, under the chairmanship of RCA President Robert Sarnoff, to lobby for the mayor's amended version of the Bundy Plan. At the same time, it appears that the mayor did not play as forceful a role as he could have in pushing for passage of the bill. It has been said that the mayor did not feel the white community, already divided in its support, backed his efforts sufficiently to enable him to push harder.

In the attempt to set up an effective decentralization plan, a compromise bill was worked out by State Commissioner of Education Allen and the New York State Board of Regents; it renewed hope that the legislature would pass a strong measure. The bill had the support of the mayor, the governor, and leaders of the legislature. While the governor, the state commissioner of education, and the Regents supported a more moderate plan for decentralization, there was nonetheless only a minimum of legislative backing for it. The more liberal, or reform, city democrats in the legislature and the few black legislators were a small coalition operating for passage. Most of the members were ill-informed on the matter and were especially susceptible to pressure from the various groups lobbying in the capital.

The UFT successfully coupled a threat of political vengeance with the fear of extremism over the involuntary transfer of nineteen educators from the Ocean Hill–Brownsville experimental district. As a result, the legislators, all up for re-election in the fall, merely postponed action for a year, empowering a hostile city school board to draw up another decentralization plan. In order to placate the pro-decentralization forces, the legislature increased the membership of the nine-member city board to thirteen. Although the legislative battle was postponed to the 1969 session, a new campaign was begun by the UFT in the fall of 1968.

The defeat of both the Bundy Plan and the Regents Plan ended the first phase of the political decentralization struggle. The escalation of the Ocean Hill–Brownsville controversy by the UFT into a city-wide strike marked the beginning of the second phase, which pitted white and black against each other in a racial confrontation.

The opening thrust was a not-too-subtle CSA–UFT campaign that charged the Ocean Hill–Brownsville district with encouraging racial extremism and anti-Semitism; it proved very successful. The Jewish community in the city became supportive and grew increasingly militant in its demands for redress. Leaflets and flyers, distributed throughout the city by the UFT and the CSA, quoted from materials purported to have been circulating in the Ocean Hill–Brownsville district. Some of the material was later proven to have been falsified; none of it was ever proven to have come from the district. Mass circulation of this propaganda fed existing fears and latent racism, as the atmosphere in the city became more charged with the passing of each day of the strike.

Although the mayor attempted to balance the interests of both sides during the strike, he was committed to the preservation of the Ocean Hill–Brownsville district and of decentralization, and this pitted him against the UFT–CSA, creating a political stalemate. The solid alignment of labor in support of the UFT was a major element in the controversy. The Central Labor Council threatened a general strike and forced the mayor to make a series of concessions to the union. The mayor appeared to have no political leverage in dealing with the union and was unable to use any of his normal political powers to de-escalate the union's demands or to force a settlement. Additionally, new efforts to develop institutional muscle for decentralization through the Committee to Save Decentralization and Community Control were slow in getting off the ground, although several sources of support, particularly church groups, were successfully tapped.

The future of school decentralization in the State Legislature this year will mark the third phase of the dispute. Legislators who were merely ill-informed in 1968 are now solidly opposed to decentralization. The New York City Democrats have largely been supportive of the union and would like nothing better than to pin the mayor's ears back. The governor, while publicly in favor of decentralization, is also not anxious to stick his neck out or to enhance in any way the career of John Lindsay.

Reformism and Community Control

It is apparent from this brief rundown of the politics of community control in New York City that traditional reform concepts developed in the first half of the twentieth century are a source of much of the opposition rhetoric. The failure of neoreformers to challenge these outdated concepts has allowed their opposition to use the rhetoric of reform against them. These traditional concepts are reflected in the professionals' defense of their role and in the white middle-class reactions to community control. Historically, the reform movement distrusted machine politics. The movement was a reaction to widespread corruption in government, and professionalism was the panacea that it developed to replace "political" or public decision-making. Citizen participation was to be satisfied by public voting in referenda and the creation of watchdog civic groups. Consequently, any challenge to professionalism, or any attempt to strengthen community control, would be an anathema to middle-class and professional attitudes. Neoreformers in the city have not been emphatic enough in arguing that much has happened in the last two decades to prove that the traditional reform mechanisms and battle lines are no longer meaningful. Because of the radical changes in the character of large-city populations and the ever increasing expansion of city functions and responsibilities, with a concurrent growth in city bureaucracy, reform must take on a new character. We cannot ignore the fact that increasingly large segments of our city population are alienated from formal policy-makers as well as from old-style civic reformers. Consequently, they have been unable to use the traditional and limited mechanisms for public participation and influence.

The Ghetto and Community Control

The ghetto communities and their leaders are not "hung-up" on professionalism. They have adequate proof that the school system and the professionals who run it have failed. In fact, the frustrations engendered by the unwillingness of the educators to yield power within the system has led to more broad-based demands for fundamental change. In two recent conferences, the Five State Organizing Committee for Community Control reaffirmed as one of its objectives absolute community control of school administrative and fiscal policies.[11] It rejected the idea of a subsystem within the city school system; such a subsystem would be a violation of self-determination because "basic control remains with the white establishment." Harlem CORE has been working on a proposal, which is gathering increased support, for a Harlem school district under state aegis. Its characterization of the present system states: "The present structure of the New York City school system as it manifests itself in Harlem does not allow the utilization of positive factors and rich resources in the Harlem community as a lever in the education of Harlem children."[12] It is their contention that only a wholly independent district can draw on community resources and engage the public in meaningful participation. The kinds of social change they seek can evolve only from effective community control.

Opposition to the Concept

The arguments against community control tend to center around two themes—the parochialism that might result from neighborhood districts' controlling the schools and the lack of qualifications of community people and their inability to cope with the highly technical problems in education.

The concern with the dangers of parochialism usually relates to fears of the emergence of black racism and separatism. State legislation and administrative regulations now prescribe certain limitations, but it is possible that new protective controls will prove necessary; these could be worked out as the need suggests. The concern with black racism is more often a misinterpretation of the movement toward creating a sense of community identity; it is evidence of a lack of understanding of the ghetto community's desire to increase the number of black teachers and administrators in local schools. In fact, there is no evidence in any of the three demonstration projects that there is any unusual stress in this area.

Local rivalries and ethnic conflicts may be intensified by local control and this should be anticipated. However, the ability to deal with, and resolve or compromise, these conflicts locally may well be an important part of the participatory process. Conflict does not necessarily have to be viewed as dangerous; rather, it may stimulate increased public and group participation in the affairs of the community. The advantages to be gained from encouraging community identity and consciousness, particularly in the ghetto, may well outweigh any negative aspects of parochialism. There is empirical evidence that participation and involvement increase when group identity is stronger: Alinsky identified greater worker participation in a worker-identified community; the experience in Norway with a workers' party showed similar results.[13] The group identity factor probably supersedes Socio-Economic-Status (SES) and racial background as an influence on the kind and extent of community participation. In fact, from the reactions and responses in the three demonstration school projects, it appears that community control has already stimulated wider local participation. Election returns in governing-board elections, although somewhat influenced by lack of publicity, inability to attain registration lists from the Board of Education, and absence of experience in conducting political campaigns, are higher than the responses in other local political elections in the same districts. Estimates of eligible parent voters who participated in the three districts were, approximately, 20 per cent in the 201 complex, 30 per cent in Ocean Hill–Brownsville, and 50 per cent in the Two Bridges district. There are also indications of wider parent interest and involvement in school meetings and school organizations in these three communities. The background of governing-board members suggests that low SES has not deterred extensive participation in the policy process— when the group can exercise power. This experience may offer important evidence to suggest that low participation by level of income or SES reflects the failure of our political system to provide either the means for participation or the direct power to lower-class groups. Given both a political structure with which the ghetto resident can identify and a delegation of effective power in decision-making, his involvement is substantially increased.

Participation should be defined in two general categories: first, as involvement or expressed interest, as reflected in attendance at meetings or voting; second, as direct engagement in the policy-making process and in the exercise of power. The latter experience should provide the basis for testing the effect of community control as a mechanism for achieving social and institutional change in the system. The limited evidence in the three demonstration projects strongly supports the hypothesis that community control in the ghetto is a source of social change.

Serious opposition to community control stems from a lack of confidence in the ability of community people to make decisions that may require some technical competence. A corollary to that position is the fear that community control denies or negates professionalism. In fact, public attitudes often attribute far too much to the ability of the professionals to come up with answers to problems. Community control must embody decision-making power vested in community representatives. Those representatives, however, must, to some extent, still rely on both professionals and nonprofessionals for inputs into the policy process.

In addition, technical resources must be made readily available to the community, to be used at its discretion. Such resources should be integral to any projected plan for community control. It should also be noted that there is advantage to injecting the dimension of community nonprofessional experience and expertise, which is now excluded from the policy process; in many ways, the parents of school children have insights into needs and values that can contribute significantly to a more viable educational program.[14] A broader concept of education, one that goes beyond the four-walls classroom concept and extends into the larger community, can gain particularly from that experience.

Again, the experience of the three demonstration projects suggests that community control does not deny professional involvement; rather, it broadens it, tapping new professional resources. However, achieving the proper balance between a professional and a public role is a continuing process that can only be defined in a practical setting.

Community control of education is only one aspect of the general movement toward expanded community involvement. Underlying the effort toward this goal is the desire to guarantee a meaningful redistribution of power in our cities. Although the community-at-large has suffered from the insulation of the policy process in the bureaucratic structure, it is the ghetto population that has recognized the problem and pressed for change. The ends that they seek and the thrust of their actions may benefit the political system and the larger community as a whole.

Notes

1. Robert A. Dahl, *Who Governs? Democracy and Power in an American City* (New Haven: Yale University Press, 1961); Edward C. Banfield, *Political Influence* (New York: The Free Press of Glencoe, 1961); Wallace S. Sayre and Herbert Kaufman, *Governing New York City: Politics in the Metropolis* (New York: Russell Sage Foundation, 1960); and Nelson W. Polsby, *Community Power and Political Theory* (New Haven: Yale University Press, 1963).

2. Lester W. Milbrath, *Political Participation: How and Why Do People Get Involved in Politics* (Chicago: Rand McNally Co., 1965); Gabriel A. Almond and Sidney Verba, *The Civic Culture: Political Attitudes and Democracy in Five Nations* (Boston: Little, Brown & Co., 1963); and Robert E. Lane, *Political Life: Why and How People Get Involved in Politics* (Glencoe, Ill.: The Free Press, 1959), particularly chap. vi. The data in these studies are generally supportive of the correlation between Socio-Economic-Status and participation, concluding that middle-class, educated people are more likely to participate. Participation is largely defined as voting and there are only limited surveys of other types of participation and/or differences among such culture groups under different circumstances. The general assumption that moderate or low participation indicates consensus has undoubtedly conditioned the character and limited scope of research on participation.

3. The critics of the democratic elitist theories have thus far been notably unsuccessful in their efforts to undermine the rationalization for replacing concepts of participatory democracy. There are obvious reasons for that failure; most important is that they have not developed empirical data to support their position. The bulk of the studies in political behavior are oriented to the reinforcement of the newly defined concepts of pluralism, as reflected in multiple-elite structure. Political scientists have generally avoided research on participation. The democratic elitists, after all, structured their defense of a new definition of pluralism on findings from the most current behavioral research. Such studies, from voting-behavior analysis to decision-making indicated an increasingly limited role for public participants. How then could one justify a traditional concept of participatory democracy in the face of a declining participatory system. The democratic elitists have stressed simplistic pluralistic elements in the system, i.e., the existence of many elites within a political system and the lack of overlapping of these groups. In addition, they have stressed the varied sources of recruitment of elites and the potential ability of anyone to enter those elites. Few have addressed themselves to the issue of the effects of increasing noninvolvement. Certainly the cities are a significant laboratory for gathering supportive empirical evidence to begin to challenge the democratic elitist theories. See Peter Bachrach, *The Theory of Democratic Elitism* (Boston: Little, Brown & Co., 1967); Jack L. Walker, "A Critique of the Elitist Theory of Democracy," in Chapter I, above; and Robert A. Dahl, "Further Reflections on 'The Elitist Theory of Democracy,'" *American Political Science Review*, LX (June, 1966), 296–305.

4. George Counts, *Decision-Making and American Values in School Administration* (New York: Teachers College, Columbia University, 1954). Published for the Cooperative Program in Educational Administration, Middle Atlantic Region, by the Bureau of Publications.

5. Peter Schrag, "Boston: Education's Last Hurrah," in Chapter III, above; Herbert Kohl, *36 Children* (N.Y.: New American Library, 1967); Peter Schrag, *Village School Downtown* (Boston: Beacon Press, 1967); Jonathan Kozol, *Death at an Early Age: The Destruction of the Hearts and Minds of Negro Children in the Boston Public Schools* (Boston: Houghton Mifflin Co., 1967); and Bel Kaufman, *Up the Down Staircase* (Englewood Cliffs, N.J.: Prentice-Hall, 1964).

6. Marilyn Gittell, *Participants and Participation* (New York: Frederick A.

Praeger, 1967); and Marilyn Gittell and T. Edward Hollander, *Six Urban School Districts* (New York: Frederick A. Praeger, 1967).

7. Marilyn Gittell, "Teacher Power and Its Implications for Urban Education," *Theory Into Practice* (April, 1968).

8. The redistribution of power is an important element in social change. The further enhancement of new power sources in a political system in turn provides the opportunity for achieving other changes in the system and related institutions. See Marilyn Gittell, "A Typology of Power for Measuring Social Change," *American Behavioral Scientist*, IX (April, 1966), 23–28.

9. A recent court action has held that these appointments were illegal since they were made in violation of state law. The case is presently on appeal.

10. Mayor's Advisory Panel on Decentralization of the New York City Schools, *Reconnection for Learning: A Community School System for New York City* (November, 1967), excerpts of which appear in Chapter IV, above.

11. Five State Organizing Committee for Community Control to the Office of Metropolitan Educational Sub-systems, *Position Statement* (January 25, 1968), p. 3.

12. New York Harlem CORE, *Questions and Answers Regarding the Autonomous Harlem School System* (1967), p. 2.

13. Lane, *op. cit.* A Norwegian study indicated higher turnout in elections where socio-economic status of an area is more homogeneous; see Stein Rokkan, "The Comparative Study of Political Participation: Notes Toward a Perspective on Current Research," in Austin Ranney (ed.), *Essays on the Behavioral Study of Politics* (Urbana, Ill.: University of Illinois Press, 1962), pp. 47–90. See also Herbert J. Gans, *The Urban Villagers. Group and Class in the Life of Italian Americans* (New York: The Free Press of Glencoe, 1965), pp. 106–10.

14. Curriculum experts now suggest the value of wider participation in the development of school curriculum; see George A. Beauchamp, *Planning the Elementary School Curriculum* (Englewood Cliffs, N.J.: Allyn and Bacon, 1956), p. 10.

CONTRIBUTORS

ROBERT L. CRAIN, formerly Senior Study Director of the National Opinion Research Center and presently Assistant Professor of Social Relations at Johns Hopkins University, is the author of *The Politics of School Desegregation*. ROBERT A. DAHL, Sterling Professor of Political Science at Yale University, is the author of *Congress and Foreign Policy*, *A Preface to Democratic Theory*, *Who Governs?*, and *Modern Political Analysis*. Professor of Political Science at Florida State University, THOMAS R. DYE is the author of *Politics, Economics, and the Public*. JASON EPSTEIN, editor and Vice President at Random House, is a New Yorker whose reviews and articles on education have appeared in *The New York Review of Books*. Program Officer at The Ford Foundation, MARIO FANTINI headed the staff that prepared the *Bundy Report*. MARILYN GITTELL, Director of the Institute for Community Studies and Professor of Political Science at Queens College of the City University of New York, is the author of *Participants and Participation*, co-author of *Six Urban School Districts*, and editor of *Educating an Urban Population*. ROBERT J. HAVIGHURST, Professor of Education and Human Development at the University of Chicago, is the author of *The Public Schools of Chicago: A Survey Report*. STEPHEN P. HENCLEY is Dean of the Graduate School of Education at the University of Utah, co-author of *Educational Research* and *Secondary School Administration*, and co-editor of *The Politics of Education*. ALAN G. HEVESI, Assistant Director of the Institute for Community Studies, teaches in the Department of Political Science, Queens College of the City University of New York. T. EDWARD HOLLANDER, co-author of *Six Urban School Districts* and an Associate Professor at the Bernard M. Baruch School of Business and Public Administration of the City College of the City University of New York, served as Studies Director of the Education Task Force of the Mayor's Temporary Commission on City Finances. Assistant Professor of English at Goucher College, FLORENCE HOWE is the co-author of *Education for Freedom*. JAMES K. KENT, a doctoral member of the Colloquium Board of the Harvard Graduate School of Education, is presently Administrative Assistant to the Superintendent of the Minneapolis public schools. PAUL LAUTER, of the Antioch-Putney Graduate School of Education, is co-author of *Education for Freedom*. Assistant Professor of Political Science at UCLA, RICHARD MERELMAN is currently completing a study of political socialization in two California school districts. WILLIAM R. ODELL, of Stanford University's School of Education, directed the Educational Survey of Philadelphia Public Schools in 1963-64. A. HARRY PASSOW, Professor of Education at Teachers College, Columbia University, and Chairman of the Teachers College Committee on Urban Education, was Director of the Teachers College study of the Washington, D.C., public school system. Author of *Community Power and Political Theory* and *Congress and the Presidency* and co-editor of *New Perspectives on the House of Representatives*, NELSON POLSBY is Professor of Political Science at the University of California at Berkeley. Associate Professor of Sociology and Management at the Graduate School of Business Administration of New York University, DAVID ROGERS is the author of *110 Livingston Street: Politics and Bureaucracy in the New York City Schools*. PETER SCHRAG, Executive Editor of *The Saturday Review*, is the author of *Village School Downtown* and *Voices in the Classroom*. ADOLPH STONE is Chairman of the Academic Department of the High School of Art and Design in New York City. DAVID STREET, Associate Professor of Sociology at the University of Chicago, has served as the Director of Russell Sage Project on Large City Schools. JACK L. WALKER is Assistant Professor of Political Science at the University of Michigan.

INDEX